The Costs of Justice

CONTEMPORARY EUROPEAN POLITICS AND SOCIETY

Anthony M. Messina, series editor

The

COSTS of
JUSTICE

How New Leaders Respond

to Previous Rights Abuses

BRIAN K. GRODSKY

University of Notre Dame Press

Notre Dame, Indiana

Library of Congress Cataloging-in-Publication Data

Grodsky, Brian K., 1974–
    The costs of justice : how new leaders respond to previous rights abuses /
Brian K. Grodsky.
        p.   cm. — (Contemporary European politics and society)
    Includes bibliographical references and index.
    ISBN-13: 978-0-268-02977-7 (pbk. : alk. paper)
    ISBN-10: 0-268-02977-6 (pbk. : alk. paper)
    1. Transitional justice—Case studies.   2. Human rights—Case studies.
3. Transitional justice—Europe, Eastern.   4. Human rights—Europe,
Eastern.   5. Transitional justice—Uzbekistan   6. Human rights—
Uzbekistan.   7. Post-communism—Case studies.   I. Title.
    JC571. G7831   2010
    320.01'1—dc22

                                                    2010024331

To my wife, Gosia, and daughter, Ania,
whose support has made each page possible.

Contents

PART II

Acknowledgments

I would especially like to thank Zvi Gitelman and Bill Zimmerman for their extraordinarily insightful comments and advice during the fieldwork and writing of this book. I would also like to thank for their helpful comments at various stages Susan Waltz, Monika Nalepa, Sarah Croco, Tom Flores, Joel Simmons, Jana von Stein, Rob Salmond, Devin Hagerty, Eileen Babbitt, Vladimir Tismaneanu, Ed Schatz, Mackenzie Whipps, and Barbara Koremenos, as well as the anonymous reviewers for the University of Notre Dame Press.

Also I would like to express my considerable debt to those organizations that have provided me with the financial support that has made this book possible. These include the following awards: Woodrow Wilson International Center for Scholars, East European Studies Research Scholar; United States Department of Education, Fulbright-Hays Doctoral Dissertation Research Abroad Program; American Council of Learned Societies Dissertation Fellowship; Harold Jacobson Fellowship, Political Science Department, University of Michigan; ACTR/ACCELS (American Councils) Combined Research and Language Training Program—Uzbekistan; Academy for Educational Development, National Security Education Program, David L. Boren Graduate Fellowship; Center for Russian and East European Studies Research, Internship and Fellowship Program Grant; and a Thesis Grant, Political Science Department, University of Michigan.

Finally, I am most grateful to the many interviewees who kindly and graciously gave their time and thoughts to me as I travelled through Poland, Uzbekistan, Serbia, and Croatia in a search for understanding the process of transitional justice in each country. From freedom fighters of yesterday to those still facing repressive regimes today, these extraordinarily busy and influential individuals shared with me their personal stories and the stories of their countries. These men and women have my great appreciation, and my good wishes go out to those for whom the transition they seek has yet to materialize.

Introduction

What Is Transitional Justice
and Why Should We Care?

The dramatic end of the Cold War in the late 1980s marked a fascinating twist in the study of transitional justice, those responses to a former regime's repressive acts following a change in political systems. First, the death of ideological bipolarity allowed for the creation of new norms and the strengthening of older but long-ignored ones with regard to justice. Countries emerging from dictatorships in the last period of the "third wave" were no longer so constrained in their internal decisions by the broader geopolitical factors that had dogged their predecessors. Second, the sheer scale of communism's collapse led to an unprecedented number of states—more than two dozen—suddenly faced with accounting for decades of dictatorship. Third, the trajectories of these postcommunist states demonstrated the tentativeness of democratization, upon which transitional justice is ostensibly based. While some postcommunist states immediately lurched in the direction of free-market democracies, other nominally new democracies (that is, those where members of the old regime continued to rule, claiming to be on a new political trajectory) clamped down rather than let up on opposition, and still other states disintegrated into bloody regional and civil wars that further complicated any reckoning with the past.

This book, based largely on elite interviews and media analyses conducted in the four postcommunist countries of Poland, Serbia, Croatia, and Uzbekistan, draws on the experiences of a diverse group of states from one of the most monumental political transitions in recent history in order to explore a fundamental question: What determines how a (nominally) new regime will pursue transitional justice following a period of repression? This question is an important component of the broader democratization discourse. Yet at a time when the U.S. government spends hundreds of millions of dollars annually to promote democratization and human rights accountability around the world, we know relatively little about how to shape the desired outcome. The American-backed trial of Saddam Hussein in 2005–2006, largely criticized as a miscarriage of justice and an inspiration for Sunni insurgents in Iraq, highlights the weight of this dilemma.

The Saddam Hussein trial is also a reminder of the staying power of transitional justice. Scarcely a day passes before another story appears in the national press about commemorations for victims of injustice, a truth commission's newest findings, or the next ex-dictator standing trial. At a time of momentous international challenges, from global warming and pervasive hunger to terrorism and war, this attention is not frivolous, but rather a sign of the times. A glance at the U.S. State Department's Web site is enough to realize that dialogue concerning transitional justice has reached a new level. The primary U.S. foreign policy body identifies among its human rights objectives the need to "promote the rule of law, seek accountability, and change cultures of impunity."[1] To back up these words, the Office of War Crimes Issues has been established to pressure states to ensure criminal justice for their worst offenders. The State Department's Bureau of Diplomatic Security, in turn, offers bounties for war criminals. The U.S. government's $5 million reward for the (recently captured) former Bosnian Serb president, Radovan Karadžić, is equal to that paid for many terrorists on the very same site.[2]

Cynics might still question the determination of U.S. officials who profess to care about transitional justice, particularly given lingering questions concerning how and why it fits into the "national interest."[3] Yet official U.S. positions in this sphere are symptomatic of a more global phenomenon. The international community is increasingly speaking out on the need to address past abuses. While intergovernmental bodies have always been somewhat equivocal about the need for justice versus peace, the

United Nations (UN) and the Intra-American Commission on Human Rights (IACHR), in particular, have condemned impunity and begun to view domestic amnesties as inconsistent with international human rights norms and laws.[4] The Cold War's explosive end resulted in the first international tribunal since Nuremberg and Tokyo: the International Criminal Tribunal for the Former Yugoslavia (1993), which was quickly followed by the International Criminal Tribunal for Rwanda (1994). Since then, the United Nations has taken an active role in establishing and supporting other criminal trials in East Timor (2000), Sierra Leone (2002), and Cambodia (2003). This process culminated in the recent establishment of the International Criminal Court, designed in part to encourage and enable criminal accountability for the world's worst violators.[5]

This trend is also evidenced by local courts' ever-increasing attempts to try crimes that took place at home or on foreign soil. This might involve stripping local rights abusers from the old regime of self-granted immunity and pursuing criminal cases against them in courts on the terrain that they once controlled.[6] It also includes a concept called "universal jurisdiction," which enables (or may even, at least in principle, require) states to pursue criminal cases for certain crimes, no matter where or against whom they were committed.[7] The term was initially coined in 1945, based on the understanding that war crimes were "offenses against the conscience of the civilized world, and every nation therefore had an interest in their punishment."[8] Since then, it has been expanded by international bodies such as the UN's advisory International Law Commission, which in 1996 confirmed universal jurisdiction's applicability to war crimes as well as to genocide, crimes against humanity, torture, and crimes against the United Nations or UN personnel.[9]

Domestic courts have begun prosecutions in defense of the international legal order in an increasing number of countries, including (but not limited to) the United States, Italy, France, Senegal, Switzerland, Sweden, England, Belgium, Luxemburg, Denmark, Ecuador, New Zealand, Israel, the Netherlands, and Spain. The Spanish demand for the extradition of former Chilean dictator Augusto Pinochet represented a dramatic application of universal jurisdiction. While Pinochet never actually stood trial because of his deteriorating health, Spanish courts arguably brought justice to a new level, even in opposition to their own government, which was seemingly more concerned with maintaining friendly diplomatic relations with their unsupportive Chilean counterparts.[10] Punishment for past crimes has become increasingly ensconced in customary law. As former UN Secretary General Kofi Annan declared in his 2004 report, "The Rule of Law and Transitional Justice in Conflict and Post-Conflict Societies," justice now means "the prevention and punishment of wrongs."[11]

Transitional justice has thus returned to the international agenda with a zeal not seen since Nuremberg. Yet even as the field of transitional justice blossoms, the very term remains only vaguely defined in the literature. Most broadly, the International Center for Transitional Justice generically defines it as "a response to systematic or widespread violations of human rights."[12] Jon Elster, in an invaluable contribution to the field, refers to transitional justice in his abstract as "retribution and reparation after a change of political regime," and then in his opening pages as "the processes of trials, purges, and reparations that take place after the transition from one political regime to another."[13] While Elster places justice on a continuum ranging from legal justice to political justice, others, such as Ruti Teitel, define transitional justice more exclusively as "legal responses" to past wrongdoings during periods of political change.[14]

In this book, I define transitional justice as a new or nominally new regime's legal and symbolic responses to past human rights violations. By legal responses, I mean restorative and retributive forms of individual accountability for past abuses, such as compensation (aimed at concrete victims of repression) and criminal trials (for individual perpetrators). By contrast, I characterize symbolic responses as those that entail a broader, less personal form of address, such as condemnations or apologies, which emphasize a moral attack on the past without necessarily affecting particular individuals. In practice, the lines between restorative and retributive or legal and symbolic are frequently unclear. Take, for example, rehabilitation of a former victim. This can be seen as a legal, restorative act with practical ramifications, since clearing the victim of alleged crimes may be a precondition to regaining certain civil or economic rights, such as a pension. At the same time, it can also be seen as a symbolic, retributive intervention, an indirect attack on the former system and a potentially humiliating repudiation of those involved. In this book, I focus on seven frequently utilized types of transitional justice, discussed in detail in chapter 2.

My inclusion of "new or nominally new regime" in this definition is a deliberate attempt to broaden our understanding of transitional justice in practice. There is a tendency in the literature to assume that transitional justice measures occur in the context of a complete (or at least intended) transition from nondemocratic rule to democracy.[15] This is perhaps not surprising given the plethora of normative arguments for justice in the literature. But even broad studies assessing cynical reasons for justice, such as populism, revenge, and narrowing the political playing field, also tend to assume that a new, democratically oriented leadership has taken power.[16] While the fact that repressive leaderships also engage in transitional justice has been acknowledged with a surprising degree of disinterest, I believe that these cases can actually help us to understand broader motivations and determinants of justice.[17] For this reason I include the case of Uzbekistan (chapter 8), governed by a nominally new regime, in this study.

DETERMINANTS OF JUSTICE

Although there is a rich, interdisciplinary literature that addresses the value of various transitional justice mechanisms, theoretical arguments concerning conditions under which we should expect to see specific measures implemented are limited. The existing literature, born as oppressive regimes from Latin America to Eastern Europe fell in the 1970s, 1980s, and 1990s, has quickly become dated. While this literature is quite vast and varied with respect to the independent variables responsible for the employment of justice mechanisms, a common thread running through most of these arguments is power-based constraints. The degree to which new elites are able to impose harsh methods of justice, the argument goes, is largely a function of their strength relative to that of the outgoing regime. The logic of the argument is intuitively appealing; it is easier to imagine Vladimir Lenin holding the head of deposed tsar Nicholas II than Boris Yeltsin holding that of Mikhail Gorbachev.

Clearly, a new regime's formal power structure, perhaps impacted by the transition process itself, will have at least some effect on new elites' justice policies. This approach, however, may be overly focused on short-term outcomes and too fixated on the domestic stage. Relative power arguments provide a useful framework for elucidating some constraints encountered by new elites faced with transitional justice, but such theories discount internal and external incentive structures that may strengthen or weaken the overall effect of this variable. By pitting old versus new elites, relative power arguments in many ways ignore the realities of governing in a democratic state where leaders are held accountable to today's electoral constituency. While attitudes toward transitional justice may vary, the provision of core political goods and services, defined here as economic or security policies that produce tangible change, is essential to a ruling elite's political viability.[18] But how does the provision of core political goods and services relate to the process of transitional justice?

In this book, I argue that a new regime's will to pursue transitional justice is closely linked to its capacity to provide these political goods and services, and that institutional variation plays an important role in determining how this process plays out. The mechanisms employed by new elites to enhance their long-term political viability should, according to this "strategic argument," depend on their institutional constraints. While those in constitutionally weak institutions may or may not support a given justice policy based on private preferences or on the overall popularity of the measure, those in constitutionally powerful institutions should be focused particularly on how justice (and a range of other policies) affects their bottom line—their ability to provide those political goods and services that constituents expect from them. This is in some ways a more nuanced application of Graham Allison's bureaucratic model, according to which "where they stand depends on where they sit."[19] Rather than simply pitting new elites against their predecessors, transitional justice may split new elites along institutionally defined lines.

This study builds upon numerous others that have examined why and how new political leaders pursue transitional justice. It differs from those studies in two important respects. First, I challenge the conventional view that justice is primarily a function of power. Instead, I explain the pursuit of justice as inextricable from a broader political framework where leaders eager to maintain their positions continually have one eye on their constituents. Justice policy is not, however, defined merely by popularity. In fact, political elites might pursue highly unpopular justice policies that they personally favor. But the path they choose will be shaped by the degree to which rulers believe that their constituents *perceive* that these policies will either endanger or enhance the delivery of bread-and-butter goods and services that politicians are charged with overseeing.

Second, this book includes new empirical evidence from four postcommunist states coping with various aspects of justice: Poland, Serbia, Croatia, and Uzbekistan. These cases provide readers with a new understanding of how states with such diversity—in terms of everything from political system and geography to religion and culture—confront fundamentally similar questions. Based on more than 250 interviews with actors key to policy debates, coupled with an analysis of thousands of international and local media reports from these countries, I offer an in-depth look at one of the most contentious and enduring political issues in the postcommunist world. In countries where everyone was touched in some way by the repressive apparatus of the state, this book relates how political leaders charged with resolving the question of how to deal with past rights violations and violators made the choices they did.

ORGANIZATION

This book is divided into two parts. In the first part, beginning with chapter 1, I examine theoretical arguments in the literature and expand on the strategic argument proposed. Chapters 2 and 3 are primarily methodological. In chapter 2, I propose a tool to assess transitional justice theories and discuss how this study was carried out. More specifically, I explain the development and use of a "transitional justice spectrum" based on a hierarchical arrangement of possible justice mechanisms and designed to allow researchers to conduct more rigorous, cross-national tests of justice arguments. In chapter 3, I discuss the specific nature of crime and punishment in postcommunist states, including an overview of lustration there. In chapter 4, I provide a broad methodological overview, including case selection, data collection, and method of analysis.

The second part of this book is composed of four country chapters (5–8), in which I analyze the path of justice in Poland, Serbia and Montenegro, Croatia, and Uzbekistan, and chapters 9 and 10, in which I pursue cross-national lessons. My first country study, Poland, is in many ways the quintessential Central European case, where the worst years of repression ended in the 1950s and where the communists ultimately negotiated power away to the Solidarity opposition group. In this chapter, I explore how and why Poland's new elites successfully pressed for criminal and other measures of justice, despite their apparent weakness. I find that most new elites approached the past with little concern about direct reactions from communists and their associates, but with much trepidation over public perceptions that they concentrated too much on "political games" and not enough on economic reform.

In chapter 6, I use my second country study, Serbia and Montenegro, to introduce a case characterized by multiple periods of repression, the last and most violent one involving victims primarily regarded by the public as enemies. How do pro-justice leaders from the former opposition movement balance external demands for justice with internal pressures against it? I find that elites in Serbia and Montenegro have pursued harsh forms of justice—namely, cooperation with the International Criminal Tribunal for the former Yugoslavia (ICTY)—when they calculated that these measures, exchanged for Western-conditioned aid, might ultimately enhance their political positions.

The same chapter raises the question of whether, without Western incentives, these leaders would have nevertheless moved against old elites, as they say they would have, in the form of less controversial domestic trials. In chapter 7, I look at factors that led Croatia's new elites to pursue justice under circumstances very similar to their counterparts in Serbia, differentiated primarily by the extent and types of Western pressure for ICTY cooperation. I find that Croatia's new elites, not subject to the Western-conditioned aid necessary to buy off their constituents, resisted unpopular ICTY extraditions despite elites' private preferences in favor of cooperation. Instead, they launched a small number of domestic trials intended to placate international actors without stepping on the toes of local voters.

Unlike the previous chapters, the case of Uzbekistan in chapter 8 demonstrates how even where old elites continue to dominate the new system, they may use transitional justice to redefine history in a way intended to vindicate both their past and present use of repression, and thus ensure for their regime the provision of external, otherwise unavailable goods. In this chapter, I also analyze the motivations behind President Islam Karimov's little-known 1999 truth commission. Apart from looking at transitional justice in contemporary Uzbekistan, I also initiate an inquiry into how today's oppositionists envision justice should they take power tomorrow, thus giving readers insight into early planning in the justice sphere.

In the final two chapters, I offer a comparative analysis of the four case studies and discussion of the methodological and practical implications of this study's findings. I begin with a survey of results from each of my case studies and conclude with methodological lessons and policy implications that arise from this effort.

This study of the process by which policymakers decide which path(s) of justice to pursue is important for several reasons. First, if international norms concerning justice continue to develop along their current trajectory, issues of accountability for rights violations may persist in their move from the exclusively domestic sphere to an important component of international relations. Attempts by external state and non-state actors to pressure target states into pursuing particular forms of justice will be more successful and less destabilizing if we better understand how decision makers are likely to interpret the dilemma. Second, understanding the conditions under which regimes employ justice might help us to clarify the reasons for the success or failure of the particular justice policies employed. For example, if we find a large number of cases where truth commissions or criminal trials appear to negatively affect regime stability, it may not be that the mechanisms per se are a poor justice tool, but rather that the specific conditions under which these mechanisms were adopted account for this impact.

Finally, and an important contribution of this book in particular, transitional justice may be more related to other policy spheres than has been previously posited. An exploration of the determinants of justice is simultaneously an exploration into the broader decision-making process in transition states. If new elites are wary of justice policies that might directly or indirectly affect former rulers, they might be equally wary of adopting, for example, economic policies detrimental to former power holders. In the pages that follow, I thus explore a process that has ramifications for the study of transitional justice in particular and the path of transition more generally.

PART I

1

Explaining Justice

*What Are the Key Determinants
of Transitional Justice Policy?*

In this chapter, I explore the rationale for justice and theoretical arguments designed to explain under what conditions new regimes choose particular justice policies. It is worth prefacing this chapter with a reminder of my definition of transitional justice: a new or nominally new regime's legal and symbolic responses to past human rights violations. These responses can be broadly understood as memory, truth, and justice in the more classic sense. The root mechanisms aimed at each of these categories involve fundamental words and deeds that in some way create divisions—between new and old, powerless and powerful, victim and perpetrator. Formal rebukes, truth commissions, and criminal trials all share this inherently punitive capacity and pose a risk to other apparently unrelated reform processes. Whenever this occurs, justice is uncertain.

I begin this chapter with a review of arguments for and against pursuing justice. Next, I explore the literature concerning determinants of justice, focusing on relative power arguments, which have gained such an enormous following that they are frequently treated as common sense assumptions. I continue by elaborating on a new way of explaining justice, incorporating broader political strategy. More specifically, I argue that justice cannot be disconnected from electoral politics and the role of economics. In the subsequent chapters of this book, I will evaluate the strengths and weaknesses of these arguments.

WHY PURSUE JUSTICE? AN ASSESSMENT OF PROS AND CONS

Studies of transitional justice are frequently centered on or around the threat of criminal justice, rooted in the logic that imposing sentences today will deter rights violations tomorrow. The challenge of empirically proving this claim, left largely to the realm of counterfactuals, is extraordinarily difficult. As a result, one scholar notes, the deterrence argument "has to be regarded almost as an article of faith rather than something that has been clearly demonstrated by an examination of specific historical evidence."[1] Transitional justice is clearly not just about criminal retribution. In the words of Kofi Annan, "Justice implies regard for the rights of the accused, for the interests of victims, and for the well-being of society at large."[2] If not for the pleasure of revenge or the hope of deterrence, what is the purpose of justice?

Transitional justice, of course, encompasses more than just criminal prosecutions. An underlying theme articulated by transitional justice scholars, who frequently approach their subject equipped with legal and normative arguments for why new elites might pursue various forms of justice, is the need for the new state to acknowledge the former regime's role in human rights abuses.[3] This can be done indirectly through a variety of mechanisms, from restorative measures, such as rehabilitation and compensation, to retributive measures, such as administrative purges and criminal prosecutions. Whatever the method, justice as described in the vast literature seems designed to facilitate two broad, interrelated objectives: societal reconciliation and democratic consolidation. By individualizing victims and, especially, perpetrators, justice policies can end the "dangerous culture of collective guilt"[4] that contributes to long-term instability, thus putting society back on track for constructive engagement in a new political order.

The transitional justice literature is overwhelmingly focused on the idea that various forms of justice can enhance reconciliation within post-conflict societies. Reconciliation might be defined as "a process through which a society moves from a divided past to a shared future."[5] Others conceptualize it more broadly, on a spectrum spanning from bare coexistence to democratic reciprocity (characterized by open policy debates) and finally forgiveness.[6] In any case, achieving reconciliation necessitates altering postconflict relations from those "based on antagonism, distrust, disrespect, and, quite possibly, hurt and hatred" to those centered on "respect-based relations of cooperation" that are also essential to instilling trust in the new system and hence to democratic stability.[7] Reconciliation is, in short, a process of "social repair."[8]

Reconciliation takes place on two planes: at the individual level, focused on alleviating personal hostility and guilt; and at the societal one, involving the reconstruction of intrasocietal relations, including within communities and between political groups and factions.[9] In cases where societies or societal elites are confident that investigations into past abuses would further polarize rather than bring together social actors, an explicit policy of "reconciliation based on forgetting" might be the best road to take.[10] In other cases where, similarly, the past is a can of worms that few wish to open, political elites might pursue reconciliation not so much by drawing a curtain on the past as by focusing on the future, attempting to create "all-inclusive identities" by building a new political discourse "around concepts of human and political rights, legality, individual responsibility, personal rights."[11] For many advocates of transitional justice, however, a more pro-active policy of addressing the past is an essential first step to moving on.

Reconciliation itself, and the very mechanisms said to make it possible, may strengthen the likelihood of successful democratic consolidation, which Philippe Schmitter defines as "the process of transforming the accidental arrangements, prudential norms, and contingent solutions that have emerged during the transition into relations of cooperation and competition that are reliably known, regularly practiced, and voluntarily accepted by those persons or collectivities (i.e., politicians and citizens) that participate in democratic governance."[12] Democratic consolidation involves the creation of institutions that both politicians and their publics support. Without some degree of societal reconciliation, justice scholars argue, "negative relations will work to undermine even the best system of governance."[13]

There is little agreement as to which justice mechanisms are most capable of bringing about reconciliation and democratic consolidation. This debate is most dramatic with respect to criminal prosecutions, which are often presented in black-and-white terms. "Purists," including such influential human rights organizations as Amnesty International and Human Rights Watch, tend to advocate for criminal prosecutions in the belief that reconciliation is a consequence of establishing a clear rule of law.[14] For purists, the soil must be thoroughly turned and neatly raked before the seeds of democracy can be planted. "Pragmatists," by contrast, frequently argue for the necessity of amnesty because, they say, "rule of law itself can take root only in a society that is sufficiently stable and reconciled."[15] The fields may be littered with debris, but with the right seeds and proper care, they will eventually nourish a flowering garden.

Transitional justice scholars generally agree that various forms of justice can signal the start of institutional reforms, demonstrate that all citizens are liable under the same law, and encourage public support for previously absent democratic values, such as equality and participation.[16] Justice can help to forge a common historical understanding, demonstrate new elites' institutional disapproval of rights violations, and even enable a new government to enhance its own legitimacy by constructing a wall between itself and the former regime.[17] To do this, chosen justice policies must represent the "will of the people," as identified through democratic means.[18] Justice can thus be both a function of, and an instrument to strengthen, democracy. Just as justice can help repair victims' feelings of loss and harm, it can also establish new leaders as "moral authorities that can claim to represent entire communities."[19]

Authors differ on precisely which forms of justice are the most beneficial and the least harmful under which conditions. Proponents of criminal accountability hold that charging individuals for their roles in yesterday's crimes is the most important step in reducing collective guilt and placing society back on an equal footing.[20] Justice can be dramatic and demonstrate a new commitment to those liberal rules and values that did not exist earlier, perhaps even where criminal prosecutions take place in illiberal or procedurally flawed environments that effectively ensure that top leaders will be convicted.[21] Trials mark a break with the past, underscoring the message that principles adhered to under the former regime were reprehensible, and thereby instilling a firm historical memory in citizen observers.[22]

Despite the possible benefits, the threat of punishment may be enough to marginalize supporters of the old regime and turn them from potential converts into hostile enemies of the new order.[23] The extent to which justice is targeted at particular institutions may affect democratic consolidation.[24] Though legal scholars question the legitimacy of potentially unpopular blanket amnesties,[25] new elites from Argentina to South Africa have refrained from extensive prosecutions in the hope of bringing closure in a more amicable and less threatening way.[26] Still, scholars warn that while clemency may be appropriate under certain circumstances, a failure to expose past injustices can prove fatal for democratic consolidation: "By refusing to confront and to purge itself of its worst fears and resentments, such a society would be burying not just its past but the very ethical values it needs to make its future livable."[27]

Perpetrators' acknowledgments of guilt and expressions of remorse may also be a precondition for reconciliation.[28] Truth commissions, official bodies established to investigate past abuses, might serve as a forum for such pronouncements.[29] These proceedings can also be beneficial for reconciliation in other ways. Priscilla Hayner highlights the important role that perceptions of "truth" play in a stratified, post-transition society, suggesting that disparate versions of a country's repressive history fuel political tensions that may turn violent.[30] The very act of procedural justice, the telling and hearing of truth about previous abuses, may allow victims to forgive or to at least move on.[31] This is, some argue, particularly true when the truth process is designed to apportion blame to all the guilty parties.[32]

Yet others warn that uncovering some facts may increase friction rather than bring about reconciliation, concluding that "sometimes it is better that some facts about the past remain unknown."[33] South Africa's last apartheid leader, F. W. de Klerk, suggested that there were worries among whites that a truth commission might not aim toward reconciliation but instead generate narratives that would serve "as the basis for further recrimination, demonization, and persecution."[34] Restricting criminal trials to a few of the worst offenders may undermine attempts at uncovering the whole truth. By concentrating blame on the most guilty, criminal trials can assist complicit elements within a society in the whitewashing of their own personal histories.[35] The perpetrators on trial may deflect blame, struggling to find explanations and excuses. Leigh Payne noted, in regard to Chile: "We all create myths or 'vital lies' that keep our images of ourselves and our acts intact. Public confessions, and the desire for absolution, tend to exacerbate that process."[36] Even if Slobodan Milošević and Saddam Hussein were guilty in the court of world opinion, both men stood defiant, with no signs of remorse, during months of televised trials. It is difficult to see any evidence that either trial resulted in reconciliation, at least in the near term.[37]

In the long term, some forms of justice may help to clear the way for democratic consolidation by creating a common historical memory. Radical movements that arise to contest democratic states in democracies new and old may be fueled by the failure to deal honestly and effectively with the past. The lack of systematic justice in wartime occupied Europe following the defeat of Germany, for example, allowed non-German societies over time to create more flattering histories.[38] "If Germans were guilty, then 'we' were innocent," Tony Judt writes. "No one had an interest in denying it — and within two years, to do so was anyway no longer possible—the story took root."[39]

The rise of the xenophobic right in countries from Austria to the Netherlands in the 1990s might in some ways be traced to this phenomenon.[40] A similar "mismemory of communism" allowed people to praise anticommunists no matter how disagreeable and outright criminal their own deeds may have been.[41] Two of the most recent cases of genocide, in Rwanda and Yugoslavia, appear to have been at least partly rooted in previous mass abuses that were left unaddressed for decades. Again, however, concerns about sidestepping the truth must be balanced with the awareness that if the public was widely complicit in past abuses, pointing fingers might jeopardize societal reconciliation and weaken support for the new, democratic regime.[42]

Each of the mechanisms of justice mentioned above invites contestation, most basically at the level of *whose* truth is being established.[43] This is particularly important because the truth found might inspire or influence other forms of justice. Criminal prosecutions and other official processes designed to investigate the past might help to clear the way for more restorative, victim-oriented forms of justice, such as compensation.[44] Compensation provides the state with an opportunity to elevate formerly oppressed elements of the population without necessarily stepping on the toes of the oppressor (though it does also involve a redistributive element). For some scholars, compensation is an essential first stage in putting all members of society on equal ground, making victims whole, and initiating a process of reconciliation.[45] Yet, given the high levels of inequality and poverty characteristic of many (post-)repressive states, providing adequate compensation may be too monumental a task for any new government.[46]

This brief glimpse into transitional justice is designed to illustrate just some of the questions that emerge as new elites determine how best to deal with the past, an issue covered in more detail in chapters 2 and 3. What we have learned from the literature to date is that no form of addressing the past is especially easy, and there is no guarantee that any particular mechanism of justice will be a panacea for the difficult transition from nondemocracy to democracy. Crowning all of the dilemmas discussed above is the fear that any specific form of transitional justice, even one that appears quite moderate, might cause political instability sufficient to derail democratization.[47] This remark takes us into the next sphere of debate: Given the various pros and cons of justice, what are the primary determinants of how new elites deal with their repressive predecessors?

TRANSITIONAL JUSTICE AND HUMAN RIGHTS ACCOUNTABILITY: DETERMINANTS OF ACTION

The dilemmas discussed above are not new; for centuries, emerging political elites have struggled with the question of how to account for human rights violations from a former period.[48] More contemporary debate can be traced back to the immediate post–World War II era, when the victorious Allied forces applied still-evolving international judicial norms to those vanquished powers accused of heinous war crimes.[49] Yet just as the Nuremberg and Tokyo trials were a leap in international human rights, they took place under "exceptional political conditions" that disappeared within only a few years.[50] The next phase in transitional justice occurred during the Cold War, when bipolar power struggles stunted the growth of the nascent transitional justice movement.[51] As harsh authoritarian regimes in Latin America, Africa, and Eastern Europe fell in the 1970s and 1980s, incoming elites sought to balance the norms of justice that emerged in the postwar era with political constraints present in the absence of all-out military victory. Retributive measures, such as mass criminal trials, were frequently replaced with more lenient policies, including truth commissions and blanket amnesties.

Perhaps conditioned by these systemic observations, theoretical arguments designed to identify key determinants of justice in post-repressive states are bound by a common thread: a focus on the relative power of incoming and outgoing elites.[52] Put simply, the greater the relative strength of the old elites compared to the new, the less likely we should see new elites pursue "harsh" forms of justice.[53] Strands of this relative power hypothesis are differentiated by definitions of power and underlying processes. I focus my discussion on three particular types of relative power arguments, centered on political transition, state structures, and public support.

One of the most widely cited explanations in the transitional justice literature focuses on the mode of transition from authoritarianism to democracy.[54] According to this elite-level argument, the path of transition affects justice in two ways. First, it demarcates on a normative level what policies may or may not be acceptable, as the result of a "gentleman's agreement" that might have occurred between negotiating parties. Second, and more important, it suggests that transition type influences the post-transition distribution of political power and, hence, the types of policies available to new elites. According to Samuel Huntington, elites rising to power through revolution are most likely to implement harsh forms of retributive justice, since the former regime's power base (and its ability to cause trouble in the new state) is presumably destroyed. By contrast, political elites emerging from a negotiated transition often give explicit or implicit amnesties to members of the still-powerful old regime and should therefore exercise more restraint in the justice sphere. The least aggressive attempts to deal with the past should occur in states where old elites voluntarily hand over the keys to the new rulers (a "transformation"). As Huntington summarizes his assortment of cases, "Justice was a function of political power. Officials of strong authoritarian regimes that voluntarily ended themselves were not prosecuted; officials of weak authoritarian regimes that collapsed were punished."[55]

Numerous scholars have signed onto Huntington's typology. For some, transition dictates the terms of justice by diffusing power between old and new elites in such a way that no one set of actors can impose its will on others.[56] Only where new elites have victoriously defeated their predecessors can they pursue more aggressive justice policies.[57] Supporters of this argument tend to focus on the veto powers of old elites, who can block prosecutions, as well as the threat of a violent backlash by still-strong perpetrators.[58] In cases of negotiated transition, new elites are said to be "too vulnerable to discard clemency."[59] Supporters of Huntington's theory find an apparently ideal case in the widely studied transition of South Africa, where departing political elites forced amnesty onto the negotiating table in the form of a constitutional amendment.[60] As outgoing president de Klerk plainly explained, "The South African government had not been defeated in battle and the ANC [African National Congress] was not in a position to dictate terms to it."[61]

Other scholars adhering to the relative power logic define power more broadly, taking into account state structures. Guillermo O'Donnell and Philippe Schmitter, for example, emphasize the continued presence in key power ministries of those actors who were complicit in prior abuses.[62] In the South American context, the military is particularly relevant; in Eastern Europe, the police and secret security forces might receive more attention.[63] Their power, as an ostensibly cohesive, armed group, gives these actors the means to disrupt the transition.[64] Presumably, those at higher levels command the significant influence and resources that make justice difficult, though it is feasible that large numbers of lower-level officials acting as a collective might pose the same threat. Loyalties to the old regime and potential feelings of complicity among members of the broader bureaucracy (as well as the judiciary) supply them with the motive for action. The combination could have important ramifications for new elites' capacity to rule, much less to engage in transitional justice.

In practice, the structural argument is largely focused on military regimes, making it sometimes difficult to separate the structure-based elites from the political elites emphasized in the transition-based argument. Supporting evidence for the structural argument is often found in Latin American cases, where military leaders led the negotiation process by which they left executive office but not the military itself, thus positioning them to be, in the words of one well-known Chilean human rights lawyer, a "formidable factor to reckon with." [65] According to this theory, there is a strong fear by new elites that the military might reenter the political sphere if justice is pursued aggressively, particularly given the cohesive nature of the military as an institution.[66] As Tina Rosenberg commented, "powerful militaries still have those guns, the support of the influential upper class, and the arrogance that justified their abuses."[67]

The structural argument is also relevant to nonmilitary dictatorships. Returning to the apparently clear-cut South African case, some in the opposition felt constrained not merely by former elite leaders, but also by those who ran their oppressive apparatus. "The security forces were concerned about their future," an aide to the African National Congress's chief negotiator recalled. "They were not going to go along with an agreement that would put them before a firing squad; why should they?"[68] In this second version of events, South Africa's negotiated settlement demanded compromise and consensus to obtain the loyalty and cooperation not so much of the former ruling class, but of their institutional strong arm.[69]

Finally, others apply an even broader definition of power, based on public support. This argument is in part premised on the notion that new elites shy away from justice measures that could inflame public opinion and increase instability, where significant sectors of society were previously aligned with the old regime.[70] Some proponents of justice have argued that individual criminal accountability can enhance civic unity by transforming collective guilt into a narrower "stigmatization of the political and military leaders who planned the atrocities."[71] But others warn of the opposite: justice can lead to feelings of unfair collective punishment and increasing societal polarization, forcing some societal groups into a hole from which it is difficult to emerge.[72] José Zalaquett presents non-elites as a potentially violent constraint, arguing that a state's social (for example, ethnic, religious) structure may preclude certain types of justice if such policies could antagonize intrasocietal relations, thus "exacerbating divisions that may threaten national unity."[73] Even Huntington, despite his succinct typology, acknowledges this, referring frequently to referenda on justice measures and quoting one Romanian government official as saying, "If we publish the [secret police] files as some people have suggested, there could literally be something worse than a civil war, with friend turning against friend once they find out what is contained in them."[74]

The degree of public acceptance or hostility for an accounting of the past, in turn, may depend partly on the nature and timing of repression.

Decisions on how to deal with the more recent past can arouse strong feelings among societal actors, particularly where high degrees of complicity in past injustices create an atmosphere of what one scholar refers to as "dirty togetherness."[75] Yet the policy dictated by these emotions is unclear. Some observers, such as Zalaquett, have argued that, precisely at this time, justice is most risky and should be put on hold. Others argue that over the long term, as the intensity of emotions fades, there will be less support for aggressive justice, which ostensibly will make justice more difficult to pursue later as opposed to earlier.[76] As a result, crimes committed a relatively long time ago, or those involving less egregious abuses, might be easier to forgive and forget.[77] Of course, the real world does not always fit neatly with these predictions. A Spanish judge recently branded Franco's Spain, where 114,000 were sentenced to death during the 1930s civil war, a "crime against humanity" and launched a series of prosecutions.[78] Yet in Spain there has never been a strong public desire to account for that past, even in the immediate post-Franco years.[79]

It should be highlighted that this Spanish case represents an isolated judicial decision rather than a formal political one. The public support argument might be better applied to yet a third interpretation of the South African case, where some have seen de Klerk's efforts at amnesty as a tactic to minimize public strife and "head off trouble from the militant, vulnerable, white right-wingers."[80] Still, it is clear that public opinion cannot always predict justice policy, perhaps because not all elites interpret or respond the same way to public demands. For example, Argentina's leadership sought immediately after the 1983 elections to placate public opinion by prosecuting senior military officers and establishing agencies to uncover previous abuses.[81] Yet their successors six years later issued mass pardons to those criminals, despite widespread disapproval for the move.[82] In other cases, such as in neighboring Chile, where citizens do not support aggressive justice,[83] some have argued for "public moral leadership that depends ultimately on persuading the people of the correctness of a position, not merely forcing them to submit to it."[84]

This review of relative power arguments, as well as the various interpretations of the South African case, demonstrates differing degrees of overlap between the particular strands. Still, they differ not only with respect to *who* determines the relative power of old and new, but also with regard to the implicit or explicit mechanisms that make relative power a serious constraint. Huntington's transition-based argument seems in part to adhere to normative aspects of the bargaining process (the necessity of upholding informal agreements established just prior to a democratic breakthrough). But it also seems to imply, as do proponents of the structural argument, that if relatively weak new elites pursue retributive justice, they risk a coup or failed state (marked by the inability of new elites to implement policies). By contrast, those focused on societal conditions warn that aggressive justice could lead to civic unrest and even civil war, depending on the attitudes, and perhaps level of complicity, of the broader society. Ultimately, however, all of these arguments center on new elite fears that powerful elements implicated in yesterday's rights violations can (violently) destabilize the political sphere if they perceive justice policies as threatening.

These various relative power arguments all point astutely to possible risks of transitional justice, but each comes with a set of potential weaknesses. Challengers to elite-level, transition arguments might ask why post-oppositionists should respect deals made through arm-twisting by illegitimate outgoing elites, particularly in cases where new elites rapidly and democratically accrue more political power than predicted by transition type.[85] As Zalaquett notes, "political situations are far from static, and if the new government consistently follows the best possible approach, despite being limited by the circumstances it faces, new possibilities may open up along the way."[86] While state-structure explanations address some of the shortfalls in elite-level theories, they leave unaddressed important questions about the cohesiveness of institutional actors, the majority of whom were probably not directly complicit in past violations.[87] Structuralists also sidestep the issue of mass participation in the initial regime change, a factor that may embolden members of the former democratic opposition.

The most obvious weakness of public support explanations is, as with each of the preceding strains of relative power, a lack of elasticity. Are public attitudes non-malleable, structurally determined by experiences and perceptions of past injustices? Or are they more dynamic, influenced by perceptions of present governmental successes and failures,[88] or are they even subject to elite persuasion?[89] Moreover, to what degree is the public directly or indirectly involved in choosing the path of justice? And, finally, are societal conflict and polarization an inevitable result of justice in democratiz-

ing states where institutions allow for mechanisms of peaceful conflict resolution and where political identities can be quite fluid?[90] In many cases, it
appears that even the most aggressive forms of justice are designed primarily
by and for elites themselves.[91]

MOVING FORWARD: THE STRATEGIC ARGUMENT

Relative power arguments dominate the literature in part because they
are so intuitively appealing and seem, at least on the surface, to adequately
reflect the way the world works. However, these arguments are largely un-
tested and plagued by methodological concerns discussed in the next chapter. Moreover, while relative power is largely backward-looking, there is
reason to believe that "weight of the past" explanations (such as transition
type and nature of past violations) cannot be considered in isolation from
"politics of the present" ones (such as contemporary political setting and
other contextual factors).[92] Studies incorporating the two have raised challenges to relative power in the context of previously well-researched cases.
For example, in an analysis of three Latin American states, David Pion-
Berlin found that while the nature of rights violations and relative power
issues helped to set the boundaries for political action, elite preferences and
strategic calculation shaped concrete policy outcomes within these con-
fines.[93] Such studies in part lend credence to the growing belief that there
is no single determinant of justice out there.[94]

These studies also pave the way for a relatively new direction of inquiry in which important elements of the contemporary political environment may influence justice: what Elster refers to as the "more or less
ordinary struggles" characteristic of daily politics.[95] For Elster, such ordinary struggles include efforts at excluding or tainting groups connected to
(or soft on) the former repressors. Some scholars looking beyond the past
have found that everyday coalition politics, characterized by a messy game
of give-and-take, has an important influence on justice.[96] Others focus on
the more concrete side effects of justice that might occur, such as deterio-
rated administrative capacity and depleted resources, which may affect
new elites' ability to efficiently govern.[97] Still others point more directly to
fears among political elites that justice might be seen by their constituents

as a distraction that prevents politicians from tackling more serious, current problems.[98] While these ideas tend to be supported only anecdotally, they represent an important step forward in how we think about justice.

A reexamination of the constraints on transitional justice thus forces us to place the dilemma in a broader strategic framework, where new elites are seen not merely as defenders of the new status quo, but also as political actors striving to maintain power through at least the next elections. Transitional justice can be a plus or a minus in the broader battle for political survival, which, according to the strategic argument, involves balancing inherited constraints with incentives for (in)action created by the everyday political environment. This environment may include transition-based constraints when old elites continue to share political office with new elites, or structure-based constraints when old elites continue to dominate in the power ministries responsible for previous abuses. But the greatest constraint, I argue, emerges in part from public support–based relative power arguments. Leaders whose positions depend on their ability to satisfy their constituents must constantly keep one eye on the public's perceptions and preferences.

The strategic argument differs from the public support argument in two important ways. First, the strategic argument is based on the understanding that justice policies, like other public policies, are multidimensional and can be judged along several criteria.[99] Political elites can frame issues in ways that undermine rigid public support arguments. For example, leaders may effectively bury the most disputed aspects of policies while simultaneously demonstrating how abstract or controversial policies will have a positive impact on people's daily lives.[100] Second, and related, according to the strategic argument, new elites pursue justice policies for which, they calculate, given this multidimensionality, citizens will not vote them out of office. The strategic argument essentially posits that justice is akin to a commodity that can be traded for other policies. Leaders calculate whether they can use the multidimensionality of the policy process to make otherwise unacceptable policies feasible and even advantageous. Finally, while public support arguments focus on the risk of violent intrasocietal schisms based on citizen relationships to past violations, the strategic argument's focus is more on the risk that particular justice policies may cause constituents to become disaffected with a specific political party (or politics altogether) based on their expectations of how these policies affect broader governance (which can also include justice).

I preface this argument with two basic assumptions. First, I assume that a significant portion of new elites, whether motivated by morality, pragmatism, or vengeance,[101] shares private preferences (that is, a personal desire) for harsh justice, insofar as such a policy does not jeopardize their own political survival. Criminal accountability can enhance democratic consolidation (and hence is in the long-term interest of new elites) in a number of ways, from demonstrating a split with the past and equality under the law, to forging common historical understandings and reducing perceptions of collective guilt that might fuel long-term instability.[102] Other forms of justice, including truth commissions, victim compensation, and apologies/condemnations, may satisfy some of these objectives, though harsher mechanisms such as administrative purges and criminal accountability have the added plus of eliminating political opponents. The infrequency of explicit references to this assumption may result from the sharp divide between scholars primarily interested in theoretical determinants of transitional justice and those who advocate transitional justice for a long list of moral, ethical, or practical reasons.[103]

Second, I assume that there are various sources of (potentially conflicting) pressures for and against justice: domestic non-elites, domestic elites, and—often overlooked in the contemporary literature—international elites. States,[104] intergovernmental organizations,[105] and nongovernmental organizations (NGOs)[106] undermine state autonomy in a variety of spheres today, and in the past two decades they have openly expressed preferences for particular types of justice and provided tangible and nontangible pressures to pursue these ends.[107]

In order to maintain power, new elites must thus cater to various interests, which may include the general public, former elites, and international actors. Ultimately, it is the first group that decides who will rule tomorrow. The strategic argument is based on the understanding that democratic leaders are accountable to constituents who expect government to provide essential goods and services. These may be public goods, such as order, security, and civil liberties,[108] or "political goods," from which the broad public benefits, such as anti-inflationary or pro-employment economic policies, or membership in international organizations (and their respective security or economic dividends). The provision of these political goods is a central feature of political viability in democratic states,[109] and features prominently in the good-government literature.[110] Political leaders concerned primarily with their own political survival must ensure that justice policies are perceived to further, or at a minimum to not interfere with, the provision of goods that these leaders can influence.

The strategic approach shares some features of standard rational choice arguments, including the assumption that individuals act first and foremost in pursuit of their own advancement (whether measured in power, money, or prestige) and then act on a coherent set of preferences ranked by the degree to which each policy furthers these objectives.[111] But in contrast to rigid institutional approaches, according to which policy preferences are largely determined by the institutional setting in which a leader finds him or herself, I argue that politicians' preferences may be set prior to taking office, leaving new political elites with the task of balancing personal preferences with institutional constraints.[112] Elites construct policy based on their internal calculation of what they need to provide citizens to be reelected; what they themselves prefer in terms of (justice) policy; and how their (justice) policies might be perceived by constituents to affect delivery of the first.

According to the strategic argument, transitional justice policies are the result of a two-stage process, the first focused on institutionally determined reward structures and the second on institutional competition. This argument takes into account the degree to which political elites are accountable to the public, the types of goods and services that they are expected to provide, and how they anticipate public reactions to their policy choices in particular circumstances.

I focus on two basic types of institutions that play a key role in determining justice policy: constitutionally authoritative *primary* institutions that directly determine the provision of public-regarding goods (for example, a prime minister in a parliamentary system); and constitutionally weak *secondary* institutions that have only an advisory or symbolic role in the allocation of these goods (for example, a president in the classic parliamentary system).

Constitutional status plays a critical role in defining the rules of the game that various governing elites must play to stay in power. Among the important factors influenced by the constitution are terms and constituencies. A president with a guaranteed term might, for example, be more willing to defy constituent demands in the short term than would a prime minister subject to the constant threat of a vote of confidence. Similarly, constitutional delimitations into national versus local constituencies can impact actor preferences, perhaps differentiating prime ministers accountable to aggregated preferences from individual legislators accountable to more local demands. But the most important aspect of constitutional status, I argue, is delegation of authority. Institutional context, even in new democracies, affects how individuals attribute political responsibility for policy success or failure.[113] It is the constitutionally empowered who suffer most when citizen expectations and policy outcomes are out of sync.[114] Different perceptions about constituent demands, even when those constituencies are identically composed, should influence the policy preferences of new elites in different institutions.

The idea that elites rely on their own perceptions, rather than on actual indicators, of public opinion is an important point worth emphasizing. While polling data might indicate where citizens stand on particular issues, there tend to be very few studies that provide data on specific attitudes toward various forms of justice and the salience of those attitudes. This is particularly true in transition states where institutions designed to elucidate citizen preferences may be nonexistent or suspect. There is also evidence that elites may misjudge public opinion based on a more narrow perception of constituency demands and that even with available information, elites sometimes act inconsistently with those demands concerning issues that they judge to be less salient than others.[115] Under these circumstances, leaders take it upon themselves to calculate how justice is likely to be interpreted, taking into account social, economic, and political conditions.

At the first stage of the strategic argument, institutionally based reward structures play a critical role (see Figure 1.1). Since primary actors are responsible for effectively providing political goods, citizen expectations of them are very high. In these institutions, justice policies will be largely dictated by the bottom line: when justice is seen as an impediment to the delivery of goods, it should be avoided; whereas, when it is viewed as beneficial, it should be pursued. Impediments are measured in perceived

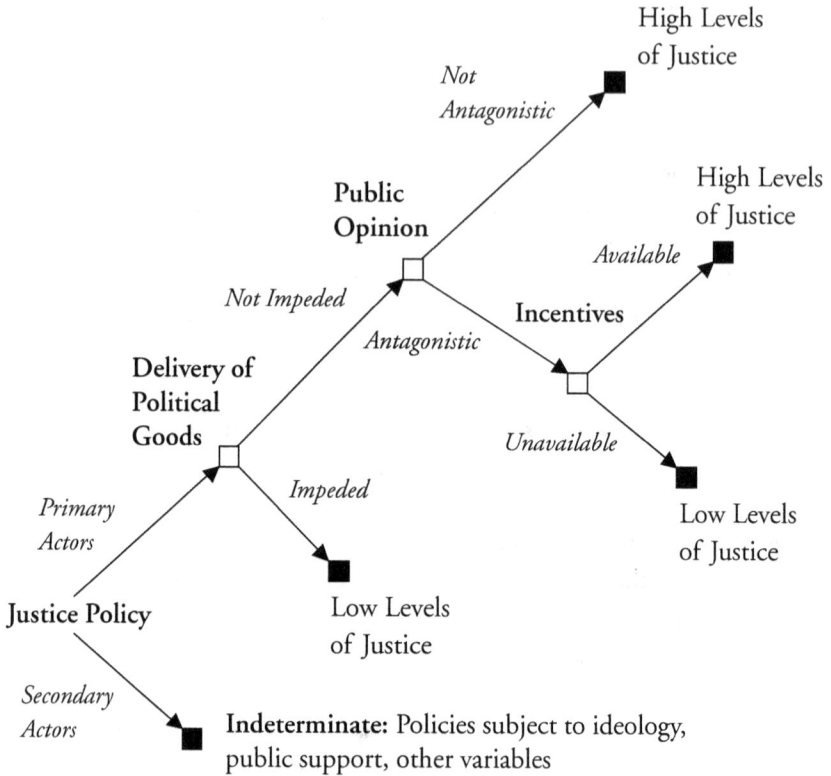

FIGURE 1.1 The Role of Political Goods in Justice Preferences

opportunity costs; even if justice has very little monetary cost, it may be seen as politically costly if it is viewed, for example, as an excessive policy-maker preoccupation. Public attitudes toward justice govern the relationship between goods and justice policies. If the public is neutral or in favor of particular justice measures, elites must simply demonstrate that such measures do not interfere with the provision of goods or may actually comprise an important political good. If the public is staunchly opposed to these measures, primary actors will only be able to pursue justice if they can explicitly link the chosen justice policies to their ability to better provide core political goods, in essence buying off their constituents.

Preferences of Secondary Actors

	High	Low
High	Expedited	Sluggish
Low	Abortive	Impeded

Preferences of Primary Actors

FIGURE 1.2   The Role of Preferences in Justice Policy Outcomes

The behavior of secondary actors is less predictable. As with primary actors, secondary actors must calculate what they must provide to be re-elected, their own justice preferences, and likely constituent perceptions of their justice policies. But, critically, the weakness of their institution reduces citizen expectations with respect to the sorts of political goods that second-ary actors can offer. This, in turn, frees secondary actors from a key policy-making constraint. So while policy choices could be mediated by politi-cal strategy (for example, populism), lower public expectations create more room in which secondary actors' private preferences and ideology may play a role. Even though these secondary actors are constitutionally incapable of halting the will of primary actors, they can employ agenda setting, issue linkages, and public political pressure to increase or decrease primary actors' costs of pursuing justice. The introduction of justice legislation or public statements, appeals, and campaigns might force primary actors to alter their policies.

At the second phase of the strategic argument, configuration of cross-institutional preferences shapes policy outcome (see Figure 1.2). When both primary and secondary actors share preferences for criminal account-ability, the political outcome should be facilitated (*expedited*). Similarly, a cross-institutional antipathy to such harsh justice should close the books on that option until such preferences change (*impeded*). Where primary actors support a process that secondary actors oppose, we should find slow and cautious implementation of criminal accountability (*sluggish*). Where the roles are reversed, primary actors should behave as veto players, blocking or watering down aggressive efforts at justice favored by secondary actors (*abortive*). An abortive outcome may be reflected in more lenient forms of justice, such as truth commissions, efforts at victim compensation, or general condemnations of perceived abusers.

In summary, the strategic argument suggests that justice policy can be less a function of new and old elite power than it is a consequence of institutionally motivated preferences. The path of transition and other aspects of the past, such as public attitudes and the presence of old elites in decision-making bodies, may place some constraints on justice.[116] But these constraints should not be exaggerated. Leaders tasked with running the country will pursue their preferred justice policies when these pose minimal political or economic risk (or are seen as advantageous), and they will eschew justice when it is seen as potentially costly. Justice policies may not be chosen to explicitly advance political careers or personal fortunes, but the more likely these policies are to undermine those objectives, the more likely they will be avoided. Levels of policy authority can help to account for diverging justice preferences across institutions and between governmental bodies. Those political elites with less policy authority may influence policy output through a variety of mechanisms, bringing it more in line with their own preferences. Justice is a compromise between new elites facing divergent, institutionally defined demands from their constituencies, as well as their own preferences, not simply between new elites and their former oppressors.

LIKE OTHER APPROACHES to transitional justice, the strategic approach is a simplified model seeking to explain a complex phenomenon. The strategic argument is meant to complement, not replace, relative power arguments. The two share a common logic: political leaders must take into account the implications of justice policies on their broader goals, which might include maintaining (or attaining) power and acting on individual, private preferences. Justice policies have implications beyond the direct outcome of a particular mechanism, so just as the decision to launch criminal prosecutions might result in societal reconciliation or civil war, it might indirectly signal the start of an economic boom (for example, thanks to renewed faith in the rule of law) or an economic crisis (caused by fear of political instability).

I have consciously structured the strategic argument in a way designed to incorporate relative power concerns. For example, primary actors determined to balance justice policies with the provision of political goods will obviously act differently when new elites completely rule the primary institutions versus when they share power with old elites. In the case of the former, new elites might be able to more aggressively pursue justice than in the latter, where they might be forced to make compromises to ensure that their colleagues from the old regime support other (political goods) policies also on the agenda.

Other aspects of justice also find a place in the strategic argument, acting as implicit constraints on, or incentives for, particular forms of justice. Justice frequently plays a role in identity politics, for example. The degree to which citizens identify with and support justice should impact on new elites' internal calculations of what they must provide to win reelection. Where publics are enthusiastic justice supporters, new elites might be able to pursue more aggressive measures without the risk that their constituents will perceive these policies as overly cumbersome and as an obstacle to the provision of other political goods, because justice itself could be seen as a political good in this context. Where publics are less interested in opening up the past, new elites face a more difficult balancing act.

By focusing on new elites' internal calculations of what publics want and expect from them, the strategic argument allows us to take into consideration a range of variables not explicitly addressed, which help set new elites' parameters of movement. In one country, justice may face public opposition due to high levels of complicity; in another, it may be intimately linked to identity; and in a third, the public may have little interest at all. In each case, the degree of perceived public support will indirectly affect new elites' internal calculus of how much people are willing to pay for justice. Structural constraints, including the explicit costs and the opportunity costs of a particular justice policy (which may in part result from the power that old elites continue to wield), must be balanced against this internal calculus to inform elites what forms of justice are politically feasible. In the next chapter, I discuss seven specific types of justice that are frequently undertaken in post-repressive states. These justice measures make up the "transitional justice spectrum" that serves as my basic dependent variable in each of the case studies that follows.

2

The Justice Spectrum

A New Methodological Approach
to Studying Transitional Justice

In this chapter, I discuss methodological problems that currently hinder us from effectively analyzing key determinants of justice policies, and propose a new tool to help us overcome these problems. More specifically, I argue that underspecification of the dependent variable (justice) makes it difficult to produce hypotheses and empirical observations that succinctly correlate power to justice type. The tool that I propose here, referred to as the "transitional justice spectrum," is designed to minimize this problem and thus allow researchers to conduct more rigorous, cross-national tests of transitional justice arguments. This spectrum is intended to serve as a yardstick to assess causality in transitional justice decision making, an analytical tool that will impose greater clarity on what, and subsequently how, these researchers are measuring.

I begin this chapter by discussing methodological shortcomings in the current literature. Next, I explain the theoretical rationale for my transitional justice spectrum before I break the spectrum down into its component parts, briefly exploring each measure and discussing its placement. In the next chapter, I will discuss in detail the research design for this book, explaining how this study uses the transitional justice spectrum to explore key determinants of transitional justice in the cases of Poland, Serbia, Croatia, and Uzbekistan.

THE WEAKNESSES OF RELATIVE POWER

In chapter 1, I raised a number of challenges to the various relative power arguments before presenting my own strategic argument. One purpose of highlighting these challenges is to suggest the need for more vigorous scrutiny. The enumerated shortcomings demonstrate the types of holes and inconsistencies that are prone to fester in theories not tested empirically using clear measures. Indeed, perhaps because of the natural appeal of relative power explanations, scholars frequently defend them by largely anecdotal evidence. Samuel Huntington, for example, evaluates his popular argument by referring to a range of cases, from the Philippines to Romania, which appear to support his thesis. To pick one example, I look at the case of Uruguay, which Huntington claims had, under military rule, the highest proportion of political prisoners in the world.[1] According to Huntington, the transitional justice policies of Uruguay's new leaders, who came to power through negotiations, were severely constrained by the prevailing power of military officers who first promised to obstruct criminal prosecutions and then made threats in order to influence (successfully, Huntington says) a public referendum on the subject.[2] Similarly, the new regime's relative weakness left it unable to pursue a truth commission, which, according to one general, would have compromised the amnesty that military leaders assured themselves by handing over power.

Instructive as this study is, Huntington is guilty of oversimplification, and he rests his theory that, across cases, "justice was a function of political power" on the observation of only two aspects of justice: criminal prosecutions and truth commissions.[3] Even arguments intended to look beyond relative power frequently revert to this truncated indicator. Luc Huyse, for example, concludes that "the need to avoid confrontation"[4] prompts new elites to exchange criminal prosecutions for truth commissions as "the least unsatisfactory solution."[5] Michelle Sieff and Leslie Wright, who argue that relative power sets "the parameters for the application of the norms of justice," similarly conclude that if new elites believe that peace and justice are reconcilable, they will prosecute, but otherwise they will opt for truth commissions.[6]

This focus on the "usual suspects" of transitional justice (criminal trials, amnesties, or truth commissions) is problematic. First, these terms may marginalize other justice measures that have been employed (perhaps successfully) by political elites around the world. Indeed, scholars have explored the pros and cons of a whole gamut of intermediate policies, including public apologies, victim compensation, and banning perpetrators from public office.[7]

More important, underspecification of the dependent variable makes it difficult to produce hypotheses and empirical observations that succinctly correlate power to justice type. How can one correlate transitional justice and power when there is no clear understanding of how the many transitional justice measures relate to one another? How do these policies compare to one another qualitatively, and under what conditions will a new leadership decide to implement which steps? While relative power might correlate nicely with the likelihood of criminal prosecutions, this does not provide strong evidence that justice is a function of power—only that one type of justice appears to be affected by this particular independent variable. If transitional justice policies are a function of relative power, it seems that both the primary independent variable (old-new elite power) and the dependent variable (justice type) should be defined incrementally. If, for example, we begin doing this and go on to concede that prosecutions and administrative purges are "harsher" than truth commissions, then relative power proponents might expect a weak, new elite leadership to launch truth commissions rather than prosecutions or purges. But what if, for example, the new leadership instead conducts purges but finds itself unable to launch an independent truth commission? This may suggest that something other than (and perhaps exclusive of) relative power is at work.

Scholars addressing the broad range of transitional justice options to date tend to refrain from outlining a clear policy hierarchy.[8] Rankings tend to be restricted to the obvious, when discussion touches on only two or three policy options (especially blanket amnesties, truth commissions, and criminal prosecutions), and general policy guidelines remain limited to the *how to*, rather than the *when to* or *when not to*, of one specific justice

Lenient • (1) Cessation and codification of human rights
violations

• (2) Rebuke of the old system

• (3) Rehabilitation and compensation for victims

• (4) Creation of a truth commission

• (5) Purging human rights abusers from public
function

• (6) Criminal prosecution of "executors"
(those lower on the chain-of-command)

• (7) Criminal prosecution of commanders
Harsh (those higher on the chain-of-command)

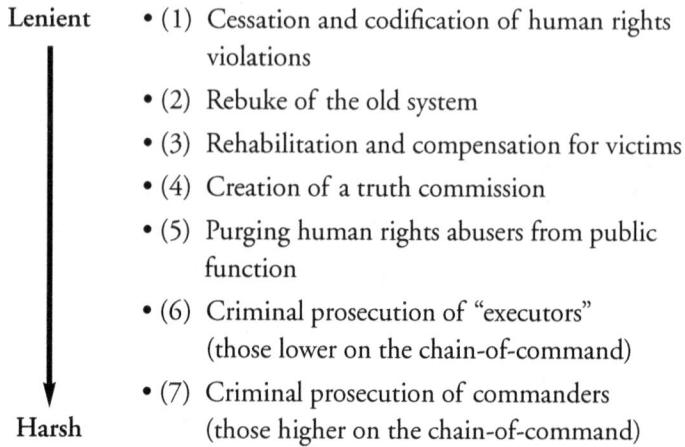

FIGURE 2.1   Transitional Justice Spectrum

policy.[9] Authors are clearly cognizant of the different risk levels involved
in the policy options, but there has been no attempt to systematically address this. Yet without explicitly defining the dependent variable in ways
that allow one to measure risk, it is difficult to have confidence in the widespread consensus that relative power is the key determinant of justice.

The goal of this chapter is therefore to suggest ways of testing relative
power arguments and other theoretical arguments concerning transitional
justice. The first step toward this objective involves specifying the dependent variable: the justice mechanisms available to a new regime. There exists a range of possible actions that leaders can undertake in order to pursue accountability for human rights violations. Through a review of the
democratization and transitional justice literatures, I have identified seven
frequently used policies and placed them in what I call a transitional justice spectrum (see Figure 2.1). These mechanisms are ranked by the degree
to which they personalize responsibility, as well as by the severity of each
policy's repercussions for the perpetrators. These measures co-vary early in
the spectrum, but, after type 4, when concrete individuals are already targeted, severity continues to rise independently.

The logic of the spectrum is twofold. Most broadly, it organizes justice mechanisms along a continuum that gradually proceeds from restorative (alleviating victims' pain) to retributive (punishing perpetrators). At the same time, and not coincidentally, this spectrum incorporates a relative power logic, since each incremental step up the justice ladder involves the implementation of a more provocative, or threatening, policy, with respect to members of the old regime. This spectrum operationalizes risk in ways that should explicitly allow transitional justice scholars to observe the strengths and weaknesses of relative power arguments, which should dictate the highest level of justice feasible for a new leadership. The argument here is not that criminal justice necessarily trumps all other forms of justice, but that it is potentially the most risky. In the straightforward case of Huntington, for instance, extremely weak regimes (for example, those handed power by old elites) should refrain from any measures other than type 1; moderately strong regimes might pursue up to type 4; and only the strongest regimes (for example, those arising out of revolution) would be able to pursue types 5 through 7. In cases where these expectations are not met, use of this spectrum might suggest other determinants.

This spectrum is necessarily limited. Transitional justice in practice touches on truth, memory, reconciliation, and other important dimensions, some of which have been omitted here. Just a few examples of the omitted policies include amnesties, various aspects of historical accounting (such as the opening of museums and the revision of history textbooks), and, most notably, lustration (a phenomenon to which I devote chapter 3). These omissions were made for several reasons. First, in order to keep the spectrum both manageable in terms of data collection (see chapter 4) and generalizable across regions, I avoid mechanisms largely specific to any particular region, such as property restitution and public identification of former secret agents common in the postcommunist space.

Second, and more important, I understand justice to be multidimensional; some of the measures I have focused on are closely related to others that I have omitted. My omission of amnesties, for example, is based on the understanding that the conscious choice to avoid criminal prosecutions (and, arguably, administrative purges) amounts to a de facto amnesty (which anyway can be later annulled). More generally, I have attempted to operationalize various forms of justice so they are represented on the spectrum at least indirectly. So while this study omits many mechanisms specific to the politics of memory, for example, it includes others that fundamentally affect this sphere of activity (such as rebukes and truth commissions); and while it leaves out property restitution, it includes other forms of victim compensation. Such categorizations are not unusual. In the postcommunist context, scholars have lumped together such potentially disparate measures as truth commissions, lustration, and declassification of police files.[10] The overlap can be even broader, as James Booth noted, fusing criminal trials and textbook revisions: "The great fear for memory-justice is that the crime will be allowed to slip into oblivion, into the forgotten; that the passage of time will, like a natural solvent or a willed forgetting, free the perpetrators and weaken the already weak hold of justice in the world. A trial is one forum of resistance to this; it is a venue for seeking the victory of the memory of justice over the will to forget, for seeking, in a sense, the rule of law."[11]

Finally, in keeping with international norms, the only punitive forms of justice characterized by material consequences (such as criminal trials and purges) included on this spectrum involve individual and not group guilt. Administrative cleansings must rely on evidence of individual wrongdoings and include a process of appeal (elements that lustration frequently falls short of). This is not to say that other forms of justice here are not retributive; indeed, I argue that there are retributive elements to even mechanisms traditionally characterized as restorative. And almost every mechanism of transitional justice can arguably lead to innocent victims. Even property restitution, for example, can negatively affect third parties who bought confiscated property from the state.[12] But I limit those measures involving the greatest deprivation of civil or political rights to those that are designed to punish individuals rather than groups.

Below, I describe each step on the proposed spectrum, including a brief discussion of the measure's pros and cons, a theoretical rationale for its risk-assessment rating, and a series of examples illustrating how this measure has been carried out in practice, as well as the types of threats associated with it. While readers may disagree with the order of these measures (for example, preferring to switch types 2 and 3 or 6 and 7), this should not detract from the use of this spectrum as a general tool. Moreover, such disagreements—and especially empirical evidence indicating that a re-ordering is necessary—could generate further discussion that would only strengthen future versions of this instrument. While I defend the particular placement below, for the purpose of my broader study, we can simply express justice as "lenient" (types 1–3), "moderate" (type 4), and "harsh" (types 5–7) (see Figure 2.1).

TYPE 1. CESSATION AND CODIFICATION OF HUMAN RIGHTS VIOLATIONS

In a democratizing state, a basic task for the new regime is to halt human rights violations. One way in which new leaders can codify the most brutal violations orchestrated by the previous political power holders, such as torture and illegal arrest or detention (chapters 5 and 9, respectively, of the Universal Declaration on Human Rights), is by signing, ratifying, and integrating into domestic law major international human rights conventions. The purpose of integrating international law is not to advance other forms of transitional justice, but rather to express disapproval for past activities and emphasize a break by the new regime. The cessation of human rights violations is the critical and obvious first step in justice, and the one that least taxes a new regime's resources.

Adoption of international laws can advance domestic human rights in several ways that may be more elusive when rights are honored solely in domestic constitutions, which were frequently beautifully written in fact but were ignored by the preceding regime in practice. On the international stage, states often base future cooperation on potential partner reputation, that is, on how they upheld past international commitments, including those in the human rights sphere.[13] The heavy investment involved in treaty negotiation and ratification also suggests that participating parties generally intend to remain true to their promises.[14] International treaties can also result in new domestic institutions (for example, subunits responsible for treaty implementation) that have a large stake in legal observance and eventually serve as a pressure point on the signatory state.[15] Ratification of international rights agreements can also alter internal political opportunity structures, directly emboldening opposition groups and indirectly expanding their collective action repertoire in ways that make them more formidable opponents to potential rights violators.[16]

Because this first step of justice involves exclusively positive steps, it is essentially risk-free for a new democratic leadership. The cessation of rights violations and the adoption of basic international rights norms and laws mark a new course in a country's politics, but they do not necessarily threaten the old power holders. New political elites do not confront (either directly or indirectly) members of the former regime or rights abusers who linger in the state apparatus. At the same time, they assure pro-justice forces in society that their most essential judicial needs are being addressed.

A review of signatories to the International Covenant on Civil and Political Rights (ICCPR), the ICCPR's first protocol allowing the Human Rights Committee to accept private citizen complaints, and the Convention against Torture suggests that incoming regimes do use international human rights agreements to signal a new era of liberty.[17] During a major period of liberalization in Algeria (1989), for example, the country's new leaders passed all of these agreements in a three-month span. A similar pattern is clear in such diverse states as Angola (1992, as the country embarked on multiparty elections), Sudan (1986, just after the fall of President Nu-meiry), Argentina (1986, following the country's "dirty war"), and Benin (1992, following democratic elections that ended decades of military rule). Soon after the fall of communism, most former Soviet and Eastern Bloc states signed onto at least one human rights convention protecting political rights formerly denied.

It should be noted that the first type of justice is frequently enacted by violator regimes themselves, often in an attempt to enhance their legitimacy on the world stage and, consequently, at home.[18] Formalized obligations signed by repressive leaders frequently mark the beginning of the end for human rights-violating regimes, which fall victim to the influential mechanisms described above, including rising domestic demands for compliance.[19] The Helsinki Final Act, for example, became a point of departure for opposition human rights demands in the communist Eastern Bloc. It is also clear, however, that some countries that have signed international agreements have made little effort to implement them, whether because the signing leaders no longer found implementation to be in their best interest or, as in the case of Sudan, successive regime changes empowered leaders with differing preferences.[20] This serves as a reminder that the authority of international institutions remains relatively weak and that the first type of justice can be perceived as low-cost on the part of both rights-violating regimes and incoming democratic ones.

TYPE 2. REBUKE OF THE OLD SYSTEM

The noncritical nature of type 1 justice is supplanted by a broad and impersonal attack on the former system in the second type. A rebuke, in the form of a general condemnation of, or apology for, the old system can come in a variety of forms, from parliamentary laws and resolutions to public speeches by high-level members of the new government. Like type 1 justice, apologies serve as a recognition of the state's duty to respect human rights.[21] The goal of rebukes should be, according to Karl Jaspers, to make "a clear distinction between the transitional government and the previous regime."[22] Condemnation and apologies are essentially restorative; they open the door to public discussion about what the preceding regime was and what it was not.[23] As such, a rebuke of past abuses may also be a first step toward social reconciliation.[24]

Apologies and condemnations are declarations that concede that past actions were inexcusable and that assign a guilty side.[25] They involve an acknowledgment of responsibility and can "correct a public record, afford public acknowledgment of a violation, assign responsibility, and reassert the moral baseline to define violations of basic norms."[26] Acknowledging an offense can be even more important to victims than reparations.[27] Often collective apologies, like condemnations, are more expressions of sympathy than actual apologies.[28] The significance of an apology might be affected by both substantive factors (explaining what occurred and requesting forgiveness) and contextual ones (where, how, and by whom the apology is delivered).[29]

Condemnations and apologies, moreover, can also serve a retributive function, as a gateway to culpability. Apologies can be used as a form of retribution when issued by the guilty party.[30] When issued by the wrongdoer, an apology allows for a role reversal, forcing a perpetrator to "bring himself low" by "begging for forgiveness."[31] Yet, by condemning the system rather than specific actors, new elites avoid threatening their predecessors or those associated with them. This leeway reduces the risk of aggressive defense; members of the old elite remain protected by ambiguity. Anonymous actors from repressive bureaucracies can offset any responsibility by claiming to be mere cogs in the machine who were unaware of what was ultimately being cranked out. Those with higher profiles can (re)define themselves as reformers, doing their best to improve a bad system from within.[32] Since a vague denunciation is unlikely to convey shocking new information to a society that witnessed oppression, rebukes may be problematic, but they are not incriminating.[33]

A newly empowered regime logically faces greater risk from this second type of justice than it did from the legal regulation of type 1. Rebukes create an indirect punitive effect, where those associated with the target regime are subject to political humiliation. The heavy weight of such rebukes is illustrated by the fierce resistance put up by states to impersonal rebukes of their countries on the international stage.[34] At the United Nations, for example, Security Council resolutions with no legal enforcement power are protested in tense debates, walkouts, and even official vetoes.[35] On the domestic stage, condemnation may be met with tolerance or even repentance on the side of the condemned, but it can also draw negative reactions.[36] Members of the old elite can contest rebukes in a variety of ways, from the veto of an official declaration by groups still in power, to grassroots efforts by excluded or weak opposition movements to delegitimize accusations.

In practice, former leaders of repressive states frequently show at least some resistance to rebukes, if only symbolic. When Argentina's President Carlos Menem pardoned ex-general and former ruler Jorge Videla, who had been sentenced to life in prison in 1985 for his role in hundreds of murders, abductions, and tortures, the general indignantly called for "the army's vindication and the reparation of military honors."[37] Similarly, when Chile's new democratic government in 1990 held a state funeral for former president Salvador Allende, who had been killed and left in an unmarked grave during General Augusto Pinochet's 1973 coup, military leaders (still under Pinochet) refused to grant him military honors.[38] In Spain, right-wing parties were politically embarrassed by a 1996 left-wing move to pass a condemnation of the rightist Franco regime, more than twenty years after the

Spanish dictator had died.[39] They agreed to the measure in 2002, after almost six years of debate. In all of these cases, those persons associated with the former regime claimed that they were not involved in any wrongdoing and resisted public rebuke.

TYPE 3. REHABILITATION AND COMPENSATION FOR VICTIMS

Rehabilitation, or legal restoration, and compensation are two restorative measures aimed primarily at improving the lives of those who suffered unjustly under the former regime.[40] As with rebukes, rehabilitation and compensation can mark a break with the past. Of the two measures, rehabilitation, including the annulment of sentences issued in the context of political repression, appears to be the least costly and controversial. Victim compensation can be more difficult, requiring potentially heavy state financial allocations. The latter has received considerable attention from transitional justice scholars, who argue that fiscal resources can "right" past wrongs materially as well as symbolically. Some say that compensation should be aimed at "restoring victims to something approaching their status quo ante,"[41] while others go so far as to argue that victims' "well-being should not be sacrificed in the interest of national reconciliation."[42] Several intergovernmental organizations have claimed that post-repressive states have a legal obligation to offer legal and financial redress to former victims.[43]

While rehabilitation and compensation appear purely restorative, affiliates of the former regime may interpret them as an indirect attack. Unlike impersonal rebukes discussed in type 2, however, attacks on specific violations of the past era can introduce the concept of personal accountability. If this family suffered, who inflicted the pain? Perhaps for this reason, the commander-in-chief of the Chilean navy responded to a presidential promise to provide reparations by rejecting "payment of compensation as a foolish and offensive way of dealing with established concepts and rules such as security, intelligence, due obedience, and others."[44] Similarly, when the Spanish right-wing Popular Party finally agreed to accept a condemnation of the Franco regime, it stood firm in its opposition to clauses that mandated rehabilitation and reparations for the dictator's victims,[45] perhaps reflecting fears of the political ramifications inherent in public expenditures in their name.[46] Personal emotions may have also played a role. Some former communists and judicial authorities in Central Europe expressed skepticism and earnest surprise at new laws that would reverse their previous decisions.[47] Others protested when their faces were shown in an exhibition connected with Stalinist-era victims who had later been rehabilitated.[48]

Increased risks that come with rehabilitation and compensation may lead to watered-down measures. Sri Lankan officials, for example, promised in the early 1990s to compensate those persons who had suffered in the government campaign against Marxist rebels, but, in an apparent bid to ward off critics, they required them to have a death certificate, which the government would not issue in the thousands of cases where a family member's fate was "unknown."[49] Similarly, when the Argentinean government agreed to compensation in late 1992, reparations were limited to people who had been convicted by military courts or detained under emergency powers. Political prisoners convicted by civilian courts, those held in secret prisons, and families of the thousands of the "disappeared" were ineligible.[50] Economic conditions in those states engaged in radical economic reforms have also resulted in serious flaws in the compensation process. In 1990, for example, the Czechoslovak parliament promised more than $800 million to "resistance heroes" who had suffered as a result of their opposition to the communist regime after 1948. Because the state lacked the cash to support the measure, however, compensation took the form of shares in privatized state companies.[51]

TYPE 4. CREATION OF A TRUTH COMMISSION

Truth commissions, or officially sanctioned, temporary bodies established to create a public record of past abuses, are frequently cited as a "third way" between criminal prosecutions and blanket amnesties.[52] Priscilla Hayner defines truth commissions as "official bodies set up to investigate a past period of human rights abuses or violations of international humanitarian law" and suggests that they share four primary elements.[53] First, they are temporary; and second, they are given the authority to dig into the past. Third, this is an effort to create a general picture of a repressive period of time rather than a single event. And fourth, they can exist as solely domestic projects or can be sponsored by international organizations. As Hayner notes, "By their very nature, truth commissions are quite pliable, and can be created in almost any shape or size, and to fit any number of agendas, depending on the circumstances and who holds the most influence over their design and operation."[54] This broad definition qualifies as truth commissions numerous types of public investigations into the past.

These commissions perform several functions, from providing an environment in which victims and/or perpetrators can tell their stories to supplying a forum for "a meaningful acknowledgment of past abuses by an official body perceived domestically and internationally as legitimate and impartial."[55] They can be public or private; designed to actively conduct investigations or passively hear testimony; empowered with legal rights of forgiveness (amnesty); or deprived of such authority. Truth commissions have been ascribed with purposes that range from the functional (establishing the official death records necessary for relatives to obtain benefits) to the metaphysical (establishing a historical record that might lower intrasocietal tensions).[56] Commission hearings are often said to be victim-oriented, providing what David Crocker calls a "public platform for victims," where they "receive sympathy for their suffering."[57] They can also be understood as society-oriented, to the degree that they aim to promote reconciliation; or policy-oriented, when they document abuse patterns that are useful in reforming the political system or specific institutions.

Though usually branded as restorative mechanisms, truth commissions mark the transition from previously described justice measures that assigned only broad or indirect responsibility, to subsequent measures on this spectrum designed to personalize blame. In cases where victims or perpetrators discuss the role of individuals in a public forum, they are inherently punitive. While retributive aspects of truth commissions are subtle (rights violators are not formally deprived of their freedom or livelihoods), the profound effects of public humiliation,[58] ranging from social ostracism in the private sphere to political defeat in the public one, have led some scholars to label this "concealed retribution."[59] While alleged perpetrators may be dismissive of charges,[60] identification of former human rights violators, particularly in public truth commissions, is one step up the ladder toward personal accountability, and it may pose a direct threat to those aligned with the former system.

A closer analysis of the South African case illustrates the risks facing the new government over transitional justice in 1994. In a 1999 autobiography, former president F. W. de Klerk cited power politics as key to attaining (conditional) amnesty for his constituents.[61] Acknowledging this, ANC negotiators were squeezed between their own constituents, who rejected blanket amnesty, and those of the National Party, who threatened to hinder negotiations if faced with criminal prosecution.[62] In an effort to compromise, ANC leaders eventually settled for a state truth commission that would include amnesty for all who confessed to politically motivated rights violations.

Some South African whites saw the truth commission as a threat rather than a bargain. Archbishop Desmond Tutu opened the commission, acknowledging that many whites viewed it as "an Inquisition, a witch-hunt."[63] Some past violators, especially in the potentially dangerous security services, chose not to come forward, fearing that the commission would deny them amnesty and send them to court.[64] The perception by whites that public attention was focused on only white perpetrators brought National Party criticism and, according to de Klerk, led to anger and vows for vengeance among blacks, as well as a dangerously "unhealthy self-image among many whites."[65] Social tensions remained high even after the commission handed over its final report, admitted its deputy chairman.[66] A majority of South Africans remained opposed to the amnesty, even though it was instrumental in bringing about confessions.[67]

The experiences of other truth commissions, as in the South African case, suggest that they can alternate between frailty and threat. In the former category, a Ugandan commission established by President Yoweri Museveni in 1986 was so deprived of funding that its inquiry dragged on for a decade, during which time it lost the public's confidence and interest.[68] Limited support for the commission may have reflected hypocrisy, given the Museveni regime's ongoing use of torture and extrajudicial killings, but it may also have been an under-the-table gesture to political parties (some run by military officers) in exchange for respecting Museveni's "non-party" democratic rules.[69] Some truth commissions, such as those in Bolivia and Ecuador, were disbanded before they even published a report.[70] Still others have been the subject of public consternation from senior officials under investigation. In response to a UN-sponsored truth commission in El Salvador, military officers, accused of most of the violations, expressed common opposition, complaining that "because of a few bad [members], an entire institution is being judged."[71]

TYPE 5. PURGING OF HUMAN RIGHTS ABUSERS FROM PUBLIC POSITIONS

The first act of tangible punishment in this spectrum is the purging of human rights abusers from public positions. Scholars cite several benefits of replacing former, tainted functionaries with new personnel. Staffing important security organs with people unaffiliated with past rights violations can increase the public's trust in institutions necessary for a young state's survival.[72] This is particularly important when the changes affect key law-enforcement bodies, such as judicial institutions and the police, which are often associated with past state crimes. New leaders can also use purges of the government payroll to reinforce the line between past and present political orders, enhancing rule-of-law concepts and their overall legitimacy. Finally, institutional cleansing is not only a retributive act against past violators, but also a restorative one for past victims. Authorities can put into place people who previously may have been denied positions because of their political views, thus, in effect, creating a form of affirmative action.[73]

While post-turnover purges are not uncommon, they can be destabilizing.[74] A large-scale vetting can tax the resources of an already weak state, for example, by overloading the court system or dismantling important elements of state security. This is especially painful in transition states where the very institutions employed to do the vetting are those being vetted. A second danger is that large groups of the purged may come together in opposition to the new order. This depends in part on who (what ministries, for example) is the target of vetting, a question that itself poses practical and ethical problems.[75] In his analysis of lustration in Czechoslovakia, Andrew Rigby warns that even mild forms of lustration can suddenly turn into widespread purges that are difficult to control.[76] In an effort to stave off this possibility, some international bodies have attempted to create guidelines for post-transformation administrative restructuring.[77]

While types 1 through 4 of this justice spectrum spare former rights abusers any formal sanction, employment bans at type 5 for the first time impinge on their civil liberties. Because large groups of unitary actors may be threatened, the risk of collective action is increased. As provocative as this measure may seem to some elites, however, there are ways to lower the risk of destabilizing collective action. Older functionaries, for example, may be able to transition into early retirement, while the younger ones may either have less experience with the former regime (and therefore will be allowed to stay in their positions) or will find another source of income relatively easily.[78] By adopting an alternative profession or accepting a lesser role in public life, members of the former regime may continue to enjoy freedom and avoid criminal liability. At the same time, human rights offenders are punished for their actions and separated from the new government.

Purges following World War II were common and often extended into occupational groups not generally associated with rights violations. In France, for example, 1,000 politicians and 500 diplomats were vetted, but so, too, were 6,000 teachers.[79] At the same time, many of the postwar purges, which Allied victors encouraged or actively participated in, were short-lived. For example, purges of "active exponents of militarism and militant nationalism" enforced by the American occupation in Japan were reversed once the victors had left, leaving less than 9,000 of the 202,000 originally purged still punished.[80] Italians also purged some 2,000 government employees but reinstated most of them under a 1948 amnesty. In all cases, the risk of injustice loomed because evidence was frequently difficult to obtain, and those people who were pursuing the purges often had a personal stake in the outcomes, as, for example, in the Netherlands.[81]

Cases from after the immediate postwar period illustrate the nuances and dangers of purges, particularly when they involve former military rulers. The Karamanlis government in Greece immediately dismissed senior-level ministry personnel and subsequently went about vetting virtually all elements of the bureaucracy, which culminated in 108,000 disciplinary actions, mostly involving termination, in only a few months.[82] Yet the Greeks were much more cautious with regard to the military. Only in January 1975, after the brigadier general loyal to the former regime had been retired and the risks of a coup were perceived to have diminished, did the new defense minister feel secure enough to purge the military ranks, retiring more than

200 army officers, including eighteen out of twenty-eight of the army's major generals and most of the division commanders.[83] In El Salvador, when a three-member civilian commission concluded an investigation of 250 high-ranking officers accused of rights violations and corruption, its list of recommended dismissals sent rumors of a military coup throughout the country. There were also fears that military personnel could disrupt democracy in other ways, such as by publicizing reputation-damaging intelligence files at their disposal: "The biggest danger is not a coup d'état because that makes no sense," said opposition politician Rubén Zamora. "The danger is that they unleash a dirty war." [84] Such fears were also common in postcommunist states.[85]

New elites in a variety of post-authoritarian states face similar risks as those successors of brutal military regimes. Depending on the nature of the repressive state, human rights violations could have been carried out by the formal military officers, paramilitary organizations loyal to the government, intelligence apparatuses, or police units—which may remain intact following political transition and thus have the potential for collective action. In countries of the former Eastern Bloc, for example, intelligence services responsible for numerous human rights violations during the communist period remained largely intact after the Communist Party fell. Newly elected leaders were forced to use a variety of methods to minimize the risk of collective opposition from these circles as they were being disassembled. These strategies included offering rewards, rather than punishment, in exchange for exits (such as early retirement), depoliticizing the process (such as listing certain departments that were simply not needed in the new regime), and allowing former functionaries to find work in other agencies of the government.[86]

TYPE 6. CRIMINAL PROSECUTION OF "EXECUTORS" (THOSE LOWER ON THE CHAIN OF COMMAND)

Since the Nuremberg trials of Nazi leaders following World War II, international law has promoted the prosecution of human rights criminals. The Allied Control Council Law No. 10 and the International Military Tribunal Charter, which allowed for the first international war-crime tribunals at Nuremberg and Tokyo, established legal precedents for justice.[87] International human rights norms gradually became codified in an international Bill of Rights, made up of the Universal Declaration on Human Rights (1948), the International Covenant on Civil and Political Rights (1966), and the International Covenant on Economic, Social, and Cultural Rights (1966). More important, the Convention on the Prevention and Punishment of the Crime of Genocide (1948) and the Convention against Torture (1984), which specifically provide for individual criminal liability, have served as the legal basis for peacetime justice. Intergovernmental organizations and local courts have increasingly justified and encouraged criminal prosecutions based on international human rights law, with both international and domestic trials finding a variety of advocates.[88]

Scholars point to diverse benefits from prosecuting human rights violators.[89] Punishment can show that all citizens answer to the same law, and it can also gather public support for democratic values, push a new political culture into being, and, like truth commissions, establish a public record that is difficult to refute. Moreover, criminal trials are evidence that violators are individuals (rather than anonymous cogs in the machine) who bear personal responsibility for their actions. By pursuing these individuals, the state can reject the "dangerous culture of collective guilt and retribution that often produces further cycles of resentment and violence."[90] Moreover, criminal trials can give victims a psychological sense of justice and demonstrate that courts are legitimate, respectable, and dependable institutions in the new order.[91] Jaspers also claims that by showing "institutional disapproval of individual behavior," new states can expedite reforms in institutions responsible for criminal acts, such as the military and police force.[92] This, in turn, may prevent noninstitutionalized processes or vigilante justice.[93]

New states may have difficulty in carrying out criminal trials for a variety of reasons. Trials may be logistically difficult in states where there is a lack of qualified lawyers, a problem that can be compounded when there are large numbers of defendants. For example, some 2,200 ex-soldiers and communist activists in Ethiopia spent almost six years in prison before the government officially charged them in 1997 with various human rights violations.[94] In postwar Rwanda, where 95 percent of the judges and lawyers had been killed in the country's 1994 genocide, tens of thousands of their alleged killers languished in prison for years with few members of the judiciary available to try them.[95] Fair trials can also be difficult in countries such as postwar Germany, where the unreformed judiciary played a vital role in the former regime's repressive apparatus.[96] As one Polish politician noted in 1992, "the prosecutor has to execute the decisions of government but the judges are from another era."[97] And there are also legal questions related to what critics refer to as "retroactive justice," that is, trying individuals for acts that were not necessarily domestic crimes when they were committed.[98]

In addition to being legally and logistically difficult, criminal trials elevate personal accountability to a higher level, thus raising the stakes thrown down by the new regime. Threats to former functionaries accused of human rights abuses may provoke these targeted persons, particularly at the upper echelons, to take aggressive action to stop the trials. Depending on the institutional culture, these threats can result in organized opposition from bodies of which the targeted functionaries are members. They can also increase the fear of witch-hunts, which makes organized resistance more likely.

The case of Argentina is particularly instructive here. In early 1986, as 300 military officers awaited their day in court, the defense minister ordered their trials to be expedited for fear that the large number of cases and slow rate of their resolution would create "an image of collective judgment" that could provoke military unrest.[99] Indeed, the navy's commander-in-chief expressed resentment at the new democratic leadership, as well as at those Argentineans who "turned their backs on us." Military men, he continued, "know what it is to suffer the pain of incomprehension and (in)gratitude." Between 1983 and 1992, the army successfully encouraged three mutinies to force the government to eventually cease prosecutions.[100] Soon after President Carlos Menem came to power in 1989, he pardoned the thirty-nine senior officers who had eventually been convicted. Perhaps operating on the premise that former leaders had been weakened by time, President Néstor Kirchner in 2003 pushed through Parliament a law that would annul immunity for some 2,000 military men believed to be connected with pre-1983 human rights abuses.[101]

Other new leaders have also seen the dangers of punishing rights abusers from the former regime. For example, when a 1980 congressional commission in Ecuador issued a report concerning human rights and other crimes under the former military regime, Admiral Alfredo Poveda Burbano publicly warned military personnel "to be alert to the strict observance of justice."[102] Other high-ranking officers expressed their disapproval of the commission, claiming that it was more interested in finding scapegoats than in the truth. Similarly, the commander-in-chief of the Chilean navy angrily accused the country's Truth and Reconciliation Commission of exceeding its legal authority by demanding annulment of a 1978 amnesty, which the president agreed to do.[103] When the United Nations in 2002 called for the opening of a special criminal court to go after former rights abusers in Sierra Leone,[104] one local newspaper warned that "no one knows for sure whether the [former rebel force] RUF actually gave up all the weapons they had or reserved some in secret locations in case the cream turns sour."[105]

TYPE 7. CRIMINAL PROSECUTION OF COMMANDERS (THOSE HIGHER ON THE CHAIN OF COMMAND)

In countries whose fragile judicial systems cannot bear the load of mass criminal trials, or where widescale trials could disrupt the operations of the state or otherwise threaten stability, new elites may turn to a more limited set of trials that indicates their belief in justice without draining the state's resources to the same degree.[106] Particularly when there are pressures for some form of retributive justice, Neil Kritz argues, a "symbolic or representative number of prosecutions of those most culpable" may be satisfactory. The most culpable, according to Kritz, are "the leaders who gave the orders to commit war crimes and those who actually carried out the worst offenses."[107] While this process may lack deterrent value for lower-level functionaries, who draw the lesson that "they are free to act as they choose so long as they avoid becoming too prominent,"[108] it could protect them from the feeling that they are being tried as scapegoats.[109]

Yet there is also an extraordinarily high risk associated with trying high-level officials for human rights violations. First, lower-ranking ones affiliated with the former regime's rights violations may view this as the beginning of a witch-hunt, rather than a one-time event.[110] Second, just as in the case of lower-ranking functionaries, senior-level leaders may command respect and organizational loyalty, and their arrests can thus create a ripple effect that stirs to action former associates from various levels. Third, the ripple effect may not stop there. Even the world's most brutal dictators seem capable of inspiring immense emotional solidarity in their former subjects. The powerful reaction to Joseph Stalin's death, with his funeral drawing tens of thousands of mourners, illustrates this fact. Fifty years afterward, a retiree who attended Stalin's funeral recalled, "It was as if we lost the father of the family, the person who took care of us. We felt like orphans."[111]

The risk of upsetting a delicate social balance by pursuing the top leaders from a former repressive regime is illustrated by the 2001 arrest and extradition of ousted Yugoslav dictator Slobodan Milošević. Weeks before the new Serbian government moved to arrest Milošević, accused of ordering human rights violations during three Balkan wars, nearly 1,000 supporters had already formed a "people's guard" in front of his home in Belgrade to protect him.[112] According to two opinion polls taken just after he was pushed from power, only 11 percent of Yugoslavs favored Milošević's extradition; and, less than a year later, two indicted war criminals (Bosnian Serb president Radovan Karadžić and General Ratko Mladić) were most often described as the "greatest defenders of the Serb nation."[113] Prime Minister Zoran Đinđić (Western spelling, Djindjic), a former leader of the democratic opposition widely known for his attempts to comply with extraditions, warned that high-profile extraditions could even lead to civil war.[114] Moreover, this emotional bond can linger for years. Pinochet's 1998 arrest by British authorities, eight years after he left power, drew sharp reactions in Santiago, where 3,000 pro-Pinochet demonstrators took to the streets.[115] Similarly, former South African president P. W. Botha, who rejected the new government's Truth and Reconciliation Commission, warned newly elected president Nelson Mandela that he would "awaken the tiger in the Afrikaner" by prosecuting apartheid-era leaders.[116]

Institutional responses, whether due to personal loyalty or fear of larger-scale investigations, are also common defense mechanisms for former leaders. In early 1975, the young Greek government was confronted with a failed military coup "by a few unrepenting officers," including six generals and thirty-one others, who allegedly aimed to secure an amnesty for imprisoned leaders of the former junta.[117] Under pressure, the government later reversed a death penalty sentence for three of the convicted 1967 coup plotters.[118] Similarly, while five out of nine Argentinean junta members and ex-commanders were convicted of human rights crimes by a civilian court, a series of army mutinies resulted in the 1989 pardon that freed them all.[119] Just as former Malawian ruler Hastings Kamuzu Banda was to appear in court in 1995 for his role in several political murders, Malawi's army headquarters announced the arrest of six soldiers and the search for a senior officer purported to be planning a coup.[120] Thus, pursuing former leaders for human rights violations can set into motion a wave of unrest involving institutional leaders and lower-ranking members affiliated with the former regime, if not broader groups in society still loyal to it.

BY IDENTIFYING AND theoretically rank-ordering a range of justice policies, this transitional justice spectrum qualifies the vague labels of "lenient" and "harsh" prevalent in the literature and allows researchers to empirically test causal theories of transitional justice decision making across cases. I have provided evidence that each incremental step up the spectrum involves more personalized responsibility and more severe repercussions for old elites. As mentioned above, this spectrum can be used to indicate the success of the relative power argument, because—according to that logic—states with the strongest old elites should eschew the harshest retributive measures. The simple, generic nature of the spectrum is designed to make it applicable across spatial or temporal contexts. For example, while the passage of time or the nature of abuses might affect the type of justice pursued, each incremental step up the spectrum should, at any point in time, be more provocative than the previous type. In other words, truth commissions will always be less provocative (or risky) than purges, which will always be less confrontational than prosecutions.

In practice, various forms of justice are frequently interconnected so that one mechanism may increase or decrease the likelihood of another. For example, truth commissions may provide material that leads to criminal prosecutions, as in Argentina, or incorporate legal guarantees that limit trials, as in South Africa. For the purposes of this study, the greater concern is where one mechanism precludes another, as in the latter case. This is not particularly debilitating for two reasons. First, we can still test the theoretical arguments by asking what prompted new elites initially to choose such a constraining form of justice (and therefore purposely sidestep other justice mechanisms). And second, such connections may be weaker than they appear. The South African case is an excellent illustration of this phenomenon. While the truth commission apparently served as a constraint on future criminal prosecutions, the large number of alleged perpetrators who did not apply or qualify for amnesty leaves open the possibility of criminal prosecutions there (which, indeed, are currently taking place).

Just as individual justice mechanisms can be interrelated, similar mechanisms may manifest themselves differently across cases. New elites in one state may issue rebukes repeatedly in the local media, while in another they may reserve condemnations or apologies for a foreign trip. Truth commissions can have multimillion-dollar budgets and enormous staffs in one country and only a handful of under-resourced volunteers in another. Qualitative aspects of the mechanisms employed may be symptomatic of genuine constraints or represent a crisis of genuineness. Motivations for pursuing a given mechanism or set of mechanisms can vary from a deep-seated desire for justice to the cynical need to weaken political enemies, and these rationales can impact on the depth and credibility of the process. For the researcher this necessitates in-depth exploration and a transparent assessment of the process. But if justice is in part a function of constraints, these should be detectable across cases. In chapter 4, I discuss in more detail the application of this spectrum. I preface this chapter with a discussion of lustration in the postcommunist context.

3

The Peculiarities of Postcommunist Justice

Addressing Lustration

This book evaluates seven frequently utilized mechanisms of justice but purposely omits one mechanism particular to postcommunist countries: lustration. I have not included lustration for several reasons. Perhaps most important, many observers have expressed valid concerns that lustration, based on questionable evidence that blurs the distinction between various types of crimes and degrees of guilt, is less a mode of justice than one of injustice. While administrative purges involve disqualifying those persons for whom there exists evidence of malfeasance, lustration involves punishment based merely on association. In addition, lustration is in many ways unique to postcommunist countries, perhaps as a result of the type of repression found in the post-Stalinist period. The addition of lustration to the justice spectrum would be an inclusion of a method of dealing with the past that is not particularly common at all, thus arguably weakening the spectrum as a tool. Also, though of considerably less importance, lustration is by far the most researched justice policy of the postcommunist world, which has left other areas underanalyzed. By gathering and analyzing data on these other important forms of justice I seek to integrate postcommunist countries into the broader literature.

Given the prevalence of lustration measures, however, any study of transitional justice in postcommunist states must consider this issue. I begin this chapter with a discussion of the types of rights abuses found under communism, which may be one explanation for the frequency of lustration processes. Next, I discuss the meaning of lustration, highlight some of its dilemmas, and provide a brief overview of its processes in a sampling of postcommunist countries. Finally, I evaluate some of the theoretical arguments concerning the topic. In my later discussion (chapter 9), I return to the question of lustration with respect to my four country case studies.

POLITICAL REPRESSION: THE COMMUNIST EXPERIENCE

That countries emerging from communism carried the weight of a repressive past is quite clear. But political repression, defined as the "use or threat of coercion in varying degrees applied by government against opponents or potential opponents to weaken their resistance to the will of the authorities,"[1] is rarely linear over several decades. Political elites can employ organs such as the military, police, intelligence services, and judiciary to deprive their adversaries of fundamental human rights, but repression can vary in form from consistent and steady pressure to acute and sporadic bursts of violence.[2] While there are well-known and horrific examples of massive, indiscriminate terror, state coercion is typically targeted at active opposition members and is contingent upon the magnitude of the perceived threat, where lower threats are met with lesser levels of coercion.[3] Since most despotic leaders depend on public acceptance, if not support, they tend to shy away from excessive levels of force that could jeopardize broad-based loyalty.[4] While excessive coercion can signal to non-elites that political passivity is no longer enough to keep the state at bay, moderate intimidation may weaken public support for any opposition movements.[5] Members of a repressive state generally know where it is safe to tread and where it is not.[6]

The Stalinist totalitarian system in place in the communist world prior to 1956 was characterized by massive repression, including extrajudicial murders, routine torture, and lengthy imprisonments stemming from political charges. But in the post-totalitarian period (after 1956), outright repression gradually mutated into more subtle forms of state control over society, including a strong police presence and widespread informant networks designed to keep the opposition in check.[7] The scope of (secret) police activity, not consistent across states, was correlated with the ruling regime's perceived legitimacy, which was usually linked to the economic situation. The degree of repression also varied, perhaps based on precommunist-era political life, making some (for example, those states with a historically weak Communist Party relative to other opposition groups) more reliant on co-optation than on coercion and even willing to permit occasional contestation.[8] Scholars have generally referred to the post-totalitarian period as "civilized violence"[9] or "selective repression," ranging from workplace dismissals and bans on foreign travel to the destruction of property, death threats, and abductions for the regime's most-feared opponents.[10]

Most citizens of post-Stalinist communist states could usually, by keeping a low profile, avoid harsh repression.[11] The rights abuses regularly witnessed by the masses were more akin to corruption than to state violence.[12] The former order restricted access to privileges, frequently making personal connections essential for professional opportunities and everyday necessities ranging from "luxuries" such as meat or liquor to basic essentials such as an apartment. People's rights were abused in that they were forced to maintain the outward appearance of support for a system that they truly did not back, a phenomenon Timur Kuran refers to as "preference falsification."[13] As Giuseppe di Palma notes, "protection was bought at the price of civil and political rights."[14] Public acceptance, derived from outward expressions of support and widespread acquiescence to elite-imposed rules, was sufficient to keep a series of despotic leaders in power for decades, entangle citizens in a web of culpability, and severely disrupt various societal institutions from the media to culture.[15] Vaclav Havel, a former Czech dissident and playwright, described how millions of Central and Eastern Europeans propped up the communist system through passive collaboration:

> [T]he overwhelming majority of shopkeepers never think about the [communist] slogans they put in their windows, nor do they use them to express real opinions. . . . [The greengrocer] put them all into the windows simply because it has been done that way for years, because everyone does it, and because that is the way it has to be. . . .

It is one of the thousands of details that guarantee him a relatively tranquil life in "harmony with society," as they say.[16]

Memories of Stalinism demonstrated the extent to which the system was capable of abuse in order to secure the status quo, and they may have played a role in tempering subsequent mass demands for change.[17] These memories were reinforced by the occasional use of harsh repression reminiscent of the Stalinist period. The police and military were sporadically deployed to brutally repress those who were demanding change, and even the threat of direct Soviet intervention was intimidating: "Driving a tank through the street was one highly effective means of sowing terror and panic in the population."[18] The omnipresent nature of the Communist Party, involved in everything from national politics to the workplace and apartment availability, made the state monopoly a clear and visible reminder of one's position in society.[19] As J. C. Sharman notes, "people had very little that could not be taken away with a minimum of effort by the state apparatus."[20]

But communist states were not constructed solely from sticks. Rather, leaders balanced political repression with a variety of economic carrots designed to raise their legitimacy. As Jacques Rupnik explains, "from social control it is a short step to an implicit 'social contract' between the state and the citizen."[21] Indeed, citizens gave up certain individual and collective rights in exchange for steady economic growth. Communism's subjects were the beneficiaries of a sprawling state-controlled social safety net, characterized by low unemployment rates and free (if substandard) social services, such as health care and education. And the system was far from static. Early demands for change, in Hungary (1956), Czechoslovakia (1968), and repeatedly in Poland (1956, 1968, 1970, 1976, 1981), for example, challenged certain Communist Party policies, especially economic ones, rather than the system of party rule.[22] Ruling elites in the post-totalitarian period had no illusions of omnipotence, and they usually promised concessions that would reduce political tensions.

The legitimacy of the communist state was ultimately questioned by those who saw that it was no longer capable of delivering the services it promised, and they increasingly realized that there would be no true economic reform without political reform.[23] Opposition movements were complex bodies, with their members fighting in the name of varying, overlapping principles ranging from Western-style democracy and capitalism to nationalism.[24] But while oppositionists were praised in the Western world for their political convictions, there is evidence that many of their constituents, in the words of one Hungarian intellectual, were "dreaming of the 'good king,' not of the mature responsibilities of democracy."[25] This observation raises questions about what postcommunist citizens sought and the sorts of rights they held dear.

Given the large numbers complicit in the regime's milder forms of repression, it is no surprise (at least in retrospect) that the most publicly charged debate has centered on how to deal with secret police collaborators. Where large groups of people were responsible for relatively low-level abuses, mass criminal trials were frequently seen as either inappropriate or ineffective.[26] As Tina Rosenberg noted, in differentiating Europe's postcommunist dictatorships from those in Latin America, criminal trials were not so easy for those "men and women who opened their letters, taught them lies in the guise of history, designed their pitiful Trabant automobiles, and took their passports."[27] The apparently obvious answer was lustration.

THE DILEMMAS OF LUSTRATION

In his editor's introduction to a 1995 special edition dedicated to the question of lustration, Peter Siegelman confessed, "The reader will soon see that we are still searching for the appropriate vocabulary with which to frame and analyze the problems of lustration. Is it a human rights issue? Or a legal question? Or one of practical politics?"[28] Reaching back to the term's Roman roots, Arthur Stinchcombe at the time broadly defined lustration as "drawing a ritual boundary between a new clean democratic regime and a bad old warlike, terrorist, totalitarian, and corrupt regime," possibly by banning members of the former from holding office in the latter.[29] The vagueness of these descriptions reflected a lack of clarity in the literature—and, indeed, in the practice—of what precisely lustration is and is not.

Almost fifteen years later, we have a modest literature on lustration and a general consensus that its processes are, most basically, aimed at identifying and somehow punishing people who belonged to or worked with the communist-era secret police, who were the key rights abusers of the period.[30] Yet much of this literature either comes from a period before this consensus was reached or is based on particular cases of lustration that lead researchers to differ as to its punitive dimensions. For example, while some argue that lustration's consequences may be limited to "serious moral punishment,"[31] others associate it with an automatic employment ban,[32] and still others (somewhat puzzlingly) argue that it should not be perceived "as a punishment" at all.[33]

The debate has been further complicated by the ostensible objects of lustration. Scholars of transitional justice, and lustration in particular, have often associated lustration with "perpetrators" involved directly in human rights violations, frequently conflating the relatively minor violations of which some of these individuals may have been culpable (such as the right to privacy) with much more serious abuses.[34] The argument that "lustration is a way to sidestep criminal prosecution" in postcommunist states,[35] is directed at "the organs of terror of that regime,"[36] or is one way to decide "what should be done with the secret police, torturers, death squads, informers, and collaborators from the old regime,"[37] obfuscates the nature of the crimes and, more important, the objects of lustration. Most targets of lustration had little or nothing to do with violent rights abuses, which were, anyway, relatively uncommon after Stalinism. Lustration is clearly not a process of "putting on trial those who were responsible for the old regime,"[38] nor is it synonymous with decommunization, the removal of people from public office for having served as (especially high-ranking) functionaries of the Communist Party or its related institutions.[39] Integrating these various concepts, consciously or unconsciously, distorts the process as well as the nature of guilt in postcommunist societies.[40]

Proponents of lustration, whether as a process of public clarification of records or automatic employment bans for former collaborators, have frequently claimed that it is necessary in order to morally cleanse the state.[41] Former Czech president Vaclav Havel, for instance, argued that "our society has a great need to face that past, to get rid of the people who had terrorized the nation and conspicuously violated human rights, to remove them from the positions that they are still holding."[42] These proponents, like those of other forms of justice, see it as a tool to separate the past from the present and to rebuild confidence in the state.[43] Pragmatists have also claimed that lustration eliminates political forces of yesterday and can thus "guarantee against the return of the old regime."[44] More often, its supporters argue that the process is designed to reduce corruption and abuse of power.[45] This argument rests on the assumption that former agents have cause to fear disclosure of their past and are therefore vulnerable to blackmail by those with access to their secret police files.[46] Lustration, then, might be considered a step toward democratic consolidation.[47]

Despite these rationales, lustration laws have, since their initial appearance, raised cries at home and abroad, with critics claiming that they violate rule-of-law and basic human rights, instead of advancing them.[48] Lustration shares some dilemmas common to other forms of transitional justice, including temporal questions, such as the retrospective nature of transitional justice, the period of inquiry and whether the old and infirmed are worthwhile targets, and spatial ones, including the scope of the inquiry.[49] Lustration has also been singled out for relying on flimsy evidence, fostering collective punishment, and proving to be easily politicized. As one former Polish dissident commented, "the concepts of lustration and decommunization that have emerged in almost all the former communist countries are not an accounting but a settling of accounts."[50]

One of the most significant lustration dilemmas concerns evidence of collaboration, usually drawn from official secret service records. In many instances, these records were at least partially destroyed by the outgoing regime or members of the security services who held onto their positions during and even after the transitions.[51] In other cases, records were sold off to, or otherwise acquired by, private individuals who might manipulate the information therein. Even where records were intact, they often proved to be deceptive or outright incorrect, given the incentives of security agents to confirm their effectiveness through demonstrating a vast (if sometimes fictitious) informant network.[52] As one Polish scholar asked, "Why should we today trust the word of a former secret police officer more than the word of a former dissident with a record of opposing the old regime—and of having suffered persecution for having done so?"[53] In fact, several well-known incidents occurred where innocent people were caught in the lustration web. Former Czech dissident Jan Kavan embodied this dilemma when he was purged from Parliament based on accusations of collaboration, only to clear his name five years later and eventually become the country's foreign minister.[54]

The case of Kavan highlights another lustration dilemma, the assumption of guilt rather than innocence.[55] As Havel noted, others faced the risk of a similar fate: "Many people do not even know whether, by accident, they might not have stepped into something."[56] Even if Kavan had somehow been involved with the secret police, his connection may have been trivial, coerced, or even purposely deceptive. Some of the most significant figures in the opposition movement—including Lech Wałęsa, who led Poland's Solidarity, and Aleksander Dubček, the leader of the 1968 reform in Czechoslovakia[57]—were alleged to have worked with the security services, thus creating an almost ridiculous situation.[58] It is no surprise, then, that Dubček, as head of the Federal Assembly in 1991, refused to sign the Czech lustration law.[59]

A third important problem of lustration is its susceptibility to politicization. In contrast to more directed forms of justice such as criminal prosecutions or the administrative purges described in chapter 2, lustration can be an instrument through which to eliminate large numbers of potential opponents from the political stage.[60] The result is lustration as "a terrain of a ruthless power struggle in countries intent simultaneously on revolution and political stabilization."[61] Some, such as Roman David, defend it as a form of affirmative action, even a type of restorative justice providing "a form of redress" and new opportunities for those previously excluded from positions due to political reasons.[62] But the risk, notes Stephen Esquith, is that those pushed out "feel that they have been the victims of a moral wrong. . . . They feel that they have played by the rules, succeeded, and then the rules have been changed in the middle of the game without their consent."[63]

Politicization of lustration varies in form. In Albania, incumbents utilized lustration to eliminate their political opponents and to subsequently solidify political control.[64] In Czechoslovakia, the center-right used it to discredit political rivals among the dissident movement, which was ostensibly filled with secret police infiltrators.[65] In Poland, some have argued that political elites worked to ensure that attitudes toward the communist past would be fundamental to political identities, more capable of arousing emotion than was simple interest-based representation.[66] Politicization of lustration has been almost commonplace. As Andrew Rigby notes, "When a political movement takes up the issue and runs with it to advance its own particular interests . . . there is every likelihood that what might have started out as a controlled process will escalate beyond the boundaries that most of us would deem acceptable in a liberal democratic state."[67] Still others have questioned the biographies of those calling loudest for lustration, deeming it "revenge for their own humiliation" from not strenuously fighting the system.[68]

Some scholars have played down the moral and political dilemmas of lustration, rejecting criticisms from such corners as the Council of Europe and the International Labor Organization as symptoms of political discomfort rather than viable legal concerns.[69] Others have explored ways in which normative dilemmas can be partly assuaged through a cleaner, more strategic lustration process. Kaminski and Nalepa, for example, argue that incentive-based, truth-revelation procedures, in which perpetrators have incentives to voluntarily testify against themselves in ways akin to plea bargaining, can at least help minimize false acquittals.[70] One implication of their analysis, which argues that such incentives ultimately reduce adjudicator workloads by getting more guilty persons to do their work for them,[71] might be that more time could be devoted to examining evidence and avoiding false convictions.

On top of the issues already raised, there are additional practical problems, including questions of whether lustration could disrupt state capacity by throwing out individuals with needed skills,[72] as well as the difficulty of finding the staff who are willing to run the controversial lustration process.[73] Numerous lustration laws have been struck down by constitutional courts, just as many judges have resisted being pulled into the highly political process.[74] Lustration has thus unfolded in an atmosphere of polarization, with some arguing it is unjust to let past villains prosper today, and with still others arguing that lustration itself leads to new injustices.[75]

LUSTRATION IN PRACTICE

Despite these dilemmas, lustration has occurred, albeit in varying forms, in many postcommunist states. In this section I mention a sampling of these processes in order to demonstrate the diversity of lustration measures. The sampling here includes cases from Lithuania to Albania and is presented in chronological order. I have devoted a special section in my general discussion (chapter 9) to Poland, Serbia, and Croatia.

Czechoslovakia and East Germany moved quickest and most aggressively with lustration laws.[76] The Czechoslovakia law, which the Czechs pursued much more rigorously than did the Slovaks following the country's division in 1992, was particularly controversial. The first cut appeared in January 1991 with parliamentary legislation that mandated screening every parliamentary deputy, minister, or deputy minister, and all employees of Parliament or the prime minister's office for cooperation with the secret police, using the latter's files. Those found guilty of collaboration would be fired or, in the case of parliamentary deputies, publicly identified.[77] This law was expanded in October 1991 to ban for five years people with certain communist-era institutional affiliations (or records of collaborating with the secret police) from taking a broad range of positions, from elected posts or judgeships to management positions in state-owned enterprises, state-run media, or academia.[78] The charismatic former oppositionist Vaclav Havel proposed amendments to the controversial bill and subsequently rejected the law's extension in 1995 and 2000, but Parliament overrode his veto.[79]

Under the 1990 German Unification Treaty, some 90,000 full-time workers of the East German secret police (Stasi) and their estimated 170,000 collaborators could be denied public-sector employment.[80] The December 1991 Law on the Documents of the State Security Service of the Former GDR, amended in 1994 and then again in 1996, overrode this treaty and established the Gauck Authority, named after its first commissioner, to manage the secret police files.[81] Employers then approached the Gauck Authority for employee screenings, which still made possible (though did not mandate) denial of jobs to those found guilty. By early 1996, there had been three million applications, a majority by employers, for verification, though many—including the police—continued to hire former Stasi workers.[82] Unlike in the Czech Republic, where those accused had quite limited rights of appeal,[83] German lustration placed the burden of proof on employers, with the courts frequently involved in wrongful-dismissal suits.[84]

Hungary passed its first lustration law in 1994, mandating the vetting of public officials in up to 12,000 positions for involvement not only in the communist-era secret police but also in the World War II–era fascist

Arrow Cross, and the specific squads responsible for crushing the 1956 revolt.[85] Those who refused to resign following findings of guilt would have their names published in the state press. In Albania, Parliament's September 1995 lustration law banned security service employees—but also communist government officials—from taking federal, parliamentary, judicial, or media positions.[86]

While Bulgaria's Parliament issued a handful of decommunization laws in 1992 (one of which blocked former communists from holding leading academic positions until its 1995 repeal), its first lustration law did not appear until mid-1997, when a supervisory body was created to evaluate whether high-level government officials, parliamentarians, or members of the judiciary had cooperated with the secret police (with the sanction of public announcement).[87] The constitutional court limited the scope of this law and completely blocked a subsequent one in 1998 that would have banned former top-ranking communists, secret service officials, or collaborators from serving in high-level government or civil service slots for five years.[88]

Lithuania's first attempt to pass a lustration law failed when it was revealed that its author was a former KGB agent, and it was not until 1999 that the country's first lustration law went into effect, which made former KGB officers ineligible to work in a number of government and private-sector jobs for ten years from the law's enactment.[89] According to a second law passed in 1999, residents of Lithuania were urged to privately confess their previous KGB collaboration or, if they did not do so by 2000, information about their collaboration could be made public. High-ranking government officials and those running for certain offices would automatically have their ties to the KGB publicly announced.

As is apparent from these examples, lustration varied considerably between countries. In some, such as Czechoslovakia and East Germany, cooperation with the secret services was sufficient to block someone from holding certain positions in the public sector, including at state-owned companies.[90] In Bulgaria, as in East Germany, the employment ban extended into institutions of teaching and research.[91] But in other states, the positions subject to vetting were far more restricted. The numbers thus diverged enormously, from around 250,000 positions in East Germany to 10,000 to 12,000 in Hungary and only 300 in Lithuania.[92] As a result of the Czech lustration law's repeated extension, by 2001 the interior minister had processed more than 400,000 lustration certificates, of which about 3 percent came back negative.[93]

EXPLAINING LUSTRATION

Much of the literature on transitional justice in postcommunist states is confined to this one mechanism, lustration, and subsequently is largely restricted to one subregion, Central Europe (plus the three neighboring Baltic countries). It has been generally accepted that since most of the more contemporary rights violations were characterized by low-level repression supported by extensive informant networks, lustration should be the naturally expected policy of choice.[94] Broadly speaking, theoretical arguments concerning the timing and shape of lustration can be classified, following Helga Welsh, along two dimensions: "weight of the past," and "politics of the present."[95]

"Weight of the past" arguments are those focused on historical factors such as level of communist-era repression and mode of transition.[96] Some scholars, such as Natalia Letki, rely primarily on the latter, and her argument is rooted in Samuel Huntington's transition-based theory.[97] Letki's most compelling evidence is the frequent observation that two of the most far-reaching lustration policies unfolded in two states where the communist regime rapidly collapsed.[98] Nadya Nedelsky, by contrast, focuses on level of repression to explain differences in lustration policies in the Czech Republic and Slovakia, arguing that Slovaks were generally more sheltered from, and thus more supportive of, the communist regime.[99] John Moran, also centered on "weight of the past" explanations, argues that justice is influenced by psychological determinants based on the degree to which opponents in the former system could voice their opposition or else emigrate.[100]

Most scholars of lustration tend to incorporate into their analysis the "politics of the present": political setting, such as the strength of postcommunists, and contextual factors, such as fading memories as well as reevaluations of the communist period.[101] In their study of the Czech Republic, Hungary, and Poland, for example, Williams, Fowler, and Szczerbiak follow from Welsh and question the degree to which earlier scholars neglected the contemporary political environment.[102] In their cases, they argue that lustration laws are a function of the ability to assemble pro-lustration coalitions in the legislature. Aleks Szczerbiak, while agreeing that transition type kept lustration off the table in Poland during the early years of transition, similarly argues in a separate piece that it took a centrist coalition to sufficiently moderate the form of lustration to the point where it became politically feasible.[103] In the same vein, Noel Calhoun claims that the adoption of liberal democratic values by postcommunist states results in a more lenient (and thus more politically acceptable to postcommunists) lustration process.[104]

Scholars focused on postcommunist states have admirably sought to engage with the broader transitional justice literature, pointing out shortcomings such as overemphasis on the past[105] or short-term policies.[106] But these studies are also notable for their own deficits. First, arguments tend to be applied to limited cases, sometimes only to one, at other times to two or three. Those that go beyond this either tend to do so incompletely, focusing on one or two cases and then summarizing how others from the subregion might fit in, or simply providing basic summary information about sometimes quite complex processes. This results in inconsistencies. One example is Nedelsky's contention that Poland did not pursue lustration early on as a result of profound societal schisms, a view that runs counter to the evidence that most Poles supported it almost from the start.[107] Another is Letki's transition-based argument, which does little to explain lustration in countries such as Romania.[108]

A second, and equally important, shortcoming is that overemphasis on just one policy makes for theoretical accounts that explain very little about justice more generally. Lustration-focused studies sometimes mention, though usually sparingly, the use of other transitional justice mechanisms in the postcommunist world. For example, Kaminski and Nalepa claim that virtually all postcommunist states at least initiated declarations that the former period was illegal, though these were sometimes dropped because of legal confusion or, they argue, to "uphold former political commitments."[109] For those who maintained these laws, they were used both as political denunciations and in pursuit of criminal prosecutions. For example, the Czech July 1993 law declaring the communist regime illegitimate extended the statute of limitations to allow for prosecutions of crimes that took place between 1948 and 1989, something the country's constitutional court upheld.[110] The law paved the way for the 1995 establishment of the Office for the Documentation and Investigation of the Crimes of Communism (UDV), which by August 2001 had looked into more than 3,000 cases and prepared 160 for prosecution.[111]

The fact that the Czechs, infamous for lustration, have also pushed for criminal prosecutions is a reminder that lustration is no more suitable than other forms of justice. The relatively mild communist regime of the most recent past was, in fact, the finale to a much longer and harsher period of repression. Thanks to systemic continuity, much of the history of communism could never be thoroughly revealed until the system collapsed. Once society emerged from the ruins, it was presented with the first opportunity to earnestly explore the truth behind earlier, darker times. Lustration for injustice from the immediate past is just one of many policies that leaders of postcommunist states have followed. For while the past few decades may have been shaped by less brutal infringements, these abuses were also sometimes used to forcibly mask more painful questions and memories dating back to Stalinism itself, World War II, and even earlier abuses by communists as well as by their opponents. The fall of communism therefore marked the unleashing of a massive wave of confusion and anger that was sometimes more concerned with the more distant, and far harsher, past. And even after the period of Stalinism ended around 1956, while the most visible form of repression was mass surveillance, certain groups and individuals faced a much more aggressive state. Some people were denied freedom of movement, some were imprisoned or repeatedly detained, some faced beatings and other forms of torture, and some were executed.

Despite the overwhelming focus on lustration, there is evidence that criminal prosecutions have occurred elsewhere, as well. Attempts in Hungary to lift the statute of limitations on crimes committed from 1944 to 1990 were overturned by the Constitutional Court, which did, however, allow for prosecutions related to the 1956 events, classified as "crimes against humanity" or "war crimes."[112] Even in Romania and Bulgaria at least a handful of trials were held. In Romania they centered on the violence that occurred at the time of the 1989 transition.[113] In Bulgaria, criminal prosecutions, facilitated by a 1990 law extending the statute of limitations, were largely focused on only a few individuals and on crimes that were economic (such as corruption) rather than on core human rights violations.[114] Certainly, greater examination might reveal a longer list of cases in these and other countries.

In addition to criminal trials of about 150 (largely lower-level) border guards and security service officials, the East Germans also pursued a truth commission, which published its report in 1994.[115] Other forms of retributive justice, such as low-key administrative reorganizations aimed at weeding out malfeasance, were initiated before lustration in countries such as Czechoslovakia and Poland, and they were administered in "a tolerant and non-vengeful way," including generous conditions of release.[116] Still other states, such as Slovakia, established institutions to document communist crimes in order to facilitate victim rehabilitation and compensation.[117]

This list is far from exhaustive; it merely highlights the varied forms of justice incompletely accounted for in the lustration-focused literature. A third and critical limitation in this literature is underspecification. There may be an emerging consensus that politics of yesterday and today affect transitional justice (or at least lustration) in postcommunist states, but what are the variables that have the most impact? One variable might be public opinion, but the evidence is unclear. For example, some scholars have claimed that there is no correlation in Poland between periods of high support and opposition toward lustration and the actual passage of lustration measures,[118] while others argue that significant public support has helped make it practical there.[119] The contradictory evidence in these studies, which focus on this broad understanding of politics of the present rather than treating public opinion as an important independent variable that must be measured, is unconvincing.

Another possible explanation, closely linked to my argument but thus far not thoroughly explored, is the role of economics in transitional justice. In some cases, scholars have found that economic hardship led to more aggressive forms of accountability.[120] But again, evidence has been incomplete and contradictory. David Ost, for example, argues that "witch-hunting former communists has proved good (i.e., electable) politics in Hungary, Czechoslovakia, Poland, and the former GDR, and the tendency grows as economic problems get worse."[121] Yet some cases of lustration, including in at least two of the cases that Ost proposes, occurred under conditions of strong economic growth. Based on World Bank figures, I have found that lustration measures were passed in Hungary during that country's first period of positive GDP growth (3 percent) since the transition began. In Poland, the 1997 lustration law was passed at a period of record GDP growth (7.1 percent), which was more than 2.5 times higher than the 1992 rate of growth (2.6 percent), marking the last full year prior to 1997 that former oppositionists to the communist regime controlled Parliament. Both extensions of the Czech lustration law were passed during periods of strong economic growth (6 percent in 1995 and 3.6 percent in 2000). These cases provide at least preliminary (if incomplete) support for arguments contending that economic concerns actually push justice into the background.[122] The remaining chapters attempt to make this argument for a broader range of justice policies.

IN HIS FOREWORD to a monumental three-volume book devoted to transitional justice, Neil Kritz recalled a conference in the early 1990s in which Latin Americans and Europeans came together: "In words spoken and unspoken, in skeptical glances and general body language, the Latin Americans and Europeans seemed to be expressing the same thing to one another: the suffering of our people during the old regime and the difficulties resulting from our legacy [are] far worse than any hardship you endured. Ours is the greater pain; there is little we can learn from your experience."[123] The Latin Americans had endured relatively brief but extremely destructive military dictatorships, while residents of postcommunist states awoke from an extended period of diminished freedom anchored in an extraordinarily violent, yet more distant, past.

Scholars have explored one of the most prominent and controversial mechanisms of dealing with the past in the postcommunist space: lustration. In the process they have engaged with the broader transitional justice literature in a uniquely postcommunist way. Given the great extent of collaboration with the repressive secret police in many postcommunist states, this is in some ways not surprising. Yet as Kritz's comments remind us, the communist world was not merely one of neighbors' whispers of and confiscated passports. It was also, depending on the time and place, a world of torture, murder, imprisonment, and social engineering. As Claus Offe noted, members of the old order "regularly violated their own legality in the service of the regime," thus making individual criminal cases feasible.[124] The nature of communist-era abuses (as well as postcommunist ones) does not therefore necessarily lend itself to one particular process. Indeed, the fact that the 1989 opening led to investigations of a period preceding communism (from tsarism in Central Asia to World War II in many parts of Central and Eastern Europe) reminds us that the postcommunist world has much to account for, and many ways in which to do it.

My choice not to formally include lustration in this study is partly out of normative and legal concerns, and partly for theoretical reasons. On a normative and legal level, many scholars have questioned the fairness of lustration, suggesting that it is more akin to vengeance than justice. Lustration is a retributive mechanism that uses questionable evidence to similarly punish people who range from the torturers to the tortured. The retributive portion of this transitional justice study focuses on individual accountability for those persons guilty of planning or actually taking part in abuses. On a more theoretical level, this study seeks to connect justice in the postcommunist world to more global patterns. While previous scholars of Central and Eastern Europe have shed light on where lustration might fit into the theoretical literature, these individual and comparative cases provide little data concerning other mechanisms, and the narrow definition of justice taken makes generalizability difficult. Both the weight of the past and, for many, the politics of the present appear to be important factors. The puzzle remains, however, how precisely these variables come together to facilitate or thwart various forms of transitional justice.

4

The Method of Study

*Using Qualitative Data to Uncover
the Path of Justice*

This book relies on a case study approach, using interview and archival data from four diverse postcommunist countries to explore the central research question. This study stands out in several respects, including the novel application of the justice spectrum discussed in chapter 2, the geographic and political range of cases involved, and the depth of fieldwork, which involved nearly two years on the ground in the four countries, preceded by several years of language studies (Polish, Croatian/Serbian, Russian, and Uzbek). The result is a thorough analysis of several broadly comparable states, the lessons of which may be pertinent to scores of other states undergoing various transitions from nondemocracy. In this chapter, I explain the research design utilized for this book, focusing on case selection, data collection, and data analysis.

CASE SELECTION

Using the spectrum proposed in chapter 2, I evaluate determinants of justice in four states facing various aspects of justice: Poland, Serbia, Croatia, and Uzbekistan.

I rely on case studies rather than large-N analysis for several reasons. First and foremost, the objective is to evaluate elite motivations for particular justice processes. In conducting this study, I attempted to gather data that address every type of influence that may have impacted elite decision making. Second, there is currently no dataset that classifies the subcomponents of my dependent variable and provides the detail necessary to evaluate this argument. My research necessarily begins by gathering new data, which will, I hope, be useful to others who subsequently look at these countries.

Rather than using the standard "comparative method," which involves establishing "general empirical relationships among two or more variables" while controlling for all others, I have adopted a theory confirming/infirming case study method.[1] This approach, which comprises "an intensive study of a single unit for the purpose of understanding a larger class of (similar) units," has its tradeoffs, namely, between comparability and representativeness.[2] The in-depth case study approach is particularly helpful when, as John Gerring notes, "insight into causal mechanisms is more important than insight into causal effects."[3] For my central research question— "What prompts leaders of a post-repressive state to pursue or eschew various types of accountability?" (and, importantly, not "What accounts for the difference between highly comparable states X and Y with regards to their justice policies?")—I chose to independently test my model on a diverse set of states. The idea was to use the replication logic, that is, to look for the presence of similar patterns in each case.[4]

Unlike with most previous groundbreaking studies, such as those of Samuel Huntington, Guillermo O'Donnell and Philippe Schmitter, and Neil Kritz, which tend to highlight general trends in various countries, this book includes a detailed analysis of why precise forms of justice were and were not carried out in each case. As noted in chapter 2, the transitional justice spectrum, an important organizational element in this study, allows me to compare each one of my cases using a common yardstick. Rather than merely note the presence of one particular form of justice in each one of my cases, I look for evidence indicating why decision makers made the choices they did concerning a series of possible mechanisms. The data are thus much richer and more thorough, allowing for an in-depth analysis of justice determinants.

Moreover, while many previous studies focus on only one or two countries, often with considerable similarities, I have chosen four with quite
different features. Previous analyses of the postcommunist world overwhelmingly center on lustration and tend to be focused on a single case,[5]
two or three cases from the same subregion,[6] or interesting but incomplete
studies of more countries from a subregion.[7] By contrast, this study is an in-
depth analysis of seven different justice mechanisms in four states from
different postcommunist subregions. The diversity is highlighted by an an-
ecdote. When Uzbek interlocutors heard that I was relocating my family to
Serbia for the next phase of research, they reacted with horror when I told
them that I was taking my six-month-old infant to such a dangerous place.
Similarly, when I arrived in Serbia, locals expressed shock that I had brought
my daughter to a country as unstable as Uzbekistan. Despite their many
similarities, these countries are, in numerous ways, worlds apart.

Given this diversity and a lack of detailed justice research in these cases,
I had a limited understanding of the actual justice outcomes before I began
my research. What I did know was that these cases are broadly comparable.
All have faced transitional justice issues in the context of radical political and
economic reform. They also share a legacy of relatively similar communist-
era rights abuses, the persistence of formerly abusive institutions in the new
system, and many elements of political culture. The previous repressive political system was one in which, willingly or not, subjects of communism
traded political rights for certain economic guarantees, thus creating particular understandings of the role of the state. Indeed, this seems a feature
common to many states developing under tyranny.

While transitional justice is commonly viewed as one of the many
political processes facing new elites, in the postcommunist world these
new elites were forced to grapple with their political past and future while
simultaneously managing radical economic transitions. The cases chosen
are brought together by the fact that each one faced its past in "a context of
ideological collapse, imperial demise, and social and economic change."[8]
The simultaneity of these processes meant that citizens were rarely disin-
terested actors in the new regime. Rather, new elites faced societal pressures
for quick improvements in countries where inflation, unemployment, and
a decline in living standards were common. There is evidence that demand

for higher living standards, just as new elites forced cuts in unsustainable communist-era social benefits, may have affected the degree of public support for dealing with the past.[9]

As new elites balanced political and economic reforms, they were confronted with a second common challenge: how to address hitherto unreformed institutions of terror and persecution from the old system. The apparatus of fear was designed similarly in each state, with the Communist Party heavily influencing the intelligence and judicial organs, as well as the police and military. While rights abuses varied by timing, quality, extent, and location, the persistent threat of coercion was similar across cases. Stalinist (and Tito)-era repression may have been an anomaly in scope, but similar mechanisms—powerful political leaders, nontransparent and unscrupulous security services, and corrupt judicial personnel—were used effectively to keep citizens in check across the communist world for almost a half-century. In some of my cases, these institutions also have been involved in rights violations during the transition period.

These states, moreover, are characterized by relatively similar political cultures, broadly understood. At the time of the most recent political changes, few residents had more than childhood memories of democratic rule, and all had lived for decades in a system where allegiance was rewarded and outspokenness punished. Politics was dominated by, and viewed as belonging to, a narrow group of elites who officially espoused democratic norms while habitually violating them. Vertical links between citizen and state were forged, while horizontal links between non-elites, necessary for the creation and maintenance of a vibrant civil society, were discouraged.[10] Political rights were exchanged for economic ones, which had long-term implications for citizen expectations of government.

Just as these cases are broadly similar in their communist histories, they diverge in ways that provide for a broad-scoped test of the arguments posited here. They differ with respect to transition type as well as to temporal and qualitative aspects of human rights violations, making them representative of postcommunist diversity and useful in understanding similar problems outside of the communist world. To account for this diversity I have included the largest countries (measured by population) in three general subregions: Central Europe, Central Asia, and Southeastern Europe.

Poland, a postcommunist democracy dealing with communist-era crimes, is similar to most Central European states, as well as to the post-Soviet Baltic countries. These states shared an initially bumpy transition characterized by steep economic decline and often by fragmented political systems. But they also quickly remedied many of these problems, by restructuring their economies and political institutions, which led to a quick reversal that gave them high economic growth rates and the rank of consolidated democracies. Many of them entered both the European Union and NATO in the almost two decades since communism collapsed. For these countries, an accounting of the past frequently begins with World War II (when the Iron Curtain was forged) and ends around 1989 (when the curtain fell).

Uzbekistan, a nondemocracy still engaged in human rights abuses, is representative of most Central Asian states and other nondemocratic postcommunist countries, such as Belorussia. From the perspective of justice, Uzbekistan might also be characteristic of a broader range of countries where democratic consolidation has generally not been successful and where the leaders of yesterday remain the rulers (in both person and style) of today. The extended list, taking into account differences in the timing and extent of the slide toward nondemocratic rule, might include most of the former Soviet Union apart from the Baltic states (and perhaps Ukraine and Georgia). In all of these cases, political and economic restructuring were only partial, and majorities in many of these countries struggle under various degrees of poverty and authoritarianism. Justice in these countries might be limited to the Soviet period or extend from the pre-Soviet (tsarist) period all the way to today.

Finally, countries of the former Yugoslavia allow for comparison with somewhat democratic states that have faced human rights violations from the communist or precommunist period, as well as in the context of civil or international conflict in the early postcommunist period, when communism was replaced by a violent breed of nationalism. I include two former Yugoslav states here, Serbia and Croatia. While I initially planned to study only Serbia, prior to beginning my fieldwork I decided to add Croatia to control for the specific nature of justice, which includes international criminal prosecutions. Other former Yugoslav states, such as Bosnia-Herzegovina or Macedonia, but also less consolidated democracies of other subregions, such as Georgia and Armenia, might also fit into this category. For these states, justice might involve human rights violations committed during or preceding communism as well as the bloody years of the early postcommunist transition.

To compensate for the small-N characteristic of the case study method, I have leveraged these cases by using intra-case comparisons, the result of what might be seen as natural experiments over time. The period of analysis in Poland includes a time when actors with apparently similar preferences (1989) suddenly diverged along institutional lines as a result of new conditions (the post-1989 focus on economic reform). In the case of Serbia, the anti-Hague president (2000–2003) became a quiet proponent of extraditions after moving to the slot of prime minister (post-2004). A similar story is observed in Croatia, where the leader of the late president Franjo Tuđman's nationalist party led demonstrations against ICTY (International Criminal Tribunal for the former Yugoslavia) handovers (2000–2004), only to assist in the capture of the general whom he had once defended after becoming prime minister (post-2004). While intra-case comparisons can be complicated (especially where earlier policies might appear to preclude later ones), I found no limitations in my case studies. Indeed, even in the most obvious occurrences, where early amnesties appear to make criminal prosecutions impossible, there are examples of new elites simply annulling their predecessors' decisions.[11]

DATA COLLECTION

My methods, media analyses, and, especially, elite interviews were designed to determine what (regardless of the array of similar and dissimilar independent variables) the key determinants of justice were. In each of my case studies, the first stage of research involved conducting a media review, which provided a contextual framework by illuminating the timing and circumstances of transitional justice reforms. An in-depth content analysis of domestic reporting was helpful in gaining strong institutional knowledge (locating particular pressures for and against aspects of the human rights agenda), gauging public discourse on the subject, and becoming acquainted with key local players. Given the lack of research on the subjects dealt with here, domestic reporting was sometimes a key source of background information. This portion of the study concentrated predominantly on the national press, since most justice issues were rarely the subjects of local or regional reporting. International press reports were also gleaned to highlight international and even domestic events that for some reason garnered little attention in the national press but nonetheless may have been important to domestic decision makers. A critical role of this media analysis was to develop a justice timeline and to generate hypothetical linkages between justice reforms and various domestic and international events.

The media analysis was organized "top-down," focusing first on international media and then on national newspapers. International media reviews involved broad keyword searches on *Lexis-Nexis,* including North American and European newspapers and wire services, as well as select translations of national media articles. I kept the search terms extraordinarily wide in order to cast as broad a net as possible. For example, in the case of Serbia, I searched not only for specific mechanisms (for example, "Yugoslavia and truth commission") but also for the more general "Yugoslavia and crimes" (rather than "Yugoslavia and 'war crimes'"), which would encompass any article referring to the former Yugoslavia and criminal activity. The advantage of this, of course, is inclusivity; the disadvantage is the time-consuming process of weeding through the data for relevant articles. Ultimately, I preferred to err on the side of caution and collected thousands of international and translated national reports on justice in Serbia and Croatia, though these were primarily focused on just three types of justice (criminal accountability for executors and for perpetrators, as well as truth commissions). Far fewer articles were available on Uzbekistan and Poland, where international attention is directed considerably less often.

I followed up the international media analysis with a search through national newspapers. I delved into at least two publications in three of my cases: *Gazeta Wyborcza* and *Rzeczpospolita* (Poland, in the Polish language); *Narodnoye Slovo, Pravda Vostoka, Khalq So'zi,* and *O'zbekiston Ovozi* (Uzbekistan, in the Uzbek and Russian languages);[12] and *Danas* and *Politika* (Serbia, in the Serbian language). The national media analysis proved critical in the Polish case, where there has been significant activity in the justice sphere without much outside reporting. In Uzbekistan, by contrast, an exhaustive search of national (state-censored) media confirmed the hypothesis that justice has been largely sidestepped or conducted outside the public purview. Finally, in Serbia, I found the media review useful in adding color to my study, but not substantively influential. This is not surprising given the thorough international reporting on the former Yugoslavia. As a result, and due to time constraints, I carried out only an international media review (which, as in the case of Serbia, was very thorough and included many translated domestic sources) for the case of Croatia.

Appropriate local media sources were chosen after consultations with local academics and nongovernmental actors. The publications were chosen primarily based on their depth of national coverage, which might include justice issues. In Poland, this led me to two of the largest daily newspapers, while in Serbia it prompted me to explore one daily and one weekly with more limited readerships. In Uzbekistan, I began my study with the understanding that it was likely to be the proverbial search for a needle in a haystack. I therefore hunted through more newspapers, with the help of two local research assistants. Without indices or online availability for most of my sources, I scanned publications in their entirety, page by page.

My media analysis spanned from the time of political change to the period when I was conducting research. For Poland, I began a few months before the first semi-democratic elections in 1989 and completed my research in 2004. The comprehensive media analysis in Serbia began with the start of democratic (opposition) rule in 2000 and ended in late 2004, with international media used to continue observing the case through 2007. The international media review for Croatia went from 1996 (after the implementation of the Dayton peace accords) to 2005. For Uzbekistan, the analysis began with the warming of U.S.-Uzbek bilateral relations in 1995 and ended in 2003.

The media analysis is useful for establishing a history of critical events and formulating hypotheses, but the primary evidence for or against these arguments is elite perceptions. What motivates policymakers to pursue various accountability measures? And what factors discourage them? Elite interviews provide evidence for or against media-based hypotheses. Therefore, I conducted interviews with four kinds of actors directly concerned with human rights developments and justice issues in each state: members of the (former) opposition movements and current ruling elites, leaders of locally active nongovernmental human rights organizations, representatives of foreign missions and intergovernmental organizations, and members of the (former) regime accused of rights violations. My focus was on the first two groups. For example, most of my Poland interviews were with former members of the Solidarity-led opposition who later became political leaders, but I also talked to several members of the Helsinki Committee, a human rights organization, who did not formally enter politics but were closely involved in the political process. In Uzbekistan, where the opposition remains underground, I observed an overlap between members of opposition parties and members of human rights organizations whom I interviewed, frequently finding these groups practically synonymous. In Serbia and Croatia, there was a relatively equal split between rights organizations members and political elites.

Interviewee selection in each country was determined in two phases. In the first one, I identified from my media review and other primary sources (such as parliamentary records) actors and organizations particularly involved in, or outspoken for or against, specific justice measures. In the second phase, I relied on the "snowball effect," concluding interviews from my initial list by asking for the names of other actors actively involved in the debate. I usually facilitated meetings with these respondents as well, carrying out interviews until I had reached a point of "saturation," where the narratives neatly fit into a small number of clear, explanatory categories. The number of interviews therefore differs by case, with by far the largest number conducted in Poland (where justice has been on the table much longer), followed by Uzbekistan (where I primarily spoke to current oppositionists about type 1 justice and future plans for other forms of accounting), Serbia, and then Croatia.

My interviews, held in Russian, Polish, Serbian/Croatian, and English, were loosely structured and based on a broad list of questions, most of which were open-ended. My main goal was to gauge personal perceptions or private views about why certain justice measures were put into place, while others were not. In each country, I went through the justice spectrum point by point, asking respondents for their perceptions of the extent to which the justice measure was (not) pursued and the reasons for pursuing it in the way chosen. Questions regarding each measure included country-specific elements derived from the media review, secondary sources, or, on occasion, other interviewee responses. For example, after inquiring generally about the incidence of apologies and factors that may have hastened or impeded such apologies, I asked respondents in Serbia more specifically why their federal president had issued his apology when he did. In addition, interviews with actors intimately involved in a specific justice mechanism were largely restricted to understanding the details of the decision-making process from that actor's point of view. For instance, when meeting with the former Polish interior minister and the former chief advisor to the Serbian interior minister, I used our limited time together to focus on the purge of the ministry and criminal prosecutions, rather than to discuss with them at length the full gamut of mechanisms.

In all cases except for Uzbekistan, I generally inquired about motivations for or against implementing various aspects of justice (types 2 to 7 on my spectrum). In the case of Uzbekistan, I probed oppositionists more deeply about the successes and failures of various internal and external pressures for type 1, and I sought to understand the goals, tactics, and constituencies of the domestic human rights organizations. I also inquired about Uzbek perceptions toward later steps on the justice spectrum, in the event that the opposition might eventually take power.

I was rarely given only "official" information about the preferences and policies of institutions that the interviewee represented. Rather, interviewees seemed eager to underscore the point that their answers were theirs alone, leaving it up to me to assess whether others felt the same way. In some cases, there was wide consensus on why certain policies were implemented and why others were not. In other cases, it appears that political elites were acting under different assumptions and for different reasons. This occurred even within specific organizations, where I occasionally interviewed two or more representatives in search of a deeper understanding of institutional influences on their thinking.

I must emphasize this study's focus on elite perceptions. While public opinion polls or raw economic data might serve as surrogate variables where elite perceptions cannot be obtained (for example, in large-N studies), they represent only one small piece of the puzzle and are more suggestive than predictive of elite attitudes. Public polls in the case of justice rarely, if ever, capture support levels for all of the various mechanisms available and are even less likely to elucidate the several dimensions that affect citizen attitudes toward any given policy. As a result, elites may find little value in the

TABLE 4.1 Elite Interviews

	TOTAL	*Political Elites*	*NGOs*	*Other*
Uzbekistan	63	**	41	22
Serbia	53	19	21	13
Croatia	31	8	14	9
Poland	68	40	15	13

results. Similarly, economic indicators may shine some light on this, but they are elusive since they are not indicative of specific concerns and debates, and they underestimate the complexity of strategic calculation and incentive structures. A state in the throes of a major economic crisis, for example, may be more likely than a prosperous one to pursue justice if the former is given side-payments from internal or external interest groups for this purpose. Observable conditions, in short, are less important than how elites interpret them.

In total, in the four countries I conducted approximately 220 elite interviews (see Table 4.1), as well as nearly thirty in Washington, D.C., with U.S. foreign policy elites. Perhaps surprisingly, almost all of my respondents (including those in Uzbekistan) chose to put their comments on the record. Due to deteriorating political conditions in Uzbekistan since the time of my fieldwork, however, I have chosen to remove labels identifying respondents from that country.

The numbers easily conceal the time-consuming process of arranging these face-to-face meetings. This was most complicated in Poland, where many new elites (especially government and parliamentary leaders) from the early period of transition had long since left public life. My task was made more difficult by Polish regulations that allow telephone directory agents to release contact information only when callers have detailed addresses of the person in question. As a result, I usually began my quest for specific interviewees by Internet searches to find those who had stayed in the political realm or to identify past workplaces for others who had left. In the latter case, I was sometimes able (by contacting various former employers) to find the person's current whereabouts. A second source I relied on was a 1990 official guide to Solidarity members in Parliament, which included their addresses.[13] Unfortunately, many of those who were once politically active had changed their addresses in the past decade. In some of these instances I was able to gain more information from various political party headquarters or from other interviewees. A final important note: a significant number of former political elites are no longer living or have become critically ill and unavailable. One figure demonstrates these various difficulties: of the eleven 1989–era senators initially selected for interviews, five had died in the preceding decade, and contact information for three others could not be found.

Arranging interviews in the other three countries was generally simpler. In Uzbekistan, where oppositionists are eager to get information out, interviews could be scheduled on short notice and for extensive periods. There, international NGOs and foreign state actors as well as fellow oppositionists themselves (given the relatively small opposition community) were helpful in identifying and finding key organizations and leaders. Only two officials connected to the Tashkent government agreed to speak with me, however, and one asked for our meeting (which elicited little more than official propaganda lines) to be completely off the record. In Serbia and Croatia, most actors could be found via their organization's or institution's Web page or through political party offices. While interviews were easy to arrange in Croatia, a distinct problem emerged in Serbia: interviewee fatigue. Many actors were willing to meet with me, but it quickly became clear that in these early years of the transition they were inundated with curious guests. Numerous interviews (about one in four) had to be rescheduled when interviewees failed to show up, and a few interviewees openly expressed frustration that so much of their time was spent talking with researchers and reporters.

The nature of this fieldwork helps to explain my decision to limit the spectrum to a handful of justice mechanisms. Given the time-intensive nature of the data collection process—not only for me, but also especially for my respondents—it would have been impractical to include the vast array of justice mechanisms available, such as passage of amnesties, exploration of constitutional processes, creation of monuments and museums, renaming of streets, and property restitution. This is, unfortunately, a necessary limitation, but one that, I believe, the justice spectrum's design renders relatively harmless.

DATA ANALYSIS

The seven-measure justice spectrum not only serves as the yardstick for my analysis, but also provides an organizational framework for interviews and analysis, a useful (if basic) checklist of important justice policies that have been implemented around the world. More important, when combined with the qualitative methods described above, it can be used to differentiate motives for one type of justice over another and thus systematically evaluate the theoretical arguments discussed in chapter 1.

I use the spectrum as an ordinal scale, depicting severity of justice, and look for correlations between the highest type of justice systematically pursued and the independent variables described in chapter 1. The term "systematically" indicates that there must be evidence that implementation is designed to cover an entire sector rather than a few individuals. So, for a country to qualify as having systematically pursued type 6 criminal trials, criminal investigations must have been authorized for a significant percentage of those suspected of crimes. Similarly, to qualify as having pursued type 5 purges, personnel investigations must have encompassed an entire administrative unit or units. One or two criminal prosecutions of low-level perpetrators or twenty investigations of a 10,000–person administrative unit—where far more people are known to have been involved in rights abuses—are insufficient.

I use the term "pursued" in the above criteria to focus the burden of evidence on political will. While pursued and "implemented" are not mutually exclusive, I rely on the former because this is a study of political decision making, not state capacity. The fact that new elites mandate prosecutors to initiate criminal trials into past abuses is more important here than the effectiveness of these investigations and subsequent trials, which political leaders in transition states may have less ability to influence. Measurement of "systematically pursued" is based largely on common sense. I would, for example, not consider the cases of criminal trials in Bulgaria or Romania, where prosecutions could be counted on one hand, to be systematic, given the significant degree of communist-era repression in these states. By contrast, cases in which political leaders authorized officials to examine and prepare for trial any cases that seemed suspect would count as systematic even if there were only a few trials that proceeded. Though room for interpretation means potential analytical pitfalls, I mitigate these by explicitly documenting evidence and criteria used in each case, thus allowing readers to draw their own conclusions.

It is important to bear in mind that there need not be a single justice policy chosen. (In fact, justice is usually pursued in multiple types, either sequentially or simultaneously.) But what is critical here is the harshest form of justice systematically pursued. Since the placement of particular measures may be debatable, for the purposes of this study I divide the justice spectrum into three general categories: "lenient" (types 1–3), "moderate" (type 4), and "harsh" (types 5–7). Given that the spectrum is built on relative power logic, it essentially posits relative power as the null hypothesis. Following the relative power argument based on transition type, we should expect to see only those new elites coming to power through revolution to pursue harsh justice. By contrast, those rising to power through negotiated transition should pursue no more than moderate justice, while new elites who were explicitly given power by their predecessors should go no further than type 3. Relative power theorists focused more on state structure might vary from the above hypotheses depending on the extent to which members of key institutions persist after political elites step aside.

I return to the case of Uruguay mentioned in chapter 2. According to Huntington, Uruguayan new elites coming to power through negotiations were constrained by the strength of outgoing military leaders, who used their institutional powers to effectively influence a public referendum on lifting the amnesty as well as to avoid a truth commission.[14] If Huntington applied this more complete spectrum of mechanisms to the case of Uruguay, he might well find that relative power was the key determinant of justice policy. But if, for example, purges of the military (an aspect of the dependent variable that Huntington does not mention here) were instigated in the absence of truth commissions, this would highlight a weakness in his theory. Using the spectrum as a checklist in a more thorough qualitative study, Huntington might find that other factors, aside from relative power, had an important effect. Perhaps new elites somewhat supportive of lifting the amnesty did not actively push for a "yes" vote in the referendum, believing that a campaign for this cause would be seen by constituents as too much energy spent on the problems of the past rather than on the problems of today. Or perhaps voters who upheld the military amnesty in the referendum were not swayed by comments from the military, but by perceptions that the justice system already had its hands full, perhaps fighting corruption. If earlier, less risky stages on the spectrum—such as legal rehabilitation or condemnation—were also left unaddressed, this might point to the perception among political elites that the public was simply uninterested in justice.

With respect to the four countries studied in this book the different relative power arguments sometimes produce diverging hypotheses (see Table 4.2). According to transition-based relative power arguments, only in the case of Croatia, characterized by an "electoral revolution," should we expect harsh justice to be feasible. By contrast, justice should be at its most moderate in the cases of Poland and Serbia, where the transitions were negotiated. In Uzbekistan, where the regime is new only in a nominal sense, justice should not have occurred at all.

The hypotheses should be quite similar according to structure-based relative power arguments, since the departure of old elites was accompanied by practically no exodus of institutional power holders at lower levels. As a result, in all four states, justice should be moderate at best, though perhaps we might expect to see resistance to even moderate forms of justice in the more militarized states (where the armies were involved in widespread atrocities) of the former Yugoslavia and certainly in Uzbekistan.

It is more difficult to establish explicit hypotheses with respect to the third relative power argument, focused more on public support. Given the nature of the communist system, we might surmise that high levels of social complicity make even moderate forms of justice difficult, since they would pit small pockets of society against other groups. As a result, only lenient forms seem feasible with respect to the communist period. The same can be said with respect to accounting for crimes in the former Yugoslavia after 1989. In countries where most citizens during the war years did little to stop their governments' abuses next door and then after the war expressed

TABLE 4.2 Justice Type Based on Relative Power and Strategic Theories

	Harsh Justice	*Non-Harsh Justice*
Transition-based	Croatia	Poland, Serbia, Uzbekistan
Structure-based	None	Croatia, Poland, Serbia, Uzbekistan
Public Support–based	None	Croatia, Poland, Serbia, Uzbekistan
Strategic	Poland, Serbia, Uzbekistan	Croatia

disbelief that their military sons and fathers could be guilty of abuses worthy of scorn or prosecution, leniency seems likely.

The strategic argument, focused on a different set of constraints, results in quite different hypotheses. Here, we assume that new elites prefer to implement the harshest type of justice they can, so long as it does not run the risk of arousing public consternation due to its impact on the provision of goods and services. This should create variability in justice depending on who is in power and in the practical (especially economic) tasks they face while governing. In Poland we might expect to see harsh forms of justice in the immediate post-1989 election period until economic reforms begin. In Serbia, where international criminal justice could be traded for major economic bonuses, harsh justice also should have occurred, while in Croatia, where international criminal justice during the first period of new elite rule offered fewer concrete rewards, harsh justice should have been eschewed. In Uzbekistan, we should expect to find any form of justice—whether lenient or harsh—that the nondemocratic leader believes will pay off.

THE FOUR CASE STUDIES provide for an intriguing examination of justice determinants. My analysis, rich with quotations cited to highlight arguments found in the field, is organized around the spectrum described in chapter 2. I begin with my investigation of Poland, the first state to end communist rule and hence the one with the longest experience of pursuing (or eschewing) justice in the region. From Poland, a country characterized by relatively moderate rights violations in the recent era and where pressures for justice have been almost exclusively domestic, I move to southern Europe. My analysis of Serbia and Croatia differs from Poland in that justice in the post-Yugoslav states is focused on egregious abuses carried out after the fall of communism and is in many ways an international affair. Finally, I move my study to Uzbekistan, where rights abuses of yesterday are juxtaposed with those of today, and where accountability appears to be largely a function of the international pressures that have such a mixed record in the former Yugoslavia.

Because relative power arguments are not determinative (they are designed to show what should not occur rather than what should), the raw results from these country studies do not necessarily refute these arguments. Relative power arguments make no explicit prediction for what should occur, only for what should and should not be permissible. For example, transition-based arguments suggest that Croatian elites, having emerged from an electoral revolution, might pursue any one of the seven types of justice discussed. It is therefore theoretically not illuminating that Croatian leaders chose to launch a truth commission or shied away from aggressively pursuing criminal justice, just as it would not be particularly interesting if we found Croatia pursuing mass extraditions to the Hague. Yet the arguments are based on process, critical to theory-building.[15] Even in cases where relative power and strategic arguments are not predictive, we can evaluate them based on the applicability of their process.

A final note: readers will observe a disparity in the size of the chapters, with the earlier country chapters in Part II generally longer than the later ones. This is largely linked to the phenomenon of justice in each state. Over the more than fifteen years covered in the Polish chapter, elites pursued the full range of justice policies. By contrast, in the five or so years covered in the Serbia chapter, Serbs were primarily focused on criminal prosecutions. The Serbia chapter is, in turn, longer than the one on Croatia because a majority of war crimes trials concerned the former, not the latter. The Uzbek case, based on the second-largest number of interviews, is the shortest, thus reflecting the narrow path of justice taken there.

PART II

5

Poland

Justice, Economics,
and the End of Solidarity

In 1989, following negotiations between members of the Communist Party and the Solidarity opposition movement, Poland became the first Eastern Bloc country to abandon communism. Between the 1989 semi-democratic elections and the 1991 free elections, post-Solidarity elites and postcommunist forces shared power. Since 1991, the two sides have taken turns running the country, with post-Solidarity elites dominating politics between 1991 and 1993 and from 1997 through 2001, and postcommunists controlling the government between 1993 and 1997 and from 2001 through 2005. For much of the postcommunist period, justice for communist-era rights violations has been an important, and highly charged, feature on the Polish political stage. Throughout this chapter, I refer to Poland's opposition-era Solidarity leaders as "post-Solidarity" elites, though they have been represented in a variety of parties, beginning with the Civic Parliamentary Club (Obywatelski Klub Parlamentarny, OKP), which was formed for the 1989 elections.

Polish post-Solidarity elites, like their colleagues in much of Central Europe, faced two main transitional justice issues: communist-era violations and World War II atrocities. The latter issue was already on the agenda during the communist period, but there were, of course, limitations to communist-era attempts to investigate wartime rights violations, since many violations were carried out by Soviet or Polish communist troops.[1] As a result, post-Solidarity elites did make numerous attempts to deal with World War II violations, but they focused specifically on those abuses that took place toward the end of the war and were instigated by communists. In this way, the examination of wartime violations served as a natural bridge by which to explore the most recent period of abuse—the period in which many post-Solidarity elites were themselves victims.

As in other parts of the communist world, the worst period of rights abuses in Poland occurred during Stalinism, in the late 1940s and early 1950s, when political imprisonment, torture, and state-sponsored killings took place regularly. During the post-Stalinist period beginning in 1956, core human rights abuses were generally less common, occurring in episodes rather than on an everyday basis. The events in Poznań in 1956, when scores of people were killed during the state's operation to end strikes initiated by factory workers, marked the first and bloodiest period of episodic rights violations that took place throughout the 1980s. Other such violations, usually involving state security services who were shooting or attacking unarmed demonstrators, broke out in 1968, 1970, 1976, and at the start of martial law in 1981. While there were sporadic episodes of political imprisonment and even extrajudicial killings during these years, these problems escalated as the communist regime set about destroying the opposition Solidarity labor union. Under martial law (1981–1983), scores of oppositionists were killed and thousands were imprisoned. This pattern of political imprisonments and detentions continued throughout the 1980s, as Solidarity continued to function underground, until the government renewed negotiations with its leaders in 1988.

In contrast to the other cases analyzed in this study, there was practically no foreign input (much less pressure) concerning transitional justice in Poland. Rather, justice was a phenomenon motivated by and primarily concerning post-Solidarity elites. Given the exclusively domestic nature of justice influences, the Polish case represents a straightforward test of the arguments posited here. Poland's democratic breakthrough followed a negotiated transition between Solidarity activists and Communist Party leaders. As part of the settlement, former communists guaranteed themselves (or members of their former satellite parties) a place in the new government and 65 percent of seats in the primary, lower house of Parliament (Sejm). Post-Solidarity elites were left with 35 percent of the Sejm and almost total control (99/100 seats) in the freely contested, but secondary, upper house (Senat). The presidency initially remained in the hands of General Wojciech Jaruzelski, who ruled Poland during the 1980s; and several communist-era leaders served in key positions — including as defense minister, foreign minister, and internal affairs minister — in the post-Solidarity government of Tadeusz Mazowiecki. Finally, society was perceived to be split on the problem of how to deal with the past, with millions having been card-carrying members of the Communist Party.

Under such conditions, and according to transition- and structure-based relative power arguments, Poland's new elites might have been expected to act with caution and to have avoided such harsh methods of justice as purges and criminal accountability. Instead, just two months after taking power, post-Solidarity members launched a truth commission that led directly to criminal accountability for former functionaries as well as for their leaders. Perhaps more surprising, in the period of post-Solidarity power consolidation (1991–1993), when relative power arguments might project the harshest forms of justice, justice was practically off the agenda. In this chapter, I explain the path of justice reforms from 1989 to 2004. My findings indicate that broad political strategy, rather than simply relative power, played a central role in determining the type of transitional justice in postcommunist Poland.

TYPE 1. CESSATION AND CODIFICATION OF HUMAN RIGHTS VIOLATIONS

Since beginning its transition to democracy, Poland has significantly strengthened human rights both on paper and in practice.[2] While Warsaw signed the Convention against Torture at a time when allegations of torture and murder by the security services were still being heard (January 13, 1986), the convention was not ratified until summer 1989, just after the first, semi-democratic elections. In November 1990, Poland signed the first optional protocol of the International Covenant on Civil and Political Rights (ICCPR), recognizing the Human Rights Commission's authority to receive and investigate citizen complaints (ratified February 1992). This was less than one year after Poland passed an amnesty that had released the few prisoners of conscience who still remained behind bars at the end of the 1980s (and who appear to have been formally charged with nonpolitical crimes).[3] Also in 1990, the Warsaw government signed the Convention on Rights of the Child (January 1990, ratified in 1991). More recently, it moved closer to its European partners, signing the Rome Statute of the International Criminal Court in 1999 and the ICCPR's second protocol banning the death penalty in 2000. In trials of communist-era human rights violations, Polish courts have cited international law in their arguments.

TYPE 2. REBUKE OF THE OLD SYSTEM

There have been two general kinds of condemnation in the Polish case: condemnation for episodic incidents of repression and broader condemnation of entire periods of repression. By episodic incidents of repression, I refer to the particularly brutal events noted above that, while not common methods of everyday intimidation, were significant in demonstrating the extent to which the system was capable of abuse in order to secure the status quo.[4] I focus here on five well-known, specific incidents of large-scale rights violations: Poznań, 1956; the anti-Semitic campaign, 1968; Baltic coast, 1970; Radom, 1976; and Wujek miners, 1981. Broader condemnations can also be broken down into three periods: pre-1956 Stalinism; martial law during the 1980s; and the entire communist era.

During the first years of post-Solidarity rule, there were no initiatives to condemn episodic violations. Just months after the 1989 elections, however, General Jaruzelski traveled to southern Poland to lay a wreath under a cross at the Wujek mine, where troops of his government had killed and wounded protesting miners during the first days of martial law in 1981. While not an apology or statement of condemnation, Jaruzelski silently placed a message at this site that read: "Polish blood flowed through the Silesian lands. That which was poured here we could have avoided. Let the memory of it be a warning for the living and a tribute to the dead." When approached by a survivor who demanded an investigation into who had ordered the soldiers to fire, Jaruzelski responded: "The very fact that I am here today among you and bow my head is testament to the fact that I have the best of intentions to clear up this issue."[5]

Only in December 1995, two years after Solidarity had lost power, did the Sejm pass a resolution sponsored by post-Solidarity elites that condemned communist suppression of the December 1970 demonstrations along the Baltic coast. The resolution encountered no opposition from the postcommunist-dominated Parliament and was followed by a June 1996 Sejm resolution in remembrance of the fortieth anniversary of the brutal suppression of workers in Poznań in 1956 (a second resolution, paying respect to the victims, was passed in June 2001). In March 1998 the Sejm passed a resolution condemning the former regime for the anti-Semitic campaign begun in March 1968, declaring that "the harm done as a result of the March events should be corrected." In June 2001, on the twenty-fifth anniversary of the abuses against protesting workers in Radom in 1976, the Sejm passed a resolution demanding that those responsible for the attacks should be punished.[6]

Broader rebukes of the former regime came first for the Stalinist period, which was decried in early legislation calling for victim rehabilitation (1991) and criminal prosecution of perpetrators (1991). There were also repeated parliamentary attempts to condemn the 1980s martial law period. In contrast to general elite support for condemnations of episodic violations and Stalin-era atrocities, a sweeping condemnation of the 1980s policies ran into consistent opposition from old elites still in power, many of whom were personally associated with that period and thus attacked proposals, even walking out on a number of votes (in 1991, 1992, 1994, and 1995). As a result of these tensions, members of the Sejm in October 1991 voted 191:28 (30 abstentions) merely to "pay respect to the victims of 1981–1989."[7] In the following February, after a lengthy and volatile debate, the Sejm adopted a resolution introduced by the right-wing Confederation for an Independent Poland (KPN) declaring martial law illegal (220:6, 16 abstentions) and calling for a Commission on Constitutional Responsibility to assess criminal responsibility.[8]

The changing political tide that brought postcommunists back to power from 1993 to 1997 left watered-down resolutions concerning martial law.

For example, in December 1994, the postcommunist Democratic Left Alliance (SLD) amended a proposed center-right resolution condemning as unconstitutional the imposition of martial law and citing deaths and political prisoners. The final version, which merely offered to "pay respect" to victims of the fight for freedom, prompted right forces to walk out of Parliament, leaving the resolution dead for lack of a quorum.[9] One year later, when the Sejm moved to pass a post-Solidarity resolution saying that it "condemns the imposers of martial law and expresses hope that their illegal activities will be justly tried," the dominant SLD opposed the resolution on the grounds that it would bias the Commission on Constitutional Responsibility's examination of martial law's legality.[10] Only in December 2002 did the Sejm manage—without objections, abstentions, or walkouts—to pass a resolution declaring December 13, the anniversary of the martial law's imposition, a national day of remembrance.[11]

Despite the fact that Poland's post-Solidarity elites dominated politics from 1991 to 1993, it took almost a decade after the start of political changes for them to pass a resolution condemning the entire communist period. The 1998 resolution was carried in the relatively weak Senat, which helped to relegate it to political (and social) irrelevance.[12] Only two of my elite respondents appear to have been aware of the resolution: Senators Zbigniew Romaszewski and Piotr Andrzejewski, both of whom had served on the Senat's Human Rights and Rule of Law Committee that drafted the resolution. The more publicized rebuke came from the postcommunists themselves, after the fall 1993 electoral victory, when then-SLD leader (and later Polish president) Aleksander Kwaśniewski told Parliament, "I apologize to all, some of whom are in this hall, who experienced harm and wrongdoing by the authorities and the system before 1989."[13]

Post-Solidarity elites are divided in their explanation for why their rebuke policy took shape so gradually. In contrast to their replies to questions concerning other justice measures, Polish political elites tended to react to this question with great uncertainty, with responses coming off as spur-of-the-moment, as if this were something that they had never reflected upon. According to some, and lending some support to the role of relative power, symbolic attacks on the old regime were at first limited by the new elites' share of seats in the lower house of Parliament and the government, and the obvious difficulty of convincing members of the old elite to approve legislation that would assign them broad responsibility for communist-era repression.[14] Former communists now acknowledge that they could not accept such repudiation, which could undermine reconciliation. "Both sides deserve respect because neither was trying to go against the national interest. I happened to take this road. I am not ashamed of my résumé," one former high-ranking Communist said.[15] Yet the fact that a Solidarity-ruled Senat (1989–1991) and then Parliament and the government (1991–1993) also refrained from issuing blanket condemnations renders this explanation weak.

Alternatively, other post-Solidarity actors have argued that condemnations, with little practical repercussions, were unimportant during a period of profound political and economic changes. One former senator, noting that a massive overhaul of the system was itself a form of rebuke, asked, "Did this really need an official condemnation?"[16] The argument that resolutions were an inefficient use of time and energy,[17] while plausible, begs the question of why there were fifty-six parliamentary resolutions passed in 1992 alone. Moreover, most of those resolutions came out of the Sejm, which immediately after coming to power had taken the time to condemn more geographically and temporally distant incidents, such as the 1968 intervention in Czechoslovakia and the postwar repression of the Polish underground.[18]

It seems, instead, that there was, in the words of one past and current senator, "no political will to give this a higher priority."[19] Elite sensitivity to widespread social sympathy to the former regime appears to be the critical reason for this lack of political will. Post-Solidarity elites had a limited mandate to deal with the past, according to some post-Solidarity respondents. While Solidarity leaders had in the 1980s called for "liquidation of the legal system," they had not promised to end socialism, much less condemn the system in which so many Poles had participated.[20] This lends some credence to the public support–based relative power argument. Indeed, post-Solidarity elites did not celebrate their dramatic victory in Poland's first fully free 1991 elections by lashing out against the old system, as the relative power argument might predict.[21] Instead, one participant in the debate said that "we carefully picked the words" of condemnations to avoid social opposition.[22] Yet, in support of the strategic argument, interviewees made it clear that they did not fear violent social rifts or street demonstrations in protest. Instead, post-Solidarity elites were afraid that voters would view their denunciation, directed at a system that was apparently more capable of securing economic stability than was the new one, as a cheap political reckoning at a time when there were more important practical issues to be resolved.

TYPE 3. REHABILITATION AND COMPENSATION FOR VICTIMS

Rehabilitation and compensation laws were passed in Poland for practical as well as for moral and political reasons. Former prisoners (and families of deceased prisoners) from the Stalinist period began to flood the courts in 1989 in an effort to clear their names and records, and by 1990 some former victims were demanding compensation. Contradictions quickly arose. For example, in 1990 one court awarded damages to the wife of a Polish fighter from the World War II pro-independence army (known as the Home Army, or Armia Krajowa), who had been killed in 1953 after being convicted on political charges.[23] Yet in other cases the ombudsman had to step in to challenge court decisions that denied victim compensation on the basis that the convictions had occurred so long ago.[24] A new law was needed to ease the courts' burden and ensure standardized justice.

The Senat reacted in late 1990 by passing a bill nullifying politically motivated criminal sentences issued between May 1943, when Stalin created a Polish army under General Zygmunt Berling, and 1989.[25] The Sejm then responded a few months later by slashing the scope of the bill to the narrow 1944–1956 period and voting down 85:161 (37 abstentions) an amendment expanding the law to 1989.[26] After a debate that touched on institutional powers, political futures, and historical obligations, senators finally voted to accept the Sejm's date change by a vote of 31:21 (5 abstentions) and ultimately passed the law 42:14 (6 abstentions). Realists in the Senat reasoned that without passage of the amendments, the entire bill would be thrown out, leaving justice for none.[27] The new law streamlined payments to those whose rights were violated pre-1957 and allowed former political prisoners to count their years in jail as time during which they were employed, thus qualifying for retirement benefits.[28]

In many ways, Poland's new law, like the debate that preceded it, was largely symbolic; under article 487 of the criminal code, anyone was entitled to compensation for illegal imprisonment, regardless of when it occurred.[29] The law did streamline the process, however. Within a year and a half, military and civilian courts had already conducted more than 2,200 judicial reviews and awarded more than zł. 257 billion ($19 million).[30] Within three years, authorities had reviewed 30,000 cases of rehabilitation and compensation.[31] This long list led to court backlogs that delayed rulings for years, ultimately leading some victims to sue the Polish state at the European Court of Human Rights. In two separate cases the European body forced Polish authorities to compensate the brother and wife of Stalin-era victims, concluding that the right to a hearing "within a reasonable time" had been denied.[32]

While pre-1957 rights victims were, at least in theory, provided with streamlined compensation processes through the 1991 legislation, challenges from victims who had suffered during the 1980s proved more controversial. In June 1991, two former opposition activists from Łódź became the first to receive compensation for prison sentences served under martial law.[33] Over time, however, compensation for victims of particular post-1956 rights violations was streamlined as well. In April 1992, for example, the internal affairs minister permitted the local police department in Legnica to pay millions of złoty to victims and families of victims of the 1981 Lubin attack.[34] Several months after the first compensation case for the December 1970 attacks on the Baltic coast went to court,[35] the Senat in early 1996 similarly voted 42:26 to send zł. 2.5 million (approximately $1 million) to the cities of Gdańsk, Gdynia, Elbląg, and Szczecin to compensate the December 1970 victims, to whom the Sejm subsequently awarded veterans' benefits in cases where severe injuries had been incurred.[36] A 1993 law also made those Polish citizens repressed between 1944 and 1956 for "independence activities" by Soviet courts (and not only Polish organs of repression) eligible for compensation, though diplomatic pressure for Russia to accept financial responsibility for its historic injustices proved impossible.[37]

The dramatic difference between the Senat's and the Sejm's versions of the groundbreaking 1991 bill appears to be linked to institutional differences. Members of the Sejm, who were forced to consider how the majority in society (who would receive no benefits from the legislation) would be affected by the bill, saw clear dangers. Many of these elites opposed extending the law through 1989 since streamlining payments for all communist-era victims could threaten the stability of Poland's extraordinarily fragile economy.[38] During debate, one OKP member asked, "Do we have the right to stick the bill to the generation of our grandchildren?"[39]

Yet perhaps more important was an elite fear of public perceptions. One former Solidarity parliamentarian commented that her constituents would be infuriated by a sweeping law since "compensation would have come at the expense of taxpayers. If this were to come from [former internal affairs minister Czesław] Kiszczak's personal income, that would be another story."[40] This perception was reinforced by the fact that by extending privileges through 1989, numerous post-Solidarity elites in power would be directly providing themselves and their close colleagues outside of Parliament with benefits. According to my own calculations based on biographies of post-Solidarity parliamentarians, more than 60 percent of post-Solidarity Sejm members had their rights violated (from politically inspired layoffs to jail time) under communism. In fact, more than 50 percent of the members were interned or imprisoned after 1956.[41] The proportion is virtually the same in the Senat, where 60 percent were victimized during communism, including 49 percent who were incarcerated at some point (9 percent before Solidarity became active in 1980). This apparent conflict of interest, which post-Solidarity elites feared would outrage their constituents, led many to object. "We fought for a free Poland, not for tips," commented then-parliamentarian Adam Michnik, a former political prisoner who is currently editor of the daily, *Gazeta Wyborcza*.[42]

Despite facing the same dilemma, senators, far removed from the aftermath of policy output, lobbied for a more extensive bill. Senators on the human rights committee believed that a bill including violations through 1989 would be seen as an indirect attack on the entire communist period, and they charged that by ending rehabilitation at 1956, their Sejm colleagues were kowtowing to the communists. One post-Solidarity senator noted during debate that a bill including the 1980s martial law period would make it more difficult to simply blame all communist-era rights violations on Soviet actors, thus setting off "a general discussion on the subject of guilt and punishment." [43] Protesting the rollback, senators argued that "political trials did not end definitively after the passage of the Stalinist period, but lasted through the entire time of real socialism."[44] Redemption, according to one prominent voice in the debate, should be applied to all those who were punished while acting in the name of "human rights and civil freedom."[45] Senators thought that the Sejm's revisions were designed to help postcommunists across the aisle save face. Senator Ryszard Juszkiewicz declared: "If we accept the date of December 31, 1956, then we *ex cathedra* state that after this date there was no repression, there were no illegitimate sentences, and there was no communist system."[46]

In the end, both sets of actors relied on symbolic arguments to defend their version of the rehabilitation and compensation law, which, as noted earlier, was in many ways itself symbolic. Sejm members replied to Juszkiewicz that there must be a distinction between brutal and systematic rights violations from the Stalinist era and the less methodical post-Stalinist abuses. Stefan Niesiołowski, a former opposition member who spent more than five years in jail between 1970 and 1981, summarized this argument succinctly: "I was never beaten in jail. I was treated well. Before 1956 I would not have left jail alive."[47]

While questions of morality, ideology, and personality might all be used to explain why rehabilitation and compensation proceeded the way that it did, Solidarity's very clear split along institutional lines strongly suggests a more systematic process. New elites did not act with unified restraint, as various relative power arguments might predict, but were fragmented between members of the Senat, who favored a bill implicating then-empowered postcommunists in past violations, and members of the Sejm, who cringed at appearing to be out for the spoils of revolution and were weary of picking fights with members of the old elite, whose votes were needed on other issues. Strategic considerations left early Polish efforts at victim rehabilitation and compensation quite narrow.

TYPE 4. CREATION OF A TRUTH COMMISSION

Despite the fact that they were a minority, and in stark contrast to relative power predictions, post-Solidarity leaders in the Sejm just two months after the 1989 elections forced postcommunists to accept a truth process that led directly to criminal investigations of both high- and low-level members of the former regime. The Special Commission to Investigate the Ministry of Internal Affairs was tasked with analyzing more than one hundred unsolved 1980s deaths attributed to the security services and other branches of the ministry.[48] The Special Commission's function was primarily retributive. Its mandate included collecting evidence that would be used directly for disciplinary action or sent on to public prosecutors for further investigation and possible trial.[49] As a result of concessions to those postcommunists dominating the Sejm, the Special Commission was structurally weak. It was broken down into working groups that each included one postcommunist. Moreover, the commissioners lacked the authority necessary to thoroughly perform their legislated functions, including analyzing government documents (which they often could not access) and interviewing witnesses, victims, and alleged perpetrators (who could be neither forced through subpoenas nor encouraged through amnesties).[50]

While the Special Commission (also known as the Rokita Commission after its chair, Jan Rokita) ultimately proved unable to guarantee widespread criminal accountability, it did send eighty-eight cases of unexplained deaths—some of which had never been investigated, others in which investigations were determined to be faulty—back to the prosecutor's office.[51] Few of these investigations resulted in a prosecution, much less a conviction. Poland's first noncommunist general prosecutor, Aleksander Herzog, denies reports that prosecutors acted purposely to reduce the effectiveness of investigations, instead attributing shortcomings to the complicated nature of delving into crimes committed long ago—though he concedes that some prosecutors may have neglected these old cases to concentrate on contemporary crimes.[52] Concurring, former internal affairs minister Krzysztof Kozłowski compared the trials emerging from the Rokita Commission to an American movie, where the good cop knows that the smug bandit is up to no good but cannot find the legal proof required to arrest him: "In terms of proving who did this, the courts are helpless."[53] The Justice Ministry's delegate to the Special Commission (who was himself repressed during communism) was less sanguine, arguing that most of the charges represented a post-1989 politicization of the otherwise common deaths of Solidarity members.[54] Still, for those sure that communist authorities had their hand in such deaths, failed prosecutions prompted anger.

"There was lots of disappointment with the Rokita Commission," concluded one former parliamentarian. "It did not clarify anything."[55]

Even if the investigations failed to satisfy many pro-justice actors (leading to promises to initiate another, less restrained commission in the future),[56] the truth commission's inauguration was almost revolutionary. Given its focus on criminal accountability, the Special Commission (like many around the world) was in many ways similar to types 6 and 7 on the spectrum. For many post-Solidarity activists, it was proof that post-Solidarity elites were quick to deal with questions of justice.[57] As Solidarity's then political leader Bronisław Geremek noted, the Special Commission embodied the belief that "crimes should be punished."[58] Former communists at first resisted it on the grounds that allegations of wrongdoing were false and, regardless, should be handled by already existing judicial institutions.[59] Ultimately, however, they conceded to a truth process that they could at least partially influence—and one that, added the Justice Ministry's liaison to the Special Commission, at least facilitated the opening of criminal investigations that otherwise would likely have remained closed.[60]

While relative power arguments accurately predict the constraints placed on the Special Commission at its inception, it seems that its mandate to essentially initiate criminal prosecutions oversteps the limits that relative power should have set. I argue that three factors allowed Solidarity members in the Sejm to support the Special Commission. Most important was the fact that it was launched in summer 1989, well before serious economic reform bills were on the floor. Post-Solidarity members in the Sejm did not yet need the support of postcommunists to pass core goods legislation at the time. In essence, post-Solidarity elites in both the Sejm and in the Senat felt comfortable antagonizing the post-communists with little fear of an adverse reaction. This effect was essential and follows directly from the strategic argument.

Yet two other explanations demonstrate the confluence of the strategic argument with relative power. First, the surprisingly strong showing of Solidarity in the June 1989 elections convinced postcommunist elites that although post-Solidarity elites remained proportionally weak in the Sejm, they were a political force quickly on the rise. Unlike rigid indicators of relative strength that elite-level relative power arguments frequently emphasize, political actors in Poland measured their own strength based on their perceptions of popular attitudes. Postcommunists would be better off with a justice policy that they could influence and that targeted individual rights abusers, than with a more sweeping one forced upon them in the event of a subsequent post-Solidarity electoral victory. As one post-Solidarity parliamentarian recalled with regard to another aggressive form of justice, "They knew there would be new elections and that they would lose. . . . Blocking the [justice policy] could end in a lustration law."[61]

In addition, the Special Commission was established during a period when public opposition to criminal accountability was relatively low. While key actors in the government were unenthusiastic about launching a process that would vilify their postcommunist partners in such power ministries as Internal Affairs, Defense, and the presidency, a decision was made to leave transitional justice to Parliament.[62] Prime Minister Mazowiecki might have feared that harsh justice could even lead to a counterrevolution,[63] but he found it politically wiser to avoid angering loud pro-justice voices: "[Certain cases were] so drastic and socially painful that even if I thought that, politically, we should wait, I could not have come out and said so."[64] If relative power of the old elites was a consideration for Mazowiecki, voter power was a more important one.

TYPE 5. PURGING OF HUMAN RIGHTS ABUSERS FROM PUBLIC POSITIONS

Post-Solidarity forces sought to remove rights abusers from the public payroll in two primary institutions: the security services within the Internal Affairs Ministry, and the judicial branch.[65] At first, former Solidarity activists were somewhat cautious, wary that an all-out purge of the ministry would, in the words of Senator Zbigniew Romaszewski, "complicate the ministry's situation."[66] Yet within just a few months, post-Solidarity elites introduced into the Sejm six separate reform bills demanding a cleansing of the Internal Affairs Ministry.[67] Politicians' demands for guilty functionaries "to act with honor and resign" appeared to resonate, as various high-level ministry officials left in 1990.[68] That same year, a benign-looking bill to restructure the 24,000–person Security Services (SB) into the Office of

State Protection (UOP) paved the way for a cleansing of one of the most brutal elements of the old system.

For those in charge, the very general terms provided in the 1990 legislation left much to the imagination. "When one does not know what he is doing, and I swear I did not, the only thing that comes to mind is to try the most simple, even primitive, method," recalled Kozłowski, then internal affairs minister.[69] With an eye toward eliminating mass resistance, Kozłowski pursued policies that would fragment the SB. First, all SB officers older than 55 were given early retirement, eliminating all but twenty of the 138-member SB leadership. Certain administrative sections, including the Third Department (focusing on internal groups/opposition), Fourth Department (monitoring the Church), Fifth Department (dealing with the unions), and Sixth Department (controlling rural activists), were eliminated on the grounds that in the new political order they were no longer necessary. Finally, Kozłowski was left with just under 14,000, primarily lower-ranking SB personnel who chose to retain their positions in the renamed organization, the UOP. These actors faced background investigations (known as "verifications") designed to eliminate persons connected with rights abuses and other transgressions.

The purge of the ministry was complicated by several factors. First, as discussed above, the legislation was so general that the minister in charge had no practical road map for proceeding. Second, Kozłowski faced conflicting pressures. The ombudsman, for example, warned him against collective punishment, while outspoken elites demanded a thorough vetting that would leave no former members in the new service. This was known as the "zero option."[70] Finally, those responsible for governing the state feared that too "thorough" a reckoning would cripple Poland's intelligence and counterintelligence capabilities for up to five years during a period of extraordinary change and regional instability.[71]

The SB verification process was, as a result, neither thorough nor systematic. Central authorities ordered committees created in each of Poland's forty-nine local administrative units (called *województwa*) to run their own verification processes. In the absence of clear criteria and anything more than circumstantial evidence, each unit acted differently. One Solidarity labor activist who served on his local SB verification committee in

the town of Toruń recalls having limited tools, especially a lack of witnesses: "We could base our judgments only on our own experience, direct
contact with these SB officers."[72] Some verification committees assumed
innocence (resulting in only 15 percent dismissals in the Gdańsk *wojewódstwo*), while others assumed guilt (leading to 86 percent dismissed in the
Tarnobrzeg *wojewódstwo*).[73] Minister Kozłowski's Central Verification Committee reviewed and altered a large number of decisions (according to one
source, 73 percent of negative *wojewódstwo* decisions were overturned),[74]
eventually leaving about half of the total positively verified or freed from
guilt.[75] There was no verification of the 100,000–man militia, also under
the jurisdiction of the Internal Affairs Ministry, and some scholars contend
that negatively verified SB officers (those found guilty) simply shifted to
police work.[76]

Officials in the judiciary, which under communism was often used
as a tool of repression, carried out a similar cleansing process.[77] Herzog,
the general prosecutor, was given just three months to dismiss all 4,000 national prosecutors and subsequently rehire a full staff. Like Kozłowski,
Herzog complained that his legislative orders were vague, that outside demands for justice varied, and that time constraints were incompatible with
a thorough vetting.[78] He translated the vague criteria (based on unfitting
"character") into more specific behaviors, ranging from alcoholism to political prosecutions and brutality. As with the SB verification, however, the
decision to retain or force out prosecutors was made largely on hearsay. "It
was on the principle of 'someone said something,' 'someone wrote something,'" Herzog recalled.[79] At the end of the three-month process, nearly
11 percent of Poland's prosecutors were negatively verified.[80] "This really
was not a true verification," Herzog concluded in retrospect. "There were
too few criteria and not enough time."

Because of shortcomings in early initiatives, these bureaucratic cleansings continued for more than a decade. An Internal Affairs Ministry special commission was created in late 1991 to review the activities of some
seventy prosecutors who had been active during martial law and who continued to work at the Justice Ministry, for example.[81] President Lech Wałęsa
single-handedly attempted to recall judges for previous partiality, a move
opposed by the ombudsman and struck down by the Constitutional Tribunal in late 1993.[82] In April 1997, Parliament passed a law denying spe-

cial retirement benefits to judges or their next-of-kin who had participated in Stalinist repression.[83] More controversial was a 1998 law (passed 275:7 with 109 abstentions) that called for the investigation and punishment of judges alleged to have yielded to political influence from 1944 to 1989.[84] Fewer than one hundred investigations, based exclusively on complaints from former defendants,[85] were carried out during the implementation period (through 2002), and less than twenty resulted in disciplinary hearings. By 2003, the community of judges responsible for the investigations had found fifty-nine of the seventy-six accused of Stalinist-era repression to be guilty and rescinded their retirement benefits.

Rather than avoid harsh cleansing processes, as the relative power argument would predict, Poland's new elites merely devised vague legislation that would allow their colleagues in the executive branch to follow aggressive policies. In other words, by keeping pre-1991 laws imprecise, they ensured their passage through a postcommunist-controlled Sejm.[86] Once indistinct bills became law, post-Solidarity leaders in their respective ministries were essentially given free rein over the purge. This use of constructive ambiguity engendered possibilities but also challenges. Each implementer struggled with similar problems: creating legitimate criteria, finding evidence, and satisfying diverse audiences. This task was frequently a thankless one, and both Internal Affairs Minister Kozłowski and General Prosecutor Herzog recall widespread disapproval of the processes that they executed. Yet only Kozłowski had any fear of revolt from the formerly repressive structures.[87] He compared the target security services (SB) to two armed military divisions desperate to maintain their status and livelihoods. "If we threw them all out in one day," he asked, "what would they do?" In retrospect, Kozłowski acknowledged, "This degree of danger was an illusion of mine." And it did not stop him from launching the widespread investigations described above.

Perhaps more interesting is the question of why early legislation for a purge of the judiciary, which had targeted both prosecutors and judges, was amended to include only the former. The answer appears to be a mix of ideology and pragmatism. Some thought that subjecting judges to verification would create an atmosphere of judicial partiality in the new Poland.[88] A number of legal professionals (who accounted for nearly 15 percent of post-Solidarity elites in Parliament from 1989 to 1991) also feared that by attacking a tight network of judges, they would risk never winning a court case again. "Revenge from the courts was brutal," one former Sejm member and lawyer commented.[89]

Apparently the most important consideration from the majority outside the legal profession was expert testimony. Opposition members with either no legal background or limited contact with judges trusted the opinion of Deputy Minister of Justice Adam Strzembosz, who promised Parliament that the National Council of Judges (Krajowa Rada Sądownictwa), ruled by a new administrative body including post-Solidarity members, would cleanse itself.[90] When an effort was made to pursue judges eight years later, postcommunists charged that the right was simply trying to humiliate them,[91] and even justice proponents questioned the practical use of the measure. "This was like serving mustard after lunch was already over," former prime minister Jan Olszewski said.[92]

TYPES 6 AND 7. CRIMINAL PROSECUTION OF "EXECUTORS" AND COMMANDERS

Because criminal accountability in Poland rarely differentiated between executor and commander, I have merged these two types into one for this chapter. There was only one attempt to seek criminal accountability solely for senior-level leaders; other measures for criminal accountability included both kinds of actors. There were several (often simultaneous) efforts to hold both lower-level functionaries and "commanders" of communist-era rights violations criminally accountable.[93] While the outgoing regime passed an amnesty that made certain political crimes impossible to punish and vindicated (or reduced sentences of) those found guilty of certain other crimes,[94] in only two months after taking power post-Solidarity elites launched a truth process initiating criminal investigations. A fall 1990 debate[95] on broader criminal accountability led to a 1991 law expanding the Chief Commission for the Investigation of Hitlerite Atrocities to the broader Commission for the Prosecution of Crimes against the Polish Nation, including pre-1957 communist-era rights violations, referred to here as GK, from the Polish acronym, Główna Komisja.[96]

Unlike the Rokita Commission, composed of political leaders who sought to publicize their investigations, the GK was set up and run by prosecutors with the exclusive aim of criminal accountability. While legislation gave the GK new authority, those in charge claim that they were already looking into Stalin-era cases before the passage of a formal law.[97] The cases begun even after the new law took effect quickly ran into legal problems since the statute of limitations had expired. To facilitate criminal prosecutions, post-Solidarity members in 1995 pushed through the postcommunist-dominated Parliament (181:108, 51 abstentions) a law resetting the clock on the statute of limitations to January 1, 1990, for crimes committed between 1944 and 1989.[98] The passage of this bill coincided with the National Constitutional Commission's decision to annul in the new constitution the statute of limitations for crimes against humanity, war crimes, and crimes committed by public functionaries previously not prosecuted due to political conditions.[99] A June 1996 law "on removing certain bills on amnesty and abolition for perpetrators of certain crimes, not pursued for political reasons from 1944 to 1989" ensured that PRL functionaries who had committed particularly brutal crimes, but were previously protected by the ruling regime, would be ineligible for amnesties issued before December 7, 1989.[100]

While the 1995 law turned out to be the first of a series of steps to clear the way for prosecutions of abusers from the former regime, circumstances surrounding the vote indicate the awkwardness with which those who inherit political guilt deal with it. While postcommunists voted in large numbers against the bill, news reports illustrate that SLD members were uncomfortable with taking a public stand.[101] For example, one SLD member, Zbigniew Siemiatkowski, commented to journalists, "I voted for this, the crimes should be pursued. This should have been done long ago." When reporters pointed out that the voting record showed that he had actually voted against the bill, Siemiatkowski responded that the record was incorrect, that he had actually abstained. Also, SLD chair Aleksander Kwaśniewski claimed that he "was in the hall but did not vote. I was busy"; but the record also showed his opposition vote, like that of the remaining SLD leadership, apart from Vice Marshal Włodzimierz Cimoszewicz. The SLD leaders subsequently took to the Constitutional Court the law that they had publicly claimed to support.[102]

In reality, practical constraints ensured that pre-1997 legal initiatives had more bark than bite. While general prosecutors were granted increasing authority to punish former rights perpetrators, there was little opportunity to pursue such cases given the enormous backlog of current ones.[103] The dilemma was compounded by the fact that the 1991 GK law authorizing criminal investigations for pre-1957 crimes did not create a prosecutorial team within the GK; it merely allowed the GK to forward completed investigations to the already overburdened general prosecutors. Between 1991 and 1995, the GK had completed more than 500 inquiries, 20 percent of which were sent on to prosecutors.[104] The Polish legal system could not keep pace.

After center-right post-Solidarity forces retook control of Parliament in 1997 (following four years of postcommunist control), they sought in part to remedy these difficulties by launching a bill that would provide the new Institute of National Remembrance (IPN, which absorbed the GK) with full prosecutorial powers.[105] Following bitter debate, the IPN bill was passed into law in September 1998,[106] vetoed by the president in December, and then, overriding the veto by a vote of 282:164, quickly passed again.[107]

Alongside broad legislative attempts to ensure criminal accountability for all guilty members of the former regime, political elites used post-Solidarity consolidation of power (1991–1993) to target one group of senior-level communist elites. In February 1992, post-Solidarity members passed a resolution declaring martial law illegal and establishing a special commission to evaluate its effects as well as draft a bill to facilitate punishing criminals from that time.[108] After interrogating political leaders responsible for martial law, and before Parliament expired in 1993, the commission demanded that senior PRL actors stand before the Constitutional Tribunal for the crime of destroying evidence.[109] Months later, following the postcommunist electoral victory, a new commission connected to the former regime reversed this decision;[110] and more than four years after the process began, the Sejm voted to drop the case.[111] Supporters decried this decision, noting the irony of a haphazard policy where trials were sporadically held for those tasked with executing abusive policies under martial law, while those presiding over the martial law policy were sometimes left alone.

Even while political elites decided the fate of senior-level functionaries, public prosecutors were investigating a number of post-1956 communist-era rights abuses, some of which came out of the Rokita Commission's investigations.[112] Several cases involving lower-ranking functionaries ended in convictions,[113] and the Polish state even pursued former violators living abroad.[114] Yet serious problems arose in prosecuting these crimes. Some cases were quietly dropped for lack of evidence,[115] while others went on for years, only to end (repeatedly) without convictions.[116] Even in cases where convictions were handed down, those persons found guilty frequently avoided jail time.[117] Few communist leaders or former state functionaries have sat in prison, even for Poland's most public and large-scale rights violations.[118]

Practical immunity for rights abusers resulted from procedural errors, the advanced age and poor health of defendants, failed investigations, previous amnesties, expiring statutes of limitations, and the generally tortuously slow pace of Poland's judicial system. Some of these problems, as predicted by the strategic argument, resulted from new elites' reluctance to devote large sums of public resources to a relatively unpopular process at a time of financial strain. In a 1994 opinion piece published in Poland's largest daily newspaper, former GK director Ryszard Juszkiewicz complained that in spite of the 1991 GK law, the Solidarity-led administration had showed a lack of genuine interest in pursuing criminal accountability, as demonstrated by the meager resources given to the GK.[119] Juszkiewicz's 1992 public appeal for private contributions provides evidence of the extent of these resource problems.[120]

Some of the difficulties are emblematic of more complex problems typical in transition states. For example, prosecutors often hesitated to investigate old cases for a variety of reasons, including an institutional atmosphere of collusion and the threat of being ostracized from legal circles,[121] difficulties in collecting evidence for crimes committed years earlier,[122] and the prospect of an increased workload, given ongoing criminal activity. While Poland's first noncommunist general prosecutor agreed that prosecutors may have carried out many of these cases "with no personal commitment," this was sometimes a function of limited resources, rather than intentional neglect. "We had a huge rise in criminal activity," Herzog said. "Maybe for some people the current issues were more important than those from the past."[123] The IPN's head agreed that most prosecutors simply preferred to pursue recent crimes, rather than search for historic justice: "That is what public opinion demanded. People want to feel safe."[124] Accused of internal resistance, prosecutors expressed weariness at being pulled once more into a political process.[125] When, as chief of the GK in the early 1990s, Juszkiewicz asked one prosecutor to expedite investigations into communist-era political crimes, the prosecutor responded: "Mr. Senator, are you sure that in two years they won't have *us* standing before a court?"[126]

Even since the IPN took over in 2000, equipped with a staff of unusually highly paid prosecutors, the vast majority of its 800 cases have continued to focus on the Stalinist period.[127] Examination of every IPN bureau's "ongoing investigations" indicated that only 11 percent of the 310 investigations published at the end of 2003 targeted post-Stalinist rights violations, with the others primarily focused on the Stalinist period, as well as alleged rights violations conducted by Soviet soldiers during World War II.[128] Momentum is partly to blame, because the IPN is obliged to finish all cases that the GK opened. The IPN staff are also battling mortality and are devoted to delivering justice while it is still feasible. "We have this feeling that we are racing against time," explained the head of the GK. "We first want to deal with those cases in which perpetrators and witnesses are dying of old age."[129] The phenomenon is also symptomatic of the IPN's political and financial dependence on political players. Its officials between 2001 and 2005 appear to have raised the bar for evidence against postcommunists, who could (while in power at the time of my field research) determine their institution's existence. "We can't allow for a mistake, losing a case, especially one against politicians," conceded the IPN head at that time.[130]

The IPN's delicate situation is symbolic of the entire criminal accountability debate in Poland, which showed contradictions from the start. Even as his party was pushing through Parliament a mechanism for pursuing criminal accountability in the form of the Rokita Commission, Prime Minister Mazowiecki issued his infamous promise to "distinguish the past with a thick line."[131] To many, his speech was interpreted to mean that Poland's new elites should look toward the future and not the past—amounting to an informal amnesty for former crimes. In fact, Mazowiecki and his former advisors acknowledge that the "thick line" was originally meant to ensure that Solidarity would not be held accountable for communism's economic legacy; it was not to signal that there would be no looking back at past abuses.[132] The speech was apparently (and perhaps purposely) misunderstood by many political elites.[133] Even more interesting, Mazowiecki half-heartedly signed onto the new meaning, which quickly won him considerable praise at home and abroad. "This also sent a symbolic message that the changes in Poland would be gradual, that there would be no witch-hunts," he recently said.[134] The ambiguity of Mazowiecki's words, as well as his reluctance to explain them, are emblematic of a conflicted new elite.

As in the case of rehabilitation and compensation for victims (type 3), Solidarity was split along institutional lines concerning how best to extend the GK in 1991. Senators favored criminal accountability for all crimes committed through 1989, while Solidarity members in the Sejm supported accountability for crimes committed only through 1956. Respondents from the former Sejm most often attribute their decision to differences in the quality of rights violations prior to, and after, 1956.[135] Moreover, post-Solidarity elites in the Sejm also had an eye squarely on their constituents, highlighting elements of the strategic argument. Post-Solidarity leaders hoped that limiting accountability to pre-1957 rights violators (then mostly dead or retired) would aid in the process of elite-level healing and minimize the risk of legislative deadlock in other critical spheres.[136] Some also pointed out that by extending the bill to 1989, post-Solidarity elites would shoot themselves in the foot by implicitly acknowledging that "we sat down with criminals" to negotiate a transfer of power.[137] Both of these explanations suggest that political strategy was a stronger motivation than fear of the old regime.

According to relative power logic, we might have seen an IPN established upon post-Solidarity consolidation of power (1991–1993), when postcommunists were a minority in the new Parliament and various governments. This did not occur for several reasons. Apparently most important was the collapse of the Solidarity umbrella, which led to a high level of political instability, as evidenced by the hasty rise and fall of governments, and which encouraged post-Solidarity elites (who could be subject to elections at any moment) to focus on economic reforms—the issues perceived to be most valuable for voters. While unknown to most, Prime Minister Olszewski actually intended to create a special criminal court to deal with the worst rights abusers, a plan that would include offers of immunity to functionaries willing to give evidence against those "who inspired or ordered" the crimes.[138] Instead, his government fell within months, after releasing a list of suspected secret police collaborators that included prominent Solidarity elites.

While postcommunists from 1993 to 1997 could have directly blocked justice initiatives, and according to relative power arguments should have done so, they did not. Most notable is the passage of legislation that extended the statute of limitations on communist-era crimes, legislation that postcommunists found sufficiently politically embarrassing and insufficiently threatening to vote down. Once center-right forces regained power in 1997, at a time of relative prosperity when Poland was hailed as Central Europe's "tiger" economy, they pursued forms of justice that had never been attempted earlier. As predicted by the strategic argument, pro-justice forces, less concerned now than in 1991 about urgently alleviating economic suffering, had more room to maneuver, and they immediately set out to create the IPN.

It should be noted that while the IPN legislation expanded opportunities for criminal justice, it was apparently less about criminal accountability than about highlighting the more prevalent, if less dramatic, rights violations that could be connected to postcommunist elites. Elite interviews and press accounts of the IPN debate illustrate that access to communist-era secret police files, intertwined with the matter of lustration, was the key and controversial issue in the passage of the IPN.[139] Asked whether the IPN was a direct attack on the postcommunist SLD and an effort to humiliate his political opponents (as they charge),[140] the IPN's chief architect, Janusz Pałubicki, responded that while the ultimate goal "was not to stick it to (*dołożyć*) the Reds . . . it was clear that it must hit the former communists."[141] At last, again back in power and in the black, post-Solidarity leaders were ready to aggressively reckon with the past.

DISCUSSION

Poland in many ways is the quintessential Central European case. The communist system was not a static period of endless repression, but rather one where mechanisms of repression were always available, to be exerted as a means of control when the opposition appeared to be a threat. The communists ultimately negotiated away power to this opposition, with the expectation that they could survive and even thrive in a more open democratic system. Through the process of negotiated transition, communist elites assured for themselves a high degree of institutional power in the new system, initially leaving post-Solidarity elites with a moderate degree of strength, heading the government and making up more than one-third of the constitutionally powerful lower house of Parliament. Postcommunists, in line with relative power expectations, were confident that they would face no sanctions for their prior roles. As Stanisław Ciosek, who held a prominent position in Poland's last Politburo, reasoned, "The proposals [for negotiations] came from us. What, should they now put me in jail?"[142]

According to transition- and structure-based relative power arguments, we should have expected no more than moderate justice measures in Poland. A truth commission designed to establish a history of repression there would have fit this model. The parliamentary commission that led to criminal trials, the expansion of a state institution to investigate communist-era rights violations (through 1956), and the early bureaucratic purges clearly do not. While failings in the Polish justice system limited the impact of transitional justice policies, political decisions to deal aggressively with the past were evident. And in contrast to societal-based relative power arguments, justice was primarily an elite affair. Those post-Solidarity elites who proposed and opposed various forms of justice recognized that the masses had neither little direct experience with repression nor an interest in addressing past violations. As one prominent proponent of justice legislation in the Senate admitted, "the problem of repression only concerned a certain fraction of society. . . . It was easy to forget about this—it was just the problem of a certain political elite."[143] Yet voter disinterest in reckoning did not mean a free hand. Instead, voters often served as an underlying, if not direct, constraint on justice.

Over the long term, Polish efforts at justice can be divided into four stages based loosely, as the strategic argument projects, around perceived demands for economic reform.[144] The first stage occurred in the months following the 1989 elections, when economic reforms had not yet come to dominate the political agenda and public opposition to justice was low (see Figure 5.1). During this stage, post-Solidarity forces were unified in their determination to launch a truth process that would lead to criminal accountability. The demand came from post-Solidarity elites themselves,

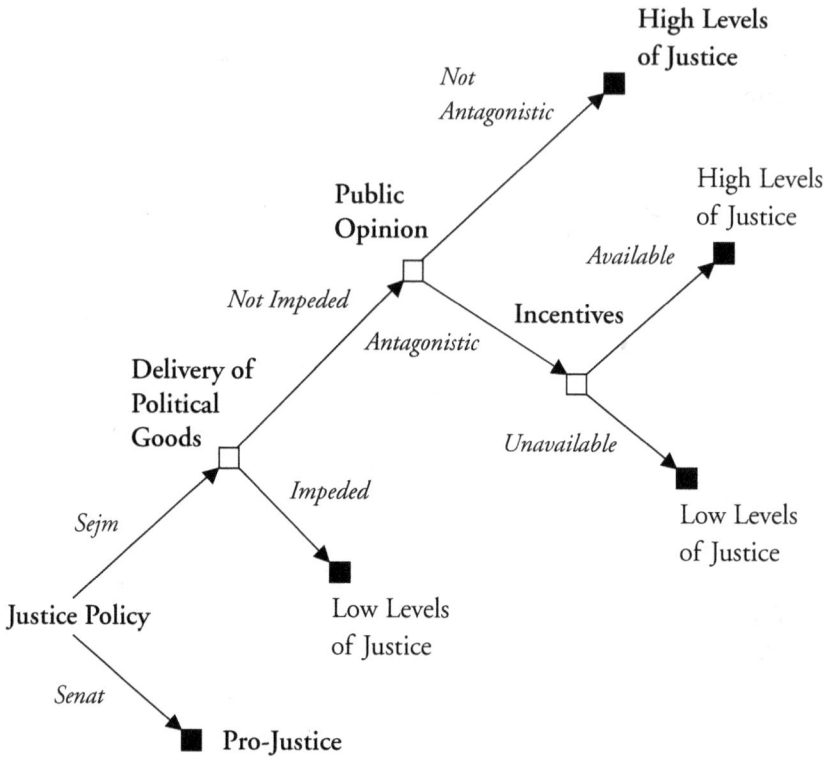

FIGURE 5.1   Justice in Poland, Summer 1989

but it was apparently sustained by general societal support or neutrality. With post-Solidarity leaders in Parliament united, the political impetus for justice was expedited.

This support appears to have worn away as the euphoria of political change dissipated and as dire economic conditions began to once again occupy voter thoughts. By late 1989, as Solidarity fractured based on institutional responsibilities, a second phase of justice began (see Figure 5.2). Senators, with little power to influence the economic situation one way or another, continued to demand harsher versions. Sejm members, faced with high public expectations for economic improvement, sought to ensure quick

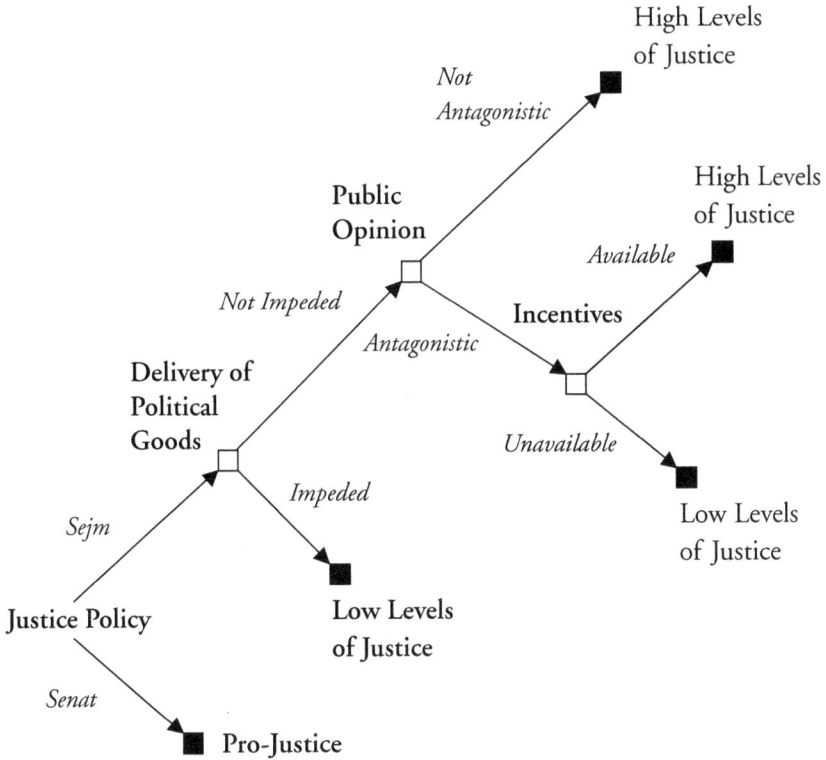

FIGURE 5.2 Justice in Poland, Fall 1989–Fall 1991

passage of bread-and-butter reforms. This required postcommunists' support, which post-Solidarity Sejm members hoped to attract by backing off in the justice sphere. The result was a form of abortive justice. In regard to rehabilitation and compensation and criminal accountability, Solidarity Sejm members moderated aggressive proposals churned out by their colleagues in the Senate. Only where justice was abstract and general, as in the case of administrative expulsions, were post-Solidarity elites in the Sejm willing to sign on.

The third phase of justice (1991–1997) began with post-Solidarity's consolidation of power (1991–1993). In contrast to expectations that former oppositionists might have been quickly positioned to "dictate the new rules" to the postcommunists who had brokered the transition, Solidarity members in the Sejm became more, rather than less, risk averse. Instead of using their strength to attack old elites, as relative power arguments suggest, post-Solidarity elites largely steered away from justice issues that could be perceived as distractions from the critical task of ending the economic crisis. The big exception to this occurred under the Olszewski government and led to its collapse. Yet it should be highlighted that Olszewski's controversial move was in the direction of lustration, a particular form of reckoning discussed in chapter 3. Once postcommunists took power (1993–1997), it was clear that justice measures would be largely overlooked. When center-right forces returned to govern, marking the fourth phase of justice (1997–2001), they took advantage of a period of relative economic prosperity to return to the initiatives from 1991, strengthening criminal accountability legislation, apparently as part of a broader attempt to ensure that postcommunists would suffer politically. Once again, Poland returned to an expedited form of justice similar to that seen in the first months of democracy in 1989 (see Figure 5.1).

What emerges in Poland is a pattern where new elites from the former opposition movement thought that they could pursue harsh forms of justice so long as they were relatively certain that their constituents would not perceive these measures as an intrusion upon current reforms and the goal of economic prosperity. But what would things have looked like under starkly different conditions? Let us suppose that there were multiple periods of repression, with the last and most violent one ending just a year or two before new elites took power; suppose that outside states dictated the form of justice; and suppose that the victims of past repression were largely regarded by the public as legitimate enemies, and the repressors were seen as heroes. In the next two chapters I will examine how former opposition elites in Serbia and Croatia dealt with questions of justice under these conditions.

6

Serbia and Montenegro

Justice as Yugoslavia's Most
Valuable Foreign Export?

Unlike their Polish counterparts, Serbia's democratic opposition emerged in 2000 not merely from a half-century of communist rule and a decade of economic decline, but also from a series of 1990s wars that amounted to the bloodiest conflict in post-1945 Europe. Although Serbia's new elites tend to gloss over rights abuses that occurred from 1945 to 1991, Yugoslavia's early communist period was at times at least as brutal as in other parts of the region. Under Josip Broz Tito's leadership, hundreds of thousands of Yugoslavs were stripped of their rights in the post–World War II period, with tens of thousands imprisoned for their political convictions or economic status.[1] Yet less than two decades after the Soviet Union split from Yugoslavia definitively in 1948, Yugoslavia was seen as a bastion of liberalism in the communist bloc. Yugoslavs could freely cross their border and had more economic rights under Tito's "self-management" system than did most of their Central and Southern European neighbors. Still, for those who opposed the League of Yugoslav Communists, or favored greater regional autonomy, Yugoslavia remained a repressive state.

By 1989, as communism collapsed across the former Eastern Bloc, occasional discussion of political repression turned into personal experiences of brutality for many of Yugoslavia's residents. The former Yugoslavia became a breeding ground for nationalism, resulting in the country's violent dismemberment, during which many sides were implicated in war atrocities. The rump Yugoslavia (composed of Serbia and Montenegro as well as Kosovo and Vojvodina) was ruled for a decade by Slobodan Milošević, an authoritarian once regarded as a good communist and subsequently devoted to building a Greater Serbia that included territory belonging to newly independent countries. During this period, Milošević's Yugoslavia was involved in multiple wars (against Croatia, Bosnia-Herzegovina, and Kosovo) that claimed tens of thousands of lives. While the data vary considerably and remain extremely controversial, casualty estimates from the Bosnia war range from 100,000 to more than 200,000.[2] The war in Croatia was estimated to cost between 10,000 and 20,000 lives, while the toll in Kosovo was also around 10,000.[3] In each of these cases, civilians made up a large proportion of casualties. and allegations of genocide and/or ethnic cleansing were made, which led to the creation of the ad hoc International Criminal Tribunal for the former Yugoslavia (ICTY) in the Hague.

As the former Yugoslavia rotted, Milošević thrived in an atmosphere of corruption and façade democracy. After years of rehearsals, in fall 2000, the Movement for a Democratic Serbia (DOS), a democratic alliance dominated by two Serbian opposition parties, Vojislav Koštunica's Democratic Party of Serbia (DSS) and Zoran Đinđić's Democratic Party (DS), helped to lead what was billed as a peaceful revolution against Milošević. Despite Milošević's ouster, the case of Serbia is best classified as a negotiated transition. The democratic opposition did take control of some federal structures in October, with Koštunica winning the post of president, a position that was to be largely representative or secondary in authority. But the incumbents did not immediately relinquish full control of the state, instead negotiating a settlement whereby members of Milošević's party would temporarily share seats with oppositionists at the top of key structures such as the police, justice, information, and financial ministries.[4] The premiership also became a shared post, pending new republic-level parliamentary elections, which, as part of the negotiations, were moved up to December. The opposition took control of the Serb republic only after winning a majority in those generally free and fair elections. Đinđić subsequently took the post of Serbia's prime minister, responsible for running the day-to-day affairs of that government, which accounted for 90 percent of Yugoslavia's populace.

Leaders of Serbia's former democratic opposition simultaneously faced three types of justice issues: communist-era violations, Milošević-era wartime violations, and Milošević-era non-war violations. With the exception of rehabilitation and, occasionally, bureaucratic turnover (connected with lustration), local elites have tended to focus transitional justice discussion on 1990s war-related violations. The communist era is frequently explained away as a period of prosperity and only minor repression. Likewise, domestic human rights violations during the Milošević period appear to be of limited concern to former opposition leaders trying to deal with massive war atrocities carried out in their name.

According to transition- and structure-based relative power arguments, Serbia's democratic opposition (referred to here as "post-oppositionists") should have gone no further than a moderate transitional justice policy, since they took positions of power through a negotiated transition that left leaders of powerful state institutions in influential positions. Prime Minister Đinđić should have settled for lenient forms of justice rather than involving himself in dangerous forms of criminal accountability. Unlike in Poland, the transitional justice process in Serbia and Montenegro has been influenced by external actors, who function as a key interest group. As external actors pressed for transfers to the ICTY, we should have seen Đinđić use domestic antagonism to convince Westerners that Hague cooperation was impossible. Instead, Đinđić in his two years in office was responsible for about twenty transfers or surrenders of high-level members of the old elite to the ICTY. Moreover, there was a split in post-opposition circles, with the prime minister's DS party (along with others, such as the Civic Alliance of Serbia, GSS) pressing for justice, as the president's DSS party led the resistance—until the president was elevated to prime minister in 2004, after which he followed Đinđić's lead. In this chapter, I explain the path of justice in Serbia and Montenegro from 2000 to 2005. According to my findings, political strategy and personality politics, mediated by institutional considerations, emerge as the key determinants for most justice processes.

TYPE 1. CESSATION AND CODIFICATION
OF HUMAN RIGHTS VIOLATIONS

Democratic forces in Serbia rapidly signed onto key international human rights documents guaranteeing basic freedoms.[5] In many cases, these were treaties that officials from the former Yugoslavia had signed and ratified, but the state's disintegration made it necessary for each new successor state to reaffirm its commitment. In the case of Serbia and Montenegro, many of these documents were signed with one broad stroke of the pen in March 2001.[6] They included the International Covenant on Civil and Political Rights (ICCPR), though optional protocols were not ratified until later that year; and the International Covenant on Economic, Social, and Cultural Rights, as well as the three Conventions against Torture, Genocide, and Racial Discrimination. The newly elected democratic regime rapidly moved to indicate its conformity to international human rights norms and laws.

TYPE 2. REBUKE OF THE OLD SYSTEM

In Serbia and Montenegro, where the most horrific human rights violations were committed against non-Serbs in the post-1991 period, international and domestic observers have expressed the need for a state apology, rather than condemnation. A few months before the 2000 elections, Montenegro's pro-reform president, Milo Đukanović, signaled that reformists might use apologies to distance themselves from the old regime when he issued the first state apology to Croatia's President Stipe Mesić—just a year and a half after Đukanović had questioned who might apologize to whom.[7] No post-oppositionists followed Đukanović's lead until three years later, when the new federal president, Svetozar Marović, issued a string of unconditional apologies, first to Croatians in September 2003,[8] then to Bosnians two months later. "I want to use this opportunity to apologize for any evil or disaster that anyone from Serbia and Montenegro caused to anyone in Bosnia-Herzegovina," he said. "The time of forgiveness is before us. We have to have enough courage to create common ground to help each other heal our wounds."[9] Finally, Marović even apologized to residents of Montenegro, a part of his own federation: "I am ready, and I wish to apologize to those who were against the war . . . and also for those who put on the uniform not in order to kill, burn, do evil unto other people, but because they deeply believed that it was their obligation to defend the land in which they were born and . . . which they believed was theirs."[10]

In late 2004, President Boris Tadić became the first ethnic Serb—and representative of the increasingly independent Serb republic—to apologize, during a visit to Bosnia. Tadić qualified his words, however, with a counter-demand: "We all owe an apology to each other. If it is necessary, I will begin."[11]

Perhaps as a testament to the saliency accorded to apologies, Serbian leaders have been extraordinarily sensitive about how their words are spoken and heard. For example, when the U.S. television news program, "60 Minutes II," in fall 2000 aired an interview where then federal president Koštunica accepted guilt in the name of the Serbs, Koštunica quickly went on the attack, saying that his words were "taken completely out of context" by "unprofessional and unethical" reporters.[12] Foreign Minister Goran Svilanović in December 2001 similarly sought to clarify a statement that he had made during a recent trip to Croatia; it was merely one of "regret" since an apology is "very complicated" and "can be made only by the president of state or someone elected at direct elections."[13]

Two interesting elements emerge from a study of these apologies. First, and perhaps anecdotal, the only two leaders from Serbia and Montenegro to issue nonqualified apologies were Montenegrins. Second, and more important, the only apologies have come from actors in secondary institutions—first the Montenegrin president, and then the federal and Serbian republic presidents. Secondary actors' private preferences and political strategy seem to account for their decisions to (not) apologize. But it is clear that the power of old elites and the composition of the public were not any more antiapology in primary institutions. Instead, in accord with the strategic argument, leaders of primary institutions have seen apologies as high in political risk and low in material returns. Given a lack of direct benefits (political goods) for apologies, which have never been a condition for European integration or foreign aid and investment, no Serbian prime minister has gambled on such a move that could infuriate his constituency.

While some post-opposition officials blame Yugoslavia's "institutional chaos," characterized by muddy foreign policy structures, for the lack of apology between 2000 and 2003,[14] the role of leadership style and incentives seems to have been more important. Neither of the senior personalities dominating Yugoslav politics was willing to apologize. Koštunica, who had condemned Đukanović's 2000 statement as a ploy to gain Western sympathy, maintained that any apology must be multilateral since "there was no innocent side in this war."[15] Similarly, Đinđić declared before taking power that he was prepared only to "accept apologies of others and [subsequently] apologize to them."[16] While Koštunica's attitude is attributed to moderate nationalist inclinations, his peers view Đinđić's reluctance as part of his matter-of-fact leadership style. According to his associates, Đinđić made some conciliatory gestures, such as when he laid flowers at a destroyed bridge during a visit to Bosnia.[17] Yet, by and large, they add, Đinđić preferred practical efforts to win over his neighbors, especially by extraditing Milošević. "He was probably killed for that," one of Đinđić's deputies said. "You have to forgive him."[18]

Political calculation appears to have played a major role in the apology process. By attacking Đukanović's 2000 apology, the extremely popular military as well as the Serbian Orthodox Church sent advance notice to other pro-justice politicians.[19] Leaders in primary institutions on both sides of the democratic divide perceive that Serbs, many of whom had supported Milošević's wars and resented international pressure for Hague cooperation, were unprepared for such a statement.[20] Đinđić, loath "to open unnecessary wars with society,"[21] openly maintained that apologies in post-Milošević Serbia were not politically feasible.[22] Đinđić's successors, Zoran Živković and then Koštunica, have also seen apologies as unnecessary political liabilities. Even as federal president, Koštunica avoided unpopular apologies, with his office staff warning that such statements could inflict "much political damage to the president and the forces leading the democratization in Yugoslavia."[23]

The apologies that eventually emerged from sympathetic actors in secondary institutions are primarily attributed to foreign pressure, whether from the West (including the United States, where Congress formally expressed the need for an apology, apparently on moral grounds) or from Serbia's neighbors.[24] Đinđić (politically constrained) and Koštunica (personally opposed) reacted to Western pressures with annoyance, with Koštunica's former human rights advisor arguing, "We need some time to see what was really happening around us."[25] But most pro-justice elites whom I interviewed thought that Tadić's conditional apology was an attempt to win international kudos without stepping on domestic toes.[26] Similarly, explanations for Marović's more direct apologies also tend to focus on international awards (if intangible) for such statements, as evidenced by Western applause following those apologies.[27] He explained his words as "confirmation that we do not live in the past anymore, but in a joint European future."[28]

Marović appears to have diminished the political risk of his statements by explaining his motives as an effort to denationalize blame, rather than to accept blame on behalf of his constituents. By apologizing himself and focusing on personal responsibility, he hoped to individualize the nature of the crimes. "I want to apologize because I do not think that peoples are guilty and that they have to apologize," Marović said in Croatia (and repeated in Bosnia).[29] Indeed, his own questionable war record—he has been accused of bolstering nationalism and "war euphoria" through his editorial comments in Montenegro during the 1990s—may have actually made an apology easier, since he could claim to nationalist critics that his sentiments were personal.[30] Certainly, repeat apologies were facilitated by the fact that his fellow democrats praised him for his actions.[31]

TYPE 3. REHABILITATION AND COMPENSATION FOR VICTIMS

Soon after the 2000 elections, the Movement for a Democratic Serbia appealed to Serbia's Justice Minister Vladan Batić to politically rehabilitate those persons sentenced in political trials between 1945 and 1999.[32] Movement officials claimed that their goals were to restore honor to those wrongfully convicted and to initiate a much-needed revision of Yugoslavia's communist history. By calling for the denationalization of property, however, the request introduced material elements. In May 2002, Batić, who simultaneously demanded a bill on denationalization, introduced into Parliament a bill for the rehabilitation of political prisoners and show-trial victims from November 1945 to 2002.[33] The legislation lacked political support and never became law; few of my interviewees even recalled this bill's existence.

While rehabilitation and compensation should have posed few problems according to relative power arguments, Serbia's post-Milošević elites have made almost no effort to rehabilitate the tens of thousands of victims from the communist era because few political actors had an interest in pressing for this issue. The primary reason appears to be the widespread belief that Yugoslavia experienced a "soft communism," with few victims to rehabilitate, certainly relative to the number who suffered under Europe's other communist regimes. The pain of communist-era victims was quickly dwarfed by the immense suffering from the 1990s wars and numerous day-to-day policy crises in post-Milošević Serbia.[34] The few (living) victims and a lack of public interest make rehabilitation and compensation "politically unimportant," even among politicians with family histories of repression.[35] Unlike in other postcommunist states, where leaders could focus their angst on the "other" (the Russians), Serbia's leaders saw little political advantage in resurrecting a case of home-grown violence that might further split an already divided society.[36]

Another factor that differentiates Yugoslavia's communist-era victims from those of other postcommunist countries is that post-opposition elites frequently view Yugoslavia's pre-1991 victims with indifference and even suspicion. Victims from the early, brutal days of Tito are sometimes recalled as Stalinists, who themselves advocated a murderous system. Political prisoners after the 1950s would be called nationalists and accused of egregious war crimes during the 1990s. Indeed, the list of repressed-turned-repressor includes at least two Serbian Hague indictees, Serbian Radical Party head Vojislav Šešelj and former Bosnian Serb president Radovan Karadžić.[37] Perceptions that relatively few people suffered under communism, and that many of those who did were unworthy of purification, have led political leaders to discount both the moral and the political value of rehabilitation. As one political leader said, "Serbs are notoriously ambivalent about this."[38]

The few political leaders who express an interest in rehabilitating former victims are alternatively either motivated or put off by the perceived connection between rehabilitation and compensation. For many parliamentarians, political rehabilitation would not necessarily be objectionable, but the potential financial costs make this step forbidding. One law professor and member of Parliament estimated that between 1946 and 1953, politically based court decisions, which were used as a tool to confiscate private wealth, were imposed on thirty thousand people. As a result, he continued, "it is not only formal rehabilitation but a question of what will happen to the property." Pro-restitution groups also treat rehabilitation as a stepping-stone to their own goals, since, for them, leaving their claimants unaddressed is "another way of slowing down the whole process of restitution."[39] Given the poor state of Serbian finances, political leaders say, a law opening the way for denationalization would be fiscally dangerous.[40]

The issue of rehabilitation and compensation cannot be viewed as a direct challenge to relative power arguments, seeing that these arguments are not determinative in the first place. But the evidence from this issue does indicate that the logic of (in)action in this sphere, as with respect to rebukes of the former system, has little to do with transition- or structure-based relative power explanations. Instead, the path of rehabilitation and compensation emerges from considerations based less on the risk of civil strife emphasized by public support–based relative power arguments than on the popularity and political feasibility emphasized in the strategic argument.

TYPE 4. CREATION OF A TRUTH COMMISSION

The case of Yugoslavia's Truth and Reconciliation Commission again highlights the effects of institutional confusion, personality politics, and foreign pressure on justice. President Koštunica and his cabinet began to market a truth commission in the face of immense Western pressure to cooperate with the ICTY, publicly arguing that the commission would prepare society for criminal trials.[41] However, even as the commission became a staple of Yugoslav diplomacy months before its birth, the federal government was quietly divided over its shape.

Justice Minister Momčilo Grubač and Foreign Minister Goran Svilanović projected a strong commission with the power to grant amnesties, subpoena witnesses, and demand evidence.[42] The commission would include international experts and lead to criminal trials after only eighteen months. This working proposal was killed, however, when President Koštunica suddenly, and without his cabinet's knowledge, established a much weaker commission. "One morning I read in the paper that Koštunica had started a commission," Grubač recalled, adding that his initiative then was dead in the water.[43] Koštunica was aware of the Grubač-Svilanović project, but the judicial powers that it entailed would have called for parliamentary support, which could not be guaranteed in the short term. Yet Koštunica was under intense international pressure to advance transitional justice immediately. At least one appointed commission member claims to have been surprised to find himself on Koštunica's list of members and, along with two others, resigned soon after hearing the news.[44]

Lacking strong constitutional powers or legal authority, President Koštunica could create only a weak "consultative body" tasked with compiling information and evidence from various—mostly open—sources.[45] He handpicked the commission's nineteen members, who were almost all ethnic Serbs, eventually resulting in a second round of appointments designed to increase both the number of its representativeness and its legitimacy.[46] Perceptions that the commission was stacked with Serb nationalists discouraged regional cooperation.[47] The goal of the commission was, according to Koštunica's human rights advisor, to broadly examine the Balkan wars to "see how they were prepared, why they happened, who was involved, who was really in charge."[48] While commission members hoped to eventually create a list of war victims and a chronology of events, their mandate was much broader, encompassing communist-era aggression by ethnic Croats and Muslims, as well.[49] The commission was given a full three years to complete its work.[50]

There remains a widespread perception among Serbian elites that Koštunica's truth commission was an attempt to sidestep international pressures for ICTY cooperation.[51] Critics also objected to domestic-oriented aspects of the commission, arguing that Koštunica hoped to shine a positive light on Serbia's role in the 1990s conflicts by loading the commission with nationalists and historians who would frame 1990s suffering in the context of previous injustices committed against Serbs, especially World War II atrocities.[52] Koštunica fed this skepticism by advocating his commission as a tool to counter the "biased" "pseudo-history" and "hypocrisy" of the Hague: "We have to do everything to influence the writing of history."[53] His commission was designed to double as both a stalling tactic for Hague cooperation and an indirect attack on the Hague itself. The commission's limited powers would render even earnest members unable to conduct an in-depth investigation.[54] It was also starved of funding, though this apparently was beyond Koštunica's control.[55] Another victim of institutional chaos, Koštunica's truth commission expired with the reorganization of all federal bodies in December 2003.[56] It never published any findings.[57]

Interested foreign parties, non-DSS post-opposition parliamentarians, and human rights activists labeled Koštunica's commission "impotent" and "a whitewash" from the start.[58] Sensing that the truth commission was being used as a bargaining piece rather than a sincere community endeavor, ICTY Chief Prosecutor Karla del Ponte warned that it must not "encroach on the prerogatives of the law." [59] At the same time, domestic opponents were wary of setting up alternative structures at the DS-controlled republic level.

According to relative power logic, there seems to be no reason why Đinđić should not have launched a more aggressive inquiry into the past. The prime minister shied away from such a move, however, as a result of institutionally motivated considerations. His followers thought that undermining Koštunica by creating a new commission would provoke interparty discord. The result would be a major obstacle to cooperation that would drift across spheres, making more difficult the passage of bills critical to the economic and political reforms demanded by constituents. In order to avoid "political war," said one GSS parliamentarian, "we decided not to open the bottle."[60] Many in the governing coalition believed that pressing economic demands made too costly a bid for the less tangible goals of "truth and justice" for the new political elites. In a country of personal politics, where party leaders are discussed as if they control rather than are constrained by their parties, Đinđić's associates recall the Serbian prime minister as far too pragmatic to get involved in a quest for truth. "Đinđić was a practical man, he wanted to change everyday life," said one DS leader.[61] Đinđić essentially ignored Koštunica's truth commission as he focused on his economic platform and Euro-Atlantic integration. "We didn't have electricity when we came to power, and we weren't professional politicians," one of Đinđić's deputies explained. "We couldn't afford this."[62]

Đinđić's reluctance to launch a more objective truth commission was also a result of perceived social resistance. Post-opposition leaders admit that they lacked the public credibility to create their own truth commission. In a society that largely supported the Yugoslav wars and still celebrated alleged war criminals as heroes, any truth commission launched by the DS or more liberal parties might be read as an attempt to demonize patriotic Serbs. "Koštunica was probably the only person who could change things from that perspective—those nationalists would believe him," commented a former member of Đinđić's government.[63] Local human rights leaders, politically isolated and internally divided, also conceded: "Let them go, it's our only chance."[64] Koštunica, with little to fear from political opponents who needed his party to pass economic reforms, made the truth commission into his pet project.

TYPE 5. PURGING OF HUMAN RIGHTS ABUSERS FROM PUBLIC POSITIONS

In this section, I focus on administrative purges of the police and military, who were blamed for most of the rights abuses that took place in the 1990s.[65] With Koštunica's DSS dominating the federal government and Đinđić's DS ruling the Serb republic, bureaucratic reforms of the military and police were undertaken by different leaderships. From the start, the DSS advocated a slow, cautious pace of change, while the DS called for quicker reforms. Still, neither side was prepared to conduct sweeping investigations of the bureaucratic structures that it nominally controlled. DSS fears of upsetting a popular institution and hopes for political favors from military officers appear to have slowed personnel investigations in the military, while a lack of evidence, staff, and institutional knowledge hindered lower-level, republic-level reforms. In both cases, high-level institutional leaders were pushed out of power, indicating the need to reassess transition and structure-based relative power assumptions here. This harsh form of justice was conducted so long as it was neither costly nor characterized by high levels of public opposition.

The Military

Immediately after Milošević fell, military leaders sought to secure their positions by forcing post-opposition gratitude and swearing allegiance.[66] Democratic forces were split on the fate of the top officers; the DS demanded quick changes, while DSS leaders took the less-rushed approach that "all will come in due time."[67] In charge of the federal military, DSS leaders objected to demands for an all-out replacement since there were "not enough clean hands for a new harvest."[68] Koštunica, in turn, began gradually nudging out only certain senior officers, eventually putting sixty-four generals (70 percent of the total) on pension within his first year.[69]

The president drew the most fire for his refusal to dismiss powerful Army Chief of Staff General Nebojsa Pavković, who had held the same position under Milošević and was questioned for his role in war crimes in Kosovo. DSS officials argued that Pavković was an insider essential to military reform and that dismissing him would be destabilizing.[70] Indeed, Đinđić's call for Pavković's resignation immediately after the 2000 elections prompted military leaders to warn of "possible negative consequences of increased attacks and attempts to discredit certain individuals in the Yugoslav army."[71] On the other hand, some members of the former democratic opposition in late 2000 actually claimed that most officers opposed Pavković and that "if he isn't sacked, they may act to remove him."[72] Most pro-justice, post-opposition forces believed that politics, not fear, kept Pavković in power.[73]

A Hague suspect and subsequent indictee, Pavković became a symbol of military rot. He was accused of blocking Milošević's transfer to the Hague and then providing Milošević with secret documents for his defense. He also harbored negative attitudes toward NATO, a club that Serbia's new leaders pledged to join.[74] Koštunica dismissed Western demands for Pavković's resignation, facetiously noting that such demands "come from the ranks of those who want us to urgently face up to our recent past, admit our alleged collective guilt, play some psychodrama, and experience catharsis."[75] In mid-2002, Koštunica finally fired Pavković, allegedly for overstepping his authority. According to Pavković, however, his dismissal was a result of U.S. pressure and his refusal to take Koštunica's side in political battles with Đinđić.[76]

Most observers and active participants in Serbian politics believe that the Pavković case epitomizes a form of institutional warfare between Koštunica and Đinđić, where each attempted to use his own power ministry for personal political gain. Pavković was initially left in power, they say, so

Koštunica could convert his military information into political advantage.[77] Koštunica's allies counter that democratic forces attacking Pavković for his human rights record actually proposed to replace him with a suspected war criminal, General Momčilo Perišić, who had been indicted by the Hague and was already convicted in absentia by a Croatian court for a 1991 attack on civilians in the Croatian town of Zadar.[78] Moreover, when Koštunica finally fired Pavković, DS officials eagerly supported the general, prompting even greater cynicism from Koštunica's camp. "They don't give a shit about human rights—they're interested in just getting political supremacy," Koštunica's former human rights advisor commented. "They would take the devil on their side to fight Koštunica."[79]

Koštunica's decision to keep Pavković on board was not particularly popular. The general apparently had a poor reputation in the military (he was actually booed at Koštunica's swearing-in ceremony) and, as noted earlier, some in the military reportedly told DOS officials that releasing him would appeal to many pro-reform officers lower in the chain of command.[80] A large-scale investigation of the lower ranks would have been difficult, however, precisely because of the army's popularity among the electorate—and not, it seems, for fear of the old elites.[81] DSS leaders also believed that the majority of their armed personnel were clean, thus indicating a high degree of faith in the institution charged with killing, raping, and torturing thousands of Bosnians and Croatians. While a handful of criminal investigations were opened, Koštunica, who had come to power thanks to a popular uprising, made no major effort to purge the military of persons responsible for violations of human rights and humanitarian law.

The Police

Just as the limited military overhaul demonstrates political aspects of bureaucratic turnover, similarly, the police transition highlights a concern for practical considerations. The republic's leaders inherited the Internal Affairs Ministry housing the police, which was responsible for many operations in the Kosovo war (1998–1999) and for keeping Milošević in power. Rather than launch a sweeping investigation into human rights abuses by police personnel, the first post-Milošević internal affairs minister, Dušan Mihaj-lović, sought to eliminate corruption and incompetence at the very top.[82] He aimed to depoliticize, decriminalize, and professionalize the police, ejecting those lacking competence or those awarded positions thanks to political connections, as well as those found guilty of corruption or of violating internal regulations. According to relative power predictions, new elites coming to office through negotiations should have abstained from touching police power holders. Yet almost all thirteen directorate heads were replaced in the first three weeks of DS power and 80 percent of the 170 territorial heads were fired over the next six months. The third phase, an investigation of the rank-and-file, was largely left to the discretion of new territorial heads. Without reference to human rights, Mihajlović touted after one year that "the de-politicization of the police has been completed."[83]

Where police reforms stalled, this was primarily a result of a deficit in personnel, evidence, and knowledge of the institution in question. Ivan Đorđević, Mihajlović's former chief of staff, recalled a solitary first year in the Internal Affairs Ministry, where he and his boss "were the only ones who had come there from the outside world."[84] A result of political compromise himself, Mihajlović was only an "acting" minister, which limited his ability to appoint a full team and thus left him and Đorđević alone for much of their rule. In addition, evidence necessary for a thorough vetting had been destroyed during the early transition period, when Milošević's cronies still held power, leaving officials without "the very basic tools to tell them who were the good and bad guys."[85] The evidence dilemma was exacerbated by the fact that few in the post-opposition government had ever held power or knew the inner workings of the oft-criminalized bureaucracy, and they depended on these structures to keep institutions running and even guard the new leaders.[86] The realization that a thorough purge would likely leave these institutions bare set the stage for a "don't ask, don't tell" policy in regard to low- and mid-ranking police.[87]

Internal Affairs Ministry officials, like reformers of the military, also apparently felt little need to investigate at the lower levels.[88] Mihajlović stressed that only a "small number" of police were guilty,[89] and his advisors emphasized a "strong and clear presumption of innocence."[90] Both Mihaj-lović and Đinđić publicly promised not to transfer police to the Hague, which at the time was reportedly investigating nearly 350 of them.[91] The apparent tradeoff between fighting for human rights and fighting against corruption was exemplified by Mihajlović's appointment of General Sreten Lukić as his deputy. Lukić, a Milošević-era police officer, had commanded institutional respect even while purging criminal elements from the ministry, including suspending up to 200 police accused of criminal activity in Kosovo.[92] Most of these acts, though, were not rights-related. As a result, one former parliamentarian noted, many rank-and-file police left in place "were not linked to organized crime, but they probably did awful things in Kosovo."[93] Moreover, by 2003, Lukić was himself a Hague suspect, subsequently indicted for his role in war crimes committed in Kosovo. In spite of his indictment, Mihajlović kept Lukić on the Liberal Party list during the 2003 parliamentary elections, a choice that almost had his party thrown out of the Liberal International coalition of worldwide liberal parties.[94]

Serbian elites were not so much fearful of bureaucratic cleansings, as relative power arguments suggest, as they were bewildered by how to implement them. Moreover, they did remove high-level police functionaries, a phenomenon we should not have seen according to transition- and structure-based relative power arguments. The strategic argument helps us understand this. Serbian post-opposition elites carried out purges to the degree that they did not meet societal resistance, focusing on higher-level officials, most of whom were apparently attacked for the obviously unpopular crime of corruption. A large-scale investigation into the lower echelons, where officers were "just following orders" that may have involved rights violations against non-Serbs (for example, in Kosovo), could have been more controversial, though, in contrast to public support – relative power arguments, elite interviewees focused on electoral consequences, not the risk of civic strife. With no Western carrot or stick dangling here, Đinđić and his successors left this sector alone.

TYPE 6. CRIMINAL PROSECUTION OF "EXECUTORS"

In the case of the former Yugoslavia, most senior-level suspects have been indicted by the ICTY, leaving lower-level war criminals to the jurisdiction of local courts. Therefore, this section is separated into "international" versus "domestic" cases, rather than executors versus commanders. According to relative power logic, there should have been no attempts to pursue criminal prosecutions for functionaries of the old regime; after a negotiated transition, the old guard continued to dominate power institutions, and the public largely rejected war crimes allegations. Yet soon after the transition began, military and police leaders began a number of low-level investigations, especially for violations in Kosovo,[95] and at least two civilian courts began to look into war crimes cases.[96] These investigations did not deal with the widespread abuses documented, as administrative purges might have, but with only some of the most brutal crimes. By mid-2002, one court was investigating thirty such cases, prompting observers to dub it the "Little Hague" of Serbia.[97] But critics, including the national Judges Association, voiced fears that enormous public pressure, a lack of training for court professionals, and poor technological capabilities in the courtroom made it impossible to conduct domestic war crimes fairly.[98]

There were also fears that institutional alignments with the old regime would prejudice cases. Indeed, some members of the Little Hague were linked with attempts to illegally maintain Milošević in office following the September 2000 vote.[99] Even Justice Minister Batić admitted in late 2001 that the requisite "domestic and international faith in the judiciary" necessary to conduct war crimes trials would not exist until Milošević-era courtroom officials had been pushed out.[100] By mid-2002, prosecutors and judges involved in war crimes trials complained of political pressure and anonymous threats.[101] While most of them feared that the guilty would be set free, defendants raised their own countercharges that they were convicted as a result of international pressures. One defendant who received a nine-year sentence for Kosovo war crimes asked the court, "Who has judged me—Vladan Batić, Zoran Đinđić, or the judge?"[102] Fewer than ten war crimes trials were held in local courts, with more than half conducted under Milošević's rule when, remarked a representative of the special war crimes court, "the prosecutor and the criminal were on the same side."[103]

Following Đinđić's assassination in 2003, the new Serbian government imposed a state of emergency and quickly passed two pending bills establishing a special war crimes court and an organized crime court.[104] Supported by Western financing,[105] the war crimes court tried to attract the best, and avoid corruption, by initially offering salaries three times that of ordinary judicial wages.[106] Now, court officials are specially trained; the court is technologically advanced, equipped with computers, and a high-level security system; and a modern witness-protection program is in its place. By early 2005, one case was on trial and an additional fifty cases were in various stages of investigation. The first case concluded in December 2005, with the conviction of fourteen individuals tied to the death of more than 200 people during the 1991 battle for Vukovar, Croatia.[107]

While international monitors guarantee a high degree of insulation, the court's budget is ultimately allocated by the Justice Ministry, thus placing court officials under political pressure.[108] ICTY officials note that despite the advent of a special court for war crimes, police remain unenthusiastic about investigating such cases, and the government has failed to adequately support the court, which is "functioning in an environment that is hostile."[109] Despite tight security, one representative of the special court complained that societal pressures remain immense, sometimes taking the form of death threats: "I am afraid, at this moment, for my life."[110] As a result of these dilemmas, international and domestic actors remained only cautiously optimistic, pending the close of the first trial, and many have maintained that even the special court would be incapable of trying high-level cases such as that of Milošević or Bosnian Serb commander Ratko Mladić.[111]

The strategic argument helps to explain the occurrence of domestic prosecutions, which should have been absent according to relative power logic. Serbian post-oppositionists saw domestic trials as a politically more benign alternative to cooperation with the unpopular ICTY. This ICTY cooperation was conducted quid pro quo: Serbian leaders made domestically unpopular handovers to the Hague and, in return, received political goods from the West that they could use to gain domestic acquiescence (see type 7). Post-oppositionists would clearly be better off trading less politically costly favors (handovers to their own courts, which would incur a lower risk of voter backlash than handovers to foreign courts) in return for the same Western rewards. Indeed, post-opposition leaders put enormous energy into convincing members of the international community that they were capable of ensuring justice for war criminals at home, which would make the unpopular ICTY transfers unnecessary. Justice Minister Batić, eager to avoid politically costly Hague transfers, initially denied that domestic courts were unprepared to handle war crimes trials (in stark contrast to his remarks noted above), saying, after Milošević's transfer, "now we insist that the rest of the indictees be tried in Serbia."[112] The political and social turmoil caused by Đinđić's assassination created space for political elites to move forward quickly with plans for a domestic war crimes court, coupled with the organized crimes court, thereby making domestic prosecutions more acceptable to external actors. Serbia's new elites viewed domestic prosecutions as their own "get out of jail free" card.

TYPE 7. CRIMINAL PROSECUTION OF COMMANDERS

In contrast to relative power predictions, Serbian leaders under the first two post-Milošević governments transferred more than twenty—mostly senior ranking—indictees to the Hague.[113] The first arrest of a Yugoslav citizen came just over two months after the Serbian government changed hands, when Prime Minister Đinđić took custody of former leader Slobodan Milošević. The latter's transfer led to accusations by fellow post-oppositionist Koštunica of anti-constitutional rule, again raising the specter that even the rump Yugoslavia's stability was uncertain. The rift led to armed conflict when federal troops fired on republic police attempting to arrest Milošević.[114] This episode also marked the first open split in the DOS leadership.[115] The apparent risks of Hague cooperation were again highlighted in November 2001, when a special operations wing of the police, tacitly supported by Koštunica and the army chief of staff, protested the arrest of two indictees.[116] Less than a year and a half after the Red Berets protests, Prime Minister Đinđić was murdered, purportedly for his transfer policy.[117]

The slow rate of Hague cooperation ceased altogether during the run-up to the fall 2003 parliamentary elections, when Hague officials made public their indictment of four Serbian generals involved in war crimes in Kosovo.[118] Serbian leaders attacked the indictment for violating an informal agreement barring cases of command responsibility,[119] and several thousand police officers protested the indictments that included their deputy minister, who was running on the Liberal Party ticket.[120] When nationalist, anti-ICTY parties received considerable support in the elections, pro-justice parties bitterly blamed Western ICTY pressures.[121] Under Prime Minister Koštunica, there were no Hague arrests for most of 2004, but there were suddenly twelve "voluntary surrenders," largely regarded as handovers, in the last quarter of 2004 and the first quarter of 2005.[122]

For several reasons, both Koštunica and Đinđić should have avoided Hague cooperation between 2000 and 2003. The two most important post-opposition leaders' private preferences were clearly anti-Hague.[123] Koštunica called the ICTY a "monstrous institution," whose indictments were "despicable and counterproductive,"[124] and he repeatedly said that cooperation was "not a priority."[125] Đinđić questioned the veracity of the Hague indictments and promised to try Milošević at home for corruption before dealing with international war crimes charges.[126] While post-opposition forces wanted Milošević and his cronies imprisoned, they envisioned domestic trials for corruption (a crime against the Serb people) rather than international trials for war crimes (committed against non-Serbs).

Not coincidentally, cooperation with the Hague has also been unpopular, opposed by a majority of Serbs since post-opposition forces took power. Around the time of the Milošević arrest, only 11 percent supported his extradition for war crimes, while many times more (59 percent) said that he should face criminal prosecution at home for "abuse of office."[127] A majority of Serbs (53 percent) were also unable to cite any war crimes committed by their own forces, and they classified as heroes the Hague's most-wanted Serb war crimes suspects.[128] In 2003, Serbs called the ICTY the single greatest threat to their state's security,[129] and one year later only 11 percent supported cooperation.[130] In the eyes of their leaders, Serbs believe that they have been burdened with an unshared proportion of wartime atrocities,[131] and they view the ICTY as an attempt to pass judgment on their nation.[132] Post-opposition elites claim that, as a result of years of Milošević propaganda, their constituents have difficulty in accepting the premise that, unlike in the two world wars when they fought fascism, they were not heroes in the 1990s conflicts.[133] Moreover, Serbs are worn down by what they perceive as the "injustices, double standards" of the Hague, where only 10 percent believe that a Serb can receive a fair trial.[134] Years of rolling indictments make it very difficult, one NGO official acknowledged, "to show these people that there is light at the end of the tunnel."[135] No Serbian politician expected to win votes by advocating for this form of justice. And finally, Hague cooperation was risky. As noted earlier, Đinđić faced police protests and an armed police mutiny, and he was ultimately assassinated, likely as a result of his Hague policies.

The push for Hague cooperation resulted from a consistent stream of Western pressure. The ICTY has been near the top of U.S. and European diplomatic agendas in Serbia, acting as a counterweight to anti-ICTY public opinion.[136] Domestic politicians are encouraged to cooperate with the Hague in return for access to Western institutions and aid. The key incentive is European Union entry, tied indirectly to Hague cooperation in the rule-of-law category. Though EU officials refuse to make Hague compliance a formal condition for entry or for funding (in late 2000, EU Commissioner Chris Patten announced that "Milošević must go to the Hague, but this is not a necessary condition that Serbia must fulfill in order to be embraced into the European family"), in early 2005 they postponed accession talks with Croatia as a result of noncompliance.[137] The same message is consistently delivered in Belgrade where, according to one EU official, "if we had a meeting with Koštunica and did not make our point, they would think we were going soft. It's gotten to be ritualistic."[138] The message from the United States is the same. It has been the only power to use the threat of foreign aid cuts to pursue this agenda,[139] though the relatively paltry amount of bilateral U.S. aid at stake makes this punishment more symbolic than tangible.[140]

Institutional factors determine the extent to which Western pressure has been successful. While the attitudes of Serbia and Montenegro's secondary actors have varied, Serbian prime ministers have consistently sought to address Western demands in the hope that the resulting carrots could be used to convince otherwise antagonistic voters that they followed the correct policy. The Milošević arrest, for example, was advertised by members of the government as a step toward European and transatlantic structures and normalization of relations with Serbia's neighbors.[141] Since then, some post-opposition politicians believe, there would be few, if any, transfers without foreign pressure—especially the carrot of EU entry, a policy with strong public support.[142]

A study of Koštunica's policy transformation helps to illustrate this point. Between 2000 and 2003, Prime Minister Đinđić and other Serbian republic officials directly referred to the billions of dollars in Western aid as they prepared to make transfers,[143] whose timing also suggests that these pressures worked.[144] At the time, President Koštunica criticized Đinđić, expressing little interest in the funding.[145] "It was Đinđić who was running the finances," explained one of Đinđić's advisors. "Koštunica had absolutely no responsibility for running the country."[146] One year after Koštunica became prime minister, he was transformed from a longtime opponent of Hague cooperation to the man who brokered a series of "voluntary surrenders" ahead of an EU deadline for negotiations that would bring Serbia one step closer to entry. Koštunica appealed to the anti-Hague vote and nationalists in Parliament by promising benefits for indictees' families, offering state guarantees designed to win pre-trial release, and sending indictees off with the fanfare of heroes rather than the shame of war criminals. Still, he defied relative power predictions with his actions. One former official involved in several high-level ICTY arrests explained: "It was not dangerous. It's all about popularity."[147]

In fact, while it appears that Western pressures have been effectively used to convince post-oppositionists to deliver a form of justice that they would otherwise shun,[148] the long-term application of these pressures has had negative effects. Post-oppositionists who supported the Hague blame Westerners for the murder of one of Serbia's most pro-Western leaders and their own political defeat in the 2003 parliamentary elections, sometimes referring to ICTY Chief Prosecutor del Ponte as "an ally of the Serbian Radical Party."[149] Political leaders think that they have gambled away their political capital for locally unacceptable Western values in the hope of undelivered Western goods. "You are traitors, but you are bad traitors," one DS official assessed the public's view of his party. "Where is the money, where is the Western way of life?"[150] This focus on a quid pro quo (broken, according to Serbian elites) again highlights the merit of the strategic argument. Post-opposition elites gambled on a politically unpopular policy in the hope that they would be able to sell the material rewards (otherwise un-

available political goods) to their constituencies. Many subsequently believed that their bet was made in vain.

The fall of pro-justice, post-opposition parties in the 2003 elections,
together with the seemingly endless list of ICTY indictments, prompted
many elites to share the perceptions of their fellow Serbs, asking, "Where is
the bottom line? Where is the end of it?"[151] They questioned why so many
Serbs, relative to other nationalities, have been indicted.[152] These sentiments have led to foot dragging; Serbian leaders make the minimal number of transfers necessary to ensure Western aid without inflaming public
opinion.[153] As time passes, local political leaders say that their population
has begun to grow numb from years of threats and sanctions. "They've gotten used to it," said one. "No one really trusts that these people dealing with
us on these issues are dead serious."[154] Weaknesses in Western bargaining
power, including perceived U.S. hypocrisy[155] and public threats to withdraw support for the ICTY, have caused some elites to favor a "wait it out"
approach.[156] This may, in part, explain Koštunica's noncooperation policies in the first three quarters of 2004.

DISCUSSION

The fall of Slobodan Milošević marked an opening to scrutiny of decades of communist-era and post-communist rights violations. Just as
post-oppositionists came to power via separate mechanisms—Koštunica
through revolution, and Đinđić through a negotiated transition—they
were torn on how to address past abuses. At first glance, and in accordance
with the transition-based relative power argument, we should have expected Koštunica to take a much more aggressive approach. But a closer
look through institutional lenses demonstrates why Đinđić was ultimately
a greater proponent of harsh justice measures during this period.

Unlike the federal president, Prime Minister Đinđić's high level of institutional responsibility forced him to make unpopular choices that would
better enable him to provide voters with expected goods essential to his political survival. Western pressure for cooperation with the ICTY prompted
Đinđić to pursue criminal accountability for high-level officials responsible
for human rights violations. Until Koštunica took the prime minister's seat,

the federal president had little to gain from the unpopular policy of transfers and publicly opposed them. Similarly, Đinđić pursued those harsh justice measures when there were fewer carrots and sticks only to the degree that they would meet with relatively little societal (not former elite) resistance. While he did not hesitate to purge senior-level members of his police force charged with corruption, for example, Đinđić and his colleagues refrained from going after lower-level rights abusers who, they estimated, were seen by their constituents as protectors of the people.[157]

Because relative power arguments forecast moderate forms of justice in Serbia, types 1 through 4 are a less appropriate indicator of relative power success or failure. Yet it is noteworthy that elite respondents consistently attributed those policies to factors such as popularity and rewards for a given measure, rather than to the dangers integral to transition- or structure-based relative power arguments. Apologies appear not to have been made simply from the heart, but in the hope that the resulting international approval might somehow be reflected onto the domestic scene.[158] Rehabilitation and compensation were nonstarters due to their potentially high financial costs and to a general lack of interest among both elites and non-elites. Koštunica's truth commission was designed to thwart unpopular transfers while simultaneously establishing a socially acceptable history. There was less concern that old elites would sabotage Koštunica's DSS as a result of this innocuous initiative than there were fears that an alternative, more genuine truth commission launched by Đinđić's DS could upset the provision of political goods.

Beyond type 4, the strength of the strategic argument becomes clearer. So long as the prime minister had institutional incentives, he followed a policy of harsh justice. This holds regardless of the characteristics of the individual in power, whether a self-avowed liberal (Đinđić) or a nationalist (Koštunica). In the case of the former, the justice policy was, as predicted by the strategic argument, sluggish; Prime Minister Đinđić transferred indictees to the Hague slowly in the face of opposition from a key secondary actor (Koštunica), who sought to gain popularity from his own hardened position (see Figure 6.1). Yet when Koštunica took the premiership, he acted similarly to Đinđić and in contrast to his long-held policies (see Figure 6.2). While the result of this sluggish justice under Koštunica is not surprising from a purely institutional perspective, it does pose an interesting

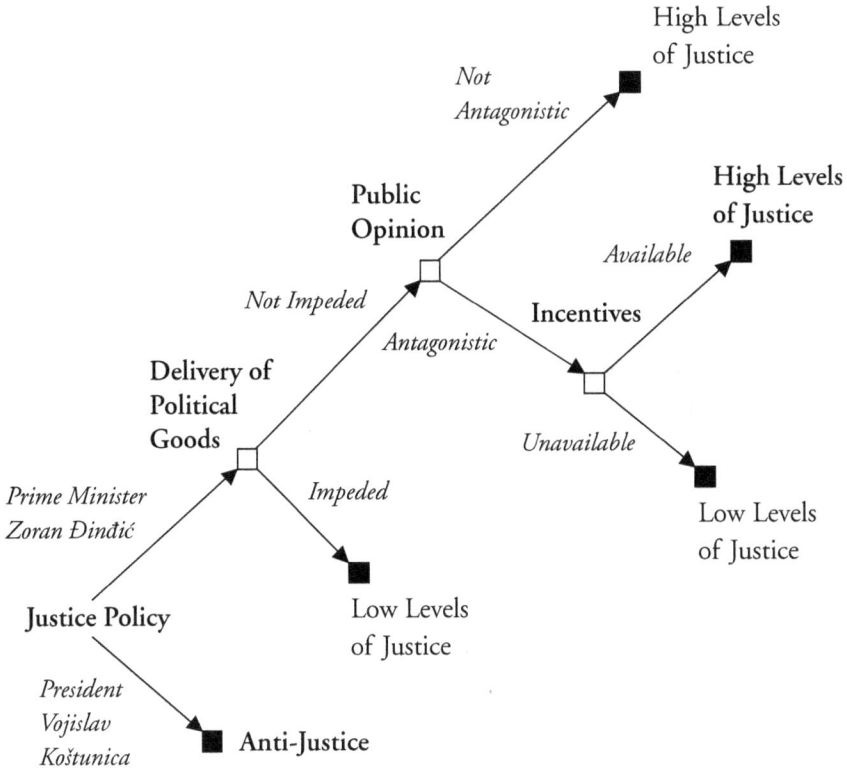

FIGURE 6.1   Justice in Serbia and Montenegro, 2000–2003

challenge to the strategic argument. For if Koštunica was institutionally prone to accept justice in return for Western goods, then the presence of a pro-justice secondary actor (President Marović) should have produced an expedited policy. The fact that Koštunica did not pursue justice more aggressively seems to reflect a weakness in this theory in dealing with private preferences and/or political reputation. In this case, it seems that Koštunica grudgingly accepted a policy that was in his own best interest but came with the potentially high price of personal distaste or public perceptions of hypocrisy. After years of taking an anti-ICTY approach, it was difficult for him to reverse course. He would, as one DS politician stated, "try to do it step by step, as little as he can."[159]

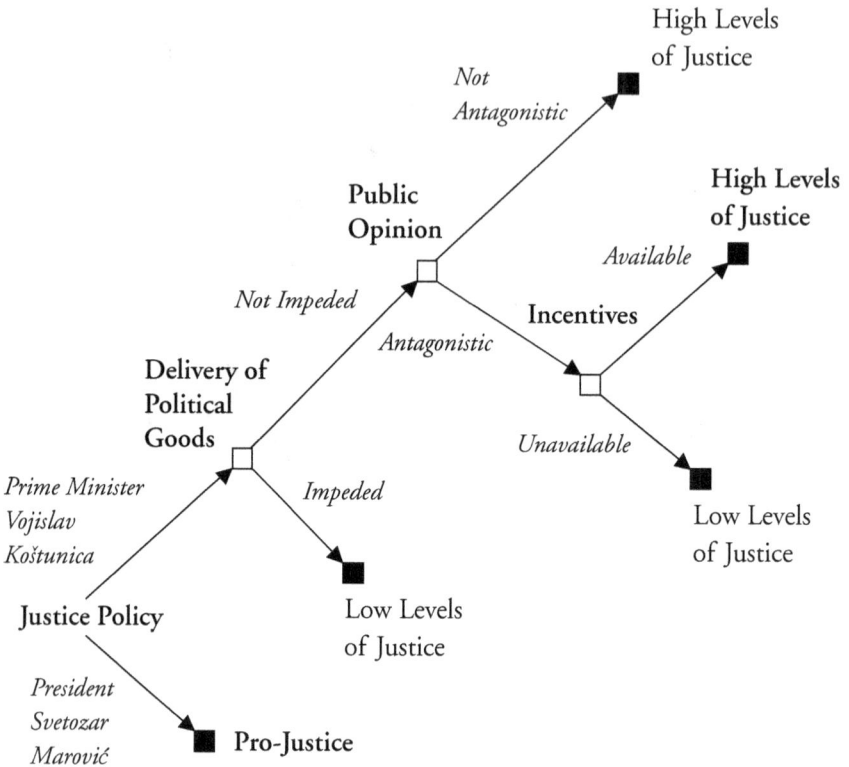

FIGURE 6.2 Justice in Serbia and Montenegro, 2003–2005

Serbian elites pursued harsh forms of justice when these measures could enhance their political positions. If there had not been Western incentives for criminal accountability in Serbia, would its leaders have nevertheless moved against old elites, as they say they would have, in the form of less controversial domestic trials?[160] While counterfactuals are a great challenge to social science, the case of Croatia brings us one step closer to answering this question. In the next chapter, I look at factors that led Croatian post-opposition elites to pursue justice under circumstances very similar to their counterparts in Serbia, differentiated primarily by the extent and types of Western pressure for Hague cooperation.

7

Croatia

When the Cost of Justice
Is Too High

Croatian pro-democracy political leaders who won power in late 1999 faced transitional justice challenges very similar to those of their one-time "brothers" in Serbia. Croatia had been a part of Yugoslavia since the end of World War II (and a component of the Kingdom of Yugoslavia from 1918 to 1941), but declared its independence in 1991. Under the nationalist and semi-authoritarian regime of President Franjo Tuđman, the country engaged in a "Homeland War" (1991–1995) against Yugoslavia and Yugoslav-backed Serb paramilitaries deep inside Croatia, as well as (less openly) ethnic Serbs and Muslims in Bosnia. Tuđman's death in December 1999 was followed by parliamentary elections that resulted in a resounding victory for the Opposition Six, a coalition of parties largely blocked from power under Tuđman. Prime Minister Ivica Račan, head of the democratic opposition's largest party (Social-Democratic Party) and the last first secretary of the League of Yugoslav Communists, formed a fragile coalition government that ran Croatia from 2000 until 2003, when the late Tuđman's party (Croatian Democratic Union, or HDZ) retook power. As in the preceding chapter, here I refer to the former democratic opposition to Tuđman as the "post-opposition."

The post-opposition leadership in Croatia was faced with three major types of justice issues that closely resemble what their Serbian counterparts would encounter one year later: communist-era violations, Tuđman-era wartime violations, and Tuđman-era non-war violations. Unlike Serbia, Croatian elites are also frequently forced to deal with a fourth justice issue: World War II rights violations. Local elites tend to agree with Serbs that the communist period was one of prosperity and that many communist-era human rights victims subsequently became rights violators with little chance of redress. While they complain of civil injustice during the Tuđman period, their attention is focused on much graver rights violations that occurred in the context of the 1990s wars. Pro-justice leaders in Croatia, like their Serbian counterparts, have faced stiff public opposition to ICTY cooperation and other justice measures, which are construed as general attacks on the 1990s war years. Unlike in Serbia, however, Croatian post-oppositionists lacked the critical Western carrots and sticks that were so effective in gaining Belgrade's compliance.

The Croatian case of an "electoral revolution" represents a challenge to transition- and structure-based relative power arguments. While from 2000 to 2003, Croatian post-opposition elites controlled the presidency (a secondary institution), the government, and 65 percent of the Parliament (primary institutions), they were unwilling or unable to systematically carry out the harsh measures of justice that were witnessed in Serbia. Instead, post-oppositionists under Račan had a spotty policy of criminal accountability (whether cooperation with the Hague or domestic criminal trials) and engaged in practically no bureaucratic cleansing of institutions suspected of committing rights violations during the 1990s. Račan, like Yugoslavia's Koštunica, launched a perfunctory truth commission apparently aimed at lowering Western pressures for criminal accountability, while simultaneously avoiding activities that could be interpreted by voters, or even his own ruling coalition, as unpatriotic. In contrast to public support–based relative power arguments, Croatia's leaders were afraid not of confronting a divided and potentially violent state, but of humiliating Croats with a reassessment of their recent war years. As in Serbia, I find that political strategy and personality politics, filtered through formal institutions, explain many of the justice decisions taken in Croatia.

TYPE 1. CESSATION AND CODIFICATION
OF HUMAN RIGHTS VIOLATIONS

Upon securing independence, authorities moved quickly to establish Croatia as a modern rule-of-law state by signing onto key international human rights agreements.[1] As in Serbia, these treaties had often been signed and ratified by officials from the former Yugoslavia, but the disintegration of the state made it necessary for each of the new successor states to reaffirm its commitment. Many of these documents, including the International Covenant on Civil and Political Rights (though optional protocols were not ratified until three years later), the International Covenant on Economic, Social, and Cultural Rights, and the three Conventions Against Torture, Genocide, and Racial Discrimination, were ratified en masse on October 12, 1992.[2] This year coincided with a temporary cessation of hostilities and efforts at normalizing relations with Yugoslavia.[3]

TYPE 2. REBUKE OF THE OLD SYSTEM

International actors have pressed Croatia for condemnations of, and apologies for, its recent history of gross human rights violations against local Serbs and Bosnian Serbs and Muslims, as well as the World War II–era murders of Jews, Serbs, and others.[4] Rather than issuing their own, Croatian politicians initially demanded apologies from Serbia and Montenegro as a condition for normalizing regional relations. Early insistence on a Montenegrin apology for the 1991 attack on Dubrovnik had very practical implications for bilateral relations,[5] as had a later proposal in which Croatia would support an end to sanctions on post-Milošević Serbia and Montenegro only after receiving a formal apology.[6] Self-perceptions among Croatian elites and non-elites of relative innocence have made it particularly difficult for their leaders to issue an apology to former aggressors.

Croatian officials apparently found it easiest to direct any apologies at temporally distant crimes. In his first year in office, President Stjepan Mesić apologized for the World War II Jasenovac concentration camp run by Croatian fascists, and later for Croatia's role in the 1990s Bosnian conflict.

In mid-2002, Prime Minister Račan laid a wreath at Jasenovac and issued his own ambiguous apology "for all victims of previous conflicts, irrespective of which ideologies prompted the crimes."[7] Finally, in 2003, Mesić replied to a formal Yugoslav apology for the 1990s wars: "In my name, I also apologize to all those who have suffered pain or damage at any time from citizens of Croatia who misused or acted against the law."[8] Račan never directly apologized for any alleged Croatian crimes during the immediate post–World War II era, despite pressures to do so.[9]

Personal factors, influenced by institutional considerations, explain the differences between Mesić's and Račan's approaches. These leaders shared professional backgrounds that may have predisposed them to reluctance. Both were former members of the League of Yugoslav Communists, seen as the antithesis to independent Croatia, and throughout the 1990s had spoken out against nationalism. It is therefore surprising that President Mesić would be more willing than the prime minister to cast doubt on his "Croatness" by issuing apologies. The record, however, is clear: Račan's apology, at the site where communists (that is, his political predecessors) killed thousands of Croat "patriots" accused of collaborating with the Nazis, was intended to reconcile communist and nationalist Croats, rather than Croats and their neighbors.[10] Moreover, the prime minister apparently spent considerably more energy than the president in trying to obtain an official apology from his eastern neighbors, even authorizing his representative at the International Court of Justice to drop genocide charges against Serbia and Montenegro if officials there publicly admitted their side's guilt.[11]

Račan's reluctance appears to result from the combination of his political background and institutional insecurity, in particular the fear of giving his (potential) enemies any ammunition that might erode his credibility and thus his ability to govern. Sheltered in his four-year term, President Mesić was less risk averse than Račan and therefore more willing to voice the private preferences once espoused by both men. Mesić accepted the fact that nationalist sympathizers would never be on his side, regardless of his actions, and he was confident that any dip in popularity at home would be short-lived. According to one of his advisors, President Mesić had little to lose from making an apology. His opponents merely thought, "What else could one expect from Mesić?"[12] People close to the Croatian president also argue that he simply believed that apologies were a moral necessity.[13]

Yet Mesić's apologies were not without cost, and sensitivity to political attacks from the right also made him cautious.[14] After being condemned for his remarks at Jasenovac,[15] for instance, Mesić waited almost one year between the time he pledged to apologize to Bosnians[16] and when he actually did so.[17] In the meantime, he made public his expectation of an apology from Serbia and Montenegro. When this did not happen, Mesić played down its significance and questioned the utility of an apology from a Yugoslavia that continued to harbor war criminals.[18] His 2003 "counter-apology" to President Marović drew fire from the center-right parties, which claimed in a parliamentary resolution that Croatians had nothing to apologize for;[19] and it was cited in late 2004 by Mesić's rival presidential contender, who said that she would "never forget who was the aggressor against Croatia."[20] Even Mesić's usual supporters in the human rights community were divided, with some saying that his apology opened "a good public discussion,"[21] and with others calling it a "waste of time for the victims."[22] One local political leader summarized the latter argument: "It's one thing when a president does this, and another when society really opens up."[23] Mesić's institutional security made him more likely than Račan to voice his private preferences, but he was not seen as speaking for Croatian society as a whole.

TYPE 3. REHABILITATION AND COMPENSATION FOR VICTIMS

Discussions of rehabilitation and compensation in Croatia took place in the early Tuđman years and revolved around suffering from the post–World War II period. In early 1992, the Tuđman-controlled Parliament passed two separate declarations providing for the symbolic, though not legal, rehabilitation of two historic figures whose pain was representative of that of "thousands of Croats" living in communist Yugoslavia.[24] The declaration to rehabilitate Cardinal Alojzij Stepinac included a condemnation of "the political trials of numerous unjustly sentenced clergymen, monks, and the faithful, thus also condemning the anti-people's communist regime."[25] The other declaration, dedicated to Andrija Hebrang, included a recognition of all "who strove for a free, democratic, and socially just Croatian state and as a consequence lost their freedom and life in thousands of staged trials in the communist and hated Yugoslavia."[26] Hebrang, who advocated for Croatian self-rule despite being a major figure in the early Yugoslav Communist Party, was accused of, and imprisoned for, supporting Stalin's Cominform resolution splitting from Yugoslavia.[27] He was later killed in prison. The two declarations were officially separated in order to establish a special place among the repressed for Stepinac and the Church.[28]

Tuđman's two rehabilitation bills served a political strategy that was designed to gain widespread support for his nationalist policies and, for similar reasons, to rewrite his own place in history. The Stepinac declaration was meant to fulfill the former function by encouraging support from the Church, a powerful social institution. To gain such support, Tuđman also needed to address his own role in the League of Yugoslav Communists. The Hebrang declaration performed this function, showing how even communists could be good nationalists. Through Hebrang, Tuđman and his allies were able to "defend their biographies,"[29] as well as cast their former system as a fundamentally benevolent one that had merely gone astray during its implementation—a phase during which they supposedly had little influence.[30]

Tuđman's rehabilitations did not pertain to the victims of the 1971 Croatian Spring (*Hrvatsko prolječe*), when a political movement made up of students and intellectuals demanding greater Croatian sovereignty launched a series of demonstrations. Both during and after those events, hundreds of demonstrators were repressed, with some sentenced to prison and others thrown out of university. Among those demonstrators was Franjo Tuđman, though the future president's relatively small role would affect his future treatment of the demonstrations. According to interviewees, Tuđman apparently avoided rehabilitating victims from these famed national events, since such actions might have undermined his own stature and given political opponents who were more active in 1971 a tool to use against him.[31] According to one parliamentarian and historian, "He did everything in his power to forget 1971."[32]

Since taking power, post-oppositionists have made no effort to revisit the question of rehabilitation and compensation. Again, as in the case of apologies, leaders' backgrounds, coupled with institutional considerations, seem to account for this outcome. If Račan, the first post-opposition prime minister and a former first secretary of the League of Yugoslav Communists, had pursued rehabilitation, he might have risked reviving unsavory memories that indicated his own guilt and that of his colleagues. One former opposition member commented, "If the state rehabilitated you, it must find who is personally guilty for the suffering. And then you will see that they are still in power."[33] Another former political prisoner, who in 1986 sought rehabilitation, blames his failure then and up to today on the presence of postcommunists in all of the major political options dominating public life.[34] Opening the can of worms of political rehabilitation might have harmed Račan's credibility and eventually hurt his ability to govern.

As in the Serbia case, post-opposition forces succeeding Tuđman also saw little value in reopening the rehabilitation issue. One of my interviewees noted that in the former Yugoslavia, where repression was homegrown and "you couldn't really blame the Russians for anything," there was little political reward in resurrecting a little-known subject, which was more discussed among returning émigrés than it was among longtime residents.[35] In fact, most of my Croatian interviewees who had experienced repression expressed no interest in pressing for their or their families' rehabilitation.[36] Furthermore, these interviewees often remarked that few of their compatriots harbor negative recollections of the communist period. Even human rights organization leaders recall Yugoslavia as much more liberal than other parts of Central Europe.[37] Indeed, they note that calls to address such historical issues are often intended to detract attention from 1990s rights violations. "I am more interested in the victims from 1995 to 2005," said one human rights organization representative, who had just returned from a small town where one hundred refugees remain in legal and economic limbo. "I really do not care about Goli Otok,"[38] the prison, on a barren island off the Croatian coast, where Tito housed political enemies in the late 1940s. Some post-opposition forces have also taken the line that the evolution of many rights victims of the 1970s and 1980s into the political leaders of the 1990s represented a de facto rehabilitation.[39] "In creating a democratic Croatia they were absolutely rehabilitated," commented Račan.[40]

Finally, as in Serbia and Montenegro, post-opposition political and nongovernmental elites frequently note that broad rehabilitations carry the risk of including the country's worst rights offenders, including the thousands of Croatian soldiers and their families, who, accused of collaborating with the fascist Ustaše regime during World War II, were in May 1945 brutally tortured and murdered by Tito's forces at Bleiberg.[41] This logic is also frequently applied to the rabid nationalists involved in atrocities during the 1990s wars. "Those people for whom we were writing petitions (under communism) later became the fascists who ruled us," exclaimed one human rights NGO leader. "They were pure criminals."[42] The issue of rehabilitation and compensation for ethnic Serbs who were persecuted during the 1990s has not received significant support in either the political or the legal system.[43]

The decision by Croatian elites to (not) issue rehabilitations, compensation, or various forms of rebuke has hinged on how voters, rather than old elites, might interpret these moves. The calculation is not a straightforward one, however. Croatian leaders have looked at their own histories, the histories of those who may be encompassed by a given form of justice, and the general attitudes of the public.

TYPE 4. CREATION OF A TRUTH COMMISSION

The process of seeking truth in Croatia has been determined largely by political strategy, with anti-justice groups in Parliament seeking the declaration of a canned version of events and pro-justice actors relegating deeper investigations to a remote, domestically irrelevant process. Members of Tuđman's right-wing HDZ, bitter at post-opposition forces for allegedly tarnishing the recent history of the Homeland War, engaged in the first effort to "produce" truth in post-opposition Croatia by introducing in October 2000 a parliamentary declaration calling the war "righteous, legitimate, defensive, and not aggressive or conquering."[44] The head of the HDZ's parliamentary branch, who introduced the bill, was apparently motivated by comments from President Mesić that a mutual apology among all former warring parties might be beneficial. Following two days of contentious debate, the resolution, which attracted vocal support from veterans' groups who had called war crimes arrests a stain on Croatia's war of independence, was adopted by a majority vote.[45] The resolution's passage prompted the HDZ to cancel a vote of no-confidence planned against Prime Minister Račan. One of the few parliamentarians to speak out against the resolution declared that everyone knew that Croatia had been an aggressor in Bosnia:

"Where we differ is whether we should face that fact or sweep it under the carpet."[46] NGO leaders sarcastically cite Parliament's truth declaration as "proof" that Croatia no longer needs to investigate the war years.[47]

Several months after passage of the highly publicized parliamentary declaration, Prime Minister Račan quietly ordered the Croatian Historical Institute, devoted to historical research, to investigate the history, scope, and nature of the victims of the Homeland War.[48] The three-year "Creation of the Croatian Republic and Homeland War" project[49] was one of the only tasks ever imposed on the institute.[50]

The similarities between the rump Yugoslavia's truth commission and the Croatian investigation are remarkable.[51] Researchers in charge of the Croatian project were charged primarily with combing through open source materials, especially newspaper accounts. They worked in relative isolation, with no input from local or international human rights or other organizations. The project included a pre-1991 component, as well as an investigation of international actors' roles during the 1990s wars, perhaps intended to spread blame or rationalize Croatian abuses. And Croatian investigators shared with their Yugoslav colleagues the perception that state funding was inadequate to accomplish the massive job set out for them. In fact, after the group completed the three-year project, it was given another three-year mandate to explore further.

As in the Serbia case, Croatia's truth mechanism appears to have been targeted solely at an international audience. In fact, researchers on the project note that it closely adheres to a subtle foreign policy strategy in which Croatian leaders have engaged for decades. Throughout the communist period, the institute was an international showpiece for free speech and published research that did not strictly conform to the ruling ideology. At the same time, it was deprived of access to the broader domestic public, which made its findings practically irrelevant on the local stage. "You could work as long as it was not published. Then they'd say, 'Look what a free country we are!'" said one researcher who has been with the institute since 1972.[52] This project, largely unknown to Croats, was destined to share "a similar fate," he added.

As in the case of Serbia, an analysis of Račan's truth commission is inseparable from that of ICTY pressures. It is a widely held view that Croatia's formal investigation was initiated as part of a government campaign to counter international demands for ICTY cooperation.[53] Others believe that the project was actually a bone thrown to right-wing forces who resented the post-opposition's criticism of the 1990s wars.[54] Račan seemed to hope that a moderate form of justice might be enough to convince foreigners that Croats could deal with the past on their own terms, which would in turn defuse the far more visible and politically costly issue of ICTY transfers. Račan himself noted that the project was an attempt to "depoliticize war crimes . . . to leave history to the historians, not to the politicians."[55] At the same time, post-oppositionists needed his truth commission to glide under the radar of most Croats, who, they suspected, would disapprove. As one politician put it, "In Croatia the truth is very simple: We were attacked by Serbs and defended ourselves."[56]

The working-level perception is that while Croatian political leaders may have been interested in launching the investigation for political ends, they were uninterested in significantly shaping its implementation. Researchers claim that there is no external pressure on them and that neither the institute's director nor the researchers are politically active—nor were they eager to take on this project. (One researcher confided that, given his other research and family commitments, he put relatively little time into it.) Instead of political interference, they complained of inadequate financial support from the state and believed that their project would attract little interest from the public. Researchers also thought that their own impotence and the post-oppositionists' reluctance to counter popular myths about the war would doom Croatia's truth mechanism to irrelevance. "Society does not give a damn," said one, adding that the government is uninterested in changing this perception. "People do not read history books."[57]

Račan's decision to launch a quiet truth process must be placed in the broader context of Croatian politics. Even the president, a strong proponent of justice, was unwilling to aggressively take on societal myths about the recent war since, according to one of his advisors, "he knows that if he did this all in one package, it would have been too much."[58] It is not surprising, then, that Račan—institutionally more exposed—sought to bury the issue. The goal of Croatia's truth process was to remove criminal justice from the central political stage, which would help preserve Račan's ability to govern with the strength necessary to deliver goods needed for him to maintain his position. The weakness of Croatia's truth commission was not determined by old elites, but rather by new elites' perceptions of their electorate.

TYPE 5. PURGING OF HUMAN RIGHTS ABUSERS
FROM PUBLIC POSITIONS

There have been practically no personnel changes as a result of human rights violations during the communist or postcommunist war period. In the early 1990s the Croatian Party of Rights (HSP) was one of the few parties to press for lustration, proposing to ban former communists from occupying certain positions. Likely due to the heavy overlap between League of Yugoslav Communists members and the ruling HDZ, the HSP proposal never became law.[59] In the post-Tuđman period, disagreements over who were more guilty—officials from the communist era or those from the Tuđman regime—led one human rights activist sympathetic to lustration to scoff at the HSP plan, commenting that "the first ones I would lustrate would be them."[60] In the late 1990s, Tuđman clearly opposed pushing out anyone for alleged violations in his great patriotic wars of 1991–1995, though it appears that he did fire some top-level military officers on other grounds.[61]

While relative power arguments are not determinative, one might expect that post-revolutionary post-oppositionists would have combed through the bureaucracy and ejected former rights abusers. Rather, facing a lack of evidence and constraints from a public that had long supported the Tuđman regime, post-oppositionists left former rights abusers both anonymous and untouched. "We couldn't do much," Račan recalled.[62] Almost one year after post-opposition forces took over in 2000, Prime Minister Račan apparently did replace a number of local Security Information Service (SIS) branch heads, who were involved in the Homeland War, with former state bureaucrats connected with the communist era, but there is no evidence that the dismissals resulted from previous rights abuses.[63] In the judiciary, the Račan government reportedly squeezed out (by refusing to reassign for new terms) only about 10 percent of court presidents.[64]

The most visible disciplinary actions took place as a result of functionaries' attacks on justice policies, rather than on the actual injustices that they had committed under the former regime. In fall 2000, President Mesić dismissed twelve generals (seven on active duty) who had, following the arrest of a dozen people suspected of war crimes, signed an open letter condemning the government for cooperating with the Hague tribunal.[65] While some of these generals were themselves suspected of war crimes (one, Ante Gotovina, was later indicted by the Hague; another, Mirko Norać, was later sentenced by a Croatian court to twelve years for his role in the murder of fifty Serb civilians in Gospić),[66] these crimes were not directly related to their removals. The dismissals led to public protests (organized by the Association of Croatian Homeland Defense War Veterans, UHVDR),[67] but the government refused to back down and, almost one year later, ejected another senior-level officer for publicly attacking the government's pro-Hague stance.[68] The many military and police personnel who were "somehow accused but never officially sentenced" for war crimes have held onto their jobs.[69]

These dismissals of generals marked the toughest administrative sanctions delivered by post-oppositionists. They were neither carried out in ways predicted by, nor in accordance with, relative power arguments. Post-oppositionists did shy away from a personnel cleanup, yet they showed no fear of confronting still powerful and highly popular military leaders from the old regime. In fact, military officers openly questioning the government were removed for fear that leaving them in place (rather than throwing them out) would be destabilizing.[70] "We were already in danger," Račan noted. "We did not want to let the generals and the military get involved in politics. This was an attack on democracy."[71] Fear of a negative public reaction, not a mutiny, appears to have been the primary consideration in not pursuing a more aggressive policy of investigations and purges.[72] A lack of evidence, coupled with concerns that some in the broad post-opposition coalition could be indirectly linked to certain rights abuses, also contributed to the reluctance to purge.[73] Finally, it should be noted that it was Mesić, rather than Račan, who ejected the generals. Housed in an institution characterized by secure terms and feeling little political need to appease members of the former regime, the president acted within his limited powers to confront the generals where Račan may have been unable to do so. The fact that the old guard was politically weakened by recent electoral defeats made Mesić's job all the easier.[74]

TYPE 6. CRIMINAL PROSECUTION OF "EXECUTORS"

As in Serbia, lower-level officials accused of human rights violations in Croatia usually faced a greater likelihood of domestic, rather than international, criminal justice. In contrast to relative power expectations of hasty prosecutions, however, Croatian post-oppositionists sought to avoid domestic trials for purported heroes of the war for independence. Instead, they attempted to diminish Western pressures for greater Croat accountability by merely cutting back on the high number of trials for ethnic Serbs. Given the logic of the institutional argument, and a lack of externally produced carrots and sticks in this sphere, local trials of ethnic Croats were a rarity. The handful that did take place were primarily designed to prove to the outside world that the Hague was superfluous, and thereby to reduce the pressure for unpopular transfers.

Since 1991, Croatian prosecutors have carried out hundreds of war crimes trials, almost all of accused Serbs.[75] Some of the accused were unsuspecting Serbs who returned to Croatia hoping to reclaim their property,[76] while others followed forced extraditions from third-party countries.[77] Single trials were frequently held for large groups of suspects. Often, between 50 percent and 100 percent of the defendants were absent for the trial, during which they were usually convicted; according to one government report from 1997, of the 500 war crimes verdicts reached, only ten defendants were acquitted.[78] International observers and local Serb leaders advocated for greater transparency, complaining that trials were conducted in near secrecy.[79] The Tuđman regime reacted to this criticism by occasionally issuing lists of war crimes suspects[80] and releasing statistics concerning the number of war crimes trials held and amnesties given.[81] Demands for more ethnic Croat war criminals to face justice have generally been contested. The official line is that Croat officials did everything they could to spare innocents; and, while isolated criminal actions may have occurred, they resulted in perhaps a few dozen deaths, not hundreds, as the ICTY maintained. More important, according to the official version, any deaths incurred took place after, not during, Croatian military and police actions.[82]

Post-oppositionists under pressure to transfer indicted Croat military officers to the Hague sought to use unpopular domestic trials as a replacement for the even more provocative international ones. The high-profile investigation of the extrajudicial murder of more than one hundred Serb civilians by Croatian soldiers at Gospić was apparently initiated as a result of international pressure.[83] When a Gospić witness was murdered, Račan reacted by launching a September 2000 crackdown on war crimes suspects.[84] As noted earlier, in February 2001, Račan had General Norać, a Hague indictee, charged with crimes at Gospić.[85]

Norać was not Račan's first arrest, but he represented the first high-level prosecution and an early attempt by Račan to fight anti-justice domestic groups.[86] The Norać case, which Račan convinced Hague authorities to transfer to Croatia, was largely regarded as a test of the state's capacity to try its own war criminals.[87] Post-opposition elites explained to their domestic audience that local prosecutions were a political necessity, given the threat of international isolation,[88] and they sold domestic trials as a way to reduce the number of Hague indictments.[89] Norać's conviction, some pro-justice elites argue, proves that Croatia is capable of delivering justice without the help of the Hague.[90]

The Norać case, however, did not set a precedent. While there were a number of other arrests of ethnic Croats under Račan,[91] critics argue that they were largely symbolic, ignored the vast majority of rights violators, and were carried out under conditions that could not guarantee justice.[92] The war crimes trials were disrupted by incidents ranging from attacks on witnesses to bomb scares.[93] Croat suspects were frequently let off or given minimum sentences because, according to one ruling judge, "they were Homeland War defenders who committed crimes during war circumstances."[94] Unable to bring ethnic Croats to justice, Račan's government moved to at least improve the situation for ethnic Serbs, installing a general prosecutor who cut the number of cases for Serbs alleged to have committed war crimes from an estimated 4,000 down to less than 2,000.[95] In late 2001, the state prosecutor announced that trials in absentia would stop, and the justice minister said that the list of charged stood at 1,522, about half of which were ongoing investigations.[96]

Račan's domestic war crimes trials may have been relatively less costly than Hague transfers, but they were still painful. The Gospić case led to political instability, including a (failed) no-confidence motion in Parliament,[97] and embittered the public. "There were huge demonstrations against me and my government," Račan recalled. "I was branded a traitor."[98] His efforts also led to more personal campaigns against him. Nationalists asserted that criminal accountability must begin with Bleiburg, where Račan's communist predecessors executed numerous alleged Croat fascists immediately following World War II.[99] Nonetheless, Račan advocated for at least some domestic trials, which were viewed as the lesser of two evils.

TYPE 7. CRIMINAL PROSECUTION OF COMMANDERS

Though Prime Minister Račan was able to convince Hague officials to transfer the Norać case to Croatian courts, he was unable to reverse several transfer orders for senior-level officials. The Opposition Six had in the run-up to the 1999 elections vowed to increase cooperation with the Hague in order to secure Croatian accession to the European Union,[100] and began the year 2000 in solid control of the government and Parliament. Furthermore, with Western pressures for ICTY cooperation, it seemed that external actors were ready to do the Croatian post-oppositionists' dirty work for them. From a transition-based relative power standpoint, there was little to stop Croatia's post-oppositionists from forcing transfers. Those taking a structure-based or public support–based relative power approach would be more likely to anticipate red flags. After all, high-level indictees retained top military positions (or had friends and colleagues in those high places) and enjoyed enormous public support. Indeed, rather than eagerly oblige with international justice, Račan promised only to balance Croatia's "international obligations" with his duty to respect "the right to freedom and actions that secured [the state]."[101] He spent four years resisting ICTY demands for transfers.

Within just months of taking power, Račan signaled that he would not cooperate closely with the Hague when he publicly questioned an ICTY sentence handed down to an ethnic Croat.[102] The Croatian government narrowly escaped UN Security Council condemnation for noncooperation.[103] Račan assured Croats in October 2000 (and again in July 2001) that "this government has not sent anyone to the Hague."[104] At the end of his first year in office he warned that the ICTY "ought not to equalize guilt" of Croats and Serbs.[105] More forcefully, Račan stated that his government would not accept indictments for the Homeland War from 1991 to 1995 or

for the 1995 operations, Flash and Storm, which returned Krajina and Slavonia to Croatian control.[106] President Mesić, by contrast, spoke out more
directly and persistently for cooperation, arguing that Croatian ICTY compliance was essential to individualize guilt.[107] "The Hague tribunal does not
sit in judgment of nations, but of suspects. Every one of them has a name
and surname. Crime has no nationality," he said.[108]

Račan, not Mesić, had the institutional responsibility and powers to
ensure cooperation. Croatia was given a much smaller list of indictments
than was Serbia, but in almost every case Račan acted in a manner inconsistent with relative power expectations that he should arrest and transfer. On one of the rare occasions when he was handed an ICTY request
for transfer, he at first refused. In June 2001, he objected to the indictment
of two Croatian generals, Rahim Ademi and Ante Gotovina. It took one
month and a personal visit by the ICTY chief prosecutor, Karla del Ponte,
to convince him to concede, by which time Gotovina had escaped or,
according to some respondents, had been allowed to go into hiding.[109]
In 2002, Račan refused to hand over another general, Janko Bobetko, on
health grounds. Račan did ultimately encourage the surrender of two indictees, Pasko Ljubičić and, after the one-month delay, Ademi.

Domestic disdain for the Hague's approach to Croatia largely determined the post-oppositionists' policies. According to elite perceptions of
public opinion, most Croats believe that they were the victims, rather than
the perpetrators, of war crimes. "The overall approach here is that Croatia was attacked by Serbia and we had a right to defend ourselves," commented the parliamentarian who had drafted Croatia's Hague cooperation
law.[110] Those who defended Croatia from secessionist Serbs are viewed as
war heroes who fought nobly for an independent state.[111] While elites believe that society has slowly begun to accept the fact that Croats could and,
at least on rare occasions, did commit crimes, Serb violators are the rule,
whereas Croat violators are the exception.[112] One Tuđman-era justice minister even called the Serb exodus from Croatian territory during the 1995
Operation Storm an act of "genocide" committed by the Yugoslav authorities, since, he claims, they organized the departure of roughly 200,000 ethnic Serbs.[113] The ICTY, therefore, represents a politicized form of justice,
where war crimes allegations against Croats unjustly cast a dark cloud over
the entire Homeland War. As in Serbia, many political elites appear to em-

pathize or even share the views they profess to be that of their constituents. Accusing ICTY prosecutors of striving to produce a "regional balance of guilt" by indicting players on all sides, Croatia's former UN representative notes: "There are differences in [the] scope of the crimes, level of intent, hierarchical level involved. Definitely no one was a saint, but Milošević was the devil."[114]

As in the case of Serbia, Croatian authorities faced diplomatic pressure for cooperation from the United States and, most important, from the European Union, seen by political elites as a club that most Croats hoped to join. Unlike in Serbia, however, diplomatic pressure was not focused. While Western pressures on Serbia have been focused on war crimes cooperation, those on Croatia have been more diffuse, also encompassing Serb refugees' right of return and justice in the domestic war crimes trials against ethnic Serbs.[115] Perhaps more important, Croatia was neither tempted with immediate rewards nor threatened with economic sanctions, thus making the benefits of cooperation and the costs of noncooperation more abstract. Diplomatic pressures have been offset by the realization that Europe does not speak with one voice. A cottage industry has arisen devoted to searching out points of difference among and within Western governments, so that the minority of Western actors less adamant about Hague cooperation play prominently in the local press.[116] For example, Austrians and Germans received enormous coverage in the press when they argued that Croatia should begin EU negotiations in March 2005 despite its failure to hand over a wanted war criminal.

When Račan did cooperate, he pointed out that the alternative was international isolation and possibly sanctions.[117] This is a remarkable statement since it appears that no country was considering economic sanctions at the time. Still, Račan's public efforts to connect noncooperation with conflict and isolation, and cooperation with European integration, are consistent with the strategic argument.[118] The distance and intangibility of EU entry made this a poor good to trade for immediate and potentially severe political concessions.

The fact that Račan sought to cooperate at all could be explained either by his personal preferences or by his hope that Croatian voters would eventually see that he was doing their country a service. Yet the net value of these actions was diminished substantially by the domestic risks they involved. The delayed decision to transfer Ademi and Gotovina led to the immediate resignation of four ministers in Račan's fragile government,[119] even though his foreign minister promised to refute "contentious elements from the indictment" over the course of the trial.[120] Račan's government survived a subsequent HDZ-led vote of no-confidence by a margin of 93:36, but the threat of having to face the Croatian electorate if his government ever collapsed in the name of extraditing national heroes was a real fear.[121] Račan knew that transfers were interpreted by society "as an attack on the Homeland War," which members of the old regime could use in the "battle for neutrals"—the electoral fight for many moderate Croatians who may have supported Račan's general policies but were wary of attacks on the war period.[122] This kept the prime minister highly sensitive to popular demonstrations in ways that the institutionally secure president did not seem to feel.[123] Račan was not ready to transfer a frail general such as Bobetko, who could easily become "a symbol for Croatian nationalists."[124] Instead, he struggled to keep ICTY cooperation at the more mundane and less public level (for example, by handing over documents).

A fascinating twist to the Croatia case occurred in 2005, a year after Ivo Sanader, a member of the HDZ, took over as prime minister. Sanader had orchestrated a 2001 protest against the Račan government in defense of General Gotovina and was considered a strong nationalist. His government was faced with a crisis, however, when, in March 2005, European Union officials indefinitely postponed accession negotiations with Croatia pending word from ICTY officials that Croatia was actively working to capture Gotovina. Faced with the specter of being responsible for locking Croatia out of Europe (EU entry being considered a political good), Sanader suddenly became a vocal proponent of Gotovina's handover. By the end of the year, Gotovina was in the Hague, thanks in part to Croatian intelligence efforts.[125]

Prime Minister Sanader's reversal on ICTY cooperation highlights the merit of the strategic argument. In fact, each case of (non)transfer provides greater evidence for this argument. In contrast to public support–based relative power arguments, Račan did ultimately press for the surrender of top-level generals, and he did so without worries of splitting society. And where he did not, as in the case of Bobetko, he openly claims that this was more out of concern for voter-level political battles than for fear of high-level military actors still in place. He certainly appears not to have felt comfortable enough in his position to aggressively pursue former abusers, as suggested by transition-based arguments. In actuality, Račan faced institutional constraints that made him wary of transfers, counterbalanced by consistent pressure from fellow post-oppositionists (especially President Mesić) to follow a path that was politically difficult and that ultimately resulted in an abortive policy.

DISCUSSION

After Tuđman's death in 1999, Croatian oppositionists were swept to power through an "electoral revolution" that, at least on paper, made them a formidable force. Post-oppositionists held the presidency, controlled a large majority of seats in Parliament, and ran the government. According to theoretical insights from the current transitional justice and democratization literatures, we might have expected harsh measures, including criminal accountability for past rights violators. Hague indictees should have been transferred, and dozens, or perhaps even hundreds, of local trials should have been held for lower-level functionaries. As in the cases of Serbia and Poland, however, institutional incentives led Croatia's post-opposition elites to behave quite differently from transition-based and structure-based relative power predictions.

Prime Minister Račan's number-one priority was political survival, and harsh justice was in many ways antithetical to this aim. He faced constant challenges to his justice initiatives, including international transfers, domestic arrests, or even apologies for 1990s war crimes. These challenges occurred on several levels. First, Račan faced the direct threat that his fragile post-opposition governing coalition would splinter over his justice policies. If this did not occur, the prime minister still faced elite-level threats from current opposition parties led by the HDZ in Parliament. Outside of the Zagreb-based, formal power structures, Račan had to deal with persistent threats of civil disobedience that could jeopardize his ability to run the country. The prime minister's capacity to provide political goods was thus subject to official constraints at the top, where instability was the overriding feature of his government; and at the bottom, where veterans' groups and others threatened to literally bring the Croatian economy to a halt through roadblocks that stopped commerce as well as threatened tourism.[126] Račan also feared the negative effects that Hague cooperation would have on his ability to govern. When asked how distracting the ICTY was for a head of state, Račan replied: "My government was not preoccupied by the Hague, but by Croatia."[127]

Unlike Serbia's Prime Minister Zoran Đinđić, Račan had little to offer his people in exchange for harsh justice. While the Serbs were periodically at risk for financial punishments and international isolation, Croats faced neither economic sanctions for noncooperation nor economic incentives for cooperation. The best that Račan could reasonably offer his constituents and fellow elites in return for Hague transfers was the distant prospect of EU and NATO entry—popular goals, but long-term objectives that he had difficulty translating into more appealing immediate pocketbook rewards. Račan himself was swayed more by the tangible domestic costs of cooperation than he was by the intangible foreign benefits. As a result, he sought to strike a balance, pressing for a handful of domestic war crimes trials and trying to stave off ICTY pressures by launching a marginal investigation into the recent war years. President Mesić, with fewer institutional responsibilities and constituent expectations, could afford to serve as a strong advocate for justice. Despite sharing a biography similar to Račan's, Mesić was a vocal and relentless proponent of Hague handovers and sacked those popular generals who opposed this policy. But for the prime minister, commented one independent parliamentarian, "it was easier to take the low road."[128]

According to the transition-based relative power argument, Croatian post-opposition elites should have been more likely than Serbian or Polish elites to pursue harsh forms of justice. Because this argument does not posit that they will *necessarily* pursue such justice, however, the Croatian case is the least significant challenge to the relative power argument. The structure-based relative power argument also fares poorly in the Croatian case, where, given the dominance of the old regime's commanders in the top ranks, we should have expected to see no high-level generals prosecuted or transferred. The Norać and Gotovina criminal cases, and the very sacking of generals publicly opposed to Hague cooperation, dramatically challenge this thesis. Still, it should be clear from this chapter that Croatian post-opposition elites, like their Serbian and Polish counterparts, followed a rationale consistent with the strategic argument, not the transition-based relative power argument. When one reporter asked about whether fears of a coup were responsible for delayed arrests, Mesić answered nonchalantly, "whenever there is a coup, someone in a foreign country is behind it, some foreign power is behind it. Tell me which foreign power would stand behind wanting to abolish democracy in Croatia."[129]

There is significant support for the public support–based relative power argument. For the new elites of Croatia, justice policy was a function of anticipated reactions from voters, not old elites, and Croatian leaders tended to shy away from measures that they calculated would inflame public opinion. But Račan did not fear pitting societal actors against each other or creating schisms. Rather, he feared alienating a group of voters whose support would be needed to keep him in power come the next election.

Moreover, the public support–based argument fails to account for why highly unpopular decisions were gradually made. For leaders in secondary institutions, such as Mesić, justice policy emerged as a balance of political sensitivities but also private preferences, relatively easy to exhibit given the nature of Mesić's institution (see Figure 7.1). For leaders in primary institutions, controversial justice decisions boiled down to political goods. Račan, a pro-justice post-oppositionist who was unable to provide constituents with otherwise unavailable goods as a result of his pro-justice policies, sought to refrain from harsh forms of justice and ultimately pursued a policy of abortive justice. Finally, once brought into the primary institution, Sanader, a former nationalist and opponent of justice, sold General Gotovina to the Hague with the expectation that political goods received in return would convince voters that he had done the right thing. Given the relatively few demands from the Hague during the period analyzed, it is difficult to classify Sanader's position as abortive or sluggish.

In the cases of Poland, Serbia, and Croatia, post-opposition leaders took power following a long period of repression and were confronted with the task of bringing to account their predecessors. The Croatian case stands out in that the post-oppositionists of today were also affiliated with the

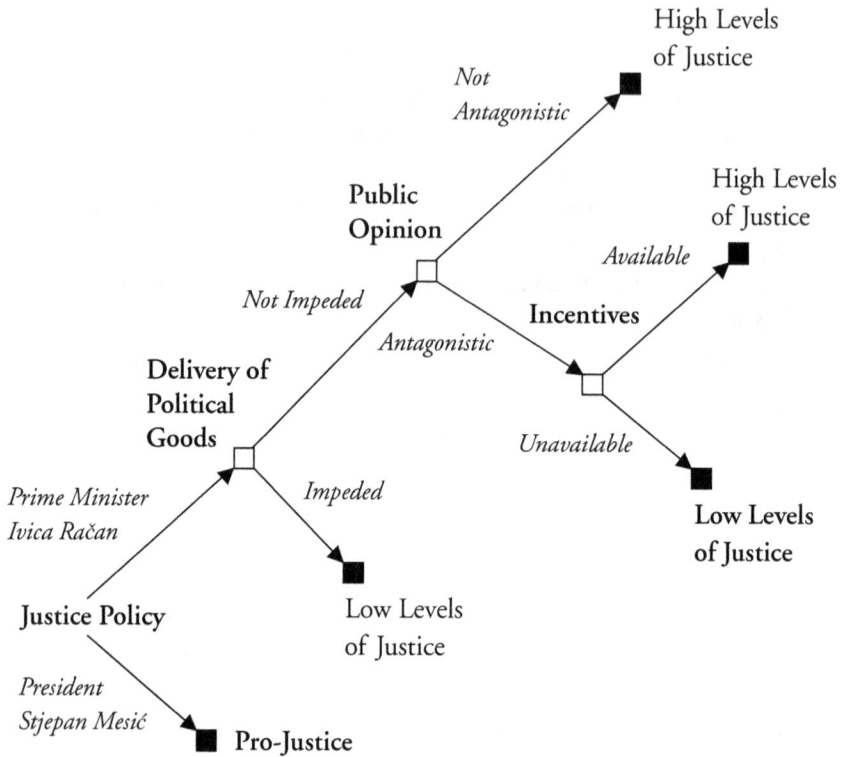

FIGURE 7.1 Justice in Croatia, 2000–2003

repressors from the day before yesterday. As a former League of Yugoslav Communists first secretary, Ivica Račan was not visibly eager to delve into communist-era rights violations, and he was equally afraid to become embroiled in the rights violations of his successors and, now, predecessors. Perhaps the latter is a problem of control. Might Račan have been more willing and politically able to exploit nationalist rights violations if he could ensure that he would emerge from the process unscathed? In the next chapter, I demonstrate how Uzbekistan's authoritarian president has used transitional justice to redefine history in a way that is intended to vindicate both his past and his present use of repression, and thus to ensure for his regime the provision of externally based, otherwise unavailable goods.

8

Uzbekistan

Exploiting Justice Today,
Facing Justice Tomorrow?

Whereas new elites took power in Poland, Serbia, and Croatia, they were incarcerated, exiled, or murdered in Uzbekistan. This was not, however, a foregone conclusion early in the process of transformation. As a Soviet republic, Uzbekistan's communist leadership faced a Moscow-directed process of political liberalization during the *glasnost* period in the second half of the 1980s. By late 1991, when Uzbekistan became independent, the country had a handful of political movements and parties poised to challenge the communists' political hegemony. Among these were Birlik, an intellectual-led movement formed in 1989; Erk, a political party offspring of Birlik, founded in 1990; the Islamic Renaissance Party, a social organization promoting the role of religion in the public sphere; and Adolat, its 1991 political party split-off.[1]

As this narrow picture of late Soviet-era politics suggests, Uzbekistan was fertile ground for multiparty democracy. The most powerful of these groups was probably Birlik, a large social movement numbering perhaps as many as 300,000 that called for a nationalist awakening of Uzbeks.[2] Birlik leaders demanded that the Uzbek language be given official status, that Uzbek soldiers serve Soviet military duty within Uzbekistan, and that the environmentally costly focus on cotton production be ended.[3] Just a year after Birlik held its 1989 founding conference, personality conflicts and strategic disagreements over how to deal best with the ruling communist authorities prompted a group of activists led by Muhammad Salih to create the rival Erk Democratic Party, registered in September 1991.[4] Birlik, registered as a party two months later,[5] and Erk had similar platforms: demanding private land ownership and quick, "shock therapy" market liberalization. They were also both seen as highly nationalistic by the country's large minority of non-Uzbeks.

Uzbekistan's last Communist Party first secretary, and then first elected president, Islam Karimov, abruptly ended this brief flirtation with democracy in late 1991 when, after being accused of rigging the December presidential elections (in which Salih won more than 12 percent of the vote), he began to actively persecute members of the opposition. Within months of Uzbekistan's independence, each of the above organizations and parties had been outlawed, and many of their members were relegated to jail cells or lives in exile. Religious organizations were most aggressively targeted and were nearly obliterated from the political scene.[6] The leaders of Birlik (Abdurahim Pulatov) and Erk (Muhammad Salih) fled the country in January 1992.[7] By 1993 both Birlik and Erk had been formally banned, and political development in Uzbekistan since then has involved the introduction of new government-controlled parties, with vague and practically identical programs.[8] Since that time, Birlik and Erk have been ruled in-country by senior-level party officials, though infighting, combined with government repression, has left Erk split into three wings and has greatly weakened Birlik. Still, those organizations, and two subsequent opposition parties (the Free Peasants Party and the Agrarian Party), found a niche in the repressive political sphere by establishing or closely cooperating with human rights organizations, through which they received foreign support and continued their political activities.[9]

Transitional justice in Uzbekistan has thus been left to the same highly repressive leadership that ruled during the communist period. While relative power arguments do not address transitional justice in cases of failed transition, such as Uzbekistan, I extend the argument logically and assume that, given the persistence of the old regime and the exclusion of those new elites who appeared as challengers only briefly in the late 1980s and early 1990s, we should expect to see virtually no transitional justice in Uzbekistan. This assumption is so commonsensical that the original purpose of this chapter was to evaluate opposition elite attitudes toward justice in the event that they should one day take power, and to focus more in depth on type 1 of the transitional justice spectrum.

Yet President Karimov has taken steps to deal with past rights violations, even as he apparently authorizes present abuses. Strategic considerations are critical to understanding the path of transitional justice in Uzbekistan. As in Serbia and Croatia, foreign demands for particularly costly types of justice have prompted Uzbekistan's political elites to pursue less costly, alternate justice measures. In particular, pressures for the cessation of rights violations carried out by the current regime have prompted a state investigation into rights violations committed under the former one. By framing justice processes in a way that depicts Uzbekistan's communists as victims rather than as oppressors, and creates a symbolic break with the past, Karimov has sought to use "truth" to transform his own image, particularly abroad, and to ensure the supply of externally based goods in the form of Western assistance. Current oppositionists and human rights activists almost universally question Karimov's attack on what they see as the benevolence of the Soviet period, but they differ in their stances toward future justice for the current regime.

In this chapter, I focus first on the types and effects of Western pressure for rights improvements in contemporary Uzbekistan and then examine motivations for Karimov-imposed transitional justice. I conclude with a discussion of excluded opposition attitudes toward transitional justice under Karimov and in a post-Karimov Uzbekistan.

TYPE 1. CESSATION AND CODIFICATION
OF HUMAN RIGHTS VIOLATIONS

For most of its short existence, independent Uzbekistan has been under intense foreign pressure to halt current rights violations. President Karimov is accused of abuses ranging from rigged elections and corruption to religious persecution and the illegal detention and torture of perceived enemies.[10] With domestic opposition held in check, only external forces have the capacity to (potentially) affect Karimov's policies. According to local human rights organization leaders and Western diplomats, the United States (followed by Great Britain and then Germany) has historically been the most active and influential player on Uzbekistan's human rights stage.[11] In this section, I illustrate the strengths and weaknesses of U.S. and other Western attempts to stop rights violations in Uzbekistan, focusing particular attention on the place of human rights in Western foreign policy toward that country.

It is important to note that Uzbekistan, during the first period of warming relations with the United States in 1995, did indicate its new-found respect for human rights by signing onto a range of international treaties. After signing the Convention on the Elimination of All Forms of Discrimination against Women in July 1995, Karimov also endorsed multiple international treaties, including the ICESCR as well as the ICCPR and its two optional protocols, the Convention on the Elimination of Racial Discrimination and the Convention against Torture in one grand motion in September 1995. It is not likely a coincidence that this spate of diplomatic activity occurred just a few months after the trip to Tashkent of U.S. Defense Secretary William Perry, the highest-level American visitor to Uzbekistan in that country's brief period of independence.[12]

Though the United States is credited with being the most aggressive international actor in regard to pressing for rights improvements in Uzbekistan, its own human rights policy is splintered. The State Department's Bureau of Democracy, Human Rights, and Labor (DRL) has historically taken a fairly hard line toward the Tashkent government, pursuing projects that other divisions of the State Department and the U.S. Agency for International Development (USAID) consider too provocative.[13] These have included (at least prior to the 2005 government massacre in the town of Andijon, which marked a sharp deterioration in U.S.-Uzbek relations) supporting opposition parties, funding politically active NGOs, and working with independent media organizations. American officials outside the DRL, who view that unit as a "competing interest," have frequently questioned the wisdom of this small office's aggressive tactics in a country where the United States has security and economic interests: "We can't just write off the region," one said.[14] In justifying the tripling of aid to Uzbekistan after the September 11, 2001, terrorist attacks, U.S. Assistant Secretary of State for European and Eurasian Affairs Elizabeth Jones exemplified mainstream executive branch preferences, proclaiming what Uzbek officials longed to hear: "security should come first."[15]

Despite internal differences, and thanks in part to congressional interest in human rights, visiting American delegations apparently place political liberalization at or near the top of talking points when interacting with their Uzbek counterparts.[16] This emphasis is particularly true during congressional meetings, which the Uzbeks participate in at the highest levels, on either side of the Aral Sea. "They're all talking about human rights. It's pretty unbalanced," one American official commented, adding that Uzbek officials feel compelled to continue meeting with U.S. delegations despite their frustration with the criticism.[17] "We have to continue to feed Congress and they understand that." At the same time, the degree to which both U.S. legislators and officials from the executive branch emphasize human rights has varied over time.[18] A review of State Department press statements concerning Uzbekistan between 1999 and 2004 indicates a shift after September 11, 2001, from human rights to security.[19] An analysis of congressional debates during the same period reveals a comparable trend away from human rights and toward security issues immediately following the attack of September 11, and then back toward human rights by 2003, as the American public's attention turned from the war in Afghanistan to the war in Iraq.[20]

The U.S. influence in Uzbekistan has historically been weakened by several factors. First, as indicated above, the United States does not speak with one voice on human rights. Not only do the executive and legislative branches frequently disagree on priorities, but there are even divisions within the executive. Second, the availability of an alternative assistance provider to Uzbekistan has made it easy for Karimov to play Washington and Moscow off one another in order to attract the most assistance at the least cost (measured in sovereignty).[21] Russia is particularly important for the supply of lethal military equipment. Ironically, Bush administration officials appear to have had the most influence in Uzbekistan immediately after they recruited Karimov into the war on terror. During this period, total U.S. assistance rose from a pre–September 11 average per year of about $40 million[22] to $220 million,[23] and Karimov made a dramatic about-face in his increasingly pro-Russia foreign policy. With $79 million designated for "security and law enforcement" programs (compared to $26 million for "democracy

programs"), U.S. officials saw a "second chance" to transform their relationship based on one-sided criticism into one that was mutually beneficial.[24]
While they may have been less outspoken on human rights issues, they were
investing in DRL-initiated projects to support political opposition and
human rights activists that had been impossible earlier. The tables again
turned as the United States began to steer its attention toward Iraq and away
from Afghanistan in 2003, and aid to Uzbekistan fell to $86 million (still
almost twice the 2001 amount), including $30 million for security and law
enforcement and $15 million for democracy programs.[25] The 2005 mas-
sacre of up to 1,000 civilians in Andijon, as noted earlier, further increased
tensions with the United States, which demanded an independent inquiry
and provided support for relocating refugees from that incident. Soon
afterward, Uzbek authorities evicted the United States from a military base
used in Afghanistan operations. The last American soldiers left Uzbekistan in December 2005.

   In contrast to the United States, the European Union has never put
much foreign policy emphasis on Central Asia. Just weeks after the September 11 attacks, EU officials admitted that they lacked the economic
strength and political will to effect change in the region.[26] European diplomats rarely go to Uzbekistan, and EU economic assistance—especially in
an area that appeals to the Tashkent government, such as security—is very
low. What aid there is tends to be in areas toward which Uzbekistan is relatively ambivalent, such as health care and education.[27] European diplomatic pressure, already limited by a lack of carrots and sticks to enforce demands, is further hampered by differing diplomatic styles and coordination
problems. Great Britain, for example, has frequently and publicly attacked
the Uzbeks,[28] whereas other EU countries have either turned away from
the issue of human rights or taken a more private approach.[29] Even confidential messages of disapproval, delivered in the form of démarches, are
weakened as a result of conflicting national interests and a lack of EU-wide
coordination. As each embassy must check in with its respective capital
and Brussels, the "combined weight" of a joint démarche is offset by the
time it takes to coordinate it.

   This situation has left Westerners unable to push for considerable
change in the human rights sphere. EU diplomats can rarely organize a

Brussels-based response to abuses, much less act with quicker American diplomats in a joint démarche, thus leaving Western actors to appear unresolved.[30] Most diplomats agree that their protests and criticisms tend to produce "unsatisfactory"—and often noncredible—responses from the Uzbeks. In 2002, for example, several European countries delivered a démarche to the Uzbeks over the death of two prisoners in the notorious Jaslik prison. While a United Kingdom pathologist concluded that burns on the bodies were consistent with the victims having been submerged in a bath or other container of boiling water, Uzbek authorities maintained that the injuries were received "in a prison fight involving a kettle."[31]

Under these conditions, progress is usually reserved to those "nonthreatening" areas, such as human trafficking and, before 2005, allowing outsiders to make confidential prison visits, which provide Uzbek officials with a low-cost method of satisfying foreign pressures. Areas of progress have also included the somewhat more risky, but closely controlled, acceptance of human rights and pro-democracy NGOs, which can benefit from "diplomatic cover," or the keen interest of Western embassies.[32] The United States, thanks in large part to the DRL, is the sole provider of assistance to Uzbek opposition and human rights organizations, which makes these groups especially susceptible to the destabilizing effects of resource dependency.[33] Just for tolerating these organizations, often only provisionally, the Uzbek leadership wins kudos. "For not doing very much they get a lot of pats on the back," commented the OSCE human rights officer in Tashkent.[34] Most Western NGOs were forced out following the Andijon massacre, which was linked by the government to nonviolent regime changes in Georgia, Ukraine, and Kyrgyzstan, purportedly masterminded by U.S.-backed NGOs.[35]

Even at its peak, U.S. power was unable to produce more than symbolic justice in Tashkent.[36] While certain prisoner amnesties between 1999 and 2003 appear to have been connected to Western pressure, human rights groups claim that they amounted to nothing more than "hostage politics," where new prisoners are subsequently used as bargaining pieces.[37] Uzbekistan's first (two) criminal trials of human rights abusers in 2002, advertised widely as evidence that the Tashkent government does not tolerate human rights abuses, were not repeated in the years after.[38] While Western pressures have been more effective at creating conditions for a pro–human rights civil society in Uzbekistan, especially by providing activists with greater security and basic organizational necessities,[39] the number of banned organizations outnumbers by several times the few local human rights organizations that have been registered. In addition, though international NGOs were allowed to operate prior to 2005, they faced the constant threat of closure, which put major constraints on their activities.[40]

Despite these shortcomings, foreign diplomats have historically been remarkably generous to the Uzbeks, grabbing at piecemeal signs of change to show that their policies were working. In a press conference marking the release of the State Department's 2003 human rights report, for example, U.S. Ambassador John Herbst pulled together each of Uzbekistan's several highly publicized rights improvements for the year, praising the Uzbeks for a March amnesty of more than 900 Hizbut Takhrir members, the prosecutions of seven authorities involved in torture and murder, and the registration of two human rights organizations.[41] In my interviews with U.S. policymakers, I frequently encountered conciliatory comments, including: "We know, honestly, it's not going to change over night"; and, "There is no basis [for democracy] there, so it is going to take a decade."[42] In a 2000 media roundtable in Uzbekistan, visiting U.S. Ambassador-at-Large for Religious Freedom Robert Seiple engaged in the standard equivocation, putting criticism in the "context of Uzbek reality": "no country has all of the answers, and no country has it absolutely perfect."[43]

Western rationalization of Uzbekistan's poor human rights record is a victory for Uzbek officials who have tirelessly defended themselves as victims of history, struggling to overcome undemocratic habits and structures inherited from the Soviet era. Their officials frequently refer to the "Soviet legacy" in their pleas for understanding from Western states.[44] They admit to lagging behind Western democracies in human rights but argue that "to reach these standards in so short a time is impossible."[45] President Karimov has for years promised the world "step by step" improvements,[46] but he has presented himself as a great reformer up against immense bureaucratic and cultural obstacles to change.[47] In 1999 he apparently decided that transitional justice for the Soviet period might allow him to demonstrate to Westerners his resolve in dealing with rights violations without relaxing his grip on power.

TYPE 4. CREATION OF A TRUTH COMMISSION

According to relative power arguments, Uzbekistan, headed by a former communist leader who never gave up power, should not have had a truth process. Yet in 1999, ten years after communism began to fall across Eastern Europe, Karimov created the Commission for the Promotion of the Memory of Victims.[48] The reason why the president engaged in any form of transitional justice, and how he chose 1999 as the year to do so, is unclear. An analysis of the commission's potential audiences, scope, and outcome suggests that Karimov's truth process was, at least initially, designed primarily to alleviate other Western human rights pressures, rather than to enhance the historical understanding of his fellow countrymen.

In fact, Karimov's truth commission appears to have been domestically irrelevant. Although the government controls the press, a review of Uzbek newspapers printed from 1995 to 2003 revealed no public discussion or demands, even at the behest of the government, concerning justice for Soviet-era crimes.[49] Indeed, "average" Uzbeks and even current opposition and pro–human rights forces appear to be genuinely uninterested in opening the books on Soviet- and tsarist-era rights abuses. In a randomly selected sample of eighteen non-elites from various parts of Tashkent, none of my interviewees recalled human rights violations under communism, and only with significant prodding did they bring up the Stalinist period.[50] Oppositionists similarly tend to argue that there were few, if any, rights violations during the Soviet era, and they are quick to claim that the scale of both political and economic rights violations has increased significantly since 1991. Most had also never heard of this commission. Given the fact that Karimov controls multiple outlets to influence public opinion, ranging from the media to local community committees (*mahallas*), this seems to demonstrate a lack of interest on the part of ruling elites in engaging the public in a discussion of the past.

The commission's peculiar timing, launched eight years after the Soviet Union collapsed, supports the argument that it was designed for a Western audience.[51] First, U.S.-Uzbek relations hit an all-time diplomatic high in 1999. The process of redirecting Uzbek foreign policy from Moscow to Washington began with Defense Secretary Perry's visit in 1995, which Karimov used to publicly condemn "the voices of imperialism in Russia."[52] This attitude developed throughout the late 1990s, when Karimov, in his book *Uzbekistan on the Threshold of the Twenty-first Century,* made thinly veiled references to Moscow as a "chauvinistic threat" and declared his goal "to search for a counterbalance" to Russian influence.[53] A new partnership with America, including formal entry into NATO's Partnership for Peace, encouraged the Uzbeks to withdraw from the Commonwealth of Independent States (CIS) security pact, to reject Russian attempts to strengthen the CIS more broadly, and to blame a Russian presence in Tajikistan for regional instability.[54] A truth commission for the Soviet era, and especially one designed to place blame for past and even present rights violations squarely on the Russians, would institutionalize this apparent foreign policy trend. Its initiation also drew complaints from Russian officials.[55]

Beyond this more general pattern, Uzbek leaders found possible short-term gains from a truth process. The sudden decision to launch the commission followed three months of high-level, public criticism from Western leaders concerning Uzbekistan's harsh crackdown on political and social groups following a spate of February 1999 bombings in Tashkent.[56] A commission of inquiry into past rights violations, coupled with an unusually timed prison amnesty in mid-May, lent support to Karimov's assertion that the government was determined to deal with contemporary rights violations (which, thanks to the truth commission's focus on Russian responsibility, could be shown to be an unfortunate side effect of colonization). Up to 300 people arrested in connection with the 1999 bombings were released in September, when the deputy chair of the government-backed Committee for the Defense of Individual Rights admitted that "many of them had had drugs and weapons planted on them."[57]

This explanation is even more compelling given that both the truth commission and amnesties seemed timed to immediately precede the rare, high-level U.S.-Uzbek Joint Commission meeting in Tashkent. The truth process was announced one week before the meeting. Meanwhile, an intensive three weeks of local reporting on the prison amnesty, including news, editorials, and analyses, ceased only after the Joint Commission's Tashkent meeting had ended, thus providing additional evidence that the amnesty was also geared to influence the United States.[58] At the much-coveted meeting, American officials rewarded the Uzbeks by promising closer cooperation on counterterrorism and narcotics control and by almost doubling the 1999 aid budget to $33 million.[59]

Alternative explanations for why Karimov launched his truth commission when he did are deficient. According to the commission's chair, for example, Karimov was motivated by reports published almost a decade earlier concerning Soviet-era repression of nationalist writers, but secrecy laws and the difficulty in accessing state archives necessitated a long waiting period before conditions were ripe for an investigation.[60] Yet this explanation is difficult to accept in an authoritarian state where the president holds supreme power and essentially rules by decree. One Western scholar suggested that nationalist demands in the early 1990s may have motivated Karimov to take control of the agenda, but this explanation again seems inadequate to account for the timing—nearly a decade later, when the explosion of nationalism characteristic of many post-Soviet states had long since faded away.

While a truth process in a democratic Uzbekistan might have exposed the old regime to opponents' attacks, Karimov's indisputable powers allowed him to launch an investigation of pre-1991 rights violations without the risk of threatening his own or his associates' reputation. In fact, he was able to design the truth commission in a way that would actually transform the history of Uzbek communists from perpetrators of rights violations to victims. He accomplished this outcome by defining the historical scope of the commission, choosing its members and tasks, and guaranteeing himself complete control over the process and output. These efforts also ensured that Uzbekistan's reckoning with its past would be purely symbolic and practically limited.

President Karimov defined the scope of the commission in a way that would simultaneously dissociate him and his colleagues from communist-era rights violations and deepen the rift that he was creating between Tashkent and Moscow. Karimov's commission focused primarily on abuses from the distant past, from the nineteenth century through the eve of World War II.[61] By coupling the Soviet and tsarist eras into one period of political dependence, he implied that the collective fate of those "unfairly convicted during the period of colonialism" was decided by the Russian "other."[62] The commission's analysis of 500 revolts against Russian rule before 1917 and the large-scale Stalinist repression allowed Karimov to depict all Uzbeks as hapless victims of chauvinism and cruelty from the north—which, he pointed out in public statements, remained a threat. Among the rights violations cited were imprisonment, deportation, and execution.

While Karimov's commission vigorously investigated the Stalinist period, it practically denied allegations of wrongdoing from the mid-1950s through the 1970s. The offensive against the Stalinist era was not particularly daring. Revision of the Stalinist past, first broached by Nikita Khrushchev during the Communist Party's 20th Party Congress in 1956, had long lost its taboo status. In 1991 the Tashkent government awarded two nationalist authors, who had been persecuted during the Stalinist period for their anti-Russian/Soviet writings, a state prize for their contributions to modern Uzbek literature and overall national identity.[63]

The commission's findings from the post–World War II period are dismissive and conclude that political repression was limited to "individual cases."[64] Detailed discussion of violations from Karimov's political lifetime was limited to the 1980s, when Leonid Brezhnev had attacked senior Uzbek Communist Party members for artificially inflating cotton production figures and embezzling massive amounts of cotton revenues. The resulting scandal had caused widespread feelings of resentment among Uzbeks, who believed that Moscow's assault was emblematic of deeper Russian injustices. President Karimov's pre-truth commission drive to rehabilitate Sharaf Rashidov, the party leader during the "cotton affair," can be seen as a "correction" of historic wrongs and the conversion of Moscow's criminal into Tashkent's champion of "Uzbek independence and strength against the overwhelming tide of Russian hegemony."[65] Karimov's truth commission transferred historical responsibility for rights abuses from the all-inclusive communists to the Russians.

The president's historic mission was facilitated by his control over the truth commission's membership and activities. Karimov appointed a nationalist, anti-Soviet literary critic, Naim Karimov (no relation to the president), to lead it. In the early 1990s, Naim Karimov had guided a literary resurrection of nationalist authors and had then attacked Soviet ideologists for attempting to destroy national histories of non-Russians in the Soviet Union.[66] Now, Naim Karimov was charged with conducting a highly symbolic investigation, but one that in many ways was pro forma.

President Karimov had essentially declared the commission's findings when he established it, and the commission was given only one month to present a comprehensive picture of Uzbekistan's victims, based on archives spanning almost 150 years. The commission's power was limited to making "suggestions and recommendations on how to perpetuate their memory," which President Karimov and his cabinet of ministers would subsequently consider.[67]

The Uzbek truth commission was President Karimov's launching pad for other forms of transitional justice. While he issued no official condemnation of the communist period, in 2000 he dedicated a memorial to the victims, and in 2001 he declared August 31—the day before Independence Day—the "Day of Remembrance for the Victims of Repression."[68] One year later, President Karimov, apparently seeing the value of promoting his new version of history, opened in Tashkent the Museum of the Victims of Repression, which presented a canned, undisputed version of the truth commission's findings.[69] The museum, like the truth commission, focuses on the period of Stalinism and includes an area devoted to the 1980s cotton affair, as well as one on the overall harmful effects of Soviet agricultural policy.[70]

While Karimov played up symbolism, he avoided more concrete forms of dealing with the past. A sweeping provision for the legal rehabilitation of communist-era victims was ruled out since, in Naim Karimov's words, "there may be people among them who were properly repressed."[71] Upon the commission's recommendation, the president in 1999 did create a victims' fund. Yet the initial budgetary allocation of $20,000 was quickly spent on administration, and, despite a lack of private donors, no state funding has since been provided. As a result, the 300 individuals who requested assistance between 1999 and 2003 were offered nothing more than "the truth" about how their relatives died and general biographical information about the victims in question.[72]

Just as President Karimov has been eager to sell the past as a period of repression against all Uzbeks, he has also hesitated to formally punish past injustices. The commission itself rejected calls by some students to eject the few Stalin-era perpetrators of rights violations who lingered in the bureaucracy, explaining that "they were, in a way, also victims" and had been intimidated into action by their superiors.[73] The commission neither examined individual criminal guilt nor discussed the role of Uzbeks in the persecution of their countrymen, for fear that this could lead to destabilizing vengeful attacks on former persecutors or their living relatives.[74]

OPPOSITION ATTITUDES TOWARD PRE- AND POST-1991 JUSTICE

Few of my elite respondents, made up largely of banned oppositionists and members of human rights organizations, had heard of President Karimov's truth commission. More striking, practically none of them believed that such a commission was justified. In part, this view may be a legacy of widespread complicity in the communist system. One high-level representative of the Agrarian Party and the Committee for the Defense of Human Rights commented that, as a former Communist Party member, "if I looked at the [period of the] Soviet Union, I would have to look at myself."[75] A representative from the Human Rights Society of Uzbekistan's Jizzak city branch, wearing Soviet military ribbons on his jacket, assured me that as a former KGB officer, he was sure that there had been no rights violations in Soviet Uzbekistan.[76]

For the most part, elite-level disinterest in justice for Soviet-era violations stems from the almost ubiquitous perception that while there were almost no abuses before 1991, there have been massive cases of abuse since then. Practically all of my respondents recalled the Soviet period favorably. "The Soviet Union took good care of its peasants. What we see now would never have been seen then," commented a representative of the Free Peasants Party.[77] One oppositionist reacted angrily to the thought of Karimov condemning the Soviet system. "The society and the authorities have no right to make accusations against the Soviet Union, to blacken its political, economic, and social policies," he said. "We do not live one bit better than we did under the Soviet Union. We live much worse."[78] The only one of my respondents who was a political prisoner during the Soviet period said that Brezhnev alone should be held criminally accountable since everyone else (including the prosecutor whom he regularly sees and greets on the street) "was just doing his job."[79]

There is considerably more diversity with respect to how opposition members would deal with the current regime if it were to collapse. Evidence from my interviews suggests that this topic has been broached only informally and may be grounds for future divisions in the already fractured opposition if and when political changes occur. Responses run the full gamut from blanket amnesty to mass criminal prosecution. The one area where there appears to be considerable agreement is that the key human rights violation to reckon with is corruption.[80]

The representative of the Free Peasants Party, which broke away from the opposition Agrarian Party, took the most radical approach, promising to pursue everyone involved in criminal behavior, from the political leadership in Tashkent all the way down to the jail guard in the infamous Jaslik prison.[81] While there is no evidence that the Agrarian Party fractured over this issue, its representative (reportedly working with the Uzbek government) took the extreme opposite position, advocating for amnesties and arguing that harsh justice measures are overly populist. "If it were possible to change the system at its roots, that would be enough for the people," he said. "We have to look ahead."[82] Another prominent human rights leader, similarly rumored to be working with the Uzbek government, was also sympathetic to amnesty, answering, "Let God punish them."[83]

Most human rights activists and other opposition leaders took middle-of-the-road positions but tended to stress a greater need to punish high-level rather than low-level officials, since widespread accusations, as suggested by the public support–based relative power argument, might threaten social stability.[84] Political actors, including the in-country leaderships of the banned Birlik and Erk opposition parties, took understandably vague stances on the issue—a difficult subject to broach at a time when oppositionists may still be considering a range of methods (possibly including amnesty) to encourage governing elites to step down. "We won't say that we will punish them," commented Birlik's in-country leader, but "they will answer to the law."[85] Apparently in conformation to public support–based arguments, Erk's leadership warned that punishment should be postponed since the large number of perpetrators could turn hasty retribution into civil strife.[86] "Many are guilty—finding those who are guilty is not the number-one priority," one Erk representative said.[87] Ironically, the only Erk leader who vowed to focus justice on Karimov and other high officials was the head of a breakaway party branch, widely thought to be government-controlled. "We don't think that everyone should be put in jail. But those in charge should be held responsible," he commented.[88] One regional leader of the Independent Human Rights Organization of Uzbekistan, also an inactive Erk member, shared this view: "One person will be held responsible: Uzbekistan's Milošević."[89]

The question of future justice gives significant insight into how political opposition and human rights leaders view current rights violations. For many respondents, government corruption is the number-one issue in need of reckoning. Often this response was explicit, such as when the in-country leader of Erk promised to focus future criminal investigations on currently corrupt officials. (Of all of the opposition parties, Erk seemed to concentrate most on corruption.)[90] Other times, the focus on corruption was less overt. One independent rights defender at first responded to the question of criminal accountability by saying, yes, "if Karimov stole $10 billion from Uzbekistan, he has to return it"; only subsequently did he add that political murders should also be investigated.[91] A broad range of justice measures was suggested to deal with the corrupt, including a truth process and general forgiveness,[92] broad purges and criminal prosecutions in only the most serious cases of corruption,[93] and criminal liability for all. "Every little bureaucrat should be held responsible," said one rights activist unaffiliated with any political party.[94] A lack of consensus on how to deal with current rights violators, and who qualifies for this label, may prove to be a point of political conflict in a post-Karimov Uzbekistan.

DISCUSSION

The case of Uzbekistan, a failed transition state, indicates a need to reassess commonly accepted assumptions about transitional justice. The current literature largely dictates that it can be pursued only during fundamental regime transformation, as its name implies. The Uzbek case suggests that both new and old elites can pursue transitional justice in ways designed to enhance their own hold on power. Old elites in Uzbekistan clearly did not act consistently with relative power logic as they sought to address communist- and procommunist-era wrongs. With a truth commission that did (if selectively) address a number of very serious rights violations, the Uzbek case is neither a fraud nor an outlier, but follows a pattern similar to other understudied truth commissions in repressive states such as Zimbabwe, Uganda, and Chad.[95]

In Uzbekistan, old elites gave birth to transitional justice as part of a broader effort to quell international demands for more costly forms of justice. These elites opposed complying with Western demands to halt rights violations, since any resulting political competition might threaten their hold on power. Pressuring states were weakened by policy fragmentation, a lack of resources, deficient interstate coordination, and competition in the region from less scrupulous state actors. These flaws may have led Uzbek elites to conclude that their standard defense—the need for change to be gradual and to take into account the roots of the problem—was an effective one. By launching a truth commission, they could recreate history in ways that supported this argument and, simultaneously, demonstrate their desire to deal with the roots of contemporary human rights violations. By addressing Western human rights concerns, President Karimov could continue to attract otherwise unavailable goods.

The case of Uzbekistan, a nondemocracy where President Karimov appears to rule by decree, fits awkwardly into the formal strategic argument posed here. As expected, Karimov apparently pursued a form of justice that would allow him to continue to accrue various forms of material and nonmaterial Western assistance. But who were the secondary actors and what was their influence? Who represents "the public" in a politically closed, post-totalitarian regime, where the incumbent's winning coalition (or that group of supporters necessary to keep him in power) is clearly more narrow than the formal electorate? While lack of transparency in the country makes a wholly satisfactory answer elusive, we can at least theoretically address this question.[96] First, perhaps outside of monarchies or sultanistic regimes, there are few one-person political shows. Rather, every incumbent has a group of supporters whom he or she must buy off using public (in the case of a democracy, where the winning coalition is quite broad) or private (in nondemocracies, where the winning coalition is relatively narrow) goods.[97] Thus, Karimov's actions may appear unilateral, but they likely require a certain degree of consensus from other members of his inner circle. Second, as a result of the inherently weak checks and balances in nondemocracies, secondary actors should play a limited role in the process of justice.

In Uzbekistan, where modern patrimonial networks were already established during the Soviet period, it seems likely that Karimov's current-day winning coalition, at least in large measure, dates back to the communist period.[98] We can assume that these actors would generally be opposed to an investigation into the past that might raise questions of their own culpability. Indeed, this is not so far afield from the Serbian and Croatian cases, where many voters who composed the winning coalitions in these newly democratic states were also guilty of supporting the previous, abusive regime to various degrees. Based on this assumption, Karimov should only have pursued justice if he could buy off these constituents (see top branch of Figure 8.1). An increase in Western assistance, which increased the legitimacy, security, and possibly wealth of the incumbent and his supporters, seems to fit these criteria well. Karimov's secondary actors would be parliamentarians, perhaps also part of his winning coalition, housed in what is in effect a rubber-stamp institution. Given the high costs of defection from a state with small winning coalitions, they should support whatever policy Karimov follows, so long as it does not directly threaten them (see bottom branch of Figure 8.1). The result is as expected: to the degree that it pays off to pursue a policy of justice, Karimov has done so.

From a strategic perspective, perhaps the most surprising aspect of justice in Uzbekistan is that Soviet-era violators were spared harsher measures such as purges and criminal accountability. After all, inasmuch as Karimov thoroughly controlled the process, he could have carefully identified perpetrators who would allow him to show that he was tough on rights violators without taking unnecessary political risks. Perhaps he believed that this might be overkill, and that such a tough line would create the image of an authoritarian leader scanning both the past and present for enemies to destroy. Alternatively, the president may have feared that attacking former rights violators would discourage current functionaries from doing the jobs that he assigned to them. Or perhaps Karimov simply saw little value in going further than he did. The decision to not pursue harsh forms of justice points to a weakness in the strategic argument, which may be better suited to democratic cases.

Karimov's path of justice was largely superficial, apparently widely regarded as unnecessary, and fairly simple. The task facing post-opposition elites who are democratically accountable to voters will be more complex.

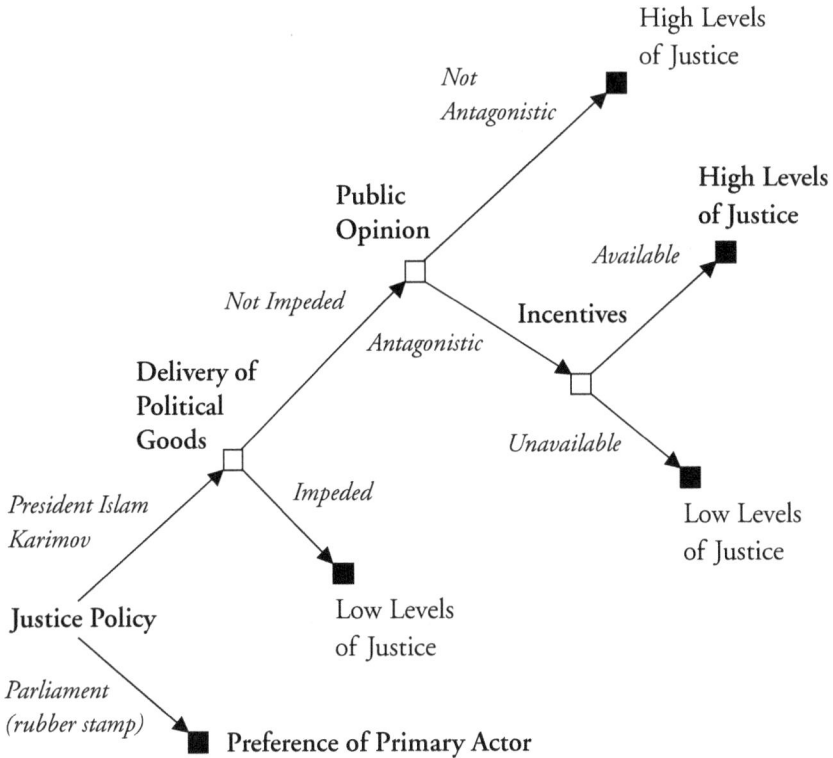

FIGURE 8.1 Justice in Uzbekistan, 1995–2000 (predicted)

As in Serbia and Croatia, future leaders in Uzbekistan will likely disregard violations from the Soviet period. How they deal with post-1991 violations will depend on a number of factors. First and foremost, it will be based on the degree of latitude that post-opposition elites believe they have to pursue harsh forms of justice without endangering their positions. As I have argued throughout this book, this will be a function of social opposition to given justice processes and new elites' ability to provide political goods while pursuing justice. Already, oppositionists seem inclined to focus on the most populist cause: corruption. Even if oppositionists are unsure of what policies to implement for whom, there does seem to be relative agreement that today's corruption will be on tomorrow's agenda.

9

Transitional Justice in
a Cross-National Perspective

Polish demonstrator Joanna Lenartowicz, Bosnian mayor Muhamed Čehajić, and Uzbek human rights activist Shovruk Ruzimuradov lived in three
worlds that at first glance appear to be far removed. These worlds violently
collided when Lenartowicz was fatally beaten (1982), Čehajić was "disappeared" (1992), and Ruzimuradov was tortured to death (2001) by authority of the ruling communist or postcommunist government. Throughout
this book, I have sought to explain how and why new elites (do not) seek to
address yesterday's rights violations. In this chapter, I bring these experiences
together and explore lessons learned. I begin with a cross-national discussion of the determinants of justice and continue by addressing the issue
of lustration, described in chapter 3. I conclude by highlighting what these
various cases tell us about justice in the postcommunist world.

As discussed in chapter 1, the dominant explanation in the literature
concerning how and why elites pursue justice revolves around the relative
power of new and old elites. This explanation can be broken down into
three primary causal arguments. First, according to elite-level, transition-
based arguments, justice should be correlated with the type of regime transition, with revolutions more likely than negotiated power transfers to produce aggressive forms of justice. Second, while transition-based arguments
are focused on political power distribution in the new system, as well as
formal and informal deals made during the power changeover, structure-

based arguments are more concerned with the distribution of power in key ministries connected with previous rights violations, such as the military and police. The less culpable these actors were in previous abuses, the more room there should be for new elites to pursue justice. And third, society-level, public support–based arguments maintain that the primary obstacle to justice should be the culpability and attitudes of various strata of the citizenry.

Each of these arguments, but especially the first two, carries a similar logic: new elites are constrained by the risk of a violent backlash to justice measures deemed overly aggressive. The consequences, whether a coup or civil strife, should persuade those new elites lacking all-out power to tread carefully. These arguments are primarily backward-looking, focused on constraints that arise from a country's history and centered on the assumption that new elites are unable to affect these variables or gain politically from pursuing justice. By contrast, the strategic approach advocated in this book envisions justice less as a wholly unique policy sphere than as a part of a broader set of interrelated political challenges. After all, among the numerous opportunity costs of pursuing criminal justice for past rights abusers might be less legislative time dedicated to agricultural reform, fewer prosecutors available to go after today's cases of corruption, and a smaller amount of funds to invest in education. Political elites must take into consideration their constituents' various daily concerns as they decide how to address yesterday's abuses.

Since relative power arguments are designed to identify what should not occur rather than what should, evidence for or against the arguments laid out here must come from the process, in addition to the outcome, of justice. In the next section, I briefly highlight the trends with regard to each of the seven types of justice across the four countries.

TYPE 1. CESSATION AND CODIFICATION OF HUMAN RIGHTS VIOLATIONS

In all of the democratic countries studied, regime change led to the immediate signing and/or ratification of major human rights agreements. In Poland, the government moved quickly to ratify the Convention against

Torture immediately after the 1989 elections and within a year had signed onto the ICCPR's first optional protocol and Convention on Rights of the Child. In Serbia, just three months after taking power, Prime Minister Đinđić had signed the ICCPR, the ICESCR, and the three Conventions against Torture, Genocide, and Racial Discrimination. In Croatia, this phenomenon occurred with the first regime change, when the country attained independence; though President Tuđman signed onto the same agreements that Serbia would nearly a decade later, he clearly violated them. There was no need or precedent for the new government under Prime Minister Račan to sign these agreements again. It is clear that in each of these cases, new regimes moved quickly to establish their strong commitment to human rights. This is a relatively cost-free form of justice that indicates a new way forward without directly harming those who were involved in past abuses or necessarily obliging the state to adopt a process that could be seen by constituents as costly and time-consuming. Unfortunately, it is also clear from the Croatia case that these commitments are not always kept.

The Uzbekistan case further underscores the difficulties in trying to force non-democratic states to stop rights violations and end impunity for rights violators. President Karimov, after signing the Convention on the Elimination of All Forms of Discrimination against Women in July 1995, signed several international treaties, including the ICESCR, the ICCPR and its two optional protocols, the Convention on the Elimination of Racial Discrimination, and the Convention against Torture, in one grand gesture in September 1995. Yet it is clear that the ruling regime, still accused by international monitors of being among the "worst of the worst," has paid little heed to these documents.

TYPE 2. REBUKE OF THE OLD SYSTEM

In each of the democratic cases examined, it appears that rebukes of the former system took place gradually as a result of elite perceptions that the voting public was either unsupportive or uninterested. Furthermore, it is clear that institutional positions had a bearing on the decision either to apologize or to condemn past abuses. In Poland, senators took the lead, eventually passing a broad condemnation of the communist period nearly a decade after communism collapsed and in a time of sustained economic growth. Prior to that, more specific condemnations were gradually passed by both the Sejm and the Senat, but these were moderated to ensure that the many voters who somehow took part in, or missed, the former system (and the better economic conditions that came with it) would not be turned off.

In both Serbia and Croatia, apologies for past abuses were also characterized by political risk and tended to be pursued by secondary actors rather than primary ones. In both of these countries, my interviewees frequently dismissed apologies, characterizing those made as political stunts designed to appeal to the West, and those omitted as a consequence of the low practicality of such a measure. In each case, observers understood political risk as voter consternation rather than confrontation with members of the old regime. Leaders feared a decline in political popularity rather than a societal schism. Without the promise of goods in return, primary actors tended to see the policy of unpopular apologies as too costly. In Uzbekistan, President Karimov waited nearly a decade after the fall of the Soviet Union to open his Museum of the Victims of Repression, which was less a rebuke of the former system than it was of the Russian colonizers.

TYPE 3. REHABILITATION AND COMPENSATION FOR VICTIMS

Rehabilitation of and, especially, compensation for victims from the previous regime have proven to be very sensitive issues in postcommunist countries. While there is no evidence that new elites feared members of the old regime who were still in power, they clearly worried about the consequences of their actions. Most important, Polish and Serbian leaders from the former democratic opposition feared public consternation at the high economic cost of reparations. This tendency was much stronger in primary institutions in Poland, where post-Solidarity elites in the Sejm fought off more extensive rehabilitation and compensation laws proposed by their Senat colleagues, largely out of budgetary concerns but perhaps also partly for fear that more aggressive measures would cause them to lose postcommunist support for other programs moving through Parliament. A similar situation occurred in Serbia, where post-oppositionists cringed at the high costs of compensation, which they thought would be unavoidable should a re-habilitation process go forward.

An interesting phenomenon took place in the former Yugoslavia, where this book's interviewees warned that the overlap between victims and abusers over time makes rehabilitation and compensation particularly diffi-cult. In both cases, some former politically repressed persons from the com-munist era themselves appeared in the immediate postcommunist period as repressors and were accused of brutal acts of ethnic cleansing and genocide. Furthermore, elites perceived that most citizens recall the communist period as one of relative tranquility and liberalism. Rehabilitation and compensa-tion thus bore potentially high political costs as a result of monetary, but also ethical, concerns. Some of these concerns were apparently mirrored in Uzbekistan, where questions emerged about whether victims indeed were deserving, and the nominally new regime proved unwilling to make more than a symbolic financial contribution to compensate them. Just as demo-cratically elected elites in Poland, Serbia, and Croatia shied away from des-ignating public funds for victims, Uzbekistan's non-democratic regime seems to have been unwilling to redistribute funds that are, in effect, treated as pri-vate goods outside of its small winning coalition.

TYPE 4. CREATION OF A TRUTH COMMISSION

At first glance, the case of truth commissions in each of these countries is quite surprising. In Poland, the fact that post-Solidarity parliamentarians went about creating such a commission so quickly, and that the commis-sion was cast as the first step in criminal justice for recent rights abuses, appears to contradict relative power arguments that predict more moder-ate forms of reckoning. Also remarkable is the appearance of unity in the post-Solidarity movement concerning this measure, as well as postcommu-nists' acceptance of the investigations. In the former Yugoslavia, both truth commissions were launched by post-oppositionists who sought to use them as shields to deflect strong external pressures for harsher, and more domes-tically unpopular, forms of justice. Similarly, in Uzbekistan, Karimov's truth commission was apparently designed to satisfy Western critics without em-barrassing the president himself or members of his inner circle. In all four cases, even where truth commissions were weak, guided by cynical motivations, and largely conducted outside of the public spotlight, the very appearance of these commissions potentially created new space for reflecting on past abuses. Moreover, given the broad definitions of truth commissions currently employed (see chapter 2), these all qualify, as well as testify to the great variety of shapes that these commissions can assume.

There was little opposition from the general public to any of them. In Serbia, Croatia, and Uzbekistan, this may be a function of each commission's relative obscurity. In the former cases, public opposition did emerge from human rights organizations and some post-opposition politicians, but these critics gradually reached a consensus that even a weak truth commission orchestrated by a nationalist was better than none. In the latter case, the ruling regime's strong hand over public debate would also hamper any criticism that might have arisen, but interviewees' responses suggest that the commission escaped the attention of even those most focused on rights abuses. In Poland, those who should have been most opposed to an investigation (postcommunist politicians, many of whom had been in power during the period of abuse) actually took part in the formulation and execution of the commission. The general public, according to interviewees, was neither strongly opposed nor particularly attentive.

While relative power arguments do not exclude such a commission in any of the democratic cases, Uzbekistan's efforts to dig into the past were quite unexpected. Moreover, the sorts of investigations that emerged in the other countries do not appear to follow from relative power explanations. The Polish case was far more aggressive, and the Croatian case less so, than transition-based or structure-based arguments would suggest. The Yugoslav truth commission, while perhaps meeting rigid criteria of moderate justice, was, like Croatia's, clearly inspired to carry out a function not foreseen in relative power arguments and, ultimately, was likely to be beneficial for former abusers.

In each of the democratic cases, concerns about voter perceptions were critical, but each process was elite-led with practically no societal input. Elites made their decisions based on their own calculations of how these measures would be perceived by voters in the broader policy debate. In Uzbekistan, Serbia, and Croatia, the calculations were relatively clear-cut, with commissions meant to serve as low-profile justice initiatives in return for high-profile Western support. In Poland, the calculus became clearer with time. While Jan Rokita, head of Poland's truth commission, declared that he would launch a new, stronger one following the 1991 elections, this lack of public interest, coupled with an overwhelming societal focus on the country's poor economic situation, left his promise unfulfilled despite the political domination of post-Solidarity elites from 1991 to 1993.

TYPE 5. PURGING OF HUMAN RIGHTS ABUSERS FROM PUBLIC POSITIONS

Regarding the first form of "harsh" justice, transition-based arguments suggest that only Croatia's new elites should have been free to conduct administrative purges, whereas Polish and Serbian leaders should have been limited by the negotiated nature of power transfer. According to structure-based arguments, none of these cases should have undergone purges. In fact, Croatia did the least, and Poland, followed by Serbia, did the most investigating of individuals. In Poland, administrative cleansings were initiated fairly early and involved extensive, if shallow, investigations of public servants in important security and justice positions. Shortcomings were largely a product of limited evidence, though the result has been a frequent return to this measure and its close associate, lustration. It is notable that those secondary actors in Serbia who came to power through revolution and who subsequently controlled the military were considerably less aggressive in their investigations than the primary actors who emerged after a negotiated transition and were responsible for the police. (As noted in chapter 6, both the police and military were accused of rights abuses.) Neither the nature of the transition nor the structure-based considerations seem to explain the decision to (not) pursue this form of justice.

While there were a variety of political considerations at work, the strength of old elites apparently had relatively little impact on policy choice. What mattered more was the public's perception. In Poland, post-Solidarity elites used vague language in Parliament to ensure that administrative justice was palatable to postcommunist officials whose support they needed in order to pass other reforms awaited by their constituents. In both Serbia and Croatia, leaders seemed to fear the public's reaction to extensive purges of those individuals who were popularly viewed as innocent. In Croatia, the most aggressive dealings occurred with respect to generals who opposed Hague extraditions, and they were carried out by a secondary actor with greater degrees of institutional security than the primary actor, who blamed a lack of evidence for his relatively lax approach to former functionaries. In Serbia, while secondary actors gently nudged senior generals out of the military, primary actors moved much more forcefully to push out leaders of the police, who were largely accused of corruption and basic rule-of-law violations. The Serbian process was notable for its failure to investigate lower-ranking police officials who may have been involved in wartime atrocities but were perceived to enjoy greater levels of public support.

TYPE 6. CRIMINAL PROSECUTION OF "EXECUTORS"

In Poland, there was little differentiation between higher-level political leaders and lower-level functionaries with regard to prosecutions; both were simultaneously targeted in the initial 1989 investigation and faced criminal trials for more than fifteen years afterward. While criminal investigations began quickly, and the scope and mechanisms for these investigations were gradually expanded throughout the 1990s, criminal accountability in Poland was weakened by several factors. These included lack of evidence and the generally poor state of the judiciary. Apart from the 1989 investigation, which in contrast to relative power arguments involved an aggressive move to deal with former abusers, criminal justice in Poland was characterized by institutional divisions. In the early 1990s, as the Warsaw government struggled to put its new economic system in order, members of the Sejm sought to weaken any criminal justice initiatives proposed by their colleagues in the Senat. Only during a period of sustained economic growth did politically powerful post-Solidarity elites move to create an institution with sweeping powers to pursue past violators.

In contrast to Poland, post-oppositionists launched domestic criminal trials in Serbia and Croatia largely in an effort to avoid the even less domestically popular option of transfers to the Hague. In both cases, local elites sought to use local trials (as with the truth commissions) to demonstrate to foreign pressure groups that they had both the will and capabilities to pursue justice without external intervention. These trials were rare and characterized by numerous problems, ranging from the technical (such as ineffective witness protection) to the political (such as questions concerning the low number of indictments and the fairness of rulings). In Croatia, they occurred in far lower numbers, and in Serbia in greater numbers, than what we might expect from transition-based arguments. In both countries, we find them more often than we should expect from structure-based or public support–based arguments. The reason they occurred at all seems to be thanks to foreign pressure, which, in turn, is connected to particular goods that elites calculated they must provide their voters.

In Uzbekistan, the nominally new elites never pursued criminal trials for past violations. However, under intense Western pressure, and in return for considerable material and nonmaterial rewards, they did launch trials for a token few present-day rights abusers.

TYPE 7. CRIMINAL PERSECUTION OF COMMANDERS

In Poland, as noted above, criminal trials for lower-level and higher-level abusers were carried out in similar fashion. In both cases, elites were wary of pursuing aggressive forms of justice that could be seen by their constituents as a waste of resources during a period when resources were thin. Only when the country's economy picked up and post-Solidarity parties made an electoral comeback, putting them in power for the first time in four years, did they pursue policies that many of them had championed earlier.

In the cases of Serbia and Croatia, domestic trials for lower-level abusers were primarily supplanted with transfers to the ICTY for those higher-level indictees. As in the case of criminal trials for lower-level officials, transfers from Croatia were fewer than might be expected based on transition-based arguments (particularly given the low number of domestic trials), while in Serbia the number of transfers was far higher than transition-, structure -, and public support–based arguments would predict. Again, international pressures were critical to justice decisions in both states. While political elites sought to avoid the appearance that they were being pushed into cooperation, they simultaneously struggled to demonstrate to their publics that without cooperation, their countries would suffer in very practical ways. Leaders hoped to show that the unpopular policies they pursued gave them additional capabilities that would benefit their citizens.

In Uzbekistan there have been no criminal trials for those responsible for ordering abuses under the current or former regime. Again, this is not a surprise, given the prevalence of these actors in the new regime.

LUSTRATION

While my justice spectrum explicitly excluded lustration (for reasons explained in chapter 3), it is important to understand how the various arguments posited here might have affected lustration policies in the region. Of the cases evaluated, and mirroring regional tendencies, the most extensive debate on this topic took place in Poland. Serbia also debated and passed a lustration measure, which was never seriously considered in Croatia or Uzbekistan.

Talk of lustration and decommunization in Poland began in earnest during the 1990 presidential campaign when Solidarity leader Lech Wałęsa advocated punishing former communists and secret service collaborators as part of an effort to differentiate himself from then Prime Minister Tadeusz Mazowiecki.[1] While Wałęsa's tone became more muted upon winning office, several right and center-right post-Solidarity parties, which had in part "built their identities around criticizing communists,"[2] kept lustration on the agenda after entering Parliament in late 1991.[3] Opinion polls taken at the time indicated that public support for lustration was on an upward trajectory, climbing from 38 percent in 1991 to 64 percent in early 1992.[4] During this period, post-Solidarity activist Jan Olszewski became prime minister, despite Wałęsa's opposition, and promised to build a government of "moral authorities."[5]

Olszewski's internal affairs minister, Antoni Macierewicz, promised quickly after the 1991 elections that once legislation was in place, he would be prepared to release the names of past secret service collaborators.[6] Despite

Parliament's failure to pass a broad lustration law, the Olszewski government used a May 1992 Sejm resolution requiring the publication of information about senior public officials to issue a list of former collaborators.[7] On June 4 the sixty-four-person "Macierewicz List," which included Poland's symbol of freedom, Lech Wałęsa, was delivered to Parliament. The list was based exclusively on evidence found in the secret police archives, but actual details of collaboration were missing and those persons named had no way to defend themselves.[8] Publication of the list led to the immediate fall of the Olszewski government, after which the Constitutional Court declared the Sejm resolution unconstitutional.[9] When a new post-Solidarity government formed under Hanna Suchocka, the Sejm began to debate six lustration proposals, two of which Sejm committees determined should be examined in more detail.[10] But as the economic crisis deepened, the bills fell off the parliamentary agenda.[11]

The 1993 electoral victory of postcommunists once again brought to the fore the question of lustration. While some political elites saw the elections as evidence of society's distaste for digging into the past,[12] for others the rise of the left only reinforced old divisions and symbolized a danger to the new, democratic Poland.[13] Post-Solidarity elites began to rely on identity politics, rather than on interest politics.[14] Eight lustration projects were initiated, but these became lost in committee until two events midway through Parliament's four-year term: the victory of a postcommunist, Aleksander Kwaśniewski, in the 1995 presidential elections; and the fall of the government of another postcommunist, Józef Oleksy, under charges of collaboration with the KGB.[15] The postcommunists had both a cause (dealing with the Oleksy public relations fiasco) and a way to steer the course of lustration.

Kwaśniewski's answer to the lustration debate was a "Commission of Public Confidence," which, those in the anti-communist bloc argued, was too weak.[16] Instead, three centrist parties (Labor Union, Freedom Union, and the SLD-allied Polish Peasants Party) pushed through Parliament a "civilized lustration" designed to increase openness in political life while promising a process that would be carried out by the judiciary and not in the political sphere.[17] The compromise bill mandated that individuals serving in certain public offices provide a written declaration indicating whether or not they had collaborated with the secret services. Unlike the infamous Czech law, collaboration itself did not entail punishment; only those filing false declarations would be banned from taking certain public offices for a period of ten years.[18]

While practically all SLD parliamentarians voted against the law, it was passed and signed by President Kwaśniewski in June 1997 and largely upheld by the Constitutional Court.[19] Still, the Polish law became unworkable because not enough judges were willing to serve on the lustration court, thus resulting in a 1998 amendment that transferred lustration duties to the Warsaw District Appeals Court.[20] A total of 23,000 public employees filed statements—only 130 of whom admitted collaboration (their names were subsequently made public)—before the judges' first decisions began to trickle down in late 1999.[21] After that period, lustration was run by the state Public Interest Spokesperson (Rzecznik Interesu Publicznego).

While the left was successful in limiting the legal powers of the Institute of National Remembrance (IPN) to conduct lustration in the 1998 law, the political right's discontent with the slow pace and minor repercussions mandated by the 1997 law ultimately led to yet another law in 2006, after center-right parties again regained political power. This law gave the IPN new powers, which now covered not only political positions from local councilor up to president, but also board members of majority state-owned companies, all academics, members of the legal community, and journalists of both the public and private media.[22] In total, the law (which again punished liars but not collaborators) covered an estimated 700,000 people and was to be administered by the IPN. It was criticized for, among other things, subjecting individuals to self-incrimination, introducing retroactive justice, and extending state power into the private sphere. In mid-2007, just days before the law was to take effect, the Constitutional Court rejected it largely on these grounds.[23]

Opposition to lustration was based chiefly on the arguments discussed in chapter 3. One communist-era human rights activist, who continued her efforts following the transition, objected to early and subsequent lustration legislation based on the supposed inaccuracy of archival evidence.[24] Another leading intellectual behind the Solidarity movement, Bronisław Geremek, believed that it would impinge on defendants' rights.[25] Others questioned the general purpose of lustration. The internal affairs minister responsible for restructuring the secret police scoffed at these bills, noting that undercover collaborators were not the equivalent of murderers. "What do we really want?" he asked.[26] Another post-oppositionist thought already in the early 1990s that "while criminal accountability would have to be carried out in the future, with respect to lustration there was nothing to deal with. The system had changed."[27]

Yet even in the first years of Polish democracy, lustration appears to have been a largely behind-the-scenes force in the broader justice debate. For some, lustration, which would encompass far more associates of the old regime than would criminal prosecutions, seemed to function as a bargaining piece to ensure that other transitional justice legislation was passed. With reference to one sample piece of legislation, a parliamentarian from the time recalled: "They knew there would be new elections and that they would lose. It was clear that they would lose and that blocking the combatant law could end in a lustration law."[28] In fact, however, early supporters of lustration (including drafters of the 1991 and 1992 bills) recognized that they had little support even within their own party.[29] Thus, as one drafter acknowledged, for most political leaders charged with a massive restructuring, lustration was ultimately relegated to the back burner: "This was not the most important thing."[30]

Following a negotiated transition, and in a country where many were forced or enticed into collaborating with the security services, post-Solidarity elites should have avoided lustration. In fact, this is precisely what happened early on. But the actual process by which it occurred does not follow from the applicable relative power arguments. Post-Solidarity elites did not hide from lustration for fear of upsetting members of the former regime who had led the transition, nor were they afraid of communist-era power structures, which they investigated directly. Lustration was also not linked directly to public support and to the risk of dividing society, since if it were, we should not have expected to see a return to lustration throughout the 1990s and especially in the highly encompassing form taken in 2006. Lustration measures were rarely populist. In fact, the Solidarity Electoral Action (AWS) coalition's policy of lustration and criminal prosecutions was largely held out of public view during the 1997 elections, when the party program included only "one insignificant sentence" about dealing with the past, despite the fact that a full-blown policy had already been developed.[31] It is of little surprise, given the strategic argument, that lustration was largely off the table during the early period of economic reform, only to return as voters' lives became gradually easier. The most aggressive form of lustration was launched seventeen years after the fall of communism and one year after Poland joined the European Union.

Unlike in Poland, where lustration has always been a national issue, the first lustration bill in Serbia and Montenegro was actually passed by the regional parliament of Vojvodina, which called in early 2003 for an employment ban for a period of up to five years for all its members and public functionaries "who violated human rights and . . . abused their own positions."[32] Lustration was brought to the national stage a few months later by the Civic Alliance of Serbia (GSS) as well as by the DS, perhaps in part motivated by a March 2003 appeal by a group of fifty intellectuals from various NGOs, who were calling the presence of former functionaries "extremely dangerous for the future of the state and for the democratic and reformist changes within it."[33] The GSS demanded a lustration law that would bring "truth to the social and political spheres" by instituting five-year employment bans for various state functionaries found to have been involved in rights violations based on information from former security service archives.[34]

Critics of the law, which was passed in May 2003, noted that the archives were incomplete and even stacked with mistruths, and early indications suggested that lustration's application would be arbitrary.[35] Some even questioned the need for lustration. While justice officials declared court cleansings necessary, for example, leaders of legal associations reckoned that individual lawsuits would be sufficient to deal with the 2 percent or so of judges who may have been guilty of rule-of-law transgressions.[36] Moreover, the presidents of the Constitutional Court and the Supreme Court both rejected lustration as unconstitutional.[37] And, following the bill's passage, the Serbian Radical Party (SRS, led by indicted war criminal Vojislav Šešelj, promised to appeal the law to the Constitutional Court since it "ruthlessly violates basic human rights and freedoms."[38] They were joined in opposition by some members of the DSS and other unlikely bedfellows, including the Fund for the Development of Democracy, who publicly agreed that the law left its targets unprotected.[39]

As in Poland, lustration in Serbia was difficult to carry out and in many ways appears to have been a hollow gesture. For starters, it proved difficult to fill the lustration commission's nine seats.[40] Moreover, the law depended on the opening up of secret personnel files and thus piggybacked on a 2001 decree that did just that. But while 350 people (out of nearly 2,000 applicants) eventually managed to see their own records, by 2003 the Constitutional Court overturned that decree, well before the commission could begin its work.[41] While the Christian Democratic Party of Serbia promised to put forward a bill in the fall of 2003 that would resolve this issue,[42] post-oppositionist losses at the polls at that time made this unfeasible. After gaining ground in the parliamentary elections, Serbian Radical Party members proposed an emergency two-article bill that would annul lustration from the day after its formal publication in the Official Gazette.[43] While the bill did not pass, one GSS parliamentarian commented that "obviously there lacks the political and social will for the 'soft' lustration that this law envisions," and that with the lustration commission still unformed nine months after the bill's passage, "it doesn't matter when it will formally be withdrawn from our legal system."[44]

Relative power arguments shed little light on the decision to go forward with lustration. From a transition-based and structure-based perspective, Serbia's new elites should have been too weak to seriously raise the issue. From a public support perspective, the similar levels of public approval and disapproval are notable; according to a public opinion poll, Serbian society was split, with 38 percent saying that the new law would lead to positive changes, and 36 percent arguing that it would lead to injustices.[45] While lustration was something that many Serbian post-oppositionists (particularly from the DS and GSS) wanted, they could not afford to be seen as preoccupied with it. As the Constitutional Court struck down the decree on secret police files, the DS-led government, still struggling to deliver essential goods and services, decided to back off. "We were coping with too many problems in too short a period," noted one of Đinđić's deputies.[46] As in Poland, the lustration measure was pushed through in Serbia only after the immediate post-transition economic crisis had somewhat abated.

An alternative and more cynical interpretation is that levels of culpability were so high among elites—and not just among the general population—that post-oppositionists undertook lustration knowing that it was doomed from the start. As another former deputy to Đinđić said, "99 percent of public officials in Serbia have broken the rule of law in the past."[47] Just as Serbia's failed lustration policy may indicate a high degree of elite-level culpability in the former regime, the same logic may explain why lustration has failed to materialize in Croatia. For some observers, the lack of lustration in Croatia is a natural result of the country's confused political scene, where communists and nationalists often shared elements of political opportunism that left few available to judge. "There is an enormous number of spoiled biographies, an incestuous relationship between right and left," one independent parliamentarian commented.[48] Thus, while a period of bitter debate on lustration appeared briefly as the communist regime collapsed in the early 1990s, Tuđman chose not to divide Croats based on their previous political affiliations but to reconcile them in ways that would strengthen his nationalist government.[49] Since 2000, there has been very little talk of lustration outside of far-right parties, which have never been able to bring up such a bill for formal debate.[50]

Not surprisingly, there has been no discussion of lustration in Uzbekistan. According to one exiled leader of the opposition party Birlik, while such a policy might have been on the agenda if the opposition had taken power in 1991, high levels of culpability in the current regime mean that the time for lustration has come and gone.[51] Still, the lessons from Poland and Serbia suggest that this line of thinking may play only a minor role in the debate, should today's oppositionists ever take power.

THE ROLE OF SECONDARY ACTORS

In each of the cases discussed, secondary actors strived to impact the justice decisions made by primary actors who sat in positions of relative power. Across cases, we have seen how these secondary actors used formal measures and public statements to put pressure on their colleagues or opponents, which had policy consequences. In Poland, after post-Solidarity members of the Sejm turned from aggressive justice to economic reform, post-Solidarity members of the Senat ensured that various justice measures, from rehabilitation and compensation to criminal prosecutions, remained on the agenda. While Sejm members were able to dilute the scope of these initiatives, they lacked the political will to remove them entirely. The result was a transition from early expedited justice to later aborted justice.

In Serbia and Croatia, secondary actors seemed to have a similar impact, at least initially. In the former, President Koštunica's anti-Hague displays raised the political costs of Hague transfers for Prime Minister Đinđić, resulting in a sluggish policy of ICTY cooperation. In the latter, President Mesić's avid support of Hague cooperation increased pressure on Prime Minister Račan to make unpopular and potentially politically destabilizing transfers, resulting in an abortive policy. Yet, when anti-Hague actors entered primary institutions and adjusted their preferences accordingly, secondary actors did not always have the expected impact. For instance, Serbia's Prime Minister Koštunica continued to pursue a policy of sluggish cooperation with the Hague, despite the fact that secondary actors in the federal- and republic-level presidencies publicly encouraged greater cooperation. While this might be a result of the potentially high costs to his reputation that Koštunica would incur for aggressively changing his justice policies, Croatia's Prime Minister Sanader apparently had few problems transitioning from General Gotovina's protector to his hunter (pursuing, along with supportive secondary actors, a policy of aggressive justice). Perhaps Koštunica's actions were in part a result of personal preferences. Thus, while institutional constraints performed as expected across these cases, the interinstitutional exchange did not lead to the expected results in Serbia.

In Uzbekistan, the impact of secondary actors—and the very definition of these actors—is more difficult to analyze. From a theoretical perspective, Uzbekistan's secondary actors should include members of the old regime who continue to oppose justice. President Karimov's truth commission initiative, designed to attract foreign aid, should be reined in to ensure that it does not pose a threat to those persons in his small winning coalition. If these people function as secondary actors, then we should expect to see a somewhat limited form of justice, just as we found.

OVERVIEW: THE ROLE OF SOCIETY IN TOP-DOWN JUSTICE

The democratic cases here highlight the role of society in transitional justice. While justice in each case was top-down, elites kept one eye on the likely reaction of their constituents. Their fear was less the relative power argument that societal groups would take to the streets to protest their decisions, pitting various social actors against one another, than that their constituents would question elites' preoccupation with a system that many supported and even associated with, albeit to varying degrees. Vaclav Havel painted this image colorfully, demonstrating how the greengrocer may have inadvertently strengthened the communist system by unceremoniously posting Communist Party slogans in his shop window.[52] After the fall of communism, Serb and Croat nationalists voted in droves for Milošević and Tuđman, who set them firmly on the warpath. My numerous Serbian interviewees commented wryly that the majority of Serbs did not blame Milošević for the bloody 1990s wars, merely for losing them. In these cases, most non-elites were, at best, unwitting supporters of the former regime, and, at worst, accomplices. As a result, new elites taking power in Poland, Serbia, and Croatia could not, for instance, easily condemn or apologize for the former system due to a high level of societal collusion.[53]

Societal complicity, either de facto or deliberate, thus prompted new elites to hesitate before adopting even relatively lenient forms of justice. In Poland, post-Solidarity elites were humbled by public perceptions that the communist system had, at least relative to the new regime, done a fairly good job of providing basic necessities. In Croatia and Serbia, post-oppositionists have had to grapple with years of public vilification by the old regime that left new elites distrusted in many circles and feeling exposed. Many observers thought that Račan's fear of extraditing national heroes was a result of his perceived need to prove his "Croatian credentials" in a still nationalist state, especially given his high-level position in the communist Yugoslavia.[54] As one presidential advisor commented, "They were afraid more than anything else that someone would call them communists again. They were afraid of their own past."[55] In both Croatia and Serbia, pro-justice forces claimed that it would be far easier for a known nationalist such as Koštunica or Sanader to cooperate with the ICTY than for someone with a more dubious "national" record. Several respondents likened this to the U.S. rapprochement with Communist China under Richard Nixon; while a hardcore anticommunist American president could get away with such a move, a less vocal anticommunist, such as Jimmy Carter, might undergo greater public scrutiny.

This phenomenon is not limited to the immediate or short term. Pro-justice elites in my three democratic cases frequently expressed a desire to enact certain measures that either have not been put into place or were poorly implemented, but they were stymied by fears of stepping on too many toes—whether those of voters or of fellow post-oppositionists, who at one point or another were somehow connected to the former regime or to its policies. The human rights literature highlights how targeted repression (rather than repression applied universally across society) is useful in maintaining a group of citizens with a stake in the system. It also creates intrasocietal divisions with respect to understandings of past violations and a desire for justice after that system falls.

At the end of the day, few post-opposition elites in Poland, Serbia, or Croatia were willing to risk upsetting their populaces by condemning the system in which they had grown up and participated. In Uzbekistan, a highly public process of condemning the past might also raise eyebrows of those elites and non-elites who miss the relatively greater economic and even political liberties that they enjoyed under communism. This may help to explain why Karimov's truth process was largely kept out of the spotlight. This factor also reinforces the underlying assumption of my justice spectrum, that harsher measures are more risky. If the masses were more interested in attacking the former regime (than, for example, focusing on economic welfare), we should expect harsh measures to be beneficial for new elites. Evidence from formal and informal discussions with non-elites supports my assumption that such conditions are the exception rather than the rule.[56]

Societal perceptions, often shared by post-oppositionists, also encouraged new elites in Serbia and Croatia to leave victims from the communist era legally and financially estranged. New elites and human rights advocates on both sides of the contentious border argued that Yugoslavia's communist period was relatively benevolent and that many of those persecuted may have actually deserved their punishment, either at the time (as former fascist collaborators or Stalinists out for others' blood) or in retrospect (as nationalists responsible for major rights violations in the 1990s). There was little political profit to be made from rehabilitation and compensation in the former Yugoslavia, where its citizens were fundamentally uninterested in dealing with long-forgotten, homegrown abuses.

While Karimov refrained from declaring a sweeping rehabilitation for some of the same reasons as the ex-Yugoslavs (namely, a belief that some

"victims" actually deserved their lot), both the Uzbeks and the Poles formally addressed communist-era victims. These cases point to another
general lesson: public opposition to justice for externally inspired crimes
appears to be weaker than for crimes of domestic origin. In both Uzbekistan and Poland, as opposed to Serbia and Croatia, elites sought to address
rights violations that were perceived to have been inflicted, or at least masterminded, by a foreign (Russian/Soviet) enemy. By limiting the beneficiaries to Stalin-era victims, new elites ensured that former communists still
in power during the transition were too young to be personally associated
with the abuses in question. For Uzbekistan's leaders, who wanted to maintain their distance from violations with which they could be associated,
and for Polish new elites, who needed to secure postcommunist approval
for economic reforms, this factor facilitated a perhaps otherwise politically
unattainable process.

Particularly notable is the fact that the Poles were less timid about
offending their postcommunist colleagues before critical economic reforms
appeared on the agenda. The August 1989 establishment of a truth commis-
sion-turned-criminal-investigation demonstrated that post-oppositionists
were eager to address post-1956 rights violations when it was politically feasible to do so. Low levels of public opposition to this process reassured post-
Solidarity politicians that they had little to lose. A truth commission was one
way in which Poland's new elites could separate themselves from, and eventually punish, communist abusers. This mechanism, however, had deeper
symbolic significance. By focusing exclusively on Solidarity victims, post-
Solidarity leaders were able to show not only that (post)communists were
the villains, but also that (post-)Solidarity activists were the heroes.

Polish elites were not unique in creating a politically flattering truth
commission. Uzbek and Serbian leaders also designed truth commissions
to portray alleged aggressors (Uzbek communists and Serb nationalists) as
victims and to transfer blame for past violations to the "other." Uzbek authorities attributed historic—and even contemporary—evils to the Russians, while Serbs sought to rationalize their 1990s war record by highlighting historic injustices on the part of Croats, Bosnian Muslims, and even
Westerners. Unlike Polish elites, however, Uzbeks, Serbs, and Croats were
motivated by significant external pressures. Governing elites in all three

states attempted to use truth as a substitute for the more radical forms of justice demanded by Westerners. Just as the Uzbeks hoped to use their commission to show international donors that they were attempting to deal with current violations, Serbs and Croats used theirs to show international actors that they were dealing with past war atrocities in ways that made unpopular transfers to the Hague unnecessary. Truth processes were calculated to secure externally generated rewards at minimal internal costs.

Harsher forms of justice, such as bureaucratic cleansings, were understandably more difficult to implement than more lenient measures. Certainly for Uzbek elites, there was little question of engaging in a bureaucratic purge since rights abusers were still put to good service. In both Croatia and Serbia, public opposition was the key determinant. Although Serbs did throw out most high-level police officers, and Croats did push out some high-level intelligence managers, these dismissals were rarely connected with the unpopular goal of weeding out human rights violators. Moreover, they stopped near the top, leaving the rank-and-file largely uninvestigated. With no rewards to offer voters in exchange for an unpopular widespread cleansing, both Croatian and Serbian elites refrained from rooting out low-level violators in states where the military and the police were regarded as having acted heroically, securing Croatians in Serb-occupied territory or rescuing ethnic Serbs from hostile non-Serb Kosovars. Only in Poland, where few citizens would speak in support of intelligence officers or prosecutors, did new elites conduct official purges of these services.

Another important similarity worth emphasizing is that in all of these cases, except Uzbekistan, bureaucratic cleansings were largely determined by executives who had no experience in running such purges. Whether these executives took the initiative themselves (in Serbia and Croatia) or were charged with implementing vague laws authorizing reform (in Poland), the cleansing process was complicated by inexperience and feelings of powerlessness. Such feelings left the Croatian bureaucracy practically untouched, except in cases where affiliates of the old regime made public their opposition to the new elites. Serbian and even Polish implementers, confounded by the task of designing and carrying out a purge that would satisfy a broad range of demands, recalled feeling weak and isolated. These actors generally recognized that their activities were not risky, as transition-

and structure-based relative power arguments would imply, but that they were complicated for other reasons.

While political considerations outlined in the strategic argument help explain how and under what conditions each justice measure evaluated here was (not) adopted, the value of the strategic argument is most obvious with respect to the harshest measures. New elites will pursue criminal justice only to the degree either that it is not a voter irritant or that it pays off. Poland's new elites pressed for criminal justice for both executors and commanders until they needed postcommunist support for much-awaited economic reforms, at which point primary actors focused new criminal justice initiatives on Stalin-era rights violations. Both Serbs and Croats attempted to sell their unpopular criminal justice policies as essential to the delivery of otherwise unavailable political goods. Only the Serbs, however, were given the tools to make this argument credible enough to ensure ICTY cooperation. Even the loudest opponents to the ICTY became willing accomplices when they governed institutions responsible for producing expected political goods that were contingent upon these policies. Serbian, Croatian, and Uzbek elites used a few symbolic domestic trials of lower-level functionaries as relatively low-cost methods to secure these otherwise unavailable political goods by assuring their foreign audience that they were dealing with the internationally recognized problem.

If society was a major constraint on justice, it was neither a direct nor an organized one. Public support set broad parameters of permissibility, but these barriers to action were porous. Elites frequently pursued unpopular justice measures that they personally favored, so long as their actions would not hurt them at the polls. Political strategy has involved caution and demanded trade-offs but has not uniformly derailed justice policies. Polish political elites who passed a late condemnation of the communist era, pursued aggressive lustration, and created an institution to go after former rights abusers did so largely without the support of (and sometimes in opposition to) their own perceptions of public opinion. Serbian and Croatian elites also crossed their constituents with respect to more lenient measures such as public rebukes. But their moves to comply with ICTY transfers make this case most clearly. While Geoffrey Best noted just after the ICTY's founding that "no state is known willingly to have extradited any alleged war criminal unless it suited national policy and did not upset national public opinion to do so," more than ten years and dozens of extraditions later, it is clear that favorable public opinion toward international justice is not a prerequisite.[57]

Another striking observation from all of these cases is the weakness of local NGOs in the justice process. In all three democratic cases, human rights organizations that long pressed for type 1 on the justice spectrum either chose not to, or were unable to, affect subsequent types. In Poland, former human rights leaders either mixed in with the new elites, after which they took various (institutionally determined) positions regarding justice, or they expressed skepticism over the new elites' ability to fairly pursue it. In both Serbia and Croatia, human rights organizations remain socially marginalized and consequently not influential in local/national politics. In the latter case, they also seem less concerned with criminal justice for past rights violations than with stemming current transgressions. In all of these states, justice processes were determined by new elites with very little input from below. What input did occur was primarily anti-justice, as is best demonstrated by the highly mobilized, anti-ICTY veterans' groups in Croatia.

Institutional factors seem to account for a significant amount of the observed variance in justice policies. The cases of Serbia and Croatia perhaps best highlight the salience of this argument. Both Serbia's Koštunica and Croatia's Sanader were staunch opponents of justice when they were outside of power or, more important, not a part of primary institutions. When each man took the position of prime minister in his respective state, both Koštunica and Sanader abandoned anti-justice stances that had been widely ascribed to personal characteristics (nationalism) or fixed political strategy (populism). Indeed, they challenged public opinion by turning into willing executors of a policy that they had previously condemned, but which offered concrete awards that could be converted into political capital. While many variables could be cited to explain earlier positions, institutional factors best account for the reversals.

In conclusion, justice in the very different postcommunist cases studied here appears to be inseparable from societal pressures. Yet, in contrast to public support–based arguments, the level of public support is neither a direct determinant of (nor constraint on) justice, nor is it a fixed variable. Rather, public support is one important element that new elites consider as they calculate their optimal policy, which is also heavily influenced by their own personal preferences, immediate institutional constraints, and the broader political context. Moreover, public support, when framed within this broader context, becomes elastic, a variable that conditions, but can also be conditioned by, elite preferences. Thus, in postcommunist states the process and logic of justice has involved a mix of public and private, political and economic. In the next chapter, I consider the implications of these findings for the broader study of transitional justice.

10

Reassessing How We Think about Justice

In many ways, transitional justice has over the past half century proved to be a misnomer. Most obviously, increased international attention has made it an ever-more permanent fixture in the international human rights regime. The rise of the International Criminal Court is only one sign of this. Another is the fact that more than sixty years after World War II ended, the United States—an opponent of the ICC—continues to hunt down Nazi war criminals.[1] A closer look at newspaper accounts indicates that even in a domestic context, the issue of justice for past violations has an amazing staying power. Japan's leaders, for example, recently reversed the acknowledgments and apologies made by their predecessors for its World War II practice of forcing women throughout Asia to work as sex slaves.[2] At about the same time, on the other side of the ocean, political elites in Chile began efforts to annul a thirty-year-old self-amnesty adopted by the Pinochet regime.[3] The consequences of these moves, from riots in China prompted by the former to an onslaught of extradition demands made possible by the latter, go beyond local boundaries. Justice is thus a long-term, dynamic process with global ramifications.

Purists would likely argue that the events described above are a consequence of the failure to deal adequately with the past in the first place. If Japan had institutionalized justice for more than merely a few symbolic

heads responsible for wartime atrocities (whether through additional criminal trials, truth commissions, or early condemnations), justice proponents
might argue, its leaders would have more trouble making public denials
today. If Chile's first post-Pinochet officials had been more aggressive in
their treatment of rights abusers soon after taking power, transitional justice
would not be a distraction today. The Polish case also demonstrates what a
long-term affair justice can be. Administrative cleansings (as well as lustration) continued to be carried out more than a decade after communism collapsed, and criminal cases are set to continue well into the future. Each of
these comments brings us back to the central question in this book: What
influences the way in which leaders in post-repressive states choose to deal
with the past?

For almost two decades, relative power arguments have held a central
position in the democratization and transitional justice literatures. These
theories, primarily elite-oriented, explain justice as a function of the power
of old and new elites, though the public support–based argument expands
the constraints into the broader public. While such arguments are intuitively
appealing, they also have shortcomings (described in my introduction), including a focus on short-term outcomes and predominantly domestic pressures. Perhaps a more essential fault is methodological: in their pursuit of
parsimony, relative power advocates have left their dependent variable under-
specified, thus making this argument difficult to test empirically.

Throughout this book, I have upheld the traditional argument that
new elites must maintain a high degree of vigilance as they pursue justice
for past abuses. At the same time, I have pressed for a more dynamic strategic argument to explain the object of their vigilance. New elites striving to
impose justice policies can view hungry voters, rather than bitter former
elites, as their greatest threat. Leaders of decision-making institutions, in
particular, constantly keep one eye on their public, making certain that political decisions are not perceived to impact negatively on the delivery of
expected political goods. Where public opposition is low and new elites are
not seen to be wasting resources on dealing with the past, justice can be relatively cheap and common. Where public opposition is high, justice costs
more and may be either deferred, or provided only with the assistance of
outside subsidies. The very fact that elites in each of the countries studied

here focused primarily on potential voter reactions, rather than on old elite reactions, lends legitimacy to the strategic argument and raises critical questions about the merit of relative power explanations.[4]

This strategic argument, of course, is not inherently in opposition to the relative power one, although it does follow a different logic. Powerful old elites can be a threat to harsh forms of justice, particularly when they have voting power in primary institutions, control the means of violence, or are capable of manipulating public opinion in the new system. Indeed, the Croatia case demonstrates the effectiveness of the latter method. But the lesson from 1989 Poland is that the formal or informal power of old elites is a poor determinant on its own. The strategic argument allows for those old elites who are featured in relative power explanations to play a role in transitional justice, but it is not necessarily the decisive role.

In this concluding chapter, I consider methodological issues, particularly the generalizability of this study, the promise and problems of the justice spectrum, and the implications of my findings. I end with a reflection on the future of transitional justice in Uzbekistan, should today's pro-democracy forces eventually take power.

GENERALIZABILITY

A study such as this, involving an in-depth investigation into a handful of states, allows researchers to delve into the details of policy making in ways that are impossible in large-N quantitative studies. Still, comparativists employing qualitative methods are often confronted with the question of whether their results are generalizable beyond the population studied. In this book, I have sought to use cases that are broadly comparable yet diverge sufficiently to allow for a wide-ranging test of the theories put forward. By choosing the largest countries of three geographically and historically distinct postcommunist subregions, and evaluating policy change over time in each one, I have attempted to leverage my cases in ways that increase the external validity of my findings. This book has explored transitional justice in democracies and nondemocracies, following negotiated transitions and revolution, in the aftermath of relatively minor and severe rights violations, and under conditions of external and internal pressure.

Nonetheless, the postcommunist world is in many ways unique. From the degree of social complicity in the old regime to the strength of democratic institutions in post-totalitarian contexts, postcommunist Eurasia appears quite different from, say, Latin America. Perhaps the most differentiating characteristic of postcommunist transitions, and one that is at the heart of the strategic argument, is the simultaneity of radical political and economic reform. With elites under enormous public pressure to bridge the transition gap between the relative economic stability provided by the communist regime and that promised by the new democrats, it is perhaps of little surprise that so much of their energy would be spent pressing for an economic correction. Would leaders of other transition states face similar tasks?

The answer, I believe, is "yes." From a purely theoretical perspective, nondemocracies are largely characterized by policies of redistribution.[5] We might picture the elite-society relationship as a series of concentric circles, with the innermost one composed of a leader's core constituency, and with those persons in the outermost one residing outside the winning coalition, or that group whose support is necessary to ensure the leader's survival. The vast majority of the population in the outermost circle provides the rents that are distributed in ever higher quantities to those who are closest to the inner circle. As these circles begin to dissolve through the process of democratization (where a majority now find themselves in the winning coalition), the distribution of political goods will be affected and those with a voice will make demands. Even where transition is not characterized by similar levels of economic change, as in postcommunist states, the newly enfranchised will want to ensure more and better access to political goods, such as schools, hospitals, and law enforcement, compared to what they had when they were effectively disenfranchised.

Moreover, if political goods are at the heart of politics in experienced democracies such as the United States, where the phrase, "It's the economy, stupid," might best characterize the defeat in 1992 of a relatively popular wartime incumbent, it seems unlikely that they should be any less salient for those undergoing a period of relative deprivation.[6] And since transitional justice has proven to be a long-term process, justice decisions can continue to occur well after democratic consolidation and economic stability have taken place. Thus, for example, primary actors in Spain confronted recently with questions about how to deal with the Franco period may have been less concerned about economic restructuring than about political stability, but they were still held to the same basic voter expectations as leaders in the postcommunist world. Relatively fewer calls for such basic political goods as employment and lower inflation were probably counterbalanced by louder demands to fight corruption, crack down on crime, or provide adequate health care. Though they may be context-dependent, the perceived impact of justice on political goods would still have been a critical consideration for pro-justice decision makers.

The international variable, largely omitted in the earlier literature, has also been shown to play a very important role in justice policy, fundamentally altering domestic considerations in two ways. First, international pressures can affect local images of new and old elites. Serbian post-oppositionists, for example, claim that Western pressures for ICTY cooperation resulted in an electoral backlash against those who obliged, and they transformed Milošević, once viewed widely as a crook, into a martyr. Second, international pressures for particular justice policies can also alter the rationale for transitional justice altogether. Serbs, Croats, and Uzbeks enacted policies that they may have never found necessary in the absence of Western demands for harsher measures. Conversely, these policies might have been adopted in a more sincere fashion had they not been rushed through to satisfy international actors.

One challenge to the strategic argument may emanate from those cases of military rule, where old governing elites left the political stage but remained at the top of security structures. The functional overlap of many former Latin American rulers may have complicated the task of pro-justice new elites in ways unseen in postcommunist states (where the military was generally distinct from, though usually subservient to, the ruling party) and more reflective of transition- and/or structure-based relative power arguments. Indeed, much of the transitional justice literature focuses on Latin American examples. At least one author, David Pion-Berlin, has raised questions about the degree to which relative power arguments explain accountability even in these cases, and the lessons from this study suggest that a reappraisal would be fruitful.[7] I would hypothesize a more significant role for political goods–based considerations than has previously been credited. Indeed, the Polish case, where General Wojciech Jaruzelski simultaneously carried out top military and civilian duties (surrounded in his civilian leadership position by other top military officers, including General Czesław Kiszczak), may partly bridge these apparently disparate worlds.

Society (and the public support–based relative power argument) may also play a more direct role in cases of recent widespread, domestic abuses. While the ex-Yugoslav cases allow us to explore how the public reacts to recent mass violations, in neither Serbia nor Croatia did the majority of citizens face abuses directed against their own countrymen. Rather, they faced recent violations directed against an ethnic "other" and a declared national enemy, a fact that plainly changes the dynamics. One Polish parliamentarian acknowledged that timing and nature played a role in justice, commenting that massive violations against Poles during Stalinism might have led Solidarity activists to take a much more aggressive approach to justice if they had taken power in 1957. Yet now, she continued, "The average Pole wants work, a good salary, and not to be embarrassed about his own government. He doesn't care about the past."[8]

The level of public support, which may be impacted by temporal and qualitative aspects of rights abuses, can vary by context. This fluctuation is not a challenge to the strategic argument, but one element that must be factored into new elites' calculations concerning whether or not to pursue particular forms of justice. It is evident from this study that public support does not dictate policy, but it can serve as an indirect constraint. How it affects justice outcomes varies, based on such factors as new elites' private preferences and institutional characteristics, as well as traditional relative power considerations such as the political and structural strength of associates from the old regime.

JUSTICE SPECTRUM

The justice spectrum, which has served as the yardstick for the theories explored in this book, has proven both useful and open to challenges. In chapter 2, I justified the order of the justice spectrum based on historical case studies. As mentioned earlier, this spectrum can be used to indicate the success of relative power arguments, because, according to that logic, states with the strongest old elites should eschew the harshest retributive

measures. The simple nature of the spectrum is also designed to make it ro-
bust across contexts. For example, while the passage of time or the nature of
abuses might affect the type of justice pursued, each incremental step up the
spectrum should at any point in time be more provocative than the preceding one. In other words, truth commissions will always be less provocative
or risky than purges, which, in turn, will be less confrontational than criminal prosecutions.

Still, the case studies described in this book, which in some ways
amount to a "test drive" of this spectrum, point to three areas of caution
relating to questions of order, reform authenticity, and interaction effects.
First, I found evidence that criminal justice for the highest- and lowest-
ranking functionaries can be perceived as more risky than for less visible,
mid-ranking leaders, at least when all of these actors share a similar degree
of public sympathy (as in Serbia and Croatia). It seems that nationally recognized figures (possibly viewed as heroes) and the "common men" lower
in the ranks are more difficult to confront than the anonymous people in
leadership roles. The Polish case also suggests that dividing the executors
from those who give the orders may not always be fruitful. Future use of
this spectrum may indicate the need to reorder, or combine, types 6 and 7.

Second, and perhaps more significant, users of this spectrum must
be aware as they code data for each country that there may be significant
differences between what I call "genuine" and "artificial" justice reforms.
For example, a truth commission conducted in democratic, post-apartheid
South Africa obviously differs substantially from one imposed in authoritarian Chad. Three of the truth commissions described in this study (Serbia, Croatia, and Uzbekistan) were launched in the face of international
pressures to institute more costly methods of justice. Authorizing leaders
designed this "moderate" form of justice in ways that would render the
outcome either irrelevant (in Croatia) or heavily biased (in Serbia and Uzbekistan). While these measures arguably had the potential to be more severe in consequence and more individually oriented in nature than earlier
types of justice, they are difficult to compare with more earnest commissions, such as the Polish one. Such insincere forms of transitional justice
demonstrate that rather than serving as merely a tool to break away from
the past, punish perpetrators, or heal society, justice measures can be used
by both old and new elites to improve their political position at home and

abroad. Context is important; and, as always, studies are only as strong as their data.

This observation leads to the third caution for using this spectrum, particularly in large-N studies: under certain conditions, there may be interaction among various components of the dependent variable that lessens the likelihood of a given policy. While this is most clear with respect to amnesties, this study highlights other conditions under which this may occur. In particular, in the relatively few cases where there are international pressures for a particular form of justice, leaders pursuing one form may argue that the enacted mechanism makes alternative policies immaterial. Serbian cooperation with the ICTY, for example, may have precluded a more aggressive bureaucratic cleansing or local criminal trials. Conversely, as noted above, there is much evidence that Yugoslav President Vojislav Koštunica launched a truth commission in order to counteract pressure for unpopular handovers to the ICTY. This interaction implies a correlation between one policy and another. Explicit descriptions of the data may help to mitigate the analytical challenges that this poses.

Finally, it should be emphasized that as much as this justice spectrum is designed to deal with a significant weakness in the current theoretical literature, it is also an invitation to begin a broader debate on this subject. In order to produce coherent theories that explain why and how leaders pursue justice for past human rights violations, we must agree on a yardstick. In this book I have proposed one such instrument and have opened the floor to suggestions for other mechanisms that may complement or substitute for this one. The collective goal of the field should be to increase our capacity to generate and test transitional justice theories in ways that are more rigorous.

IMPLICATIONS

It is clear from this study that transitional justice, like many other political decisions, is affected by societal perceptions of how policy will impact on citizens' general well-being. The slogan, "It's the economy, stupid," resonates eerily in the context of whether or not to punish someone responsible for torture or extrajudicial killings. Just as former Polish prime minister

Mazowiecki demonstrated by allowing his economic "thick line" slogan to be applied to questions of transitional justice, political goods and human rights are often more interrelated than we might deem morally or ethically proper.[9] Economic doldrums can increase new elites' leniency toward their former oppressors, at least so long as more aggressive moves might be perceived by voters as disrupting the primary business at hand. However, when there are external rewards for justice, as in Serbia, economic slumps may actually hasten justice.

If the Polish case is any indication, new elites' early inability to deal with the past may simply keep transitional justice on the agenda for the long term. Almost fifteen years after the transition began, a large number of post-Solidarity respondents voiced regret for failing to more aggressively handle the past. These leaders most often lamented the lack of a broader-reaching attack on members of old elites, which they believed would have helped avoid the corruption scandals plaguing the country today. Harsh measures of lustration would have kept disreputable postcommunists out of the public sphere long enough to establish stronger democratic values, they say. By contrast, Serb and Croat leaders who were forced to deal with the past more harshly complain that they did everything in their power and faced domestic punishment as a result. It will be fascinating to observe the path taken by justice in Serbia and Croatia over the next decade, with an eye to whether post-oppositionists quietly revisit questions of harshness, as Polish post-oppositionists did, if and when economic conditions improve.

This book has focused on domestic policy making, but the study has important foreign policy implications at a time when human rights often figure into external relations. Foreign pressures for justice can work. In order to be effective, however, these pressures must involve a combination of carrots and sticks that new elites can trade to their own domestic constituencies in exchange for public tolerance. These pressures might include both tangibles and intangibles. They should be primarily, but not exclusively, focused on primary actors. In addition, they should be imposed in a measure sufficient to make clear that benefits of acquiescence outweigh the potential negative side effects of policy implementation.

Although tangible carrots and sticks are the staple in diplomacy, this study points to the merit of intangible incentives as well. Obstructing certain forms of aid or loans is not always possible or even convincing. Serbian elites, for example, never cited U.S. bilateral aid cuts as a reason for cooperation. The most effective pressures in the case of the former Yugo-slavia were multilateral in nature, whether blocking large loans from in-stitutions such as the World Bank or threatening to block entry into the European Union. The latter example is an especially important intangible, vital because many citizens in both Serbia and Croatia see EU entry as the key to stability and prosperity. This political good was even useful in gain-ing ICTY cooperation from vocal anti-cooperation forces after they began to govern.

While I have focused my analysis on the role of primary actors (since these are the players who affect policy), the role of secondary actors can also be important. Because they are often very public figures, actors in secondary institutions can influence people's attitudes toward justice. For example, heavily criticized apologies by the presidents of Serbia and Montenegro and Croatia might have created previously nonexistent space for discussions about violence and guilt, thus making criminal trials less risky. Less visible secondary actors can also play a critical role through agenda setting. In Po-land, one might question whether primary actors in the Sejm would have supported rehabilitation and compensation or criminal justice initiatives if the members of the Senat did not put these options on the table in the first place. Future studies may find the role of secondary actors to be significant in these respects.

Pro-justice secondary actors are certainly strengthened when they can demonstrate the concrete benefits of justice. If European Union entry can be sold as a political good, as it was in Serbia and Croatia, so might a range of international clubs, ranging from economic, such as the World Trade Organization or the North American Free Trade Agreement, to military, such as the North Atlantic Treaty Organization. The value of these goods is determined by how effectively they are marketed. External actors must either convince new elites that it is in their interest to sell these political goods at home as a genuine benefit, or they must convince the target pub-lics directly.

This second policy option raises important questions about the appro-priate role of external state actors in domestic politics. Indirect pressures are not unusual. Western states annually spend millions of dollars on support for sectors of local civil society that pursue a shared agenda. Channeling funds into those organizations that press for a certain justice policy, directly or indirectly (for example, educating the public about the importance of conditioned political goods), may be an effective way to do new elites' work for them. With more targeted outside support, former Croatian prime minister Račan recalled, NGOs "absolutely could have done more" to lead public opinion and thereby lower his costs for fulfilling international demands for criminal justice.[10]

The obvious drawback to such incentives and disincentives is that they arguably lead to the instrumentalization of justice. It seems that the instrumentalization discussed above should lead to an insincere form of justice that will accomplish none of the objectives put forward for transitional justice in chapter 1. Yet this is not necessarily the case. For example, the Croatian trial of General Norac may never have occurred without ICTY pressures. While Croats initially took to the streets to defend Norac, the general's subsequent admission of guilt was to some citizens a transformative event. "This was cathartic for Croatia, a historic event," said Croatia's representative to the International Court of Justice. "Public opinion had to face the difficult truth." On the other hand, personal tragedy and political instability in Serbia resulting from Đinđić's assassination, purportedly by an anti-Hague group, highlights the serious risk posed by international pressures. Coerced justice may thus have side effects both positive and negative.

This discussion of how to persuade target elites to comply with international demands for justice begs an essential question: What is the value of transitional justice? Though much of the literature focuses on this issue, there are few empirical studies that actually measure the impact of justice, much less justice that is externally conceived. In this book, I have demonstrated that outside pressures for one type can have a ripple effect through the justice spectrum. The result can be a series of insincere policies that may breed public cynicism, rather than support for dealing with the past. If the goal of justice is deterrence, this may be immaterial. However, if the aim is to encourage reconciliation, in the belief that this will enhance stability, foreign-imposed justice may backfire tragically. In both Serbia and Croatia, elites believe that the ICTY and pressures for ICTY cooperation have deepened rather than diminished inter-ethnic and inter-regional tensions, and have negatively impacted on the process of democratization. The International Criminal Court, an embodiment of globalization in the human rights sphere, therefore faces a very difficult task.

A FINAL WORD

Countless regimes over hundreds of years have been confronted with the dilemma of how to deal with predecessors guilty of rights abuses. The study of transitional justice, and in particular determinants of justice policies, is a comparatively new phenomenon, gaining traction only in the 1980s. Scholars who have walked this path have examined variables that range from the context of political change to the nature and timing of abuses. Yet these authors have almost all adhered to one or another strand of relative power, framing transitional justice as a policy area determined by the relative strength of new elites. In this book I have built upon, but also challenged, this approach, arguing that justice is a function of political strategy, mediated by institutions in which particular policymakers are housed.

I conclude by looking forward and applying lessons learned in this book to Uzbekistan. It is likely that if current post-oppositionists attain power there, they will encounter little significant pro-justice pressure from below. In a small sample of non-elite residents of Tashkent, I found that most Uzbeks are not preoccupied with the harshest civil and political rights violations of the Karimov regime, whereas they are very sensitive to current economic deprivation. Organized civil society in the human rights sphere is likely to disintegrate as oppositionists who now make up the backbone of these organizations abandon them for government positions. As in Poland, those leading the human rights movement today are likely to be the new governing elites tomorrow. The justice debate will be largely an elite-level affair.

Those new elites who take control of Uzbekistan will have to balance their desire for justice with the risks that it entails. As noted earlier, oppositionists are already split over the optimal way to deal with the past. This divide may be attributed partly to complicity with the current regime, as well as to a fear of speaking out prematurely. It may also be a sign of political prudence. Uzbekistan's new elites might be expected to deal with justice as harshly as they can without endangering support from their democratic constituencies. A heavy focus on economic rights violations in the pre-transition period suggests that Uzbek oppositionists are already aiming for a form of justice that might double as a campaign banner. Trials may be held for political rights violators, but they seem likely to be marketed under the more socially salient guise of corruption, the same socially palatable tactic that Serb leaders had hoped to employ to minimize public opposition.

President Karimov and his associates will fare best if they succeed in joining the new system and control votes necessary for post-oppositionists to make good on material promises to their constituents. This point illustrates the intersection of the strategic and relative power arguments. Where new elites in primary institutions share power with onetime oppressors, the former may need to adjust their justice preferences in order to achieve the overriding goal of political goods provision. As the Polish case highlights, however, this is likely to be only a temporary reprieve for today's rights abusers. Indeed, it seems more likely that exile or shortcomings in the judiciary, rather than post-opposition elite considerations, offer Karimov and his close associates the best chance of avoiding prison sentences in the long term. For those lower down the chain of command, public sympathy, poverty, and impatience with democratic governing elites represent the greatest opportunities for freedom.

Finally, though transitional justice is unlikely to make or break democratic consolidation in post-Karimov Uzbekistan, it may have an impact on how political parties develop. One element of party identity is likely to be the relationship to the Karimov regime in the past and the present. Just as DS leaders in Serbia and various post-Solidarity parties in Poland sometimes sought to differentiate themselves from competitors along justice lines, Uzbekistan will likely have parties of retribution, parties of forgiveness, and parties of complicity. The salience of these identities will depend primarily on information about rights violations that eventually becomes public, as well as how elites manage that information. Judging from Uzbek perceptions today, pro-justice parties will seek to capitalize on antagonism to the old regime, based on charges of widespread corruption, while anti-justice parties will call for a focus on the future. Unless Karimov repeats his brutal suppression of the 2005 protests in Andijon, future justice in Uzbekistan will be a meat-and-potatoes issue. As Gleb, a retired computer repairman living in Tashkent, commented, "Rights can be bought for money. If you have no money, you have no rights."[11] The challenge for future post-opposition elites will be to guarantee that in the course of serving justice, they provide Gleb and the rest of Uzbekistan's voters with those expected political goods that mark an end to the types of violations that affect the majority today.

Notes

In the notes, the titles of newspaper articles and other press reports whose authors are unnamed are preceded, for convenience in shortening repeated citations, by a noun or an acronym identifying the source. Thus, for instance, AFP = *Agence France Press,* AN = *Africa News,* AP = *Associated Press,* B92 = *Radio B92,* DPA = *Deutsche Presse-Agentur,* Economist = *The Economist,* GNA = *Global News Wire—Asia Africa Intelligence Wire,* IPNSA = *Inter Press News Service Agency,* RFE/RL = *Radio Free Europe/Radio Liberty,* UPI = *United Press International.* Newspaper and press reports are not included in the select bibliography.

INTRODUCTION

1. See official site at http://www.state.gov/g/drl/hr/.

2. For more on this, see the official Web site, http://www.rewardsforjustice.net/index.cfm?page=Rewards_program&language=english.

3. Graham Allison and Morton Halperin, "Bureaucratic Politics: A Paradigm and Some Policy Implications," *World Politics* 24 (1972); Geoffrey Best, "Justice, International Relations, and Human Rights," *International Affairs* (Royal Institute of International Affairs) 71, no. 4 (1995); Sandy Vogelgesang, "What Price Principle? U.S. Policy on Human Rights," *Foreign Affairs* 56, no. 4 (1978).

4. Naomi Roht-Arriaza, "The Role of International Actors in National Accountability Processes," in *The Politics of Memory: Transitional Justice in Democratizing Societies,* ed. Alexandra Barahona De Brito, Carmen Gonzales-Enriquez, and Paloma Aguilar (Oxford: Oxford University Press, 2001), 41–43.

5. Michael J. Gilligan, "Is Enforcement Necessary for Effectiveness? A Model of the International Criminal Regime," *International Organization* 60 (2006); Chandra Lekha Sriram and Amy Ross, "Geographies of Crime and Justice: Contemporary Transitional Justice and the Creation of 'Zones of Impunity,'" *International Journal of Transitional Justice* 1, no. 1 (2007); Christopher Rudolph, "Constructing an Atrocities Regime: The Politics of War Crimes Tribunals," *International Organization* 55, no. 3 (2001).

6. Roht-Arriaza, "The Role of International Actors in National Accountability Processes," 42–43.

7. Menno T. Kamminga, "Lessons Learned from the Exercise of Universal Jurisdiction in Respect of Gross Human Rights Offenses," *Human Rights Quarterly* 23 (2001): 941.

8. Ibid., 943.

9. Ibid., 945.

10. Richard J. Wilson, "Prosecuting Pinochet: International Crimes in Spanish Domestic Law," *Human Rights Quarterly* 21, no. 4 (1999).

11. UNSC, "The Rule of Law and Transitional Justice in Conflict and Post-Conflict Societies" (United Nations Security Council, 2004), 4.

12. ICTJ, "What Is Transitional Justice?" International Center for Transitional Justice, http://www.ictj.org/en/tj/.

13. Jon Elster, *Closing the Books: Transitional Justice in Historical Perspective* (New York: Cambridge University Press, 2004), 1.

14. Ruti G. Teitel, "Transitional Justice Genealogy," *Harvard Human Rights Journal* 16 (2003): 69.

15. Neil J. Kritz, "Coming to Terms with Atrocities: A Review of Accountability Mechanisms for Mass Violations of Human Rights," *Law and Contemporary Problems* 59, no. 4 (1996); Stephan Landsman, "Alternative Responses to Serious Human Rights Abuses: Of Prosecution and Truth Commission," *Law and Contemporary Problems* 59, no. 4 (1996).

16. David Bloomfield, Teresa Barnes, and Luc Huyse, *Reconciliation after Violent Conflict: A Handbook* (Stockholm: International Institute for Democracy and Electoral Assistance, 2003), 127; Lyn Graybill, "To Punish or Pardon: A Comparison of the International Criminal Tribunal for Rwanda and the South African Truth and Reconciliation Commission," *Human Rights Review* 2, no. 4 (1999); Peter R. Baehr, "Controversies in the Current International Human Rights Debate," *Human Rights Review* 2, no. 1 (2000): 20; Audrey R. Chapman and Patrick Ball, "The Truth of Truth Commissions: Comparative Lessons from Haiti, South Africa, and Guatemala," *Human Rights Quarterly* 23 (2001).

17. Brian Grodsky, "Justice without Transition: Truth Commissions in the Context of Repressive Rule," *Human Rights Review* 9, no. 3 (2008); Priscilla B. Hayner, "Fifteen Truth Commissions, 1974 to 1994: A Comparative Study," *Human Rights Quarterly* 16, no. 4 (1994): 608.

18. Stephen B. Cornell and Joseph B. Kalt, "Successful Economic Development and the Heterogeneity of Governmental Form on American Indian Reservations," in *Getting Good Government: Capacity-Building in the Public Sectors of Developing Countries,* ed. Merilee Grindle (Cambridge, Mass.: HIID/Harvard University Press, 1997); Gary W. Cox and Mathew D. McCubbins, "Political Structure and Economic Policy: The Institutional Determinants of Policy Outcomes," in *Presidents, Parliaments, and Policy,* ed. Stephan Haggard and Mathew D. McCubbins (Cambridge: Cambridge University Press, 2001); Kathryn Stoner-Weiss, *Local Heroes: The Political Economy of Russian Regional Governance* (Princeton: Princeton University Press, 1997).

19. Graham Allison, "Conceptual Models and the Cuban Missile Crisis," *American Political Science Review* 63, no. 3 (1969), 711.

CHAPTER 1   *Explaining Justice*

1. Stephen A. Garret, "Problems of Transitional Justice: The Politics and Principles of Memory" (paper presented at the Annual Meeting of the International Studies Association, Washington, D.C., February 16–20, 1999).

2. UNSC, "The Rule of Law and Transitional Justice in Conflict and Post-Conflict Societies," 4.

3. Leslie Vinjamuri and Jack Snyder, "Advocacy and Scholarship in the Study of International War Crime Tribunals and Transitional Justice," *Annual Review of Political Science* 7 (2004).

4. Kritz, "Coming to Terms with Atrocities: A Review of Accountability Mechanisms for Mass Violations of Human Rights," 128.

5. Bloomfield, Barnes, and Huyse, *Reconciliation after Violent Conflict: A Handbook,* 12.

6. David A. Crocker, "Reckoning with the Past: A Normative Framework," *Ethics and International Affairs* 13 (1999).

7. Bloomfield, Barnes, and Huyse, *Reconciliation after Violent Conflict: A Handbook,* 11.

8. Laurel E. Fletcher and Harvey M. Weinstein, "Violence and Social Repair: Rethinking the Contribution of Justice to Reconciliation," *Human Rights Quarterly* 24, no. 3 (2002): 578.

9. Ibid.

10. Priscilla B. Hayner, "International Guidelines for the Creation and Operation of Truth Commissions: A Preliminary Proposal," *Law and Contemporary Problems* 59, no. 4 (1996): 175.

11. Grzegorz Ekiert, "Democratization Processes in East Central Europe: A Theoretical Reconsideration," *British Journal of Political Science* 21, no. 3 (1991): 306.

12. Philippe C. Schmitter, "The Consolidation of Democracy and Representation of Social Groups," *American Behavioral Scientist* 35, no. 4/5 (1992): 424.

13. Bloomfield, Barnes, and Huyse, *Reconciliation after Violent Conflict: A Handbook,* 11.

14. Michael Fehrer, "Terms of Reconciliation," in *Human Rights in Political Transitions: Gettysburg to Bosnia,* ed. Carla Hesse and Robert Post (New York: Zone Books, 1999), 325–26.

15. Ibid., 326; Samuel Huntington, *The Third Wave: Democratization in the Late Twentieth Century* (Norman: University of Oklahoma Press, 1991); Teitel, "Transitional Justice Genealogy."

16. Crocker, "Reckoning with the Past: A Normative Framework," 47–54; Graybill, "To Punish or Pardon: A Comparison of the International Criminal Tribunal for Rwanda and the South African Truth and Reconciliation Commission," 5; Huntington, *The Third Wave: Democratization in the Late Twentieth Century,* 213; Karl Jaspers, "The Question of German Guilt," in *Transitional Justice: How Emerging Democracies Reckon with Former Regimes,* ed. Neil J. Kritz (Washington, D.C.: United States Institute of Peace Press, 1995), 198–99.

17. Jaspers, "The Question of German Guilt."

18. José Zalaquett, "Confronting Human Rights Violations Committed by Former Governments: Principles Applicable and Political Constraints," in *Transitional Justice,* ed. Neil J. Kritz (Washington, D.C.: United States Institute of Peace Press, 1995), 9.

19. John Borneman, "Apologies as Performative Redress," *SAIS Review* 25, no. 2 (2005): 53.

20. Jaspers, "The Question of German Guilt," 164.

21. Eric A. Posner and Adrian Vermeule, "Transitional Justice as Ordinary Justice," in the Public Law and Legal Theory Working Paper Series (Chicago: University of Chicago Law School, 2003), 23.

22. Vojtech Cepl and Mark Gillis, "Making Amends after Communism," *Journal of Democracy* 7, no. 4 (1996): 123–24.

23. Ben Reilly, "Democratic Levers for Conflict Management," in *Democracy and Deep-Rooted Conflict: Options for Negotiators,* ed. Peter Harris, Ben Reilly,

and Mark Anstey (Stockholm: International Institute for Democracy and Electoral Assistance, 2002); Lorna McGregor, "Individual Accountability in South Africa: Cultural Optimum or Political Façade?" *American Journal of International Law* 95, no. 1 (2001): 33.

24. Terence Roehrig, *The Prosecution of Former Military Leaders in Newly Democratic Nations* (Jefferson, N.C.: McFarland & Company, 2002), 199.

25. William W. Burke-White, "Reframing Impunity: Applying Liberal International Law Theory to an Analysis of Amnesty Legislation," *Harvard International Law Journal* 42 (2001); Hayner, "International Guidelines for the Creation and Operation of Truth Commissions: A Preliminary Proposal."

26. Luis Moreno Ocampo, "Beyond Punishment: Justice in the Wake of Massive Crimes in Argentina," *Journal of International Affairs* 52, no. 2 (1999): 685; Graeme Simpson and Paul van Zyl, "South Africa's Truth and Reconciliation Commission," *Temps Modernes* 585 (1995).

27. Guillermo O'Donnell and Philippe C. Schmitter, "Tentative Conclusions about Uncertain Democracies," in *Transitions from Authoritarian Rule: Prospects for Democracy*, ed. Guillermo O'Donnell, Philippe C. Schmitter, and Laurence Whitehead (Baltimore: Johns Hopkins University Press, 1986), 30.

28. McGregor, "Individual Accountability in South Africa: Cultural Optimum or Political Façade?" 35; Geoffrey Best, "Justice, International Relations, and Human Rights," 798.

29. Leigh A. Payne, "Collaborators and the Politics of Memory in Chile," *Human Rights Review* 2, no. 3 (2001).

30. Priscilla B. Hayner, *Unspeakable Truths: Confronting State Terror and Atrocity* (New York: Routledge, 2001), 27.

31. Martha Minow, *Between Vengeance and Forgiveness* (Boston: Beacon Press, 1998), 61; James L. Gibson, "Truth, Justice, and Reconciliation: Judging the Fairness of Amnesty in South Africa," *American Journal of Political Science* 46, no. 3 (2002): 543.

32. James L. Gibson, *Overcoming Apartheid: Can Truth Reconcile a Divided Nation?* (New York: Russell Sage Foundation, 2004), 335.

33. Crocker, "Reckoning with the Past: A Normative Framework," 47.

34. F. W. de Klerk, *The Last Trek—a New Beginning: The Autobiography* (New York: St. Martin's Press, 1999), 369.

35. Tony Judt, "The Past Is Another Country: Myth and Memory in Postwar Europe," in *The Politics of Retribution in Europe: World War II and Its Aftermath*, ed. István Deák, Jan Tomasz Gross, and Tony Judt (Princeton: Princeton University Press, 2000).

36. Payne, "Collaborators and the Politics of Memory in Chile," 9.

37. Fletcher and Weinstein, "Violence and Social Repair: Rethinking the Contribution of Justice to Reconciliation."

38. Judt, "The Past Is Another Country: Myth and Memory in Postwar Europe," 296.

39. Ibid., 300.

40. In Germany, for example, one group is named the "Association for the Rehabilitation of People Persecuted for Denying the Holocaust." See Nicholas Kulish, "World Briefing: Germany: 2 Groups Banned for Neo-Nazism," *New York Times,* May 8, 2008.

41. Judt, "The Past Is Another Country: Myth and Memory in Postwar Europe," 309.

42. Huntington, *The Third Wave: Democratization in the Late Twentieth Century.*

43. Minow, *Between Vengeance and Forgiveness,* 83.

44. Landsman, "Alternative Responses to Serious Human Rights Abuses: Of Prosecution and Truth Commission," 82.

45. Fletcher and Weinstein, "Violence and Social Repair: Rethinking the Contribution of Justice to Reconciliation," 625.

46. Conway Henderson, "Conditions Affecting the Use of Political Repression," *Journal of Conflict Resolution* 35, no. 1 (1991).

47. O'Donnell and Schmitter, "Tentative Conclusions about Uncertain Democracies"; José Zalaquett, "Balancing Ethical Imperatives and Political Constraints: The Dilemma of New Democracies Confronting Past Human Rights Violations," *Hastings Law Journal* 43, no. 1425 (1992): 1431.

48. Elster, *Closing the Books: Transitional Justice in Historical Perspective.*

49. Teitel, "Transitional Justice Genealogy."

50. Ibid., 70.

51. Tony Evans, *U.S. Hegemony and the Project of Universal Human Rights* (New York: St. Martin's Press, 1996).

52. Paloma Aguilar, "Justice, Politics, and Memory in the Spanish Transition," in *The Politics of Memory: Transitional Justice in Democratizing Societies,* ed. Alexandra Barahona De Brito, Carmen Gonzales-Enriquez, and Paloma Aguilar (Oxford: Oxford University Press, 2001), 99; Alexandra Barahona De Brito, Carmen Gonzales-Enriquez, and Paloma Aguilar, "Introduction," in *The Politics of Memory: Transitional Justice in Democratizing Societies,* ed. Alexandra Barahona De Brito, Carmen Gonzales-Enriquez, and Paloma Aguilar (Oxford: Oxford University Press, 2001), 11; Jamal Benomar, "Justice after Transitions," in *Transitional Justice,* ed. Neil J. Kritz (Washington, D.C.: United States Institute of Peace Press, 1995), 41; Luc Huyse, "Justice after Transition: On the Choices Successor Elites

Make in Dealing with the Past," *Law and Social Inquiry* 20, no. 1 (1995): 63; Roehrig, *The Prosecution of Former Military Leaders in Newly Democratic Nations,* 199; Rachel Sieder, "War, Peace, and Memory Politics in Central America," in *The Politics of Memory: Transitional Justice in Democratizing Societies,* ed. Alexandra Barahona De Brito, Carmen Gonzales-Enriquez, and Paloma Aguilar (Oxford: Oxford University Press, 2001), 162; Daniel Sutter, "Settling Old Scores: Potholes along the Transition from Authoritarian Rule," *Journal of Conflict Resolution* 39, no. 1 (1995): 121; Zalaquett, "Balancing Ethical Imperatives and Political Constraints: The Dilemma of New Democracies Confronting Past Human Rights Violations," 1432.

53. Huyse, "Justice after Transition: On the Choices Successor Elites Make in Dealing with the Past," 78.

54. Huntington, *The Third Wave: Democratization in the Late Twentieth Century,* 230–31.

55. Ibid., 79.

56. Michelle Sieff and Leslie Vinjamuri Wright, "Reconciling Order and Justice? New Institutional Solutions in Post-Conflict States," *Journal of International Affairs* 52, no. 2 (1999): 759.

57. Barahona De Brito, Gonzales-Enriquez, and Aguilar, "Introduction," 11.

58. Landsman, "Alternative Responses to Serious Human Rights Abuses: Of Prosecution and Truth Commission"; Jack Snyder and Leslie Vinjamuri, "Trials and Errors: Principle and Pragmatism in Strategies of International Justice," *International Security* 28, no. 3 (2003/2004): 18; Benomar, "Justice after Transitions," 41.

59. Huyse, "Justice after Transition: On the Choices Successor Elites Make in Dealing with the Past," 75.

60. Graybill, "To Punish or Pardon: A Comparison of the International Criminal Tribunal for Rwanda and the South African Truth and Reconciliation Commission"; Simpson and van Zyl, "South Africa's Truth and Reconciliation Commission."

61. de Klerk, *The Last Trek—a New Beginning: The Autobiography,* 288.

62. O'Donnell and Schmitter, "Tentative Conclusions about Uncertain Democracies," 28.

63. Tina Rosenberg, "Overcoming the Legacies of Dictatorship," *Foreign Affairs* 74, no. 3 (1995).

64. Zalaquett, "Confronting Human Rights Violations Committed by Former Governments: Principles Applicable and Political Constraints," 18.

65. Ibid., 19.

66. Reilly, "Democratic Levers for Conflict Management"; Zalaquett, "Balancing Ethical Imperatives and Political Constraints: The Dilemma of New De-

mocracies Confronting Past Human Rights Violations"; Roehrig, *The Prosecution of Former Military Leaders in Newly Democratic Nations,* 19.

67. Rosenberg, "Overcoming the Legacies of Dictatorship," 141.

68. Patti Waldmeir, *Anatomy of a Miracle: The End of Apartheid and the Birth of the New South Africa* (New York: W. W. Norton & Company, 1997), 213.

69. Gareth Newham, "Truth and Reconciliation: Realising the Ideals," *Indicator SA* 12, no. 4 (1995).

70. Landsman, "Alternative Responses to Serious Human Rights Abuses: Of Prosecution and Truth Commission"; Fehrer, "Terms of Reconciliation," 326.

71. Fletcher and Weinstein, "Violence and Social Repair: Rethinking the Contribution of Justice to Reconciliation," 599.

72. Allison Corey and Sandra F. Joireman, "Retributive Justice: The Gacaca Courts in Rwanda," *African Affairs* 103, no. 410 (2004); Teitel, "Transitional Justice Genealogy," 70; Baehr, "Controversies in the Current International Human Rights Debate," 21.

73. Zalaquett, "Confronting Human Rights Violations Committed by Former Governments: Principles Applicable and Political Constraints," 19.

74. Huntington, *The Third Wave: Democratization in the Late Twentieth Century,* 230.

75. Andrzej S. Walicki, "Transitional Justice and the Political Struggles in Post-Communist Poland," in *Transitional Justice and the Rule of Law in New Democracies,* ed. A. James McAdams (Notre Dame, Ind.: University of Notre Dame Press, 1997), 186.

76. Jon Elster, "Introduction," in *Retribution and Reparation in the Transition to Democracy,* ed. Jon Elster (New York: Cambridge University Press, 2006), 11.

77. O'Donnell and Schmitter, "Tentative Conclusions about Uncertain Democracies," 30.

78. Giles Tremlett, "Franco Repression Ruled as a Crime against Humanity," *The Guardian,* October 17, 2008.

79. Paloma Aguilar and Carsten Humblebaek, "Collective Memory and National Identity in the Spanish Democracy: The Legacies of Francoism and the Civil War," *History and Memory* 14, no. 1–2 (2002): 123.

80. T. R. H. Davenport, *The Birth of a New South Africa* (Buffalo, N.Y.: University of Toronto Press, 1998), 33.

81. Ocampo, "Beyond Punishment: Justice in the Wake of Massive Crimes in Argentina," 681.

82. Ibid., 685.

83. Alexandra Barahona De Brito, "Truth, Justice, Memory, and Democratization in the Southern Cone," in *The Politics of Memory: Transitional Justice in*

Democratizing Societies, ed. Alexandra Barahona De Brito, Carmen Gonzales-Enriquez, and Paloma Aguilar (Oxford: Oxford University Press, 2001), 153.

84. Cepl and Gillis, "Making Amends after Communism," 123.

85. Michael McFaul, "The Fourth Wave of Democracy and Dictatorship: Noncooperative Transitions in the Postcommunist World," *World Politics* 54, no. 2 (2002): 229; Barbara Geddes, "What Do We Know about Democratization after 20 Years?" *Annual Review of Political Science* 2 (1999): 121, 137.

86. Zalaquett, "Balancing Ethical Imperatives and Political Constraints: The Dilemma of New Democracies Confronting Past Human Rights Violations," 1431.

87. Geddes, "What Do We Know about Democratization after 20 Years?" 131.

88. Stephen Holmes, "The End of Decommunization," *East European Constitutional Review* 3, no. 3–4 (1994); Walicki, "Transitional Justice and the Political Struggles in Post-Communist Poland."

89. Philip J. Powlick, "The Attitudinal Bases for Responsiveness to Public Opinion among American Foreign Policy Officials," *Journal of Conflict Resolution* 35, no. 4 (1991): 636; Eric M. Uslaner, "Trade Winds, NAFTA, and the Rational Public," *Political Behavior* 20, no. 4 (1998): 351; James A. McCann, "Electoral Choices and Core Value Change: The 1992 Presidential Campaign," *American Journal of Political Science* 41, no. 2 (1997); Timothy J. McKeown, "The Cuban Missile Crisis and Politics as Usual," *Journal of Politics* 62, no. 1 (2000): 75; Philip J. Powlick and Andrew Z. Katz, "Defining the American Public Opinion/Foreign Policy Nexus," *Mershon International Studies Review* 42, no. 1 (1998); Lawrence R. Jacobs et al., "Congressional Leadership of Public Opinion," *Political Science Quarterly* 113, no. 1 (1998): 27; Jeffrey W. Koch, "Political Rhetoric and Political Persuasion: The Changing Structure of Citizens' Preferences on Health Insurance during Policy Debate," *Public Opinion Quarterly* 62, no. 2 (1998); Lawrence R. Jacobs and Robert Y. Shapiro, "Presidential Manipulation of Polls and Public Opinion: The Nixon Administration and the Pollsters," *Political Science Quarterly* 110, no. 4 (1995–1996): 526.

90. Amartya Sen, "Civilizational Imprisonments: How to Misunderstand Everybody in the World," *The New Republic,* June 10, 2002.

91. Aguilar and Humblebaek, "Collective Memory and National Identity in the Spanish Democracy: The Legacies of Francoism and the Civil War," 186–87; Walicki, "Transitional Justice and the Political Struggles in Post-Communist Poland."

92. Helga A. Welsh, "Dealing with the Communist Past: Central and East European Experiences after 1990," *Europe-Asia Studies* 48, no. 3 (1996): 419–20.

93. David Pion-Berlin, "To Prosecute or to Pardon? Human Rights Decisions in the Latin American Southern Cone," *Human Rights Quarterly* 16, no. 1 (1994).

94. Elster, "Introduction."

95. Ibid., 12.

96. Kieran Williams, Brigid Fowler, and Aleks Szczerbiak, "Explaining Lustration in Central Europe: A 'Post-Communist Politics' Approach," *Democratization* 12, no. 1 (2005): 23.

97. Posner and Vermeule, "Transitional Justice as Ordinary Justice," 767.

98. Holmes, "The End of Decommunization."

99. Koch, "Political Rhetoric and Political Persuasion: The Changing Structure of Citizens' Preferences on Health Insurance during Policy Debate."

100. Simon Hug and Thomas Konig, "In View of Ratification: Governmental Preferences and Domestic Constraints at the Amsterdam Intergovernmental Conference," *International Organization* 56, no. 2 (2002): 471; Koch, "Political Rhetoric and Political Persuasion: The Changing Structure of Citizens' Preferences on Health Insurance during Policy Debate," 211; Powlick and Katz, "Defining the American Public Opinion/Foreign Policy Nexus."

101. Hayner, *Unspeakable Truths: Confronting State Terror and Atrocity*; Jaspers, "The Question of German Guilt"; Rajeev Bhargava, "Restoring Decency to Barbaric Societies," in *Truth v. Justice: The Morality of Truth Commissions,* ed. Robert I. Rotberg and Dennis Thompson (Princeton: Princeton University Press, 2000); David A. Crocker, "Truth Commissions, Transitional Justice, and Civil Society," in *Truth v. Justice: The Morality of Truth Commissions,* ed. Robert I. Rotberg and Dennis Thompson (Princeton: Princeton University Press, 2000); Zalaquett, "Confronting Human Rights Violations Committed by Former Governments: Principles Applicable and Political Constraints"; Minow, *Between Vengeance and Forgiveness*; Andrew Moravcsik, "The Origins of Human Rights Regimes: Democratic Delegation in Postwar Europe," *International Organization* 54, no. 2 (2000).

102. Crocker, "Reckoning with the Past: A Normative Framework," 47–54; Graybill, "To Punish or Pardon: A Comparison of the International Criminal Tribunal for Rwanda and the South African Truth and Reconciliation Commission," 5; Huntington, *The Third Wave: Democratization in the Late Twentieth Century,* 213; Jaspers, "The Question of German Guilt," 198–99; Kritz, "Coming to Terms with Atrocities: A Review of Accountability Mechanisms for Mass Violations of Human Rights," 128.

103. Snyder and Vinjamuri, "Trials and Errors: Principle and Pragmatism in Strategies of International Justice."

104. Helen Milner, "The Interaction of Domestic and International Politics," in *Double-Edged Diplomacy,* ed. Peter Evans, Harold Jacobson, and Robert Putnam (Berkeley: University of California Press, 1993); Robert Putnam, "Diplomacy and Domestic Politics: The Logic of Two-Level Games," *International Organization* 42, no. 3 (1988); Richard Cooper, "Economic Interdependence and Foreign Policy in the Seventies," *World Politics* 24 (1972); Michael Doyle, "Liberalism in World Politics," *American Political Science Review* 80 (1986).

105. Anne-Marie Burley and Walter Mattli, "Europe before the Court: A Political Theory of Legal Integration," *International Organization* 47, no. 1 (1993); Robert O. Keohane and Joseph S. Nye, "Transgovernmental Relations and International Organization," *World Politics* 27 (1974).

106. David P. Forsythe, *Human Rights in International Relations* (New York: Cambridge University Press, 2000); Margaret E. Keck and Kathryn Sikkink, *Activists beyond Borders: Advocacy Networks in International Politics* (Ithaca, N.Y.: Cornell University Press, 1998); David Held, *Global Transformations* (Stanford: Stanford University Press, 1999).

107. CE, "Resolution #1096 on Measures to Dismantle the Heritage of Former Communist Totalitarian Systems" (Council of Europe, 1996); UN, "The Right to Restitution, Compensation, and Rehabilitation for Victims of Gross Violations of Human Rights and Fundamental Freedoms" (United Nations Commission on Human Rights, 1993); UN, "Basic Principles and Guidelines on the Right to Reparation for Victims of Gross Violations of Human Rights and Humanitarian Law" (United Nations Commission on Human Rights, 1996).

108. Mancur Olson, "Dictatorship, Democracy, and Development," *American Political Science Review* 87, no. 3 (1993): 568; Albert O. Hirschman, "Exit, Voice, and the State," *World Politics* 31, no. 1 (1978): 105.

109. Bruce Bueno de Mesquita et al., "Policy Failure and Political Survival: The Contribution of Political Institutions," *Journal of Conflict Resolution* 43, no. 2 (1999); Olson, "Dictatorship, Democracy, and Development."

110. Cornell and Kalt, "Successful Economic Development and the Heterogeneity of Governmental Form on American Indian Reservations"; Cox and McCubbins, "Political Structure and Economic Policy: The Institutional Determinants of Policy Outcomes"; Stoner-Weiss, *Local Heroes: The Political Economy of Russian Regional Governance.*

111. George Klosko, Edward N. Muller, and Karl Dieter Opp, "Rebellious Collective Action Revisited," *American Political Science Review* 81, no. 2 (1987): 557; Pedro C. Magalhaes, "The Politics of Judicial Reform in Eastern Europe," *Comparative Politics* 32, no. 1 (1999): 47.

112. Donald D. Searing, "Roles, Rules, and Rationality in the New Institutionalism," *American Political Science Review* 85, no. 4 (1991): 1248.

113. Christopher Anderson, "Economic Voting and Political Context: A Comparative Perspective," *Electoral Studies* 19, no. 2 (2000); Thomas J. Rudolph, "Institutional Context and the Assignment of Political Responsibility," *Journal of Politics* 65, no. 1 (2003); Richard Rose and Doh Chull Shin, "Democratization Backwards: The Problem of Third Wave Democracies," *British Journal of Political Science* 31, no. 2 (2001): 347.

114. Rose and Shin, "Democratization Backwards: The Problem of Third Wave Democracies," 347.

115. Paul Burstein, "The Impact of Public Opinion on Public Policy: A Review and an Agenda," *Political Research Quarterly* 56, no. 1 (2003): 30; Eric M. Uslaner and Ronald E. Weber, "U.S. State Legislators' Opinions and Perceptions of Constituency Attitudes," *Legislative Studies Quarterly* 4, no. 4 (1979): 563.

116. Elster, *Closing the Books: Transitional Justice in Historical Perspective,* 188.

CHAPTER 2   *The Justice Spectrum*

An abridged version of this chapter appeared under the title "Re-Ordering Justice: Towards a New Methodological Approach to Studying Transitional Justice," *Journal of Peace Research* 46, no.6 (November 2009): 819–37.

1. Huntington, *The Third Wave: Democratization in the Late Twentieth Century,* 211.

2. Ibid., 226–29.

3. Ibid., 228.

4. Huyse, "Justice after Transition: On the Choices Successor Elites Make in Dealing with the Past," 76.

5. Ibid., 78.

6. Sieff and Wright, "Reconciling Order and Justice? New Institutional Solutions in Post-Conflict States," 759.

7. Minow, *Between Vengeance and Forgiveness,* 23; Crocker, "Reckoning with the Past: A Normative Framework"; Mark Gibney and Erik Roxstrom, "The Status of State Apologies," *Human Rights Quarterly* 23, no. 4 (2001); Reilly, "Democratic Levers for Conflict Management"; Kritz, "Coming to Terms with Atrocities: A Review of Accountability Mechanisms for Mass Violations of Human Rights."

8. Minow, *Between Vengeance and Forgiveness,* 23; Reilly, "Democratic Levers for Conflict Management."

9. Landsman, "Alternative Responses to Serious Human Rights Abuses: Of Prosecution and Truth Commission"; Hayner, "International Guidelines for the Creation and Operation of Truth Commissions: A Preliminary Proposal."

10. Marek M. Kaminski and Monika Nalepa, "Judging Transitional Justice: A New Criterion for Evaluating Truth Revelation Procedures," *Journal of Conflict Resolution* 50, no. 3 (2006): 385.

11. W. James Booth, "The Unforgotten: Memories of Justice," *American Political Science Review* 95, no. 4 (2001): 779.

12. Claus Offe, *Varieties of Transition: The East European and East German Experience,* 1st MIT Press ed., Studies in Contemporary German Social Thought (Cambridge, Mass.: MIT Press, 1997), 113.

13. Christopher Gelpi, "Crime and Punishment: The Role of Norms in International Crisis Bargaining," *American Political Science Review* 91, no. 2 (1997); Jack Donnelly, "International Human Rights: A Regime Analysis," *International Organization* 40, no. 3 (1986): 608; James D. Fearon, "Bargaining, Enforcement, and International Cooperation," *International Organization* 52, no. 2 (1998); Putnam, "Diplomacy and Domestic Politics: The Logic of Two-Level Games."

14. Abram Chayes and Antonia Handler Chayes, "On Compliance," *International Organization* 47, no. 2 (1993).

15. Burley and Mattli, "Europe before the Court: A Political Theory of Legal Integration"; Keohane and Nye, "Transgovernmental Relations and International Organization."

16. Susan J. Pharr, *Losing Face: Status Politics in Japan* (Berkeley: University of California Press, 1990); Sidney Tarrow, "'Aiming at a Moving Target': Social Science and the Recent Rebellions in Eastern Europe," *PS: Political Science and Politics* 24, no. 1 (1991); Sidney Tarrow, *Power in Movement: Social Movements, Collective Action, and Politics* (New York: Cambridge University Press, 1994).

17. UNHCHR, "Status of Ratifications for the Principal International Human Rights Treaties" (Office of the United Nations High Commissioner for Human Rights, 2004).

18. Putnam, "Diplomacy and Domestic Politics: The Logic of Two-Level Games."

19. Chayes and Chayes, "On Compliance," 197.

20. Linda Camp Keith, "The United Nations International Covenant on Civil and Political Rights: Does It Make a Difference in Human Rights Behavior?" *Journal of Peace Research* 6, no. 1 (1999).

21. Gibney and Roxstrom, "The Status of State Apologies," 914, 924, 926.

22. Jaspers, "The Question of German Guilt," 198.

23. Aaron Lazare, *On Apology* (Oxford; New York: Oxford University Press, 2004), 78; Gibney and Roxstrom, "The Status of State Apologies," 914, 924, 926.

24. McGregor, "Individual Accountability in South Africa: Cultural Optimum or Political Façade?" *American Journal of International Law* 95, no. 1 (2001).

25. Nicholas Tavuchis, *Mea Culpa: A Sociology of Apology and Reconciliation* (Stanford: Stanford University Press, 1991), 17; Nick Smith, *I Was Wrong: The Meanings of Apologies* (Cambridge: Cambridge University Press, 2008), 23.

26. Minow, *Between Vengeance and Forgiveness,* 116.

27. Lazare, *On Apology,* 67, 75.

28. Smith, *I Was Wrong: The Meanings of Apologies,* 173.

29. Ibid., 163–64; Lazare, *On Apology,* 202; Gibney and Roxstrom, "The Status of State Apologies"; Borneman, "Apologies as Performative Redress," 62.

30. Lazare, *On Apology,* 62.

31. Jeffrie G. Murphy, "Forgiveness and Resentment," in *Forgiveness and Mercy,* ed. Jeffrie G. Murphy and Jean Hampton (Cambridge: Cambridge University Press, 1988), 28.

32. Payne, "Collaborators and the Politics of Memory in Chile."

33. Kritz, "Coming to Terms with Atrocities: A Review of Accountability Mechanisms for Mass Violations of Human Rights."

34. Jack Donnelly, "Human Rights at the United Nations, 1955–1985: The Question of Bias," *International Studies Quarterly* 32, no. 3 (1988); Kenneth L. Cain, "The Rape of Dinah: Human Rights, Civil War in Liberia, and Evil Triumphant," *Human Rights Quarterly* 21, no. 2 (1999).

35. IPNSA, "Mideast: U.S. Blocks U.N. Rebuke of Israel for Assassination," *Inter Press News Service Agency,* March 23, 2004.

36. Evelin Gerda Lindner, "Humiliation and Human Rights: Mapping a Minefield," *Human Rights Review* 2, no. 3 (2001); Gilligan, "Shame, Guilt, and Violence."

37. Toronto, "Freed Argentine Junta Leader Accused of Provoking Unrest," *Toronto Star* (Reuters), January 1, 1991.

38. Leslie Crawford, "Chile Tries to Exorcise Ghosts with Public Burial of Allende," *The Sunday Times* (London), September 2, 1990.

39. Aguilar and Humblebaek, "Collective Memory and National Identity in the Spanish Democracy: The Legacies of Francoism and the Civil War," 132.

40. Eric A. Posner and Adrian Vermeule, "Transitional Justice as Ordinary Justice," *Harvard Law Review* 117, no. 3 (2004).

41. Crocker, "Reckoning with the Past: A Normative Framework," 51.

42. Landsman, "Alternative Responses to Serious Human Rights Abuses: Of Prosecution and Truth Commission," 86.

43. UN, "The Right to Restitution, Compensation, and Rehabilitation for Victims of Gross Violations of Human Rights and Fundamental Freedoms"; UN, "Basic Principles and Guidelines on the Right to Reparation for Victims of Gross Violations of Human Rights and Humanitarian Law"; CE, "Resolution #1096 on Measures to Dismantle the Heritage of Former Communist Totalitarian Systems."

44. BBC, "Chile Navy's Opinion of Rettig Report; Government Supports Report's Veracity," *BBC Summary of World Broadcasts,* April 1, 1991.

45. Aguilar and Humblebaek, "Collective Memory and National Identity in the Spanish Democracy: The Legacies of Francoism and the Civil War," 132.

46. Simpson and van Zyl, "South Africa's Truth and Reconciliation Commission."

47. Leszek Paprzycki interview, December 12, 2003; Ryszard Kalisz interview, December 22, 2003.

48. Adam Domagała, "Poznaj Te Twarze," *Gazeta Wyborcza,* September 26–27, 1998; Adam Domagała, "Winny? Niewinny?" *Gazeta Wyborcza,* December 14, 1998.

49. Christian Rees, "Lonely Vigil for the Loss of Innocents," *The Independent,* October 15, 1990.

50. Vivek Chaudhary, "Argentinians Angry at 'Selective' Compensation for Army's Victims," *The Guardian,* September 26, 1992.

51. Peter S. Green, "Czechs Agree on Payment to Victims of Stalinism," *United Press International,* November 24, 1990.

52. Hayner, *Unspeakable Truths: Confronting State Terror and Atrocity*; Hayner, "Commissioning the Truth: Further Research Questions," *Third World Quarterly* 17, no. 1 (1996); Sieff and Wright, "Reconciling Order and Justice? New Institutional Solutions in Post-Conflict States."

53. Hayner, "Fifteen Truth Commissions, 1974 to 1994: A Comparative Study," 598.

54. Hayner, "International Guidelines for the Creation and Operation of Truth Commissions: A Preliminary Proposal," 173.

55. Kritz, "Coming to Terms with Atrocities: A Review of Accountability Mechanisms for Mass Violations of Human Rights," 138.

56. Hayner, *Unspeakable Truths: Confronting State Terror and Atrocity,* 30.

57. Crocker, "Reckoning with the Past: A Normative Framework," 48; Graybill, "To Punish or Pardon: A Comparison of the International Criminal Tribunal

for Rwanda and the South African Truth and Reconciliation Commission"; Hayner, *Unspeakable Truths: Confronting State Terror and Atrocity.*

58. Dov Cohen, "The American National Conversation about (Everything but) Shame," *Social Research* 70, no. 4 (2003): 1075; Richard A. Shweder, "Toward a Deep Cultural Psychology of Shame," *Social Research* 70, no. 4 (2003); Kurt Riezler, "Comment on the Social Psychology of Shame," *American Journal of Sociology* 48, no. 4 (1943).

59. McGregor, "Individual Accountability in South Africa: Cultural Optimum or Political Façade?" 38; Hayner, *Unspeakable Truths: Confronting State Terror and Atrocity,* 24; Mark J. Osiel, "Why Prosecute? Critics of Punishment for Mass Atrocity," *Human Rights Quarterly* 22, no. 1 (2000); Zalaquett, "Confronting Human Rights Violations Committed by Former Governments: Principles Applicable and Political Constraints."

60. Payne, "Collaborators and the Politics of Memory in Chile"; David Shapiro, "The Tortured, Not the Torturers, Are Ashamed," *Social Research* 70, no. 4 (2003).

61. de Klerk, *The Last Trek—a New Beginning: The Autobiography,* 288.

62. Richard A. Wilson, *The Politics of Truth and Reconciliation in South Africa: Legitimizing the Post-Apartheid State* (New York: Cambridge University Press, 2001), 7; Waldmeir, *Anatomy of a Miracle: The End of Apartheid and the Birth of the New South Africa,* 213; Newham, "Truth and Reconciliation: Realising the Ideals"; Lindsay Michie Eades, *The End of Apartheid in South Africa* (Westport, Conn.: Greenwood Press, 1999); John Jackson, "The 1994 Election: An Analysis," in *The New South Africa: Prospects for Domestic and International Security,* ed. F. H. Toase and E. J. Yorke (New York: St. Martin's Press, 1998).

63. TRC, "Archbishop Desmond Tutu's Address to the First Gathering of the Truth and Reconciliation Commission," *Truth and Reconciliation Commission* (TRC) *Press Release,* December 16, 1995.

64. Davenport, *The Birth of a New South Africa.*

65. de Klerk, *The Last Trek—a New Beginning: The Autobiography,* 377.

66. BBC, "World: Africa—Truth Commission Admits Failures," *BBC Summary of World Broadcasts,* August 14, 1999.

67. Gibson, "Truth, Justice, and Reconciliation: Judging the Fairness of Amnesty in South Africa."

68. Kritz, "Coming to Terms with Atrocities: A Review of Accountability Mechanisms for Mass Violations of Human Rights."

69. Susan Dicklitch and Doreen Lwanga, "The Politics of Being Non-Political: Human Rights Organizations and the Creation of a Positive Human Rights Culture in Uganda," *Human Rights Quarterly* 25, no. 2 (2003).

70. Hayner, *Unspeakable Truths: Confronting State Terror and Atrocity,* 291–320.

71. Tracy Wilkinson and Marjorie Miller, "Salvador Military Awaits Probe," *Toronto Star,* October 13, 1992; Daniel Alder, "Salvadoran Judge Orders Release of Death Squad Killer," *United Press International,* April 3, 1993.

72. Kritz, "Coming to Terms with Atrocities: A Review of Accountability Mechanisms for Mass Violations of Human Rights."

73. Stephen L. Esquith, "Toward a Democratic Rule of Law: East and West," *Political Theory* 27, no. 3 (1999).

74. Kritz, "Coming to Terms with Atrocities: A Review of Accountability Mechanisms for Mass Violations of Human Rights."

75. Baehr, "Controversies in the Current International Human Rights Debate."

76. Andrew Rigby, *Justice and Reconciliation: After the Violence* (Boulder, Colo.: Lynne Rienner Publishers, 2001).

77. CE, "Resolution #1096 on Measures to Dismantle the Heritage of Former Communist Totalitarian Systems."

78. John P. Moran, "The Communist Torturers of Eastern Europe—Prosecute and Punish or Forgive and Forget," *Communist and Post-Communist Studies* 27, no. 1 (1994).

79. Kritz, "Coming to Terms with Atrocities: A Review of Accountability Mechanisms for Mass Violations of Human Rights."

80. Ved P. Nanda, "Civil and Political Sanctions as an Accountability Mechanism for Massive Violations of Human Rights," *Denver Journal of International Law and Politics* 26, no. 3 (1998): 391.

81. Peter Romijn, "'Restoration of Confidence': The Purge of Local Government in the Netherlands as a Problem of Post-War Reconstruction," in *The Politics of Retribution in Europe: World War II and Its Aftermath,* ed. István Deák, Jan Tomasz Gross, and Tony Judt (Princeton: Princeton University Press, 2000).

82. Nanda, "Civil and Political Sanctions as an Accountability Mechanism for Massive Violations of Human Rights," 391; Kritz, "Coming to Terms with Atrocities: A Review of Accountability Mechanisms for Mass Violations of Human Rights."

83. Economist, "The Army and Mr. Averoff," *The Economist,* September 20, 1975, 12.

84. Wilkinson and Miller, "Salvador Military Awaits Probe."

85. Elster, *Closing the Books: Transitional Justice in Historical Perspective*; Walicki, "Transitional Justice and the Political Struggles in Post-Communist Po-

land"; Maria Los and Andrzej Zybertowicz, "Is Revolution a Solution?" in *The Rule of Law after Communism,* ed. Martin Krygier and Adam Czarnota (Brookfield, Vt.: Dartmouth, 1999).

86. Krzysztof Kozłowski interview, January 21, 2004.

87. Steven R. Ratner and Jason S. Abrams, *Accountability for Human Rights Atrocities in International Law: Beyond the Nuremberg Legacy* (Oxford: Oxford University Press, 2001).

88. CE, "Resolution #1096 on Measures to Dismantle the Heritage of Former Communist Totalitarian Systems"; Naomi Roht-Arriaza, "Combatting Impunity: Some Thoughts on the Way Forward," *Law and Contemporary Problems* 59, no. 4 (1996); Fletcher and Weinstein, "Violence and Social Repair: Rethinking the Contribution of Justice to Reconciliation."

89. Huntington, *The Third Wave: Democratization in the Late Twentieth Century*; Jaspers, "The Question of German Guilt"; McGregor, "Individual Accountability in South Africa: Cultural Optimum or Political Façade?"; Kritz, "Coming to Terms with Atrocities: A Review of Accountability Mechanisms for Mass Violations of Human Rights."

90. Kritz, "Coming to Terms with Atrocities: A Review of Accountability Mechanisms for Mass Violations of Human Rights," 129.

91. Ibid.; McGregor, "Individual Accountability in South Africa: Cultural Optimum or Political Façade?"

92. Jaspers, "The Question of German Guilt," 199.

93. Economist, "Judge Better, Lest You Be Judged," *The Economist,* December 18, 1976, 47; McGregor, "Individual Accountability in South Africa: Cultural Optimum or Political Façade?"

94. AFP, "More Than 5,000 Ethiopians Charged with 'Red Terror' Crimes," *Agence France Presse,* February 13, 1997.

95. Kritz, "Coming to Terms with Atrocities: A Review of Accountability Mechanisms for Mass Violations of Human Rights," 133. See also Corey and Joireman, "Retributive Justice: The Gacaca Courts in Rwanda."

96. Katharina von Kellenbach, "Vanishing Acts: Perpetrators in Postwar Germany," *Holocaust and Genocide Studies* 17, no. 2 (2003).

97. Krystyna Naszkowska, "Gruba Kreska Olszewskiego," *Gazeta Wyborcza,* May 26, 1992.

98. Carlos Santiago Nino, *Radical Evil on Trial* (New Haven: Yale University Press, 1996), 166–79.

99. Bradley Graham, "Buenos Aires Presses Trials of Military; Restructuring Effort Continues to Lag," *Washington Post,* April 29, 1986.

100. John Barham, "Mothers Who Mourn Their Lost Innocents: Argentina's 'Disappeared' Children," *Financial Times,* May 9, 1992.

101. Tom Hennigan, "Argentina Lifts Ban on 'Dirty War' Military Trials," *The Times* (London), August 22, 2003.

102. LARP, "Ecuador's Former Junta Warns Accusers in Corruption Probe," *Latin American Regional Reports,* February 29, 1980.

103. BBC, "Chilean President's Address and Comments on Human Rights Violations Report," *BBC Summary of World Broadcasts,* March 6, 1991; BBC, "Chile Navy's Opinion of Rettig Report; Government Supports Report's Veracity."

104. AN, "Sierra Leone; Rights Body Welcomes UN Special Court," *Africa News,* January 22, 2002.

105. AN, "Sierra Leone; Standard Voice Let the Special Court Wait," *Africa News,* January 23, 2002.

106. McGregor, "Individual Accountability in South Africa: Cultural Optimum or Political Façade?"; Crocker, "Reckoning with the Past: A Normative Framework."

107. Kritz, "Coming to Terms with Atrocities: A Review of Accountability Mechanisms for Mass Violations of Human Rights," 134.

108. Landsman, "Alternative Responses to Serious Human Rights Abuses: Of Prosecution and Truth Commission," 86.

109. Maryam Kamali, "Accountability for Human Rights Violations: A Comparison of Transitional Justice in East Germany and South Africa," *Columbia Journal of Transnational Law* 40, no. 1 (2001): 107; Rigby, *Justice and Reconciliation: After the Violence,* 104–5; Osiel, "Why Prosecute? Critics of Punishment for Mass Atrocity," 126.

110. Roehrig, *The Prosecution of Former Military Leaders in Newly Democratic Nations,* 199.

111. Steve Rosenberg, "Shades of Spring on Stalin Legacy," *BBC News,* March 5, 2003.

112. Aleksandar Mitic, "Thousands Join Belgrade Anti-NATO Demo Two Years after Bombings," *Agence France Presse,* March 24, 2001.

113. David Holley, "Serbs Face Their Past, Dose of Truth at a Time," *Los Angeles Times,* April 17, 2001; Peter Ford, "Serbs Still Ignore Role in Atrocity," *Christian Science Monitor,* February 11, 2002.

114. RFE/RL, "Yugoslavia: Djindjic Says Serbia Will Not Extradite Mladic," *Radio Free Europe/Radio Liberty,* February 23, 2002.

115. DPA, "Chilean Police Use Fire Hoses to Control Pinochet Supporters," *Deutsche Presse-Agentur,* October 19, 1998.

116. DPA, "Former Apartheid Leader Rejects South Africa's Truth Commission," *Deutsche Presse-Agentur,* November 21, 1995.

117. Economist, "Military Coup Attempt Foiled," *The Economist,* March 1, 1975; Economist, "Blood Doesn't Cleanse," *The Economist,* August 30, 1975.

118. Economist, "The Army and Mr. Averoff."

119. Graham, "Buenos Aires Presses Trials of Military; Restructuring Effort Continues to Lag"; Barham, "Mothers Who Mourn Their Lost Innocents: Argentina's 'Disappeared' Children."

120. Felix Mponda, "Banda Murder Case Monday Puts African Democracy and Law on Trial," *Agence France Presse,* April 23, 1995; AFP, "President Muluzi Surprised at Rumors of Coup Plot," *Agence France Presse,* April 23, 1995; AFP, "Senior Army Officer Sought on Coup Plot Charges," *Agence France Presse,* April 26, 1995.

CHAPTER 3 *The Peculiarities of Postcommunist Justice*

1. Conway Henderson, "Conditions Affecting the Use of Political Repression," *Journal of Conflict Resolution* 35, no. 1 (1991): 121.

2. Ibid.; James C. Scott, *Weapons of the Weak: Everyday Forms of Peasant Resistance* (New Haven: Yale University Press, 1985).

3. Christian Davenport, "Multi-Dimensional Threat Perception and State Repression: An Inquiry into Why States Apply Negative Sanctions," *American Journal of Political Science* 39, no. 3 (1995).

4. Ronald Wintrobe, "The Tinpot and the Totalitarian: An Economic Theory of Dictatorship," *American Political Science Review* 84, no. 3 (1990).

5. T. David Mason and Dale A. Krane, "The Political Economy of Death Squads: Toward a Theory of the Impact of State-Sanctioned Terror," *International Studies Quarterly* 33 (1989): 175; Will H. Moore, "The Repression of Dissent: A Substitution Model of Government Coercion," *Journal of Conflict Resolution* 44, no. 1 (2000).

6. Grant Wardlaw, *Political Terrorism: Theory, Tactics, and Counter-Measures* (New York: Cambridge University Press, 1989), 11.

7. Welsh, "Dealing with the Communist Past: Central and East European Experiences after 1990," 419–20; Karel Bartosek, "Central and Southeastern Europe," in *The Black Book of Communism,* ed. Stephane Courtois et al. (Cambridge, Mass.: Harvard University Press, 1999).

8. Herbert Kitschelt, *Post-Communist Party Systems: Competition, Representation, and Inter-Party Cooperation,* Cambridge Studies in Comparative Politics (Cambridge and New York: Cambridge University Press, 1999), 22–26.

9. Jacques Rupnik, "Totalitarianism Revisited," in *Civil Society and the State: New European Perspectives,* ed. John Keane (New York: Verso, 1988), 277.

10. Andrzej Paczkowski, "Poland, the 'Enemy Nation,'" in *The Black Book of Communism,* ed. Stephane Courtois et al. (Cambridge Mass.: Harvard University Press, 1999), 384.

11. Donna Bahry and Brian Silver, "Intimidation and the Symbolic Uses of Terror in the USSR," *American Political Science Review* 81, no. 4 (1987); Shalom H. Schwartz and Anat Bardi, "Influences of Adaptation to Communist Rule on Value Priorities in Eastern Europe," *Political Psychology* 18, no. 2 (1997).

12. Andrzej Tymowski, "The Unwanted Social Revolution: Poland in 1989," *East European Politics and Societies* 7, no. 2 (1993).

13. Timur Kuran, "Now out of Never: The Element of Surprise in the East European Revolution of 1989," *World Politics* 44, no. 1 (1991).

14. Giuseppe di Palma, "Legitimation from the Top to Civil Society: Politico-Cultural Change in Eastern Europe," *World Politics* 44, no. 1 (1991): 61.

15. Offe, *Varieties of Transition: The East European and East German Experience,* 83–84.

16. Vaclav Havel and John Keane, *The Power of the Powerless: Citizens against the State in Central-Eastern Europe* (Armonk, N.Y.: M. E. Sharpe, 1985), 27.

17. Nicolas Werth, "A State against Its People: Violence, Repression, and Terror in the Soviet Union," in *The Black Book of Communism,* ed. Stephane Courtois et al. (Cambridge Mass.: Harvard University Press, 1999).

18. Bartosek, "Central and Southeastern Europe," 438 (quote); Grzegorz Ekiert, *The State against Society: Political Crises and Their Aftermath in East Central Europe* (Princeton: Princeton University Press, 1996), 10.

19. Rupnik, "Totalitarianism Revisited."

20. J. C. Sharman, *Repression and Resistance in Communist Europe,* BASEES/RoutledgeCurzon Series on Russian and East European Studies (London; New York: Routledge Curzon, 2003), 15.

21. Rupnik, "Totalitarianism Revisited," 276.

22. Ibid.; Ekiert, *The State against Society: Political Crises and Their Aftermath in East Central Europe.*

23. Oliver MacDonald, "The Polish Vortex: Solidarity and Socialism," *New Left Review* 139 (1983); di Palma, "Legitimation from the Top to Civil Society: Politico-Cultural Change in Eastern Europe."

24. Christian Joppke, "Revisionism, Dissidence, Nationalism: Opposition in Leninist Regimes," *British Journal of Sociology* 45, no. 4 (1994).

25. M. Vajda, "East-Central European Perspectives," in *Civil Society and the State: New European Perspectives,* ed. John Keane (New York: Verso, 1988), 348.

26. Rigby, *Justice and Reconciliation: After the Violence,* 114.

27. Rosenberg, "Overcoming the Legacies of Dictatorship," 15.

28. Peter Siegelman, "The Problems of Lustration: Prosecution of Wrong-doers by Democratic Successor Regimes," *Law and Social Inquiry* 20, no. 1 (1995): 2.

29. Arthur L. Stinchcombe, "Lustration as a Problem of the Social Basis of Constitutionalism," *Law and Social Inquiry* 20 (1995): 246.

30. Aleks Szczerbiak, "Dealing with the Communist Past or the Politics of the Present? Lustration in Post-Communist Poland," *Europe-Asia Studies* 54, no. 4 (2002): 553; Roman David, "Transitional Injustice? Criteria for Conformity of Lustration to the Right to Political Expression," *Europe-Asia Studies* 56, no. 6 (2004): 789; Kaminski and Nalepa, "Judging Transitional Justice: A New Criterion for Evaluating Truth Revelation Procedures," 384.

31. Kaminski and Nalepa, "Judging Transitional Justice: A New Criterion for Evaluating Truth Revelation Procedures," 384.

32. Maria Los, "Lustration and Truth Claims: Unfinished Revolutions in Central Europe," *Law and Social Inquiry* 20 (1995): 118; Huyse, "Justice after Transition: On the Choices Successor Elites Make in Dealing with the Past," 52; Cepl and Gillis, "Making Amends after Communism," 118.

33. Natalia Letki, "Lustration and Democratization in East-Central Europe," *Europe-Asia Studies* 54, no. 4 (2002): 535.

34. Crocker, "Reckoning with the Past: A Normative Framework," 44; Roman David, "Lustration Laws in Action: The Motives and Evaluation of Lustration Policy in the Czech Republic and Poland (1989–2001)," *Law and Social Inquiry* 28, no. 2 (2003): 396.

35. Huyse, "Justice after Transition: On the Choices Successor Elites Make in Dealing with the Past," 52.

36. Stinchcombe, "Lustration as a Problem of the Social Basis of Constitutionalism," 255.

37. Stanley Cohen, "State Crimes of Previous Regimes: Knowledge, Accountability, and the Policing of the Past," *Law and Social Inquiry* 20 (1995): 9.

38. Erhard Blankenburg, "The Purge of Lawyers after the Breakdown of the East German Communist Regime," *Law and Social Inquiry* 20 (1995): 224.

39. Williams, Fowler, and Szczerbiak, "Explaining Lustration in Central Europe: A 'Post-Communist Politics' Approach," 23; Kaminski and Nalepa, "Judging Transitional Justice: A New Criterion for Evaluating Truth Revelation Procedures," 384; Szczerbiak, "Dealing with the Communist Past or the Politics of the Present? Lustration in Post-Communist Poland," 553.

40. Jaspers, "The Question of German Guilt."

41. Tina Rosenberg, *The Haunted Land: Facing Europe's Ghosts after Communism* (New York: Random House, 1995), 68.

42. Adam Michnik and Vaclav Havel, "Confronting the Past: Justice or Revenge?" *Journal of Democracy* 4, no. 1 (1993): 25.

43. Letki, "Lustration and Democratization in East-Central Europe," 535, 541; John Miller, "Settling Accounts with a Secret Police: The German Law on the Stasi Records," *Europe-Asia Studies* 50, no. 2 (1998): 318.

44. Jacques Rupnik, "The Post-Totalitarian Blues," *Journal of Democracy* 6, no. 2 (1995): 63.

45. David, "Transitional Injustice? Criteria for Conformity of Lustration to the Right to Political Expression," 789; Letki, "Lustration and Democratization in East-Central Europe," 540; C. Charles Bertschi, "Lustration and the Transition to Democracy: The Cases of Poland and Bulgaria," *East European Quarterly* 28, no. 4 (1994).

46. Williams, Fowler, and Szczerbiak, "Explaining Lustration in Central Europe: A 'Post-Communist Politics' Approach," 29–30; Kaminski and Nalepa, "Judging Transitional Justice: A New Criterion for Evaluating Truth Revelation Procedures," 384.

47. Letki, "Lustration and Democratization in East-Central Europe," 529.

48. David, "Transitional Injustice? Criteria for Conformity of Lustration to the Right to Political Expression," 789.

49. Cohen, "State Crimes of Previous Regimes: Knowledge, Accountability, and the Policing of the Past," 33; Rigby, *Justice and Reconciliation: After the Violence,* 104–5.

50. Adam Michnik, "Reflections on the Collapse of Communism," *Journal of Democracy* 11, no. 1 (2000): 125.

51. Blankenburg, "The Purge of Lawyers after the Breakdown of the East German Communist Regime"; Moran, "The Communist Torturers of Eastern Europe—Prosecute and Punish or Forgive and Forget," 108; Miller, "Settling Accounts with a Secret Police: The German Law on the Stasi Records," 308.

52. Letki, "Lustration and Democratization in East-Central Europe," 542; Rigby, *Justice and Reconciliation: After the Violence,* 104–5; Welsh, "Dealing with the Communist Past: Central and East European Experiences after 1990," 418.

53. Krzysztof Jasiewicz, "The Political-Party Landscape," *Journal of Democracy* 18, no. 4 (2007): 32.

54. Lawrence Weschler, "The Velvet Purge: The Trials of Jan Kavan," *The New Yorker* (October 19, 1992); Michnik, "Reflections on the Collapse of Communism," 125.

55. Rigby, *Justice and Reconciliation: After the Violence,* 104–5.

56. Michnik and Havel, "Confronting the Past: Justice or Revenge?" 22.

57. Michnik, "Reflections on the Collapse of Communism," 125–26.

58. Michnik and Havel, "Confronting the Past: Justice or Revenge?"

59. David, "Transitional Injustice? Criteria for Conformity of Lustration to the Right to Political Expression," 792.

60. Monika Nalepa, *Skeletons in the Closet: Transitional Justice in Post-Communist Europe* (Cambridge: Cambridge University Press, 2009).

61. Los, "Lustration and Truth Claims: Unfinished Revolutions in Central Europe," 119.

62. David, "Lustration Laws in Action: The Motives and Evaluation of Lustration Policy in the Czech Republic and Poland (1989–2001)," 395.

63. Esquith, "Toward a Democratic Rule of Law: East and West," 339.

64. John Higley, Judith Kullberg, and Jan Pakulski, "The Persistence of Post-Communist Elites," *Journal of Democracy* 7, no. 2 (1996): 138.

65. Rigby, *Justice and Reconciliation: After the Violence,* 109; Mary Kaldor and Ivan Vejvoda, "Democratization in Central and East European Countries," *International Affairs* (Royal Institute of International Affairs) 73, no. 1 (1997): 73.

66. Welsh, "Dealing with the Communist Past: Central and East European Experiences after 1990," 414; Walicki, "Transitional Justice and the Political Struggles in Post-Communist Poland," 185–86; David Ost, "The Politics of Interest in Post-Communist East Europe," *Theory and Society* 22, no. 4 (1993): 478; Szczerbiak, "Dealing with the Communist Past or the Politics of the Present? Lustration in Post-Communist Poland," 560.

67. Rigby, *Justice and Reconciliation: After the Violence,* 109.

68. Moran, "The Communist Torturers of Eastern Europe—Prosecute and Punish or Forgive and Forget," 105.

69. David, "Transitional Injustice? Criteria for Conformity of Lustration to the Right to Political Expression," 806.

70. Kaminski and Nalepa, "Judging Transitional Justice: A New Criterion for Evaluating Truth Revelation Procedures."

71. Ibid., 401.

72. Rupnik, "The Post-Totalitarian Blues," 63; Posner and Vermeule, "Transitional Justice as Ordinary Justice."

73. Letki, "Lustration and Democratization in East-Central Europe," 542.

74. Ibid.; Miller, "Settling Accounts with a Secret Police: The German Law on the Stasi Records," 309.

75. Los, "Lustration and Truth Claims: Unfinished Revolutions in Central Europe," 160.

76. Welsh, "Dealing with the Communist Past: Central and East European Experiences after 1990," 415; Grazyna Skapska, "Moral Definitions in Constitutionalism in East Central Europe: Facing Past Human Rights Violations," *International Sociology* 18, no. 1 (2003).

77. Nadya Nedelsky, "Divergent Responses to a Common Past: Transitional Justice in the Czech Republic and Slovakia," *Theory and Society* 33, no. 1 (2004): 70.

78. Ibid., 70–71; Michael Kraus, "The Czech Republic's First Decade," *Journal of Democracy* 14, no. 2 (2003): 52.

79. David, "Transitional Injustice? Criteria for Conformity of Lustration to the Right to Political Expression," 792.

80. Miller, "Settling Accounts with a Secret Police: The German Law on the Stasi Records," 307; Blankenburg, "The Purge of Lawyers after the Breakdown of the East German Communist Regime," 232.

81. Miller, "Settling Accounts with a Secret Police: The German Law on the Stasi Records," 309–10.

82. Ibid., 315.

83. Rigby, *Justice and Reconciliation: After the Violence,* 104–5.

84. Miller, "Settling Accounts with a Secret Police: The German Law on the Stasi Records," 316, 319, 321.

85. Nedelsky, "Divergent Responses to a Common Past: Transitional Justice in the Czech Republic and Slovakia," 104.

86. Higley, Kullberg, and Pakulski, "The Persistence of Post-Communist Elites," 138.

87. Wojciech Sadurski, *Rights before Courts: A Study of Constitutional Courts in Postcommunist States of Central and Eastern Europe* (Norwell, Mass.: Springer, 2005), 248.

88. Ibid., 249–50.

89. IRBC, "Lithuania: Treatment of Former KGB Agents and the Availability of State Protection (Jan. 1998–Oct. 2002)," Immigration and Refugee Board of Canada, http://www.unhcr.org/refworld/publisher,IRBC,,LTU,3f7d4dc623,0 .html.

90. Welsh, "Dealing with the Communist Past: Central and East European Experiences after 1990," 416.

91. Letki, "Lustration and Democratization in East-Central Europe," 539.

92. Ibid., 539–40; Williams, Fowler, and Szczerbiak, "Explaining Lustration in Central Europe: A 'Post-Communist Politics' Approach," 25.

93. Nedelsky, "Divergent Responses to a Common Past: Transitional Justice in the Czech Republic and Slovakia," 76.

94. Welsh, "Dealing with the Communist Past: Central and East European Experiences after 1990," 419–20.

95. Ibid.

96. Ibid.

97. Letki, "Lustration and Democratization in East-Central Europe," 546.

98. Ibid., 537.

99. Nedelsky, "Divergent Responses to a Common Past: Transitional Justice in the Czech Republic and Slovakia," 81.

100. Moran, "The Communist Torturers of Eastern Europe—Prosecute and Punish or Forgive and Forget."

101. Welsh, "Dealing with the Communist Past: Central and East European Experiences after 1990," 422–24. One argument that does not fit neatly into either category is Skapska's, whose claim that cultural factors determine the justice pursued seems to disregard the important political context; see Skapska, "Moral Definitions in Constitutionalism in East Central Europe: Facing Past Human Rights Violations," 211. Her evidence, particularly that Protestant East Germany has been much more aggressive than Catholic Poland, is also weakened by Poland's subsequent passage of a far-reaching lustration bill.

102. Williams, Fowler, and Szczerbiak, "Explaining Lustration in Central Europe: A 'Post-Communist Politics' Approach," 23.

103. Szczerbiak, "Dealing with the Communist Past or the Politics of the Present? Lustration in Post-Communist Poland," 555.

104. Noel Calhoun, "The Ideological Dilemma of Lustration in Poland," *East European Politics and Societies* 16, no. 2 (2002).

105. Welsh, "Dealing with the Communist Past: Central and East European Experiences after 1990."

106. Calhoun, "The Ideological Dilemma of Lustration in Poland."

107. Nedelsky, "Divergent Responses to a Common Past: Transitional Justice in the Czech Republic and Slovakia," 102; Williams, Fowler, and Szczerbiak, "Explaining Lustration in Central Europe: A 'Post-Communist Politics' Approach," 33.

108. Letki, "Lustration and Democratization in East-Central Europe," 546.

109. Kaminski and Nalepa, "Judging Transitional Justice: A New Criterion for Evaluating Truth Revelation Procedures," 391.

110. Welsh, "Dealing with the Communist Past: Central and East European Experiences after 1990," 417; Nedelsky, "Divergent Responses to a Common Past: Transitional Justice in the Czech Republic and Slovakia," 77.

111. Nedelsky, "Divergent Responses to a Common Past: Transitional Justice in the Czech Republic and Slovakia," 77.

112. Welsh, "Dealing with the Communist Past: Central and East European Experiences after 1990," 416; Mark Ellis, "Purging the Past: The Current State of Lustration Laws in the Former Communist Bloc," *Law and Contemporary Problems* 59, no. 4 (1996).

113. Welsh, "Dealing with the Communist Past: Central and East European Experiences after 1990," 417.

114. Moran, "The Communist Torturers of Eastern Europe—Prosecute and Punish or Forgive and Forget," 107; Welsh, "Dealing with the Communist Past: Central and East European Experiences after 1990," 416.

115. Kamali, "Accountability for Human Rights Violations: A Comparison of Transitional Justice in East Germany and South Africa," 107; Welsh, "Dealing with the Communist Past: Central and East European Experiences after 1990," 417; Rigby, *Justice and Reconciliation: After the Violence,* 114.

116. Moran, "The Communist Torturers of Eastern Europe—Prosecute and Punish or Forgive and Forget," 101 (quote); Szczerbiak, "Dealing with the Communist Past or the Politics of the Present? Lustration in Post-Communist Poland," 556–57; Nedelsky, "Divergent Responses to a Common Past: Transitional Justice in the Czech Republic and Slovakia," 69.

117. Nedelsky, "Divergent Responses to a Common Past: Transitional Justice in the Czech Republic and Slovakia," 78.

118. Letki, "Lustration and Democratization in East-Central Europe," 538.

119. Williams, Fowler, and Szczerbiak, "Explaining Lustration in Central Europe: A 'Post-Communist Politics' Approach," 33; Szczerbiak, "Dealing with the Communist Past or the Politics of the Present? Lustration in Post-Communist Poland," 559.

120. Moran, "The Communist Torturers of Eastern Europe—Prosecute and Punish or Forgive and Forget," 103; Ost, "The Politics of Interest in Post-Communist East Europe," 478.

121. Ost, "The Politics of Interest in Post-Communist East Europe," 478.

122. Bertschi, "Lustration and the Transition to Democracy: The Cases of Poland and Bulgaria"; Szczerbiak, "Dealing with the Communist Past or the Politics of the Present? Lustration in Post-Communist Poland," 558; Welsh, "Dealing with the Communist Past: Central and East European Experiences after 1990," 424.

123. Neil J. Kritz, "The Dilemmas of Transitional Justice," in *Transitional Justice: How Emerging Democracies Reckon with Former Regimes,* ed. Neil J. Kritz (Washington, D.C.: United States Institute of Peace Press, 1995), xix.

124. Offe, *Varieties of Transition: The East European and East German Experience,* 89.

CHAPTER 4   *The Method of Study*

1. Arend Lijphart, "Comparative Politics and the Comparative Method," *American Political Science Review* 65, no. 3 (1971): 683.

2. John Gerring, "What Is a Case Study and What Is It Good For?" *American Political Science Review* 98, no. 2 (2004): 342.

3. Ibid., 352; Robert K. Yin, *Case Study Research: Design and Methods* (Thousand Oaks, Calif.: Sage Publications, 1994).

4. Yin, *Case Study Research: Design and Methods,* 46.

5. Szczerbiak, "Dealing with the Communist Past or the Politics of the Present? Lustration in Post-Communist Poland"; Calhoun, "The Ideological Dilemma of Lustration in Poland."

6. Skapska, "Moral Definitions in Constitutionalism in East Central Europe: Facing Past Human Rights Violations"; Nedelsky, "Divergent Responses to a Common Past: Transitional Justice in the Czech Republic and Slovakia"; Williams, Fowler, and Szczerbiak, "Explaining Lustration in Central Europe: A 'Post-Communist Politics' Approach."

7. Welsh, "Dealing with the Communist Past: Central and East European Experiences after 1990"; Letki, "Lustration and Democratization in East-Central Europe"; Moran, "The Communist Torturers of Eastern Europe—Prosecute and Punish or Forgive and Forget."

8. Barahona De Brito, Gonzales-Enriquez, and Aguilar, "Introduction," 13.

9. Walicki, "Transitional Justice and the Political Struggles in Post-Communist Poland."

10. One can, of course, identify disparities among states. In Poland, Solidarity's rise in the early 1980s seemed to symbolize the great power of civil society. This period, however, proved ephemeral, and in postcommunist Poland there are few signs that such a powerful organization could ever arise. The fabled *mahallas,* or neighborhood committees, in Uzbekistan appear to represent organizing powers of the state rather than of the people. In Serbia and Croatia, fifteen years after the fall of communism, civil society remains marginalized and frequently suspect. In much of the postcommunist world, civil society is still perceived as anything from irrelevant to malevolent.

11. Snyder and Vinjamuri, "Trials and Errors: Principle and Pragmatism in Strategies of International Justice," 14; Pion-Berlin, "To Prosecute or to Pardon? Human Rights Decisions in the Latin American Southern Cone," 116; Barahona De Brito, "Truth, Justice, Memory, and Democratization in the Southern Cone," 121.

12. For the Uzbek case, I reviewed the entire period of *Narodnoye Slovo* and *O'zbekiston Ovozi,* and a more limited date range of *Pravda Vostoka* and *Khalq So'zi.*

I employed two research assistants to scan the Uzbek language papers, and I read through the articles they pulled out.

13. *Nasi W Sejmie I W Senacie: Posłowie I Senatorowie Wybrani Z Listy Solidarności* (Warsaw: Oficyna Wydawnicza Volumen, 1990).

14. Huntington, *The Third Wave: Democratization in the Late Twentieth Century,* 226–29.

15. Charles A. Lave and James G. March, *An Introduction to Models in the Social Sciences* (New York: Harper & Row, 1975).

CHAPTER 5   *Poland*

1. Edmund Wnuk-Lipiński, "Recydywa PRL Z Nasza Pomoca," *Gazeta Wyborcza,* July 5, 1994.

2. Signature dates in this section can be found at HRI, "Human Rights Internet: For the Record 2002—the United Nations Human Rights System," Human Rights Internet, www.hri.ca/fortherecord2002/engtext/vol5eng/polandrr .htm. For official ratification dates, I refer to the date assigned by the Office of the United Nations High Commissioner for Human Rights, "Status of Ratifications for the Principal International Human Rights Treaties" (as of June 4, 2004), available at www.unhchr.ch.

3. Purportedly the last political prisoner, a historian and journalist for the Polish Press Agency (PAP) named Józef Szaniawski, was released from prison in December 1989. Rzeczpospolita, "Ostatni Więzień Polityczny PRL," *Rzeczpospolita,* April 21–22, 1990. The amnesty released those serving two-to three-year sentences on misdemeanors (see Polish Parliament, *Dziennik Ustaw,* nr. 64, poz. 390, 1989).

4. Werth, "A State against Its People: Violence, Repression, and Terror in the Soviet Union."

5. Gazeta, "Miejsce Pod Krzyżem," *Gazeta Wyborcza,* December 4, 1989.

6. Sejm, *Monitor Polski,* nr. 21, poz. 327, June 21, 2001.

7. Gazeta, "Osądzony Stan Wojenny," *Gazeta Wyborcza,* October 7, 1991.

8. Jerzy Pilczyński, "Stan Wojenny—Nielegalny," *Rzeczpospolita,* February 3, 1992; Walicki, "Transitional Justice and the Political Struggles in Post-Communist Poland."

9. Agata Nowakowska, "Stan Wojenny Według SLD," *Gazeta Wyborcza,* December 17–18, 1994.

10. Eliza Olczyk and Jerzy Pilczyński, "Hołd i Potępienie," *Rzeczpospolita,* December 16–17, 1995; Gazeta, "Spór O Stan Wojenny," *Gazeta Wyborcza,* December 15, 1995.

11. Senat, *Monitor Polski,* nr. 59, poz. 799, December 6, 2002.

12. Senat, *Monitor Polski,* nr. 20, poz. 287, June 18, 1998.

13. Gazeta, "Przepraszam Za PRL," *Gazeta Wyborcza,* November 10–11, 1993.

14. Andrzej Zoll interview, December 17, 2003.

15. Stanisław Ciosek interview, January 30, 2004.

16. Andrzej Findeisen interview, January 23, 2004.

17. Stefan Niesiołowski interview, January 6, 2004; Zbigniew Romaszewski interview, January 19, 2004.

18. Senat, *Sprawozdanie Stenograficzne,* Kadencja I, 4 posiedzenie, August 11, 1989, 64; Senat, *Sprawozdanie Stenograficzne,* Kadencja I, 6 posiedzenie, August 30, 1989, 64.

19. Piotr Andrzejewski interview, January 29, 2004.

20. Jerzy Ciemniewski interview, December 30, 2003.

21. Relative power arguments do not directly address what would happen two years after a transition, but, by applying their general logic to a longitudinal study, we should expect to see subsequently stronger new elites pursuing more aggressive policies.

22. Jacek Taylor interview, January 9, 2004.

23. Gazeta, "Odszkodowanie Za Stalinowski Wyrok," *Gazeta Wyborcza,* November 13, 1990.

24. Krystyna Łopuchowska, "Na Rehabilitacje Zawsze Czas," *Rzeczpospolita,* July 10, 1990.

25. Gazeta, "Sprawiedliwość Dogania Niepodległość," *Gazeta Wyborcza,* November 10, 1990.

26. Rzeczpospolita, "Stalinowskie Wyroki Będą Unieważnione," *Rzeczpospolita,* February 14, 1991.

27. Senat, *Dziennik Ustaw,* Kadencja I, 45 posiedzenie, March 15, 1991, 83; see also Senator Edward Wende's and Senator Leszek Piotrowski's remarks, respectively, 42 and 36.

28. Gazeta, "Zaświadczenia O Więziennej Wysludze Lat," *Gazeta Wyborcza,* February 25, 1991.

29. At least three Sejm members pointed this out during the debate; see comments by Ujazdowski, Bednarkiewicz, and Paprzycki, January 12, in Sejm, *Sprawozdanie Stenograficzne,* Kadencja X, 49 posiedzenie, 1991, 156–91.

30. Bartosz Dobrzyński, "Zapłata Za Stalinism," *Gazeta Wyborcza*, August 17, 1992.

31. Danuta Frey, "Rehabilitacja Sądownictwa," *Rzeczpospolita*, April 29, 1994.

32. See European Court of Human Rights (ECHR), *Case of Kurzac vs. Poland*, February 22, 2001; European Court of Human Rights (ECHR), *Case of Halka and Others vs. Poland*, July 2, 2002. Available at: http://echr.coe.int/echr/

33. Gazeta, "Pieniądze Za Niewinność," *Gazeta Wyborcza*, May 31, 1991; Gazeta, "Kropiwnicki Rezygnuje Z Odszkodowania," *Gazeta Wyborcza*, August 29, 1991; Józef Kuśmierek, "Józef Kuśmierek Proponuje Zrzutkę Na Andrzeja Słowika," *Gazeta Wyborcza*, June 21, 1991.

34. Gazeta, "Ugoda Z MSW," *Gazeta Wyborcza*, April 18–20, 1992.

35. Rzeczpospolita, "Proces O Odszkodowanie Za Utratę Wzroku," *Rzeczpospolita*, October 3, 1995.

36. Gazeta, "Senat Ofiarom Grudnia '70," *Gazeta Wyborcza*, January 27–28, 1996; Gazeta, "Naprawa Zadawnionych Krzywd," *Gazeta Wyborcza*, April 25, 1997.

37. Włodzimierz Bieroń, "Wyroki Bez Pokrycia," *Rzeczpospolita*, May 21, 1993; Gazeta, "Rachunek Za Łagry," *Gazeta Wyborcza*, September 19–20, 1998.

38. Andrzej Kern interview, January 6, 2004.

39. Sejm, *Sprawozdanie Stenograficzne*, Kadencja X, 49 posiedzenie, January 12, 1991, 185.

40. Grażyna Staniszewska interview, December 17, 2003.

41. Data gathered from an analysis of individual biographies of post-Solidarity elites in the Sejm and Senat (1989–1991); see *Nasi W Sejmie I W Senacie: Posłowie I Senatorowie Wybrani Z Listy Solidarności*. See also Michnik remarks in parliamentary debate, February 23, in Sejm, *Sprawozdanie Stenograficzne*, Kadencja X, 52 posiedzenie, February 23, 1991, 365.

42. Adam Michnik interview, January 14, 2004; Staniszewska interview. Staniszewska commented, "Society would have turned its back on us if we gave this to ourselves." Interestingly, some post-Solidarity elites abandoned this principle after the postcommunists reclaimed power in the 1993 parliamentary and 1995 presidential elections. One man who had spent two years in jail in the 1980s noted that when two fellow activists received compensation for their similar suffering in the early 1990s, "this infuriated us all" (Janusz Pałubicki interview, January 7, 2004). But this idealism faded with the postcommunist victories, which prompted this former victim to claim zł. 22,000 in 1996. "For us, our point of viewed changed. This is not a normal state after all," he added.

43. Sejm, *Sprawozdanie Stenograficzne*, Kadencja X, 49 posiedzenie, 1991, 184.

44. Ibid., 161.

45. Sejm, *Sprawozdanie Stenograficzne,* Kadencja X, 52 posiedzenie, 370.

46. Senat, *Dziennik Ustaw,* Kadencja I, 45 posiedzenie, 1991, 42.

47. Niesiołowski interview. Michnik (see note 42) also spent several years in prison for his opposition activities.

48. Sejm, *Sprawozdanie Stenograficzne,* Kadencja X, 4 posiedzenie, 1989, 291–310.

49. Jerzy Jachowicz, "Spojrzenie W Ciemność," *Gazeta Wyborcza,* November 21, 1989.

50. See, for example, Waldemar Szymczyk, "Winni Zabójstwa Będą Ukarani," *Gazeta Wyborcza,* March 4, 1991; Jan Rokita's statements in Sejm, *Sprawozdanie Stenograficzne,* Kadencja X, 76 posiedzenie, 1991; and Andrzej Konopka interview, December 12, 2003.

51. Ireniusz Dudziec, "Kto Strzelał, Kto Rozkazywał," *Gazeta Wyborcza,* October 3, 1991.

52. Aleksander Herzog interview, January 9, 2004.

53. K. Kozłowski interview.

54. Kazimierz Krasny interview, February 3, 2004.

55. Paweł Łączkowski interview, January 7, 2004.

56. Rokita promised to call up a similar investigatory committee in the subsequent Parliament that would have substantially increased investigative capabilities (see Dudziec, "Kto Strzelał, Kto Rozkazywał"). A year and a half after delivering his final report, Rokita questioned the success of the commission in an open letter published in *Gazeta Wyborcza* in which he complained that "a large number of the petitions that I sent from the special Sejm commission of 1990 were ignored by the prosecutor" (Jan Rokita, "Letter to the Editor," *Gazeta Wyborcza,* May 12, 1994).

57. Maria Dmochowska interview, January 2, 2004.

58. Bronisław Geremek interview, January 20, 2004.

59. See testimony by Zbigniew Pudysza, Zbigniew Sobotka, and Jerzy Karpacz in Sejm, *Sprawozdanie Stenograficzne,* Kadencja X, 4 posiedzenie, 1989, 302.

60. Krasny interview.

61. Dmochowska interview.

62. Ciemniewski interview.

63. Tadeusz Mazowiecki claims that his fears of a communist counterrevolution did not subside until Kiszczak, the man to whom he credited democratic changes, left office in 1990 (Tadeusz Mazowiecki interview, May 19, 2004). Mazowiecki was one of a relatively small number of my respondents who feared that justice could lead to political instability.

64. Ibid.

65. There were also forced resignations in the political world. Andrzej Maj-kowski, assistant to President Kwaśniewski (Foreign Affairs), was forced to resign when it was revealed that, as head of the Union of Socialist Youth (Związek Młod-zieży Socjalistycznej) in March 1968, he had stated a need for harsher treatment of Jews: "We believe that removing them from the party and positions is only the first stage on the road to a consequential accounting for acts of people together guilty for serious perversions in political, economic, and cultural life. We demand a con-sequent cleansing of the party and party administration of Zionists and revisionists." (See Gazeta, "Żałuje Tych Kłamstw," *Gazeta Wyborcza*, March 22, 2001; Gazeta, "Przyjmę Dymisję," *Gazeta Wyborcza*, March 31–April 1, 2001.)

66. Agnieszka Jędrzejczyk, "MSW Się Przebiera," *Gazeta Wyborcza*, Janu-ary 5, 1990.

67. Gazeta, "MSW W Sejmie," *Gazeta Wyborcza*, February 10–11, 1990.

68. In January 1990, for example, a general under pressure from Solidarity activists for his role in the 1982 Wujek shootings retired from the local Kraków branch of the Internal Affairs Ministry (Gazeta, "Gen. Gruba Zrezygnował," *Gazeta Wyborcza*, January 17, 1990). Two months later, ten other generals in the ministry resigned (Jerzy Jachowicz, "Generałów Ubywa," *Gazeta Wyborcza*, March 31, 1990).

69. K. Kozłowski interview.

70. Jan Olszewski interview, January 26, 2004.

71. K. Kozłowski interview.

72. Władysław Krypeł interview, January 28, 2004. See also K. Kozłowski interview; and Los and Zybertowicz, "Is Revolution a Solution?" 283. Critics com-plained that SB verification could not be complete until victims had seen their files and knew who was involved in their cases (Romaszewski interview).

73. K. Kozłowski interview.

74. Jerzy Jachowicz, "Weryfikacja Zweryfikowanych," *Gazeta Wyborcza*, Au-gust 24, 1990.

75. K. Kozłowski interview.

76. Los and Zybertowicz, "Is Revolution a Solution?"

77. In a 1992 review of high court (SN) cases from 1982 to 1984, one author found that those charged with political crimes received much harsher penalties than others. (They were twice as likely to be sent to jail, and longer sentences were gen-erally imposed.) Wanda Falkowska, "Czy Stać Nas Dziś Na Sprawiedliwość," *Gazeta Wyborcza*, February 7, 1992.

78. Herzog interview.

79. Ibid.

80. Approximately thirty were reinstated upon appeal.

81. Gazeta, "Weryfikacja Prokuratorów," *Gazeta Wyborcza,* October 3, 1991.

82. Gazeta, "Niezawisłość Kontrolowana," *Gazeta Wyborcza,* July 16, 1993; Gazeta, "Sędziom Lżej," *Gazeta Wyborcza,* November 10–11, 1993.

83. Law available in Polish Parliament, *Dziennik Ustaw,* nr. 68, poz. 436, 1997. The 1997 law was actually an amendment to the Combatant Law of January 1991, aimed at financially punishing retirees who had benefited from their role in the former system. According to early figures, an estimated 60,000 who had participated in repression from 1944 to 1956 or had collaborated with the Germans during World War II would be deprived of special retirement supplements (Gazeta, "Sprawiedliwość Po Latach," *Gazeta Wyborcza,* February 27, 1992). In December 1992, PSL sent the issue to the ombudsman (Gazeta, "Czas Na Rzecznika," *Gazeta Wyborcza,* December 24, 1992). In February 1994 the Constitutional Tribunal ruled that the law could not be applied to people who "did not take part in fighting independence organizations" (Natalia Skipietrow, "Kombatanci Do Weryfikacji," *Gazeta Wyborcza,* February 13–14, 1993). The Sejm accepted this in a September 1994 amendment to the law (Gazeta, "Nie Chcą Zbrodniarzy," *Gazeta Wyborcza,* December 3, 1994). In December 1994 a postcommunist-dominated Parliament crafted an amended bill that would allow former employees of the Security Office (UB) to get pensions if (1) they had been ordered to join these organizations by an independence organization, or if their work there benefited independence organizations; or (2) if the internal affairs minister could vouch for the person having not repressed anyone. In January 1995, facing considerable political pressure from combatant organizations, Wałęsa vetoed the bill, which the Sejm failed to override the following month (Gazeta, "Cień UB," *Gazeta Wyborcza,* February 17, 1995).

84. Polish Parliament, *Dziennik Ustaw,* nr. 1, poz. 1, 1999; see also Gazeta, "Kara-Wydalenie," *Gazeta Wyborcza,* December 4, 1998.

85. Andrzej Jagiełło interview, January 27, 2004.

86. Kern interview. Two pressure groups emerged during this time—one, composed of old prosecutors pressing for lax vetting; and the other (Ruch Odnowy Prokuratorów), composed largely of young prosecutors in favor of a more rigorous process. According to one Justice Ministry official, these people formed the core of a union that profited professionally from the exclusion of former prosecutors.

87. There was at least one act of resistance that prompted the internal affairs minister to surround an SB training facility with police and disarm rebellious students who had commenced their training under the former regime (K. Kozłowski interview). Rather than rebel, most SB personnel cast themselves as victims of

injustice under the new elites and even created an Organization of Former Workers of the Internal Affairs Ministry to provide legal and material aid to those negatively verified (Waldemar Szymczyk, "Stowarzyszenie Byłych Tajniaków," *Gazeta Wyborcza*, August 3, 1990). Former officers were rehabilitated in court and even sought damages from the Polish treasury (case pending as of time of fieldwork; see Artur Brykner, "Esbek Wylicza Swoje Krzywdy," *Gazeta Wyborcza*, October 18–19, 2003).

88. Ciemniewski interview.

89. Łączkowski interview.

90. Olszewski interview; Józeffa Hennelowa interview, January 22, 2004; Geremek interview, Ryszard Juszkiewicz interview, January 5, 2004.

91. Bogdan Lewandowski interview, December 17, 2003.

92. Olszewski interview.

93. There were also sporadic attempts in Poland to criminalize entire organizations. A precedent had been established at Nuremberg, where members of certain German organizations were deemed criminal in specified cases (for example, those persons must have known and supported the criminal activities of the organization). See *Nuremberg Military Tribunal*, vol. 3, pp. 1029–30, available online at Mazal Library, http://www.mazal.org/archive/nmt/03/NMT03-T1030.htm. In October 1991 an OKP-supported bill in Parliament declared the Ministry of Public Security (MBP), Military Information agency (IW), Security Office (UB), and Security Service (SB) criminal organizations (Gazeta, "Osądzony Stan Wojenny"). Local initiatives also appeared episodically, such as the December 1997 resolution by the Tarnów city council (15:5, 11 abstentions) declaring the PZPR, UB, and SB criminal institutions (Gazeta, "Przestępcza PZPR," *Gazeta Wyborcza*, December 5, 1997). It is unclear to me what the precise repercussions of this would be, but it seems to make common functionaries more vulnerable. The combatant law, which also condemns certain organizations, has led to financial penalties for some of them.

94. In May 1989, just before Poland's first semi-free elections, the outgoing communist Sejm passed an act on "forgiveness and forgetting certain crimes and violations" of a political nature that had occurred after the signing of the Gdańsk Agreement, on August 31, 1981 (Polish Parliament, *Dziennik Ustaw*, nr. 34, poz. 179, 1989). According to the amnesty, all investigations and trials in process would be halted (unless the crime qualified for a sentence of more than three years) and confiscated property would be returned. The free press immediately reacted with skepticism. *Gazeta*'s Wanda Falkowska, reporting on the event as a news story, commented that the act failed to address the "essential question" of how those whose rights were violated during the investigation and trial (including "the right to defense, use of questionable evidence, and sometimes even coercive deals [*pomó-*

wieniach]") would be guaranteed justice (Wanda Falkowska, "Amnestia," *Gazeta Wyborcza,* May 30, 1989). According to Falkowska, the act raised the question of "who should forgive whom."

95. Rzeczpospolita, "Przeciwko Narodowi," *Rzeczpospolita,* October 12, 1990.

96. For the law, see Polish Parliament, *Dziennik Ustaw,* nr. 45, poz. 195, 1991. See also Gazeta, "Zbrodnia Przeciw Narodowi Nie Będą Przedawniane," *Gazeta Wyborcza,* April 5, 1991.

97. Aleksander Bentkowski interview, December 18, 2003; Jan Ordyński, "Będą Procesy Stalinowskich Zbrodniarzy," *Rzeczpospolita,* August 9, 1993.

98. Gazeta, "PRL Potępiona I Stracona W Niebyt?" *Gazeta Wyborcza,* July 1–2, 1995; Artur Domosławski, "Ścigany PRL," *Gazeta Wyborcza,* June 10–11, 1995; Krzysztof Olszewski, "Nieprzedawnianie Zbrodni PRL Według Senatorow 'Solidarności,'" *Rzeczpospolita,* January 28–29, 1995; Eliza Olczyn and Jerzy Prczyński, "Przeciw Przedawnieniu," *Rzeczpospolita,* March 3, 1995. The parliamentary vote is available at Sejm, *Sprawozdanie Stenograficzne,* Kadencja II, 51 posiedzenie, June 9, 1991, 205–6.

99. Rzeczpospolita, "Bez Przedawnienia Zbrodni," *Rzeczpospolita*, March 10, 1995.

100. Gazeta, "Czy Karać Za 13 Grudnia '81?" *Gazeta Wyborcza*, February 15, 1996; Gazeta, "Funkcjonariusze Publiczni," *Gazeta Wyborcza*, April 25, 1996; Polish Parliament, *Dziennik Ustaw,* nr. 89, poz. 400, 1996.

101. Domosławski, "Ścigany PRL."

102. Gazeta, "PRL Potępiona I Stracona W Niebyt?"

103. Jolanta Kroner, "Prawo Dogoniła Chronionych Przez Politykę," *Rzeczpospolita*, August 9, 1996.

104. Walicki, "Transitional Justice and the Political Struggles in Post-Communist Poland," 220.

105. Jan Ordyński, "Całe Śledstwo W Rękach Głównej Komisji," *Gazeta Wyborcza*, January 2, 1998.

106. The vote was 237:157, with opposition primarily from the SLD; PSL, the peasant party previously allied with postcommunists, abstained (Gazeta, "Każdemu Jego Teczki," *Gazeta Wyborcza,* September 23, 1998). A special commission working on the IPN bill rejected a presidential proposal that would allow anyone access to their secret files but would not give the IPN the power to prosecute (Rzeczpospolita, "Nim Każdy Zajrzy Do Teczki," *Rzeczpospolita*, June 3, 1998).

107. Gazeta, "Weto Na Teczki," *Gazeta Wyborcza*, December 5–6, 1998; Sejm, *Sprawozdanie Stenograficzne*, Kadencja III, 39 posiedzenie, 1998, 176–202, 245–46.

108. Pilczyński, "Stan Wojenny—Nielegalny," 158–213; Sejm, *Sprawoz-danie Stenograficzne*, Kadencja I, 7 posiedzenie, 1992.

109. Gazeta, "Przesłuchanie WRON-Y," *Gazeta Wyborcza*, September 23, 1992.

110. Wojciech Zaluska, "Adwokaci Generałów," *Gazeta Wyborcza*, February 2, 1994; Wojciech Załuska, "Palenie Nie Wzrbonione," *Gazeta Wyborcza*, April 7, 1994.

111. Wojciech Załuska, "Stan Wojenny Do Umorzenia," *Gazeta Wyborcza*, February 14, 1996; Dominika Wielowieyska, "Stan Umorzenia," *Gazeta Wyborcza*, October 24, 1996.

112. At least some of these investigations were opened at the request of the Rokita Commission (Gazeta, "Wznowić Śledztwa," *Gazeta Wyborcza*, June 6, 1990), others at the request of family members or members of the government (for example, the Justice Ministry). Prosecutors opened investigations into a range of communist crimes, including the unsolved 1988 death of Mieczysław Turbaki-ewicz, who died during a factory strike at Stalowa Wola (May 1990); the 1982 killing of an opposition activist (June 1990); Gdańsk 1970 (September 1990); illegally destroying Interior Ministry files concerning SB operations (October 1990); 1945–1950 human rights crimes committed by local functionaries (No-vember 1990); the 1984 abduction of Solidarity activists in the Toruń area (April 1991); the 1981 Wujek mine shootings (October 1991); the 1982 Lubin shoot-ings (October 1991); and Radom 1976 (1995). In May and June 1990 the Jus-tice Ministry announced that it would ask prosecutors to reopen the 1983 death of opposition activist Grzegorz Przemyk, and it called for a broader investigation of the 1984 murder of Father Jerzy Popiełuszko. By October 1990, several high-ranking Internal Affairs Ministry officials had been arrested in conjunction with the latter (Gazeta, "Kto Kazał Zabić Księdza Popiełuszkę," *Gazeta Wyborcza*, Oc-tober 9, 1990).

Only two of the six incidents of major rights violations did not lead to crimi-nal prosecutions: Poznań 1956 (though a criminal investigation was launched—see Gazeta, "Sprawiedliwość Staje Się Zadość," *Gazeta Wyborcza*, September 19, 1991); and March 1968 (in 1998 a Polish emigrant demanded in a high court that the period be declared a repression, but the case was dropped due to proce-dural irregularities). The trial for Jaruzelski and eleven lower-level functionaries blamed for the December 1970 shootings on the Baltic coast that left at least 44 dead and 1,165 injured was delayed for more than a decade due to various administrative errors, defendants' illnesses, and changes of location (see Gazeta, "Grudzień 1970," *Gazeta Wyborcza*, December 17, 1991; Gazeta, "Akta Grudnia '70 Odesłane," *Gazeta Wyborcza*, July 4, 1995; Gazeta, "Po Raz Kolejny," *Gazeta*

Wyborcza, March 26, 1998; Gazeta, "Sąd Przyjdzie Do Generałów," *Gazeta Wyborcza,* November 9, 1999; Adam Zadworny, "Obrona Na 81 Stron," *Gazeta Wyborcza,* October 19, 2001). After a slow investigation, and despite prosecutors' attempts to drop the case, the first charges in conjunction with Radom 1976, when functionaries injured more than 280 protesters, came in 1999 (Magda Ciepielak, "Więzili Ludzi Bezprawnie," *Gazeta Wyborcza,* July 28, 1999; Magda Ciepielak and Renata Metzger, "Nie Przedawiać 'Ścieżek Zdrowia,'" *Gazeta Wyborcza,* November 10–11, 1999; Renata Metzger, "Czerwiec Na Wokandę," *Gazeta Wyborcza,* November 30, 1999). Two of the four defendants were found guilty and the other two were released on the basis of their immunity under the statute of limitations (Magda Ciepielak, "Niewinni Milicjanci, Niewinni Esbecy," *Gazeta Wyborcza,* August 3–4, 2002).

While former internal affairs minister Kiszczak and twenty-three others were charged in 1992 for the 1981 shootings at the Wujek mine, two trials of the lower-level functionaries ended in not-guilty verdicts, based on lack of evidence, in 1999. Kiszczak's trial, which had been carried out separately (Gazeta, "Kiszczak Uniewinniony," *Gazeta Wyborcza,* July 30, 1996), finally concluded in 2004 in a guilty verdict and a suspended two-year jail sentence, but in the following February, Kiszczak was granted an appeal (based on a judge's error in the second trial), and it was announced that a third trial would be conducted (Gazeta, "Trzeci Proces Kiszczaka Za Pacyfikację Wujka," *Gazeta Wyborcza,* February 10, 2005). Finally, the case of the 1982 Lubin shootings went to court three times since 1993, and it appeared to culminate in halved sentences (on the basis of the 1989 amnesty law) for several functionaries; prosecuting families vowed to appeal the decision, however (see Marcin Maciejewski, "Bez Kary," *Gazeta Wyborcza,* July 15–16, 1995; Katarzyna Lubiniecka, "Lubin Po Raz Drugi," *Gazeta Wyborcza,* June 12, 1997; Katarzyna Lubiniecka, "Wyrok Za Lubin," *Gazeta Wyborcza,* July 3, 1998; Gazeta, "Amnestia Nie Dla Nich," *Gazeta Wyborcza,* July 7, 1999; Malgorzata Porada, "Winni Z Lubina," *Gazeta Wyborcza,* June 25, 2003).

113. See, for example, the case of six former SB officers who abducted Solidarity activists in 1984 (Gazeta, "Wyroki Dla Toruńskich Porywaczy," *Gazeta Wyborcza,* December 6, 1991); or the Nowa Huta case (Gazeta, "10 Lat Dla Zabójcy Włosika," *Gazeta Wyborcza,* May 29, 1992; Jan Ordyński, "10 Lat to Sprawiedliwa Kara," *Rzeczpospolita,* June 9, 1994).

114. Gazeta, "Estradycja Za 'Nila,'" *Gazeta Wyborcza,* November 27, 1998.

115. There were at least two high-profile cases, including the trial for the 1977 murder of an opposition student and the 1981 Lubin attacks. Officials seem to have been aware that dropping charges would raise a public outcry, and they made their announcement only one month after the case had been closed.

116. See, for example, the case of high-ranking Internal Affairs Ministry officials Władysław Ciaston and Zenon Płatek, accused of ordering the 1984 murder of priest and opposition hero Jerzy Popiełuszko, which ended only after twelve years of trials that failed to result in convictions. The first trial, begun in 1992, ended two years later with public outrage at their proclaimed innocence. By the time the 2002 verdict was read, "the same hall was empty. Those who brought about the new consideration of the case, the lawyers of Father Jerzy's family, were not in court" (Bogdan Wróblewski, "Osądzi Historia," *Gazeta Wyborcza,* December 10, 2002).

117. Six years after the April 1997 conviction of one of the two officers accused in the 1983 beating to death of Grzegorz Przemyk, the appeals process ensured that the convicted officer had yet to be sent to jail by 2003, when it was announced that the Przemyk case would go to court for a fourth time (Gazeta, "Karta 989," *Gazeta Wyborcza,* June 6, 2003).

118. See, for example, the Ciaston and Płatek case (Gazeta, "Generałowie Wracają Do Prokuratory," *Gazeta Wyborcza,* March 18, 1998). The high rate of sickness is partly a result of the fact that crimes pursued often took place decades earlier, resulting in trials of elderly and often sick defendants. For example, the first case of a judge accused of Stalinist crimes went to court in December 1995, but the judge, too ill to attend her trial, died a free woman in January 1998 (Piotr Lipiński, "Zabójstwo Sądowe," *Gazeta Wyborcza,* December 16, 1995; Piotr Lipiński and Marcin Boguszewski, "Wszyscy Poumierają," *Gazeta Wyborcza,* January 7, 1998). The trial of former MBP investigation department director Adam Humer and eleven lower-level officers, all accused of torture during the 1950s, went on from 1992 to 1996, after which each was sentenced to between two and nine years in jail (Gazeta, "54 Dni Humera," *Gazeta Wyborcza,* March 9–10, 1996). Humer, without going to jail, appealed his case but was ruled too sick to attend the hearings and remained free two years after his conviction (Jan Ordyński, "Czy Humer Stanie Przed Sądem," *Rzeczpospolita,* May 7, 1998).

119. Ryszard Juszkiewicz, "Krzywda Nie Może Ujść Bezkarnie," *Gazeta Wyborcza,* April 1, 1994. Pointing to resource limitations, including a shortage of judges and prosecutors at GK (see also Ordyński, "Będą Procesy Stalinowskich Zbrodniarzy"), Juszkiewicz commented that the "practice has not fit, and still does not fit, with the bill."

120. Rzeczpospolita, "Ściganie Zbrodniarzy Jest Kosztowne," *Rzeczpospolita,* February 12, 1992.

121. Institutional collusion or a membership ethos within the legal community apparently had a profound impact on postcommunist accountability. Prosecutors formed a core group, which tended to band together during the period of

political uncertainty following the partial regime change in 1989. According to one member of the 1990 Sejm commission calling for prosecutor verification, "old prosecutors were closely connected with each other," and the legal community adopted a defensive posture in light of prosecutor verification (Kern interview). Even after prosecutor verification, one prominent post-Solidarity politician added that "sometimes the prosecutors were the same people who had been there before" (Geremek interview). This view is shared by others deeply involved in Polish legal circles (and those of other postcommunist countries) who agree that the 1990 verification left "judges and prosecutors who should not be working in the courtroom" (Leon Kieres interview, January 16, 2004). Zbigniew Romaszewski pointed out the clear implication for trials of communist-era crimes: "This was an apparatus of force; how could they carry out a trial of something that was their own responsibility?" (Romaszewski interview). The prosecutor who supervised investigations into cases emanating from the Rokita Commission admitted the same: "There definitely was a group of people who did not cease thinking in categories of those [earlier] authorities" (Krasny interview).

The fact that Poland's postcommunist legal system was founded on people associated with the past era meant a series of alliances between prosecutors, judges, and law enforcement/intelligence personnel. One former public prosecutor in Kraków, who felt isolated for his involvement in two high-profile trials of 1980s murders, claims that prosecutors were so established in communist institutions that they are reluctant to bring charges against their colleagues in the intelligence services or the party apparatus. "Years of activities in a certain system had an effect on these people. It is not so easy for them to change their way of thinking" (IPN, January 21, 2004). Even if they did, according to one lawyer, systemic bias became a deterrent to accept cases because "most judges would begin to fear their own role in the past and would be in solidarity with those being charged" (Olszewski interview). This is particularly true when it comes to investigations of judicial crimes, where current judges (even those active only after the fall of communism) take the stance that "people can make mistakes and that judges should have immunity" (Kieres interview). One opposition politician claimed that the prevalence of prosecutors who had themselves been involved in questionable trials under communism had led to "strong resistance" to digging into the communist past (Romaszewski interview). In a 1993 interview, Juszkiewicz confirmed that "we see among some of our workers a certain lack of initiative; they simply wait for a report [*doniesienie*], they don't search these out themselves. We hurry them along, but there are not always results" (Ordyński, "Będą Procesy Stalinowskich Zbrodniarzy").

122. Once a prosecutor did accept a case against former authorities, the struggle for evidence became crucial. Prosecutors who have pursued cases from

the 1970s and 1980s recall three obstacles in this task. First, social networks were formed to defend colleagues and weaken the prosecution's case. In cases against SB officers, for example, prosecutors were forced to go to SB sources for archival or other material relevant to the case. Their SB counterparts, often asked to unearth evidence against a colleague or a superior, were unlikely to cooperate. "They are not going to speak badly of their 'lifelines [*żywiciele*]'" commented one prosecutor involved in high-profile cases in the 1990s (IPN). Even if they were cooperative, a second obstacle was the condition of their archives. In many cases, the IPN prosecutor said, "these documents had been cleansed for years. When we got to them, they were just remnants." According to the head of the GK, this problem continues today: "sometimes an unseen hand has taken [materials] from the personnel files" (Ryszard Kulesza interview, December 18, 2003). Finally, a third challenge derived from the nature of the crimes, which were often directed by word of mouth and left no paper trail. According to the prosecutor overseeing trials that emanated from the Rokita Commission, "these cases did not come about as a direct order, but were a certain understanding [*przemówienie*]. . . . Because of the passage of time or the methods of operations, which generally left no traces, [these cases] were impossible to determine" (Krasny interview).

123. Herzog interview.

124. The IPN's president also agrees that workload is a major reason why the number of communist-era cases brought to trial in the first two years of the IPN's existence is twice as many as the twenty-eight cases brought about by general prosecutors between 1990 and 2000 (Kieres interview).

125. Olszewski interview.

126. Ordyński, "Będą Procesy Stalinowskich Zbrodniarzy."

127. Kieres interview.

128. Data found on the IPN Web site (www.ipn.gov.pl/sledztwa.html, as of December 2003). This analysis includes the thirty-five cases that were dated sometime after 1956, but excludes eight others that were undated. There are also a large number of cases from the war period, primarily against Soviet soldiers. This is not surprising, since cases against Germans would have been politically more feasible between the GK's inception and 1989, leaving investigations into communist aggression unopened until after communism fell.

129. Kulesza interview.

130. Kieres interview.

131. Gazeta, "Przeszłość Odkreślamy Grubą Linią [reprint of Prime Minister Tadeusz Mazowiecki's speech to Parliament]," *Gazeta Wyborcza*, August 25–27, 1989.

132. Mazowiecki interview. One advisor who helped to edit this speech confirmed this (Ciemniewski interview).

133. During my interview, the editor-in-chief of Poland's largest daily newspaper explained that he has always understood that the "thick line" speech did not intentionally refer to justice but is, regardless, "colloquially" used with such a meaning (Michnik interview). As another former member of Parliament from that time noted, "the 'thick line' is still living its own life, different from its original intentions" (Juliusz Braun interview, December 17, 2003).

134. Mazowiecki interview.

135. Michnik interview.

136. Henryk Wujec interview, February 3, 2004; Dmochowska interview.

137. Niesiołowski interview.

138. Olszewski interview.

139. While criminal prosecution of post-1956 crimes was also of concern to SLD members, it was not the principal one (Kalisz interview).

140. SLD opponents to the bill, who claim that the Institute's Polish acronym better stood for Institute of Political Hatred (Instytut Politycznej Nienawiści), criticized the IPN for creating a one-sided view of Polish history, being institutionally redundant and serving as a weakly camouflaged attack on the left (Ryszard Jarzębowski interview, December 18, 2003; Ciosek, Lewandowski, Kalisz interviews). "This is a reminder—that this is the left, we are carrying on the tradition" (Lewandowski interview). One IPN board member commented, "They don't like to dig in these areas, personal things can come up" (IPN, November 24, 2003). Post-Solidarity forces charge that the left has since attacked the IPN through budget cuts intended to bring about the institute's "quiet death" (Staniszewska interview). The IPN's financial dependence is a major weakness in the institute's drafting, according to some supporters of justice, leaving its fate at the hands of the governing regime.

141. It is also interesting to note that the initiator of the 1998 IPN law had only recently taken an interest in justice. Asked about how he felt when the 1991 GK bill was limited to pre-1956, Pałubicki responded that he could not recall it since "there wasn't much discussion on this issue" (Pałubicki interview). GK head Kulesza, who co-authored the bill, ducked this question, answering only that his personal motives were legal in nature: "This is the last chance we have to judge communist crimes. We worked in the belief that a law-abiding state is law-abiding not because it is written in the Constitution but through a very long process of legitimizing the state and its institutions" (Kulesza interview).

142. Ciosek interview.

143. Romaszewski interview.

144. The one element binding all four periods of justice in Poland is the locus of justice demand. Since 1989, post-Solidarity elites have been the primary— indeed, practically the only—group demanding harsh forms of transitional justice. Even in the first period, when there was at least marginal public interest in criminal accountability for 1980s violations, the impetus for action came from elites. While victim groups do exist in Poland, they are politically weak. The most consequential force, World War II veteran groups (*kombatanci*), played only a consultative role in early legislation banning some elements of the communist regime from receiving special veteran benefits. The lack of influence from organized civil society may result from the perception that there was little need for outside interference since post-Solidarity elites themselves made up a large percentage of communist-era victims.

CHAPTER 6 *Serbia and Montenegro*

1. Scholars estimate that more than thirty thousand political prisoners went through the brutal Goli Otok prison off the coast of Croatia. See Bartosek, "Central and Southeastern Europe."

2. Robert M. Hayden, "'Ethnic Cleansing' and 'Genocide,'" *European Journal of Public Health* 17, no. 6 (2007).

3. Igor Graovac interview, March 18, 2005; Laura Konda, "Victims of Kosovo War Still Searching for Loved Ones," *Voice of America,* June 11, 2008.

4. George Jahn, "Milosevic's Party Agrees to Share Power with Pro-Democracy Camp," *Associated Press,* October 16, 2000.

5. This was the one measure I did not discuss with respondents, since preliminary interviews suggested that this was theoretically uninteresting because there was such an obvious need for conformity to these laws.

6. For ratification information, see the Office of the United Nations High Commissioner for Human Rights, available at http://www.ohchr.org/english/countries/ratification/1.htm.

7. See Vesna Peric Zimonjic, "Politics—Yugoslavia: Apology to Croats Earns Wrath of Serbia," *IPS-Inter Press Service,* July 3, 2000. Đukanović's controversial 2000 apology signaled a reverse, following his 1999 statement questioning who should apologize to whom (BBC, "Official Criticizes Montenegrin President's Comments on 1991 War," *BBC Summary of World Broadcasts,* February 9, 1999).

8. Aleksandar Mitic, "Belgrade, Zagreb Apologize for Bloody War but Problems Remain," *Agence France Presse,* September 10, 2003.

9. Amra Hadziomanovic, "Belgrade Apologizes to Bosnia for 'Evil' Committed during War," *Agence France Presse,* November 13, 2003.

10. V. Kopriviča, "Marović Spreman Da Se Izvini I Crnogorcima," *Danas,* November 17, 2003.

11. FENA, "Tadic: I Apologize to All Who Have Suffered Crimes in the Name of the Serb People," *Federalna Novinska Agencija (FENA),* December 6, 2004.

12. Stefan Racin, "Kostunica Admits Serb Crimes in Kosovo," *United Press International,* October 24, 2000; Katarina Kratovac, "Kostunica Says His Words on Kosovo Were Taken out of Context," *Associated Press,* October 26, 2000.

13. BBC, "Yugoslav Foreign Minister Says He Expressed Regret, Not Apologised to Croatia," *BBC Monitoring Europe—Political,* December 20, 2001.

14. Advisor interview, February 11, 2005.

15. BBC, "Yugoslav President Says Serbian Premier Bent on 'Hasty Reforms,'" *BBC Monitoring Europe—Political,* August 5, 2002; DPA, "Mixed Reaction by Serbian Opposition to Montenegrin Apology for Shelling of Dubrovnik," *Deutsche Presse-Agentur,* June 25, 2000; Vladimir Vukičević interview, January 24, 2005.

16. GNW, "Yugoslavia Does Not Need to Apologize to Anyone: Djindjic," *Global News Wire (ONASA News Agency),* November 23, 2000.

17. Čedomir Jovanović interview, February 3, 2005; Žarko Korać interview, February 4, 2005.

18. Korać interview.

19. BBC, "Opposition Party Criticizes President for Apology to Croatia," *BBC Summary of World Broadcasts,* June 27, 2000; BBC, "Yugoslav Army Condemns Montenegrin President for Making 'Unfounded Accusations,'" *BBC Monitoring Europe—Political,* July 5, 2000.

20. Milan St. Protić interview, December 20, 2004; Vukičević, Korać interviews.

21. Dragor Hiber interview, December 16, 2004.

22. GNA, "Serbian Premier: U.S. Demand for Public Apology for War Crimes 'Inappropriate,'" *Global News Wire—Asia Africa Intelligence Wire,* May 10, 2003.

23. Kratovac, "Kostunica Says His Words on Kosovo Were Taken out of Context."

24. GNA, "Serbian Premier: U.S. Demand for Public Apology for War Crimes 'Inappropriate.'" Croatia and Bosnia also hoped for apologies at a 2002 summit, though Koštunica declined (see Mirjana Vujović, Beriz Belkić: Koštunica Bi Trebalo Da Izrazi Žaljenje, *Danas,* July 9, 2002; and Will Hardie, "Yugoslav

President Refuses to Apologize for Atrocities," *The Independent* [London], July 16, 2002). See also Advisor, St. Protić, Korać interviews.

25. Gradomir Nalić interview, January 25, 2005. On Đinđić, see GNA, "Serbian Premier: U.S. Demand for Public Apology for War Crimes 'Inappropriate.'"

26. Korać interview.

27. See AFP, "Washington Welcomes Move by Belgrade, Zagreb to Apologize over War," *Agence France Presse,* September 13, 2003; BBC, "EU's Solana Hails Apologies Exchanged by Serbia-Montenegro, Croatian Presidents," *BBC Monitoring Europe — Political,* September 12, 2003.

28. Mitic, "Belgrade, Zagreb Apologize for Bloody War but Problems Remain."

29. Ibid.

30. Koprivića, "Marović Spreman Da Se Izvini I Crnogorcima"; Korać interview.

31. Danas, "Nastavak Pozitivnog Procesa," *Danas,* September 12, 2003.

32. Z. Panović, "Revizija Političkih Procesa Od '45," *Danas,* February 8, 2001.

33. Danas, "Nova Pravda Za Stare Grehe," *Danas,* May 18, 2002. The bill, created by an expert group in the Justice Ministry, called for case reviews by a seven-member justice ministry committee and then, in addition, by either the Serbian government or the Supreme Court. Just as Batić was at the forefront of the fight for rehabilitation, he also took the offensive in the denationalization debate, declaring in August 2002 that he expected a denationalization bill to be passed by the end of the year and to go into effect at the beginning of 2003.

34. Slobodan Gavrilović interview, November 30, 2004; Rebeka Božović interview, January 28, 2005; Gordana Matković interview, December 9, 2004; Miroslav Filipović interview, February 2, 2005.

35. Ivan Janković interview, December 13, 2004. See also Dušan Petrović interview, December 9, 2004; Matković, Korać, St. Protić interviews.

36. In reference to his northern neighbors, Korać explained: "There it's simple: communism, Russia, tanks." Korać interview.

37. Filipović, Korać interviews. See also Sinisa Djuric, "Radically Better Doom," http://www.diacritica.com/sobaka/2004/seselj.html; Milos Vasic, "Vojislav Seselj, SRS Leader and Member of the Federal Parliament," *Vreme News Digest Agency,* May 23, 1994. On Karadžić, see Robert M. Kaplan, "Boundaries: Dr. Radovan Karadzic: Psychiatrist, Poet, Soccer Coach, and Genocidal Leader," *Australasian Psychiatry* 11, no. 1 (2003).

38. Korać interview.

39. Hiber interview; Bogdan Veljković interview, November 29, 2004.

40. Momčilo Grubač interview, January 27, 2005; Veran Matić interview, December 1, 2004; Nalić interview.

41. B92, "Svilanović: Uključiti Susede U Rešavanje Statusa Kosova," *Radio B92,* November 10, 2000; James Hider, "Yugoslav FM Wants Milosevic on Trial as Soon as Possible—in Serbia," *Agence France Presse,* December 20, 2000.

42. B92, "Grubač O Komisiji Za Istinu," *Radio B92,* April 5, 2001; AFP, "Yugoslavia Preparing Truth Commission: Minister," *Agence France Presse,* January 11, 2001.

43. Grubač interview.

44. Vojin Dimitrijević interview, December 28, 2004.

45. Aleksandar Lojpur interview, January 10, 2005; Dimitrijević interview; Daniel Williams, "A Faint Path to Truth in Serbia; Yugoslav Panel Probing Wars Lacks Funding, Clout," *Washington Post,* July 5, 2002.

46. Danas, "Nema Novca Za Svedočenje O Srebrenici," *Danas,* October 7, 2002.

47. Jelena Bulajić, "Organizovaćemo Javna Svedočenja O Zločinima," *Blic,* April 22, 2002.

48. Deborah Cole, "Yugoslavia Wants Truth Commission to Fight 'Public Amnesia,'" *Agence France Presse,* April 8, 2001.

49. Ivana Stevanović, "Komisija Za Istinu I Pomirenje: Iluzija Ili Stvarnost," *Radio B92,* February 18, 2003.

50. B92, "Sagledavanje Istine Preduslov Za Pomirenje U SRJ I Susedstvu," *Radio B92,* December 15, 2001.

51. Nataša Kandić interview, December 29, 2004.

52. Filipović, Matković, Hiber interviews.

53. Jean-Eudes Barbier, "Kostunica Seeks to Counter 'Pseudo-History' of Milosevic Trial," *Agence France Presse,* February 19, 2002.

54. Sonja Biserko interview, December 9, 2004; Biljana Kovačević-Vučo interview, November 17, 2004; Janković, Kandić, Matić interviews.

55. Ten months after the truth commission's inception, the government finally handed it an annual budget of $20,000, less than 15 percent of the sum requested (Peter Ford, "Serbs Still Ignore Role in Atrocity," *Christian Science Monitor,* February 11, 2002). Political opposition to the commission appears to have offset the president's attempts to gain funding. While Miroljub Labus, the federal vice president who controlled the federal budget, denies that he held back money for political reasons, in his 2002 drive for the federal presidency he openly accused Koštunica of establishing a commission that did nothing, in part because it had no money with which to function (Aide interview, January 17, 2005).

56. BBC, "Yugoslav President's Party to Vote against Law on Constitutional Charter," *BBC Monitoring Europe—Political,* January 17, 2003.

57. GNW, "Commission for Truth, Reconciliation Launches Discussions on Web Site," *Global News Wire (ONASA News Agency),* November 10, 2002. As of March 2006, when I attempted to access the site (see www.komisija.org), it had been converted to pornography.

58. Joshua Kucera, "Controversy Dogs Fact-Finding Body; Lack of Amnesty Hurts Its Mission," *Washington Times,* July 12, 2001; Ford, "Serbs Still Ignore Role in Atrocity."

59. Christophe Chatelot and Claire Trean, "No One Speaks Up for Milosevic's Victims," *Manchester Guardian Weekly,* May 16, 2001.

60. Hiber interview.

61. Petrović interview.

62. Gavrilović, Korać interviews.

63. Matković interview.

64. Ana Miljanić interview, December 9, 2004. See also Biserko interview. Various NGOs in Serbia and the region have launched their own investigations into past events, focusing on the collection of documents and personal testimonies of victims (Aleksandar Popov interview, January 27, 2005; Kandić interview). Otpor opposition movement leaders also launched an independent commission of inquiry, which was to "help the state organs, the police, and the prosecutors" ensure criminal accountability. See Danas, "Zakon, a Ne Revanšizam," *Danas,* October 28, 2000; IRI, "Otpor Delegation Luncheon Discussion at the International Republican Institute" (International Republican Institute, 2001).

65. While I do not address lustration in this chapter, I should note that a lustration law, passed in 2003, was never enacted due to procedural limitations inherent in the law and to the increased political opposition to it that followed the December 2003 elections. For more, see chapter 9.

66. Z. Miladinović, "Dokazali Da Smo Narodna I Profesionalna Vojska," *Danas,* October 24, 2000; Bojan Tončić, "Milošević Je Rekao: Ja Ovde Više Nemam Šta Tražim," *Danas,* October 27, 2000.

67. Jasminka Kočijan, "Stari Ljudi U Novoj Politici," *Danas,* November 8, 2000. See also Facts-WN, "Opposition Leader Sworn In as Yugoslav President: Kostunica Takes Office amid Discord," *Facts on File World News Digest,* October 7, 2000.

68. Jasminka Kočijan, "Tražio Sam Od Pavkovića Da Ostane," *Danas,* December 27, 2001.

69. USIP, "Serbia Still at the Crossroads," in *Special Report* (United States Institute of Peace, 2002). See also AFP, "Kostunica Purges Milosevic-Era Armed Forces Staff," *Agence France Presse,* December 30, 2000.

70. USIP, "Serbia Still at the Crossroads"; Nalić, Vukičević interviews.

71. Facts-WN, "Opposition Leader Sworn in as Yugoslav President: Kostunica Takes Office amid Discord."

72. Justin Huggler, "Kostunica Faces Fresh Clash over Army Chief," *The Independent,* October 14, 2000.

73. BBC, "Belgrade News Agency Views Current Serbian Political Scene," *BBC Monitoring Europe—Political,* November 2, 2000; Huggler, "Kostunica Faces Fresh Clash over Army Chief."

74. O. Radulović, "Pavković: Milošević Ne Koristi Podatke Vojske," *Danas,* February 28, 2002; Tončić, "Milošević Je Rekao: Ja Ovde Više Nemam Šta Trazim."

75. UPI, "Kostunica Retains Suspect Army Chief," *United Press International,* December 28, 2001.

76. Misha Savic, "President Fires Army Chief, Top General Fights Back," *Associated Press,* June 25, 2002.

77. See, for example, Gavrilović interview.

78. Huggler, "Kostunica Faces Fresh Clash over Army Chief." Not surprisingly, General Perišić, the leader of a small party within the DOS, was one of those calling for Pavković's resignation (Jonathan Steele, "The New Yugoslavia: Factory Anarchy Alarms Kostunica: Workers Hound Old Guard While Prisoners of the Milosevic Regime Still Wait for Freedom," *The Guardian* [London], October 13, 2000). Perišić surrendered to the Hague in March 2005 (Igor Jovanovic, "Former Yugoslav Army Chief of Staff Goes to the Hague," *Southeast European Times,* March 7, 2005).

79. Nalić interview. Đinđić's associates also acknowledge that the prime minister offered Pavković political protection in the hope of gaining control of military intelligence (Korać interview).

80. Huggler, "Kostunica Faces Fresh Clash over Army Chief"; Stefan Racin, "Yugoslav Army Split between Reformists, Milosevic," *United Press International,* October 16, 2000.

81. Filipović, Nalić interviews.

82. Ivan Đorđević interview, January 25, 2005.

83. Danas, "Depolitizujemo Policijiu," *Danas,* October 2, 2001.

84. Đorđević interview.

85. Advisor, Grubač interviews.

86. Korać, Filipović, Petrović interviews.

87. Korać, Č. Jovanović, Advisor interviews.

88. Đorđević explained that most police had acted professionally and were happy to see their corrupt superiors dismissed (Đorđević interview).

89. Aleksandar Roknić, "Prošlo Je Vreme Straha Građana Od Policije," *Danas,* June 5, 2001.

90. BBC, "Serbia Cannot Dismiss Policemen Who Participated in Kosovo Actions—Official," *BBC Monitoring Europe—Political,* November 29, 2001.

91. USIP, "Serbia Still at the Crossroads."

92. BBC, "Latest Hague Indictments 'Serious Problem' for Serbian Government—Agency," *BBC Monitoring Europe—Political,* October 24, 2003; DPA, "Serbian Police Rally for Chief Indicted for War Crimes," *Deutsche Presse-Agentur,* October 24, 2003.

93. Dimitrijević interview.

94. Božović interview.

95. In mid-April 2001, just after Milošević's arrest, military prosecutors began to try twenty-four personnel accused of 1999 war crimes in Kosovo (Danas, "Ratni Zločini Ustaljeni Civilnimi Sudovima," *Danas,* April 24, 2001), and a military court in the southern town of Niš had brought charges against almost 200 officers by mid-May (AP, "Nearly 200 Soldiers, Officers Being Investigated for Alleged Kosovo Atrocities," *Associated Press,* April 24, 2001; BBC, "Yugoslav Army Charges Nearly 200 Soldiers for Crimes against Kosovo Albanians," *BBC Monitoring Europe—Political,* May 12, 2001). In early 2001 police officials announced that sixty-six police officers were under investigation for crimes, ranging from murder to plunder, committed against Albanians in Kosovo in 1999. According to one former official, approximately 1,500 officers were ultimately charged for such crimes, though bribery, not human rights violations, apparently dominated (Đorđević interview).

96. M. Torov, "Dve Krivične Prijave Protiv Srba Za Ratne Zločine Počinjene Na Kosovu," *Danas,* July 21, 2001.

97. Andrej Nosov, "Postaje Li Prokuplje Domaći Hag," *Danas,* July 20, 2002.

98. Judges Association member interview, December 13, 2004; Aleksandar Resanović interview, November 10, 2004.

99. Andrej Nosov, "'Malom Hagu' Neophodna Lustracija," *Danas,* July 23, 2002.

100. Bojan Tončić, "Ratni Zločinci Će Morati Da Odgovaraju," *Danas,* November 17, 2001.

101. Andrej Nosov, "Anonimne Patriotske Pretnje," *Danas,* May 4, 2002.

102. Andrej Nosov, "Nikoliću Osam Godina," *Danas,* July 9, 2002, 3.

103. War crimes prosecutor's office interview, December 17, 2004.

104. Misha Savic, "Special Court to Try War and Other Crimes Opened," *Associated Press,* October 24, 2003.

105. The U.S. government invested at least $850,000 in the court. Ibid.

106. War crimes prosecutor's office interview.

107. Reuters, "Serbian Court Finds 14 Guilty in '91 Massacre of Croatians," *Reuters,* December 13, 2005.

108. War crimes prosecutor's office interview.

109. Aleksandra Milenov interview, January 19, 2005.

110. War crimes prosecutor's office interview.

111. Filipović interview.

112. Z. Panović, Skidanje Hipoteke Zločina, *Danas,* July 3, 2001.

113. According to an official from the Belgrade Center for Human Rights, there were twenty-three extraditions; my own calculation, based on ICTY data, was twenty-two.

114. See BBC, "Yugoslav General Staff Chief Denies Army Tried to Block Milosevic's Arrest," *BBC Monitoring Europe—Political,* April 1, 2001; BBC, "Yugoslav President: Lack of Army, Police Coordination during Milosevic Arrest," *BBC Monitoring Europe—Political,* April 3, 2001; AFP, "Yugoslav Army Obstructed Milosevic Arrest: Minister," *Agence France Presse,* March 31, 2001. Though participants say shots were fired simply due to a lack of communication (Đorđević, Č. Jovanović interviews), Koštunica made it clear that he was against Milošević's arrest and extradition (in the run-up to the fall 2003 parliamentary elections, Koštunica denied any involvement or prior knowledge about the arrest operation). See BBC, "Election Campaign, Priorities of Serbia's Leading Opposition Party Analyzed," *BBC Monitoring Europe—Political,* December 20, 2003. According to the officials involved in the seizure, Koštunica knew ahead of time that Milošević was to be arrested and, along with Đinđić and Serbian president Milutinović, signed off on it (Đorđević, Č. Jovanović, Hiber interviews).

115. Local politicians agree that the Hague sparked a conflict that was inevitable (Petrović, Božović, Grubač, Matković interviews). Given personality conflicts and the sharp political competition generated by the two dominant DOS parties, said one member of Đinđić's government, "if it was not for sending Milošević to the Hague, it would be to Kosovo or Montenegro" (Matković interview).

116. Zeljko Cvijanovic, "Serbia: Red Beret Revolt," *Balkan Crisis Report #296,* November 13, 2001; DPA, "Serbian Police Unit Ends Protest, Interior Ministry Says," *Deutsche Presse-Agentur,* November 17, 2001.

117. During interrogation, one suspect confessed to killing Đinđić "because I believed that it will stop further extradition of Serbian warriors to the Hague" (Katarina Subasic, "Serb PM Killed to Stop UN War Crimes Extraditions, Court Told," *Agence France Presse,* December 25, 2003. See also Independent, "Assassin Says Đinđić Murder Was to Be First of Many," *The Independent,* April 9, 2003. Some say that Đinđić may have been killed as a result of his links to organized crime.

118. DPA, "Decorated Serbian Police General Faces War Crimes Trial," *Deutsche Presse-Agentur,* October 20, 2003.

119. Stephen Coates, "Serbia Furious over Fresh War Crimes Indictments," *Agence France Presse,* October 21, 2003; BBC, "Serbia-Montenegro Defence Minister Says Latest Indictments 'Huge Burden,'" *BBC Monitoring Europe—Political,* October 26, 2003.

120. DPA, "Serbian Police Rally for Chief Indicted for War Crimes."

121. The Serbian Radical Party took 27 percent of the vote (82 seats), more than twice that of the Democratic Party (12.6 percent, 37 seats). Koštunica's DSS won 17.7 percent (53 seats), Labus's G-17 Plus took 11.5 percent (34 seats), and the Serbian Renewal Movement took 7.7 percent (22 seats) (GNA, "Victory in Serbia to Nationalists but Reformers in Coalition Move," *Global News Wire—Asia Africa Intelligence Wire,* December 30, 2003).

122. Ellie Tzortzi, "Serb Ex-General to Surrender to UN," *Reuters,* March 3, 2005; Nicholas Wood, "Serbia Moves a Step Closer to the European Union," *New York Times,* April 13, 2005; Reuters, "Serb General Pavkovic to Surrender to Hague," *Reuters,* April 22, 2005.

123. One reason for including private preferences here is that in a political system characterized by personal politics, where party leaders dominate the party, the lines dividing leadership personality from overall tactics are blurry. In my interviews, respondents tended to refer to "Đinđić's" or "Koštunica's" position rather than to the "party position."

124. AFP, "Vojislav Kostunica, Moderate Nationalist and Old Milosevic Foe," *Agence France Presse,* September 24, 2000.

125. BBC, "President Says Cooperation with Hague Tribunal Not Priority," *BBC Summary of World Broadcasts,* December 21, 2000.

126. DPA, "Djindjic Vows to Bring Milosevic to Justice," *Deutsche Presse-Agentur,* December 25, 2000.

127. David Holley, "Serbs Face Their Past, Dose of Truth at a Time," *Los Angeles Times,* April 17, 2001. This may have been aggravated by the fact that one year after the transfer of power, two of Yugoslavia's largest privately owned television stations were under the control of Milošević's allies (Ford, "Serbs Still Ignore Role in Atrocity").

128. Ford, "Serbs Still Ignore Role in Atrocity."

129. BCHR, "Public Opinion in Serbia: Attitudes towards the International Criminal Tribunal for the Former Yugoslavia" (Belgrade: Belgrade Center for Human Rights, 2003). The survey had a total sample size of 1,545 respondents (in Serbia, not including Kosovo).

130. USAID-funded survey conducted by the International Republican Institute in late 2004: IRI, "Survey" (International Republican Institute, 2004).

131. Božović interview. ICTY officials dismiss charges of bias, but admit that the tribunal keeps no statistics on the ethnic origins of its indictees. "I've never gone through the indictments and done a head count," Milenov said, adding that the ICTY's goal is not "to do bean counting" (Milenov interview). In fact, ICTY officials appear to be purposely looking the other way, rather than giving Serb nationalists fuel for the fire. According to my calculations, more than two-thirds of all ICTY indictees are from the Serb side. While ICTY officials react defensively to this charge, they claim that "what's important is not the ethnicity of the accused but the evidence." ICTY officials hope that by emphasizing the existence of war criminals charged for crimes against Serbs, they will be able to disarm some of these criticisms. They also argue that because Serbia was involved in three wars as opposed to only one (like Bosnia and Croatia), and because the single greatest number of war criminals (fourteen) came from the case of Serbian aggression on Srebrenica, "there isn't going to be an equal number of crimes committed on each side."

132. Svetozar Stojanović interview, December 22, 2004; Nalić, Korać interviews.

133. While the Serbs recall a long struggle against fascism during World War II, they equate the Croatians with the Ustaše, a fascist regime recalled fondly by Croatia's President Franjo Tuđman during the 1990s. See Rešanović, Božović interviews.

134. Filipović interview. See also BCHR, "Public Opinion in Serbia: Attitudes towards the International Criminal Tribunal for the Former Yugoslavia."

135. Marko Kovačević interview, December 8, 2004.

136. EU diplomat interview, December 6, 2004; EU official interview, December 2004; EU representative interview, November 16, 2004; U.S. Government official interview, December 15, 2004.

137. Elvir Bučalo, "Milošević U Hagu? Nieje Neophodno!" *Danas,* October 7, 2000. Similarly, at a December 2004 discussion on dealing with the past, the OSCE head in Belgrade repeated at least three times that Hague cooperation will affect the speed rather than the feasibility of Serbian foreign policy. Hague cooperation means "fast integration" into European and transatlantic structures (namely, the European Union and NATO), and a lack of cooperation "will slow down integration," he said (OSCE, paper presented at the Perspectives on Responsibility for Grave Violations of Human Rights in the Past, Media Center, Belgrade, December 10, 2004).

138. EU interviews.

139. Numerous interviews conducted with members of the U.S. Department of State suggest that members of the executive branch tend to agree with their European counterparts that aid cuts are counterproductive, since they frequently target programs aimed at democratization. At the same time, U.S. officials maintain that aid cuts can have an effect, putting a mark on Serbia that might give potential investors pause.

140. The strong U.S. position in multilateral lending institutions seems to have had a major impact on the Milošević arrest, in particular.

141. Advisor, Korać interviews.

142. Matković, Filipović, Gavrilović, Hiber interviews. One poll conducted by Marten Board International (sample of 1,500) indicated that 78 percent of Serbs favor joining the European Union (Nicky Star, "Poll: Serbs Want EU Membership, Consider U.S. Unfriendly," *Associated Press,* April 8, 2005).

143. U.S. support was critical to rescheduling payments on the country's $4.5 billion foreign debt, in addition to $100 million in bilateral grants (Scott Peterson, "Temporary Reprieve on Milosevic," *Christian Science Monitor,* March 30, 2001).

144. For example, one week before a March 31, 2001, U.S. congressional deadline on ICTY cooperation, the Serbian government arrested and transferred a Bosnian Serb to the Hague (AFP, "Serbia Takes First Step in Cooperating with UN War Crimes Court," *Agence France Presse,* March 23, 2001). Milošević's provocative extradition by Serbian authorities took place just days before an important donors' conference, where more than $1 billion of aid to Serbia and Montenegro was on the agenda (BBC, "Yugoslavia Might Receive up to 1.3 Billion Dollars of Aid, Bank Governor Says," *BBC Monitoring Europe,* May 1, 2001). The situation prompted one liberal Serbian newspaper to print the headline, "Milošević, Yugoslavia's most valuable foreign export" (Danas, "Milošević Kao Najskuplji Izvozni Proizvod SRJ," *Danas,* June 13, 2001).

145. See, for example, Stefan Racin, "Kostunica Condemns Transfer of Milosevic," *United Press International,* June 28, 2001; Ivan Arandelović, "Đinđić: Koštunica Čekao Da Mi Hapsimo," *Danas,* April 2, 2002.

146. Advisor interview.

147. Đorđević interview.

148. While the typical pattern involved post-opposition elites selling Western aid and membership prospects (provided only in the event of cooperation) to their constituents, there were also other dynamics involved. In the case of the Milošević handover, for instance, Đinđić apparently thought that the Western-imposed deadline pitted him against a taunting Milošević on the domestic stage. Though some might accuse Đinđić of caving in to the West by arresting and extraditing Miloše-

vić, the failure to arrest him would mean an even greater political loss of credibility for the new Serbian leadership and points for the old regime. "This was a test of our capabilities," recalled the man who negotiated Milošević's arrest (Č. Jovanović interview; see also Korać interview).

149. DPA, "Decorated Serbian Police General Faces War Crimes Trial"; BBC, "Latest Hague Indictments 'Serious Problem' for Serbian Government—Agency"; Gavrilović interview; see also GNW, "Serbian PM Takes Swipe at UN War Crimes Prosecutor," *Global News Wire (ONASA News Agency),* December 5, 2003; GNA, "Minister Blames Serbia-Montenegro's 'Political Radicalization' on ICTY," *Global News Wire—Asia Africa Intelligence Wire,* November 18, 2003.

150. Petrović interview.

151. Božović interview.

152. Matković interview.

153. Filipović interview.

154. Božović interview.

155. Washington's pressure on Serbia to exempt the United States from the International Criminal Court has helped to undermine U.S. credibility and given nationalists a weapon. Commented Korać; "Sometimes chauvinists are not really stupid" (Korać interview).

156. IRI representative interview, February 11, 2005; Kandić interview.

157. Serb police active in Kosovo were said to be protecting the Serb minority there.

158. Putnam refers to this as reverberation. See Putnam, "Diplomacy and Domestic Politics: The Logic of Two-Level Games."

159. Filipović interview.

160. Č. Jovanović, Grubač interviews.

CHAPTER 7   *Croatia*

1. As in Serbia, I did not discuss this measure with respondents, since preliminary interviews suggested that the obvious need for conformity to these laws made this theoretically uninteresting.

2. For ratification information, see the Office of the United Nations High Commissioner for Human Rights, available at http://www.ohchr.org/english/countries/ratification/1.htm.

3. See, for example, BBC, "Yugoslav-Croatian Committee Begins Work in Zagreb, Sets Up Five Commissions," *BBC Summary of World Broadcasts,* October 14, 1992.

4. Israel recognized an independent Croatia only after Tuđman edited out of the English version of his book a section in which he attempted to discount the Ustaše's murder of Jews during World War II, and after Tuđman's government issued a formal apology for Ustaše crimes. AFP, "FM Apologizes for Croatia's World War II Persecution of Jews," *Agence France Presse,* May 11, 1998.

5. Croatians even refused Montenegrin assistance during a natural disaster for lack of an official apology (BBC, "Official Rejects Montenegrin Firefighting Help Unless War Crimes Apology Given," *BBC Summary of World Broadcasts,* August 13, 1998). See also BBC, "Croatia's Support for NATO Action Improved International Position—Foreign Minister," *BBC Monitoring Europe—Political,* June 30, 1999; BBC, "President Expects Apology from Montenegro for Shelling of Dubrovnik," *BBC Summary of World Broadcasts,* June 26, 2000.

6. DPA, "Kostunica Should Apologize to Croats, Speaker Says," *Deutsche Presse-Agentur,* October 8, 2000.

7. BBC, "Croatian Premier Apologizes for All Crimes Committed by Previous Regimes," *BBC Monitoring Europe—Political,* May 14, 2002.

8. Mitic, "Belgrade, Zagreb Apologize for Bloody War but Problems Remain."

9. These pressures were from the local NGO community.

10. Ivica Račan interview, March 4, 2005; Žarko Puhovski interview, February 16, 2005.

11. Račan interview. According to the ICJ negotiator, the Croatian leadership was publicly very cautious in the face of international rejection, quietly giving the representative "a sort of yellow light" to propose this, but ensuring deniability for themselves (Ivan Šimonović interview, March 18, 2005).

12. Advisor interview, April 1, 2005; Ivo Banac interview, March 17, 2005.

13. Puhovski, Advisor interviews.

14. See, for example, BBC, "President Attempts to Clarify Controversial War Guilt Comments," *BBC Summary of World Broadcasts,* September 25, 2000.

15. GNW, "HSP Leader Lashes Out at Croatian President, Zagreb Archbishop," *Global News Wire (ONASA News Agency),* August 11, 2000.

16. GNW, "Exclusive Interview with New Croatian President," *Global News Wire (ONASA News Agency),* February 8, 2000. See also BBC, "Presidential Candidate Mesic Says Croatia Must Apologize to Bosnian Muslims," *BBC Summary of World Broadcasts,* January 28, 2000; BBC, "President Attempts to Clarify Controversial War Guilt Comments."

17. GNW, "Interview with Stipe Mesic, President of Republic of Croatia," *Global News Wire (ONASA News Agency),* September 29, 2000.

18. BBC, "President Says Croatian Army Never Officially Involved in Bosnian War," *BBC Monitoring Europe—Political,* February 27, 2001; BBC, "Croatian President, Opposition Leader on Yugoslav Foreign Minister's Apology," *BBC Monitoring Europe—Political,* December 16, 2001; BBC, "Change of Policies More Important than Apology—Croatian President," *BBC Monitoring Europe—Political,* June 24, 2002.

19. BBC, "Lower House Begins Debate on Declarations on Independence War," *BBC Summary of World Broadcasts,* October 14, 2000. See also GNW, "'Almost All' Croatian Parties Welcome S-M President's Apology for 'Wrongdoings,'" *Global News Wire (ONASA News Agency),* September 10, 2003.

20. BBC, "Croatia Should Not Apologize to Serbia for Wartime Events—Deputy Premier," *BBC Monitoring Europe—Political,* December 19, 2004.

21. Vesna Teršelić interview, February 19, 2005.

22. Representative (of Croatian human rights organization) interview, February 17, 2005.

23. Andrea Feldman interview, February 18, 2005.

24. BBC, "Assembly Condemns Communist Treatment of Cardinal Stepinac and Andrija Hebrang," *BBC Summary of World Broadcasts,* February 17, 1992.

25. Ibid.

26. Ibid.

27. For an interesting, though partial, account of Hebrang's life, see www .andrija-hebrang.com.

28. BBC, "Assembly Separate Declarations on Cardinal Stepinac and 'Rigged' Trial Victims," *BBC Summary of World Broadcasts,* February 15, 1992.

29. Banac interview.

30. Ivan Čičak interview, March 31, 2005.

31. Puhovski interview; Vesna Pusić interview, March 31, 2005; Čičak interview.

32. Banac interview.

33. Čičak interview.

34. Dobroslav Paraga interview, March 3, 2005.

35. Feldman interview.

36. Advisor, Banac, Čičak, V. Pusić interviews.

37. One respondent corrected the author, calling Croatia a socialist rather than a communist state (Nela Pamuković interview, February 17, 2005). See also Tin Gazivoda interview, February 17, 2005.

38. Representative interview.

39. V. Pusić interview.

40. Račan interview.

41. Ibid.

42. Pamuković interview.

43. Many in the human rights community also point out that in Croatia they are less concerned with pushing out the few potential rights abusers and more interested in bringing back ethnic minorities who, in the 1990s, were thrown out of the bureaucracy. Under the HDZ, Croatian authorities particularly targeted Serbs, removing them from public positions as powerful as judges and as insignificant as drivers (Zoran Pusić interview, March 17, 2005). One Serb NGO representative recalls first being told to take a few days off from his job as a state journalist, because there was not enough to do, only to be told a few days later that he had been dismissed for not showing up for work (Saša Milošević interview, April 28, 2005). I heard similar anecdotes from many Serbs whom I met in Croatia. For the few willing to go through years of legal proceedings, Croatian courts rarely rule in their favor (Branka Kašelj interview, April 28, 2005).

44. BBC, "Lower House Begins Debate on Declarations on Independence War."

45. AP, "Croatian Parliament Adopts Resolution Reaffirming Dignity of the 1991 War," *Associated Press,* October 14, 2000.

46. V. Pusić interview; quote from Robert Wright, "Learning to Live with the Neighbours: Bosnia-Herzegovina," *Financial Times* (London), June 19, 2001. See also BBC, "President Says Law Exempting War Veterans from Prosecution Not Right," *BBC Summary of World Broadcasts,* March 1, 2001.

47. V. Pusić interview. One center-right parliamentarian confirmed in an interview that a truth commission is unnecessary since the government already has all the facts (Franjo Piplović interview, March 31, 2005).

48. BBC, "Croatian Government Sets Up War Crimes Investigation Body," *BBC Monitoring Europe—Political,* March 9, 2001.

49. For more details, see their Web site: http://misp.isp.hr/suvpovproj5.html.

50. Zdenko Radelić interview, March 3, 2005.

51. I interviewed three of the eight researchers involved in this project, including the project leader.

52. Graovac interview.

53. Radelić interview.

54. Banac interview.

55. Račan interview.

56. Ivo Josipović interview, March 18, 2005. See also Čičak interview.

57. Albert Bing interview, April 28, 2005.

58. Advisor interview.

59. Čičak, Feldman, Puhovski interviews.

60. Čičak interview.

61. In mid-1997, several senior military officers were pushed out of their positions, allegedly as a result of unnamed crimes, though it appears that these were not associated with human rights abuses. More than a year later, rumors in Zagreb suggested that another major dismissal of generals was at hand, though Croatian military officers denied this. See Guardian, "Tuđman Purge," *The Guardian* (London), July 23, 1997; BBC, "Army Chief Denies 'Purges' in Croatian Army," *BBC Monitoring Europe—Political,* September 23, 1998.

62. Račan interview.

63. BBC, "Croatian Defence Ministry 'Purges' Municipal Secret Service Heads—Daily," *BBC Monitoring Europe—Political,* December 16, 2000.

64. BBC, "Croatian Justice Minister Denies 'Purge of Judicial Personnel,'" *BBC Monitoring Europe—Political,* December 18, 2003.

65. DPA, "Croatian President Sacks Seven Generals over War Crimes Letter," *Deutsche Presse-Agentur,* September 29, 2000.

66. See Reuters, "Hague Tribunal Charges Croat 'War Hero' Norac," *Reuters,* May 25, 2004.

67. BBC, "Croatia: Hard-Line Veterans' Association Expects President to Reconsider Decision to Sack Generals," *BBC Monitoring Europe—Political,* September 29, 2000.

68. AFP, "Croatia's Mesic Sacks Officer for Criticizing ICTY Cooperation," *Agence France Presse,* August 24, 2001.

69. Representative interview.

70. Advisor interview.

71. Račan interview.

72. Josipović interview.

73. Feldman, Račan interviews.

74. Advisor interview.

75. See BBC, "War Crimes Commission Holds Constituent Session," *BBC Summary of World Broadcasts,* February 8, 1997. The OSCE has produced several critical reports concerning domestic war crimes trials, available at www.osce.org.

76. The case of Jovan Romčević, a former resident of Novska (in eastern Slavonia) who left in 1991, is typical. When Romčević returned in 2000 to rebuild his house, he was arrested by police on charges filed in 1996. See BBC, "Police Arrest Returnee on Suspicion of Committing War Crimes," *BBC Summary of World Broadcasts,* October 13, 2000.

77. BBC, "Trial of War Crimes Suspect in Eastern Slavonia Begins," *BBC Summary of World Broadcasts,* April 30, 1997; BBC, "Croatia Requests Extradition

of Croat War Crimes Suspect from Canada," *BBC Monitoring Europe—Political,* March 3, 2001; AFP, "Croatian War Crimes Suspect Arrested in Germany," *Agence France Presse,* August 16, 2001; AP, "Ethnic Serb Woman Convicted in Absentia for War Crimes Is Extradited to Croatia," *Associated Press,* November 16, 2001.

78. BBC, "War Crimes Commission Holds Constituent Session"; BBC, "Croatia Puts Bosnian Embassy Official on Trial for Crimes against Humanity," *BBC Summary of World Broadcasts,* October 19, 1996; BBC, "Court in Split Tries Serb Paramilitary Members for War Crimes," *BBC Summary of World Broadcasts,* November 27, 1996; BBC, "Split Court Jails 39 Serbs for War Crimes," *BBC Summary of World Broadcasts,* May 28, 1997; BBC, "Croatia to Try Group of Serb War Crime Suspects," *BBC Monitoring Europe—Political,* March 10, 1999.

79. BBC, "President in Talks with Serbs, Promises No Revenge," *BBC Summary of World Broadcasts,* February 19, 1997.

80. AFP, "Zagreb Publishes Names of Serbs Accused of War Crimes," *Agence France Presse,* June 27, 1996.

81. In early 1997 the Croatian government's Commission for War Crimes was established, and it announced that more than 2,000 war crimes proceedings had been completed. See BBC, "War Crimes Commission Holds Constituent Session"; AP, "Government So Far Pardoned Thousands of Serbs from War-Related Charges," *Associated Press,* March 19, 1998.

82. M2, "Amnesty International: Croatia—Minister of Interior Should Answer on Specific Cases," *M2 PRESSWIRE,* August 13, 1998.

83. In an unusual case in 1998, Internal Affairs Ministry officials announced that they would begin investigating crimes committed at Gospić, after three former Croatian soldiers made public accusations that their reports of up to 120 Serb extrajudicial executions had been ignored. See AFP, "Zagreb to Investigate after Claims of Serb Executions in 1991," *Agence France Presse,* January 27, 1998; BBC, "Croatian Interior Ministry Rejects Charges of War Crimes Cover-Up," *BBC Monitoring Europe—Political,* January 28, 1998. A former deputy prime minister under Tuđman admitted that the 1991 Gospić crimes were known to government leaders, but a series of investigations were thwarted because Tuđman swept the case under the rug. BBC, "War Crimes Known about but Probe Obstructed, Says Former Minister," *BBC Summary of World Broadcasts,* September 16, 2000; DPA, "Former Croatian Premier Confirms Organised Killings of Serbs," *Deutsche Presse-Agentur,* December 1, 2000.

84. Snejana Vukic, "Croatia Arrests Two War Crimes Suspects, Other Suspected Killers," *Associated Press,* September 12, 2000.

85. DPA, "Former Croatian Army General Charged with War Crimes," *Deutsche Presse-Agentur,* February 7, 2001.

86. After a series of September 2000 arrests, Račan publicly said that he would ensure the continuation of war crimes investigations, and he spoke out against pressure from veterans' groups, calling them "a minority of radical and irresponsible people." See BBC, "Premier Pledges to Continue Investigation into War Crimes," *BBC Summary of World Broadcasts,* September 16, 2000; BBC, "Premier Says Government Will Not Cave In to Veterans' Demands," *BBC Summary of World Broadcasts,* September 18, 2000. See also BBC, "Premier Announces Harsher Measures against War Criminals," *BBC Summary of World Broadcasts,* September 4, 2000.

87. Teršelić, Feldman interviews. See also BBC, "Croatian Leaders Welcome War Crimes Suspect Being Tried in Croatia," *BBC Monitoring Europe—Political,* February 21, 2001; BBC, "Judiciary Capable of Handling War Crime Cases, Says President," *BBC Summary of World Broadcasts,* February 27, 2001; BBC, "Premier Regrets Past Decision Not to Hold War Crimes Trials in Croatia," *BBC Monitoring Europe—Political,* July 8, 2001.

88. BBC, "Retired Generals Want Referendum on Law to Ban Trials of War Veterans," *BBC Summary of World Broadcasts,* February 27, 2001; BBC, "Croatia Is against Amnesty for War Crimes, Ruling Party Chief Whip Says," *BBC Monitoring Europe—Political,* February 16, 2001.

89. BBC, "Croatian Foreign Minister Says Planned Reforms Depend on International Support," *BBC Monitoring Europe—Political,* March 23, 2000.

90. Šimonović, Josipović, Feldman interviews.

91. DPA, "Croatian Police Arrest Two War Crime Suspects," *Deutsche Presse-Agentur,* September 6, 2000; Robert Wright, "Croatia Set to Hold War Crimes Trials on Own Territory," *Financial Times* (London), September 14, 2000; DPA, "Croatian Police Arrest More War Crimes Suspects," *Deutsche Presse-Agentur,* September 6, 2001; DPA, "Three Croatian Soldiers Arrested for Alleged War Crimes," *Deutsche Presse-Agentur,* September 19, 2001; BBC, "Croatia: Six Ex-Policemen Suspected of War Crimes Arrested in Split," *BBC Monitoring Europe—Political,* September 27, 2001; BBC, "70 People 'Disappeared' from Croatian-Controlled Military Base," *Deutsche Presse-Agentur,* September 30, 2001.

92. Teršelić interview.

93. See, for example, DPA, "War Crimes Tribunal Witness Killed by Bomb in Croatia," *Deutsche Presse-Agentur,* August 28, 2000; AFP, "Croatian War Crimes Defence Attorney Shot and Wounded," *Agence France Presse,* December 31, 2000; AFP, "Croatian War Crimes Trial Suspended after Bomb Scare," *Agence France Presse,* February 5, 2002.

94. DPA, "Former Croat Military Police Sentenced for War Crimes," *Deutsche Presse-Agentur,* January 24, 2002. See also AFP, "Former Croatian Policemen

Acquitted of War Crimes Charges," *Agence France Presse,* December 20, 2001; BBC, "Croatia: Zadar Prosecutor Drops Charges against Croat War Crimes Suspect," *BBC Monitoring Europe—Political,* January 17, 2002; GNA, "Six Former Croatian Soldiers Acquitted of War Crimes for Second Time," *Global News Wire—Asia Africa Intelligence Wire,* February 13, 2002.

95. Puhovski, Čičak, Josipović, Banac interviews.

96. DPA, "Croatia to Prosecute 1,522 People for War Crimes," *Deutsche Presse-Agentur,* September 20, 2001.

97. BBC, "Main Opposition Party to Move No-Confidence Motion in Government," *BBC Summary of World Broadcasts,* September 21, 2000.

98. Račan interview.

99. BBC, "Croatian Opposition Party Deputy Calls for Government to Be 'Toppled,'" *BBC Monitoring Europe—Political,* March 11, 2001; BBC, "Croatian Parties Support Government Decision to Set up Prosecution Body," *BBC Monitoring Europe—Political,* January 12, 2001.

100. BBC, "Opposition Parties Condemn Croatia's Policy towards Hague War Crimes Tribunal," *BBC Monitoring Europe—Political,* August 27, 1999; Steven Erlanger, "Opposition Ex-Communist Favored in Croatia Vote," *New York Times,* January 1, 2000.

101. BBC, "New Premier on Croatia's Economy, Media, Relations with Hague Tribunal, Bosnia," *BBC Monitoring Europe—Political,* January 29, 2000.

102. BBC, "Bosnian Croat General's Sentence Ought to Be Re-Examined—Croatian Premier," *BBC Monitoring Europe—Political,* March 3, 2000.

103. DPA, "Croatian Parliament Approves Greater Cooperation on War Crimes," *Deutsche Presse-Agentur,* April 14, 2000; BBC, "War Crimes Tribunal to Suspend Proceedings against Croatia before UN," *BBC Monitoring Europe—Political,* April 17, 2000.

104. BBC, "Premier Says Government Does Not Prosecute Croats, Defend Serbs," *BBC Summary of World Broadcasts,* October 6, 2000; BBC, "Croatian President Defends Government's Decision on Extradition to Hague," *BBC Monitoring Europe—Political,* July 8, 2001.

105. BBC, "Croatian Government Publishes Stances on Cooperation with War Crimes Tribunal," *BBC Monitoring Europe—Political,* December 11, 2000.

106. AFP, "Croatia's PM Admits Problems in Cooperation with ICTY," *Agence France Presse,* December 11, 2001.

107. See, for example, GNW, "Exclusive Interview with New Croatian President"; BBC, "Presidential Candidate Mesicc Says Croatia Must Apologize to Bosnian Muslims"; BBC, "Croatian President on Cooperation with Hague, Differences with Premier," *BBC Monitoring Europe—Political,* April 18, 2000.

108. BBC, "Croatian President Defends Government's Decision on Extradition to Hague."

109. DPA, "Del Ponte: Racan Opposes Indictments," *Deutsche Presse-Agentur,* July 6, 2001.

110. Josipović interview.

111. Z. Pusić, Representative interviews.

112. Puhovski, Šimonović, Feldman interviews.

113. Zvonimir Šeparović interview, February 18, 2005.

114. Šimonović interview. One Tuđman-era justice minister, similarly, contended that "you cannot compare Mladić and Gotovina" (Šeparović interview).

115. Šimonović interview; U.S. government official interview, April 2005; EU official 1 interview, March 17, 2005; EU official 2 interview, April 28, 2005.

116. EU official 2, Banac interviews.

117. BBC, "Croatia: Premier Says Decision to Cooperate with Hague Tribunal Was Inevitable," *BBC Monitoring Europe—Political,* July 8, 2001.

118. See BBC, "Croatian Premier Says Country's Future Needs Cooperation with Hague Tribunal," *BBC Monitoring Europe—Political,* July 10, 2001; DPA, "Half of the Croats Support Extradition of War Crimes Suspects," *Deutsche Presse-Agentur,* July 9, 2001.

119. DPA, "Croatia to Extradite War Crimes Suspects to Hague," *Deutsche Presse-Agentur,* July 7, 2001.

120. BBC, "Foreign Minister: Croatia Will Not Allow Besmirching of Homeland War in Hague," *BBC Monitoring Europe—Political,* July 11, 2001.

121. Igor Medic, "Analysis: Croatian PM Racan Boosted after Winning Confidence Vote," *Deutsche Presse-Agentur,* July 16, 2001.

122. Račan interview.

123. In one interview concerning protests by ICTY opponents, Mesić calmly reacted: "What are 3,000 demonstrators in a country of 4.5 million? They were taken to Zagreb in buses to discredit me as the new president" (BBC, "President Calls for Rapprochement with Serbs and End to Sanctions," *BBC Summary of World Broadcasts,* April 7, 2000).

124. Račan interview.

125. See BBC, "Croatian Fugitive General Seized," *BBC News,* December 8, 2005; Nicholas Wood, "Croatian Turnaround Led to General's Arrest," *International Herald Tribune,* December 27, 2005.

126. BBC, "Croatian President Slams Protests over Gen. Norac Arrest Warrant," *BBC Monitoring Europe—Political,* February 10, 2001.

127. Račan interview.

128. Banac interview.

129. BBC, "President Says Law Exempting War Veterans from Prosecution Not Right."

CHAPTER 8. *Uzbekistan*

1. For a brief background, see Freedom House report on Uzbekistan, available at http://www.freedomhouse.org/research/freeworld/2001/countryratings/uzbekistan.htm.

2. Resul Jalcin, "The Formation of a Multi-Party System in Uzbekistan," *Central Asia and the Caucasus* 5 (2001).

3. Bakhodir Fakhritdinov, "Civilian Movements and Parties in Uzbekistan: Development Trends and Problems," *Central Asia and the Caucasus* 5 (2002).

4. Jalcin, "The Formation of a Multi-Party System in Uzbekistan."

5. Fakhritdinov, "Civilian Movements and Parties in Uzbekistan: Development Trends and Problems."

6. I attempted to locate members on several occasions by asking my local contacts (in the human rights, diplomatic, and banned opposition communities) who was still in Uzbekistan. None of my contacts could give me such information.

7. Nikolai Borisov, "Transformation in the Political Regime in Uzbekistan: Stages and Outcome," *Central Asia and the Caucasus* 6 (2005).

8. Fakhritdinov, "Civilian Movements and Parties in Uzbekistan: Development Trends and Problems." For more on the development of governmental parties, see Bakhtier Ergashev, "The Formation of a Multi-Party System in Uzbekistan: Problems and Prospects," *Central Asia and the Caucasus* 6 (2000).

9. Brian Grodsky, "Looking for Solidarność in Central Asia: The Role of Human Rights Organizations in Political Change," *Slavic Review* 66, no. 3 (2007).

10. For more on the nature of rights violations in Uzbekistan, see Uzbekistan country reports at Human Rights Watch (www.hrw.org) and the U.S. Department of State (www.state.gov).

11. The members of the human rights organizations whom I interviewed shared similar perspectives on diplomatic activities, claiming that the United States is the most active in putting pro–human rights pressure on the Uzbek government, followed by Great Britain and then Germany. Other embassies mentioned sporadically include the Swiss and French as well as the Dutch consul. In interviews with Western officials, the ranking was the same. "The Americans play an incomparable role," one German commented. "Without the influence of American diplomats I think it would be hard to get any kind of results here" (German Government official interview, March 2004).

Unlike the Americans, who have more personnel, greater financial leverage, and relatively quick reaction times to the frequent human rights policy crises on the ground, the Europeans remain small, weak, and too divided to efficiently commit to a common stance. "Definitely the Americans are the most active, the best resourced," commented one European diplomat, adding that Americans "have better access" to senior officials in key ministries (EU official interview, September 2004). One OSCE official concluded, "the only one that has some power to really push is the States" (Per Normark interview, March 10, 2004).

12. BBC, "U.S. Defense Secretary Praises Uzbekistan as 'Island of Stability,'" *BBC Summary of World Broadcasts,* April 8, 1995.

13. U.S. Government (USG; Washington, D.C.) official 7 interview, April 2003; USG official 8 interview, May 2003.

14. USG official 7 interview.

15. Zamirakhon Tolijeva, "U.S.A. to Triple Financial Aid to Uzbekistan to 160m Dollars in 2002," *Uzbek Radio,* January 30, 2002.

16. Sources in Washington say that while these talking points are delivered to all high-level officials meeting with Uzbeks in Washington or Tashkent, it is unclear how far their message gets within the Pentagon ranks. "We make the Pentagon do the human rights point. We give them the point and they say, 'Okay, we'll see'" (USG official 7 interview).

17. This understanding was likely reinforced when, in 2002, Congress amended the U.S. Foreign Appropriations Act to mandate bi-annual administration reports on all security assistance to Uzbekistan. See HRW, "Uzbekistan: Human Rights Developments 2002," Human Rights Watch, http://www.hrw.org/wr2k3/europe16.html#international_community.

18. For a closer analysis, see Brian Grodsky, "Direct Pressures for Human Rights in Uzbekistan: Understanding the U.S. Bargaining Position," *Central Asian Survey* 23 (2004).

19. These press releases are available, chronologically, at www.state.gov. In 1999 the only two press statements concerning Uzbekistan condemned the Uzbeks for the arrest of dissidents and unfair parliamentary elections. While U.S. officials in 2000 issued two press statements concerning terrorism (one noting a terrorist incursion and the other designating the Islamic Movement of Uzbekistan as a terrorist organization), their strategic interests remained balanced by human rights concerns, including a press statement attacking the Uzbek leadership for conducting flawed presidential elections. The only statement issued in pre-September 2001 concerned the death in police custody of a human rights activist. Between September 11 and December 31, 2001, the State Department issued four press statements concerning Uzbekistan, all related to security. Over the course of

2002, human rights remained a non-issue; the State Department issued three security-oriented statements and two statements about medical aid being delivered to Uzbekistan. It made no official press statements concerning Uzbekistan in 2003 or in the first half of 2004.

There are several weaknesses to using these press releases as a measure. First, Uzbekistan was mentioned relatively few times, so the number of observations is small. Second, it does not account for private meetings with Uzbek officials, but instead shows only the "public face" of diplomacy. This public aspect, however, is an important indicator of bargaining position. With decreasing public attention to Uzbek human rights issues, the U.S. government is sending a signal to the Uzbeks that its priorities, and the influence of pro–human rights domestic constraints, have changed.

20. In order to gauge the U.S. Congress's interest in Uzbekistan, I first searched the Lexis-Nexis database for congressional testimony concerning Uzbekistan within the Senate's Foreign Relations Committee and the House's International Relations Committee, between January 1999 and December 2003. Next, I scanned these debates for references to Uzbekistan. In many of these cases, Uzbekistan was mentioned only peripherally (e.g., someone giving testimony said that he had worked in several CIS countries, including Uzbekistan). After dropping these cases, I coded the remaining "significant" debates according to the context in which Uzbekistan was raised (e.g., security, human rights, economic potential). The total number of occurrences in the House and Senate committees were: 20 (1999), 14 (2000), 21 (2001), 20 (2002), 21 (2003). The total number of "significant" occurrences were: 6 (1999), 8 (2000), 14 (2001), 12 (2002), 12 (2003). More than 70 percent (10) of the significant 2001 hearings took place after September 11.

With U.S. interest in Uzbekistan relatively limited at the end of the 1990s, it is not surprising that the 1999 congressional testimony concerning that country touched on a smattering of human rights, security, and economic topics. Its dismal human rights performance gained increased attention in 2000, dominating more than half of the significant hearings concerning Uzbekistan. This trend continued in the first part of 2001, but it was suddenly and dramatically reversed immediately following the September 11 terrorist attacks. In the last quarter of 2001, the Senate became much more interested in Uzbekistan, which was discussed in five Foreign Relations Committee hearings focused almost exclusively on security issues. Congressional debate remained largely centered on security in 2002 (where security was featured in three-quarters of the hearings concerning Uzbekistan), but human rights remained on the table; and by the end of the year, some members of Congress wondered aloud why Uzbekistan was not on the Religious Freedom Report's list of "countries of particular concern." Security concerns, from Uzbekistan's role in the Afghan war to nonproliferation and transnational crime, continued to dominate in 2003 (when seven of the twelve hearings were almost exclusively focused on security), but the hearings were marked by important human rights debate as well.

21. While the Uzbeks initially used greater U.S. attention to cold-shoulder Russia and the Russian-dominated Commonwealth of Independent States (CIS), by the second half of 1999 the Uzbeks began to shift back toward Russia, which proved to be a more dependable ally against terrorist infiltrations. This move was exemplified by Uzbekistan's mid-2001 entry into the Shanghai Cooperation Organization, but it was reversed by late 2001, when the Uzbeks returned to the U.S. side to profit from the "war on terrorism." Tashkent's frequent shifts partly indicate the negligible cost of moving from one side to another. They also reflect a more fundamental problem in U.S. bargaining power with Uzbekistan: in the eyes of the Tashkent government, pro-democracy pressures within the United States result in decreased benefits (limited security assistance) and increased costs (threats to sovereignty) of dealing with Washington. For a more detailed discussion of this situation, see Brian Grodsky, "The New Game in Central Asia: Comparative Uzbek and Kazakh Foreign Policy," *Journal of Central Asian Studies* 5, no. 2 (2003).

22. Total U.S. assistance to Uzbekistan rose from $44 million in 1999 and $36.8 million in 2000 (including military aid of only $2.6 million and $2.7, respectively), to $244 million in 2001 (including $3.5 million in military aid) and $225 million in 2002 (when military aid skyrocketed to $42.1 million). See USAID, "U.S. Overseas Loans and Grants [Greenbook] 2007," United States Agency for International Development, http://qesdb.cdie.org/gbk/index.html.

23. In 2002, spending on Uzbekistan was projected at $160 million earlier in the year (see statement by Ambassador William Taylor in FNS, "Special State Department Briefing," *Federal News Service,* February 11, 2002). See also Denise Albrighton, "U.S. Praises Uzbekistan, Looks Past Poll to Extend Presidential Term," *Agence France Presse,* January 29, 2002. As the year went on, U.S. assistance continued to climb. See AFP, "Washington Gives Uzbekistan 193 Million Dollars in Financial Aid: Embassy," *Agence France Presse,* June 19, 2002. For official figures, see State Department (U.S.), "U.S. Assistance to Uzbekistan—Fiscal Year 2002," available at United States Department of State, http://www.state.gov/p/eur/rls/fs/15683.htm.

24. In addition to the obvious benefits of monetary and non-monetary aid, some U.S. officials believe that they have given the Uzbeks a much-wanted opportunity to fearlessly dismiss Russia's flirtation in the region. Uzbekistan's leadership also receives transaction benefits (primarily prestige and legitimacy) from the high-level international presence to impress their domestic audience. Photographs

of President Karimov meeting senior-level delegations are a staple in the state-controlled Uzbek press, and greater access to high-level officials—ranging from the U.S. president and vice president to the secretaries of state and defense—have been added to Karimov's trophy case. "We don't only give them assistance, we give them legitimacy," one American official commented. "That access has a price on it" (USG official 7 interview).

25. See State Department (U.S.), "U.S. Assistance to Uzbekistan—Fiscal Year 2003," available at United States Department of State, http://www.state.gov/p/eur/rls/fs/29494.htm. Even then, the Bush administration remained adamant that Uzbekistan's poor human rights record should not get in the way of security assistance. In late 2003, Secretary of State Colin Powell decertified Uzbekistan under the Cooperative Threat Reduction (CTR) program, but President George W. Bush issued a national security waiver permitting continued funding. See HRW, "Uzbekistan: Human Rights Developments 2004," Human Rights Watch, http://hrw.org/english/docs/2003/12/31/uzbeki7024.htm#4.

26. Following a report drafted by Javier Solana, the European Union's foreign policy head, EU diplomats admitted several weeks after the September 11 terrorist attacks that they lacked the economic strength and political will to press for change in Central Asia, saying instead that "our main priority is the Balkans and how to bring them closer to the EU" (Judy Dempsey, "Central Asian States Force Way into EU Consciousness," *Financial Times* [London], October 30, 2001).

27. German aid, for example, is largely in the form of social programs to fight tuberculosis and to promote German-language training, while British security aid is similarly limited to English-language instruction for military personnel. "Our leverage is not that powerful financially," one British official conceded (British Government official interview, February 2004).

28. Craig Murray, the post–September 11 ambassador who was relieved in 2004, raised eyebrows both in Tashkent and in his own capital for his aggressive, public campaign against Uzbek human rights abuses. With conditionality impossible, the "one tool that we do have," a British official noted, "is the willingness to speak publicly" (ibid.). For more on Murray and his dismissal, see Paul Reynolds, "Confession of a British Diplomat," *BBC News,* October 15, 2004.

29. One German government official commented, "Diplomacy should be more or less quiet. We understand that diplomacy can be a very long-lasting process. Communication depends very much on both sides" (German Government official interview). The difference between British and German policy is embodied in each country's human rights report. While the British (much like the Americans) use their annual report to publicly chastise Uzbekistan for serious rights abuses, the Germans' semi-annual report is reserved for internal use, the German official said.

30. I saw this personally, while trying to coordinate a U.S.-EU démarche as political officer at the U.S. Embassy in Tashkent (2000). At the last minute, a representative from the French Embassy (then representing the EU) said that he needed more time, and the démarche was carried out without full EU participation. My diplomatic contacts from U.S. and EU missions (in Tashkent and Belgrade) acknowledged that this remains a problem.

31. British Government official interview. See also Western diplomat interview, September 2004.

32. Officials with ABA/CEELI's human rights projects in Tashkent claim that the prevalence of American visitors to their sites and high-level discussion of ABA projects between U.S. and Uzbek officials provide "diplomatic cover" that makes such programs more difficult to close down (Marina Colby interview, March 3, 2004; Phyllis Oscar interview, March 3, 2004). Similarly, as a senior-level Freedom House officer at the organization's Tashkent headquarters commented, "we are so promoted by the U.S. government, which gives us extra operational security" (Ele Pawelski interview, March 10, 2004). NDI officials also said that the State Department had "given us this opening" and that continued U.S. pressure was essential for continuing local operations (Nelson Ledsky interview, May 8, 2003).

33. The U.S. government provides assistance through and/or alongside unofficial (e.g., National Democratic Institute/International Republican Institute) or even private American entities (e.g., Soros, Freedom House). While DRL expenditures in Uzbekistan for 2001 amounted to only $150,000, in 2003 and 2004 they were roughly twelve times higher (approximately $1.9 million) (USG official 1 interview, April 2003). Freedom House funding, for example, grew from $150,000 in 2001 (when it was the DRL's only Uzbekistan program) to almost $800,000 by 2003. At the same time, the DRL in late 2002 began supporting ($600,000 combined) the National Democratic Institute (NDI) and the International Republican Institute (IRI), organizations expressly charged with political party development for "opposition parties and movements." In addition, the DRL has put $500,000 into ABA/CEELI's Human Rights Law Center.

For more on resource dependency in the Uzbek context, see Brian Grodsky, "Resource Dependency and Political Opportunity: Explaining the Transformation from Excluded Political Opposition Parties to Human Rights Organizations in Post-Communist Uzbekistan," *Government and Opposition* 42, no. 1 (2007). Apart from their fear of a diplomatic backlash, the Europeans also believe that local human rights organizations and opposition parties are not a viable alternative to the current regime and, therefore, are unworthy of foreign support. While they consistently advocate for democratic reforms, the British and Germans keep their distance from excluded elites, whom Western diplomats refer to as immature, disorganized, and politically inept. "Opposition parties have not even reached the level where they have developed their own agenda," a German official commented. "They are not ready to be a reliable partner for projects" (German Government official interview). Similarly, the British have resisted putting money into human rights organizations that one British official has called "not developed" (British Government official interview).

34. Normark interview.

35. Michael McFaul, "Transitions from Postcommunism," *Journal of Democracy* 16, no. 3 (2005); Mark R. Beissinger, "Promoting Democracy: Is Exporting Revolution a Constructive Strategy?" *Dissent* (2006); Thomas Carothers, "The Backlash against Democracy Promotion: The Autocrats Push Back," *Foreign Affairs* 85, no. 2 (2006); Mark N. Katz, "Revolutionary Change in Central Asia," *World Affairs* 168, no. 4 (2007). Among key Western organizations pushed out of Uzbekistan were Freedom House, IREX, and various news organizations (e.g., BBC, RFE/RL) (FH, "Uzbek Court Suspends Freedom House Human Rights Programs in Uzbekistan," Freedom House, http://www.freedomhouse.org/template.cfm?page=70&release=322).

36. For more discussion on this topic, and more specific results, see Grodsky, "Direct Pressures for Human Rights in Uzbekistan: Understanding the U.S. Bargaining Position."

37. A review of seven major amnesties issued between 1996 and 2003 (August 1996, December 1997, May 1999, September 2000, August 2001, December 2002, and March 2003) suggests that direct Western pressures have been influential in obtaining the release of political prisoners in Uzbekistan. This analysis is based on a review of two Uzbek daily newspapers (*Narodnoye Slovo* and *O'zbekiston Ovozi*). Two local research assistants and I searched for all occurrences of articles concerning human rights developments, including prison amnesties.

38. See AFP, "Uzbek Policemen Jailed for 20 Years for Torturing Detainees," *Agence France Presse*, January 30, 2002; and AFP, "Uzbek Security Officials Tried for Torturing Suspect to Death," *Agence France Presse*, May 8, 2002. See also comments by Uzbek government officials in Vilor Niyazmatov, "Authorities Say Human Rights Abuses in Uzbekistan Not Systemic," *TASS*, March 19, 2003; GNA, "Uzbekistan Says Rights Abuses 'Not Systematic,' Pledges Actions," *Global News Wire—Asia Africa Intelligence Wire*, March 19, 2003.

39. IHRI official 1 interview, March 3, 2004; AFP, "Rights Campaigner Released from Uzbek Jail," *Agence France Presse*, July 4, 2001; GNA, "Uzbek Rights Activist Says Police Have Stopped Hounding Her," *Global News Wire—Asia Africa Intelligence Wire*, December 30, 2002. Human Rights Watch also credited U.S. threats to halt nonproliferation assistance with the release of two prominent human

rights activists (see HRW, "Uzbekistan: Human Rights Developments 2002"). Leaders of each of the three registered human rights organizations in Uzbekistan also credit their official existence to U.S. and other international pressures (CDHR official interview, March 4, 2004; IHRSU official 5 interview, March 9, 2004; AFP, "Uzbek Authorities Register Independent Human Rights Group," *Agence France Presse,* March 6, 2002; Ezgulik official and Birlik Party leader interview, March 11, 2004; GNA, "Uzbek Authorities Register Human Rights Organization," *Global News Wire—Asia Africa Intelligence Wire,* April 1, 2003). The same is true of international human rights and pro-democracy organizations, including the Red Cross, National Democratic Institute, ABA-CEELI, and Freedom House, which credit their post–September 2001 human rights and pro-democratization activities in Uzbekistan to direct U.S. pressure (Ledsky, Colby, Oscar, Pawelski interviews; International Committee of the Red Cross representative interview, February 24, 2004; HRW, "Uzbekistan: Human Rights Developments 2002"). While an agreement reached between Uzbekistan and the Red Cross in 2001 was quickly suspended for lack of Uzbek compliance, full compliance was attained in the period after September 11.

40. In spring 2004, for example, all foreign NGOs were ordered to re-register under a new regime, drawing intense criticism from the organizations and Western embassies. (Note: Since then, Russia has adopted a similar law—see Reuters, "Russia to Curb Foreign Human Rights Groups and Charities," *Reuters,* November 23, 2005.) This action led several international NGOs, including the Open Society Institute, National Democratic Institute, and International Republican Institute, to cease much of their activities for several weeks or months. The Open Society Institute was pushed out of the country, a fate shared one year later by Internews.

41. GNA, "U.S. Envoy Laments Uzbekistan's Human Rights Record," *Global News Wire—Asia Africa Intelligence Wire,* April 11, 2003. Likely due to its immense scale, the spring 2005 massacre in Andijon seemed to mark an end to this trend.

42. USG official 7, USG official 8 interviews.

43. Roundtable, "Media Roundtable with Robert Seiple, U.S. Ambassador-at-Large for Religious Freedom," http://www.osce.usia.co.at/ambseiple24may00.html.

44. Natalia Mielczarek, "Expression Not Free in Central Asia; Former Soviet Republics' Democratic Reforms Remain Only Promises," *Washington Times,* April 14, 2001; Andrew Jack and David Stern, "Region Weighs Gains in Pro-U.S. Stance," *Financial Times* (London), October 18, 2001.

45. AFP, "EU Demands Uzbek Reform Progress ahead of May Bank Meeting," *Agence France Presse,* January 27, 2003.

46. GNW, "Uzbekistan Pledges to Implement OSCE Recommendations on Human Rights," *Global News Wire—Interfax,* October 25, 1999.

47. GNA, "Uzbek Government Has Much to Do to Improve Rights Situation—Fuller," *Global News Wire—Asia Africa Intelligence Wire,* April 4, 2002. In one example, Karimov made a speech two days after two human rights advocates who had attempted to demonstrate against the government were placed in psychiatric hospitals. "I have the impression that our media, trampled by ideological and administrative control for years, have psychological problems in ridding themselves of that yoke," Karimov said. Vilor Niyazmatov, "Uzbek Pres. Urges Mass Media to Discard Ideological Control," *ITAR-TASS News Agency,* August 30, 2002. See also Bagila Bukharbayeva, "Uzbek President Urges Radical Democratic Change, Military Reform," *Associated Press,* August 29, 2002.

48. BBC, "President Orders Research into Victims of Soviet Regime," *BBC Summary of World Broadcasts,* May 17, 1999.

49. My media analysis is based on a review of human rights-related articles in two Uzbek daily newspapers (*Narodnoye Slovo* and *O'zbekiston Ovozi*) for the 1995–2003 period and in two daily newspapers (*Pravda Vostoka* and *Xalq So'zi*) for the 1995–2000 period.

50. For more, see Grodsky, "Looking for Solidarność in Central Asia: The Role of Human Rights Organizations in Political Change." For elite responses, see, for example: IHRSU official 6 interview, March 12, 2004; CDHR official interview; Ezgulik official and Birlik Party leader interview. Outside human rights groups, such as the Moscow Helsinki Group, have made a similar point (Digest, "Other Post-Soviet States—Uzbekistan," *Current Digest of the Post-Soviet Press,* October 10, 2001).

51. Karimov's concern for his international reputation has been noted by other scholars, including Laura Adams, "Winds of Change in Central Asian Politics" (paper presented at the Center for Russian and East European Studies, University of Michigan, Ann Arbor, October 5, 1995). It is evidenced in the daily front page of Uzbek newspapers, where Karimov is invariably pictured alongside some foreign dignitary.

52. DPA, "Uzbekistan 'Worried about Russian Imperialism,' Perry Is Told," *Deutsche Presse-Agentur,* April 6, 1995.

53. I. A. Karimov, *Uzbekistan on the Threshold of the Twenty-first Century* (Surrey, Eng.: Curzon, 1997), 34.

54. Bruce Pannier, "Uzbekistan: Minister Announces Plans to Quit CIS Defense Pact," *Radio Free Europe/Radio Liberty,* February 4, 1999; IPS, "Central Asia: Little Applause for Russian Military Presence," *Inter Press Service,* April 22, 1999.

55. Laura Adams, "Tashkent Museum Allows for Public Discussion of Recent Past," *Eurasianet,* November 1, 2002.

56. BBC, "Uzbek President Speaks on Bomb Attacks," *BBC Monitoring Central Asia Unit,* February 17, 1999.

57. AFP, "Uzbekistan Frees Muslim Political Activists Imprisoned on False Charges," *Agence France Presse,* September 22, 1999.

58. Articles concerning the amnesty, in news and op/ed format, were published in *Narodnoye Slovo* on May 6, May 7, May 12, May 13, May 15, May 26, and May 27, 1999.

59. Interfax, "Uzbekistan to Continue with Economic Reforms," *Interfax Russian News,* May 25, 1999.

60. Naim Karimov interview, September 23, 2004.

61. BBC, "President Orders Research into Victims of Soviet Regime"; Karimov interview.

62. BBC, "President Orders Research into Victims of Soviet Regime."

63. See Halim Kara, "Reclaiming National Literary Heritage: The Rehabilitation of Abdurauf Fitrat and Abdulhamid Sulaymon Cholpan in Uzbekistan," *Europe-Asia Studies* 54, no. 1 (2002).

64. Karimov interview.

65. Andrew F. March, "The Use and Abuse of History: 'National Ideology' as Transcendental Object in Islam Karimov's 'Ideology of National Independence,'" *Central Asian Survey* 21, no. 4 (2002): 379.

66. For more on Naim Karimov, see Kara, "Reclaiming National Literary Heritage: The Rehabilitation of Abdurauf Fitrat and Abdulhamid Sulaymon Cholpan in Uzbekistan."

67. BBC, "President Orders Research into Victims of Soviet Regime."

68. UzTV, "Uzbek Head Decrees Remembrance Day for Victims of Totalitarianism," May 2, 2001.

69. Adams, "Tashkent Museum Allows for Public Discussion of Recent Past."

70. According to Naim Karimov, who is also its director, the museum has become an important part of the educational system, with schoolchildren making up a majority of the 500,000 visitors in its first fifteen months of operation (Karimov interview).

71. Ibid.

72. Ibid.

73. Ibid.

74. Ibid.

75. CDHR official interview.

76. HRSU official 3 interview, September 17, 2004.

77. Ozod Dekhkonlar Party official interview, March 16, 2004.

78. CDHR official interview.

79. IHRSU official 3 interview, September 4, 2004.

80. This may come as a surprise to outside observers who focus primarily on political and civil rights violations, such as arbitrary detention, torture, and the closed political system. Indeed, many of these respondents center their work on these more "sellable" aspects of human rights on the grant market.

81. Ozod Dekhkonlar Party official interview. I should note that this respondent made it clear that she feels more protected than other opposition members due to her shared elite status with Karimov. "I am not their enemy—I come from up there, not from below," she said. "He can't use open repression on us." Since our conversation, however, this representative's husband was killed under suspicious circumstances, and her sister was accused of financial crimes and arrested.

82. CDHR official interview.

83. IHRSU official 5 interview. This representative, once an avid critic of the president, has staged a number of pro-Karimov events since his organization was legalized, and he is widely regarded as having joined the government side.

84. IHRI official 1 interview.

85. Ezgulik official and Birlik Party leader interview.

86. Mazlum official 3 interview, March 12, 2004; IHRSU official 2 interview, September 25, 2004. "Payday will happen sooner or later," agreed one Birlik member. "Not by us, but the following generations" (Ezgulik official 1 interview, September 2, 2004).

87. Erk Party official 2 interview, February 24, 2004.

88. IHRSU official 6 interview.

89. IHRSU official 3 interview.

90. Erk Party official 2 interview.

91. Appellyatziya official interview, September 3, 2004. The leader of Appellyatziya was arrested following the Andijon massacre and reportedly was sentenced to seven years in jail after a secret trial in Tashkent (RFE/RL, "Uzbek Court Reportedly Sentences Rights Activist over Andijon," *Radio Free Europe/Radio Liberty,* January 17, 2006).

92. IHRI official 2 interview, September 9, 2004. One advisor to Birlik agreed that while high-level officials motivated by greed must be charged to set an example, lower-level officials accused of corruption should be left alone: "when a doctor takes [a bribe], he does it to buy bread" (CDI official interview, September 7, 2004).

93. IHRSU official 1 interview, September 3, 2004; Mazlum official 2 interview, September 2, 2004.

94. IHRI official 3 interview, September 9, 2004.

95. Richard Carver, "Called to Account: How African Governments Investigate Human Rights Violations," *African Affairs* 89, no. 356 (1990); Hayner, "Fifteen Truth Commissions, 1974 to 1994: A Comparative Study."

96. Juan J. Linz and Alfred Stepan, *Problems of Democratic Transition and Consolidation: Southern Europe, South America, and Post-Communist Europe* (Baltimore: Johns Hopkins University Press, 1996); Bruce Bueno de Mesquita et al., "An Institutional Explanation of the Democratic Peace," *American Political Science Review* 93, no. 4 (1999); Larry Jay Diamond, "Thinking about Hybrid Regimes," *Journal of Democracy* 13, no. 2 (2002).

97. Geddes, "What Do We Know about Democratization after 20 Years?" 133.

98. Demian Vaisman, "Regionalism and Clan Loyalty in the Political Life of Uzbekistan," in *Muslim Eurasia: Conflicting Legacies,* ed. Yaacov Ro'i (London; Portland, Ore.: F. Cass, 1995).

CHAPTER 9 *Transitional Justice in a Cross-National Perspective*

1. Szczerbiak, "Dealing with the Communist Past or the Politics of the Present? Lustration in Post-Communist Poland," 557.

2. Calhoun, "The Ideological Dilemma of Lustration in Poland," 501.

3. Szczerbiak, "Dealing with the Communist Past or the Politics of the Present? Lustration in Post-Communist Poland," 557; Calhoun, "The Ideological Dilemma of Lustration in Poland," 501.

4. Rigby, *Justice and Reconciliation: After the Violence.*

5. Walicki, "Transitional Justice and the Political Struggles in Post-Communist Poland," 196.

6. Calhoun, "The Ideological Dilemma of Lustration in Poland."

7. Ibid.; Szczerbiak, "Dealing with the Communist Past or the Politics of the Present? Lustration in Post-Communist Poland," 557.

8. Walicki, "Transitional Justice and the Political Struggles in Post-Communist Poland," 197; Szczerbiak, "Dealing with the Communist Past or the Politics of the Present? Lustration in Post-Communist Poland," 558.

9. Walicki, "Transitional Justice and the Political Struggles in Post-Communist Poland," 198.

10. Calhoun, "The Ideological Dilemma of Lustration in Poland."

11. Walicki, "Transitional Justice and the Political Struggles in Post-Communist Poland," 198–99; Szczerbiak, "Dealing with the Communist Past or the Politics of the Present? Lustration in Post-Communist Poland," 558.

12. Szczerbiak, "Dealing with the Communist Past or the Politics of the Present? Lustration in Post-Communist Poland," 558.

13. Jack Bielasiak and David Blunck, "Past and Present in Transitional Voting: Electoral Choices in Post-Communist Poland," *Party Politics* 8, no. 5 (2002): 566.

14. David Ost, "The Weakness of Symbolic Strength: Labor and Union Identity in Poland, 1989–2000," in *Workers after Workers' States: Labor and Politics in Postcommunist Eastern Europe,* ed. Stephen Crowley and David Ost (Lanham, Md.: Rowman & Littlefield, 2001), 88.

15. Rigby, *Justice and Reconciliation: After the Violence*; Calhoun, "The Ideological Dilemma of Lustration in Poland."

16. Walicki, "Transitional Justice and the Political Struggles in Post-Communist Poland," 205.

17. Szczerbiak, "Dealing with the Communist Past or the Politics of the Present? Lustration in Post-Communist Poland," 562–64.

18. Calhoun, "The Ideological Dilemma of Lustration in Poland"; Rigby, *Justice and Reconciliation: After the Violence*; Szczerbiak, "Dealing with the Communist Past or the Politics of the Present? Lustration in Post-Communist Poland," 567–68.

19. Calhoun, "The Ideological Dilemma of Lustration in Poland," 516; Szczerbiak, "Dealing with the Communist Past or the Politics of the Present? Lustration in Post-Communist Poland," 567.

20. Szczerbiak, "Dealing with the Communist Past or the Politics of the Present? Lustration in Post-Communist Poland," 569.

21. Calhoun, "The Ideological Dilemma of Lustration in Poland," 516.

22. Jasiewicz, "The Political-Party Landscape," 31.

23. Ibid., 33.

24. Danuta Przywara interview, December 9, 2003.

25. Geremek interview.

26. Kozłowski interview.

27. Braun interview.

28. Dmochowska interview.

29. Andrzejewski interview; Alicja Grześkowiak interview, January 28, 2004.

30. Andrzejewski interview.

31. Pałubicki interview.

32. M. Males, "Kažne Za Kršenje Ljudskikh Prava," *Danas,* February 12, 2003; Danas, "Lustracija Za Sve Funkcionere," *Danas,* February 6, 2003.

33. Danas, "Obračun Sa Zlom I Istinska Lustracija," *Danas,* March 24, 2003.

34. Danas, "Kriterijum Istina, a Ne Čistke," *Danas,* May 27, 2003.

35. Grubač interview; BBC, "Serbian Commentary Sees Scope for Political Abuse of Secret Files," *BBC Monitoring Europe—Political,* September 21, 2003.

36. BBC, "Serbian Christian Democrats Reelect Vladan Batic as Party Chairman," *BBC Monitoring Europe—Political,* December 14, 2002; BBC, "Serbian Justice Minister Condemns Sentences Issued in Ibar Motorway Case," *BBC Monitoring Europe—Political,* January 31, 2003; Danas, "Nema Političke Volje Za Lustraciju," *Danas,* March 4, 2003.

37. Danas, "Vučetić: Lustracija Kao Ubiranje Političkih Poena," *Danas,* March 1, 2003.

38. GNW, "Serbia: SRS Questions Constitutionality of Lustration Law, to Initiate Inquiry," *Global News Wire,* June 2, 2003.

39. M. Jevtović, "Revanšizam Ili Korak Ka Pravdi," *Danas,* May 30, 2003; BBC, "Serbia NGO Says Lustration Law Unconstitutional," *BBC Monitoring Europe—Political,* July 14, 2003.

40. GNW, "Serbian Supreme Court Judge Rejects Membership in New Lustration Commission," *Global News Wire,* July 13, 2003; Danas, "Serbian Assembly Elects Eight Members of Lustration Commission," *BBC Monitoring Europe—Political,* July 15, 2003.

41. Resanović interview.

42. Danas, "Zakoni Za Ispravljanje Istorijskih Nepravdi," *Danas,* August 18, 2003.

43. BBC, "Serbian Radical Party Proposes Annulment of 'Anti-Constitutional' Lustration Law," *BBC Monitoring Europe—Political,* February 9, 2004; Matković interview.

44. S. Bisevać, "Zakon O Lustraciji Pred Ukidanjem?" *Danas,* March 6, 2004.

45. Danas, "Većina Građana Za Lustraciju," *Danas,* February 25, 2003.

46. Korać interview.

47. Č. Jovanović interview.

48. Banac interview.

49. Puhovski interview.

50. Gazivoda interview.

51. Pulat Ohunov interview, September 4, 2004.

52. Havel and Keane, *The Power of the Powerless: Citizens against the State in Central-Eastern Europe.*

53. This also raises questions about how non-elites define human rights. Through non-elite interviews conducted in two disparate postcommunist states (Poland and Uzbekistan), I found that non-elites tend to focus much more on economic than on political rights violations. The opposite was true of their elite counterparts. See Brian Grodsky, "On the Other Side of the Curtain: A Reassessment of

Non-Elite Human Rights Experiences and Values in Poland," *Human Rights Review* 9, no. 4 (2008).

54. V. Pusić, Advisor (to Mesić), Gazivoda, Puhovski, Banac, Z. Pusić interviews.

55. Advisor interview.

56. Grodsky, "On the Other Side of the Curtain: A Reassessment of Non-Elite Human Rights Experiences and Values in Poland."

57. Geoffrey Best, "Justice, International Relations, and Human Rights," 785.

CHAPTER 10   *Reassessing How We Think about Justice*

1. Peter Eisle, "Nazi Chasers Will Also Hunt Modern-Day Monsters," *USA Today,* December 27, 2004.

2. AP, "Japan's Abe Denies Proof of World War II Sex Slaves," *Associated Press,* March 1, 2007.

3. Larry Rohter, "Chile's Leader Attacks Amnesty Law," *Associated Press,* December 24, 2006.

4. The fact that Polish new elites started their political careers by pressing for the prosecution of a postcommunist still serving as internal affairs minister seems to be a significant jab at the relative power argument. So, too, is the opinion of those Serbian leaders responsible for carrying out Hague arrests, who claimed that criminal accountability was a function of political popularity, not danger.

5. Paul Collier, "Ethnic Diversity: An Economic Analysis," *Economic Policy* 32 (2001); Bueno de Mesquita et al., "Policy Failure and Political Survival: The Contribution of Political Institutions"; Bueno de Mesquita et al., "An Institutional Explanation of the Democratic Peace."

6. Ted Robert Gurr and Woodrow Wilson School of Public and International Affairs, Center of International Studies, *Why Men Rebel* (Princeton: Princeton University Press, 1970).

7. Pion-Berlin, "To Prosecute or to Pardon? Human Rights Decisions in the Latin American Southern Cone."

8. Staniszewska interview.

9. Interestingly, economic costs also play into the argument for or against the death penalty in the United States. See, for example, Rone Tempest, "Death Row Often Means a Long Life," *Los Angeles Times,* March 6, 2005.

10. Račan interview.

11. Gleb interview, September 2004. See Grodsky, "Looking for Solidarność in Central Asia: The Role of Human Rights Organizations in Political Change."

List of Interviews

Poland

Andrzejewski, Piotr. Former senator (1989–2001), January 29, 2004, Warsaw.

Bednarski, Jerzy. Representative of Union of Polish Combatants and Former Political Prisoners (Związek Kombatantów Rzeczpospolitej i Byłych Więźniów Politycznych), December 4, 2003, Warsaw.

Bentkowski, Aleksander. Former justice minister (1989–1991), December 18, 2003, Warsaw.

Braun, Juliusz. Former Sejm member (1989–2001) and chair of National Council for Radio and Television (Krajowa Rada Radiofonii I Telewizji), December 17, 2003, Warsaw.

Ciemniewski, Jerzy. Co-founder of Polish Helsinki Committee, former advisor to Prime Minister Tadeusz Mazowiecki, and current judge of Constitutional Court, December 30, 2003, Warsaw.

Ciosek, Stanisław. Member of Poland's last Politburo, January 30, 2004, Warsaw.

Dmochowska, Maria. Former Sejm member (1989–1997) and current advisor to president of Institute of National Memory (IPN), January 2, 2004, Warsaw.

Filipkowicz, Tadeusz. Board member of World Union of Home Army Soldiers (Światowy Związek Żołnierzy Armii Krajowej), January 19, 2004, Warsaw.

Findeisen, Andrzej. Former senator (1989–1991), January 23, 2004, Warsaw.

Geremek, Bronisław. Former head of OKP (1989–1990) and foreign minister (1997–2000), January 20, 2004, Warsaw.

Grzebski, Witold. Vice president of Union of Soldiers from the National Armed Forces (Związek Żołnierzy Narodowych Sił Zbrojnych), December 3, 2003, Warsaw.

Grześkowiak, Alicja. Former senator (1989–2001), January 28, 2004, Toruń.

Heda-Szary, Antoni. President of the World Federation of Polish Veterans (Światowa Federacja Polskich Kombatantów), December 2, 2003, Warsaw.

Hennelowa, Józeffa. Former Sejm member (1989–1993), January 22, 2004 (via telephone), Kraków.

Herzog, Aleksander. Former deputy general prosecutor (1989–1991), January 9, 2004, Warsaw.

Human rights activist and lawyer, November 20, 2003, Warsaw.

Institute of National Memory (IPN). National office, board member, November 24, 2003, Warsaw.

Institute of National Memory (IPN). Kraków, branch prosecutor, January 21, 2004, Kraków.

Institute of National Memory (IPN). Łódź, Archive Department director, January 6, 2004, Łódź.

Institute of National Memory (IPN). Łódź, branch director, January 6, 2004, Łódź.

Institute of National Memory (IPN). Łódź, Education Department director, January 6, 2004, Łódź.

Institute of National Memory (IPN). Poznań, branch director, January 7, 2004, Poznań.

Institute of National Memory (IPN). Wrocław, local representative, January 6, 2004 (via telephone), Wrocław.

Jagiełło, Andrzej. Chairman of National Council of Courts (Krajowa Rada Sądownictwa) (2000–2004), January 27, 2004, Warsaw.

Jarzębowski, Ryszard. Senator (SLD) (1991–2005) and former undersecretary at Combatant Affairs Office, December 18, 2003, Warsaw.

Józefiak, Cezary. Former senator (1989–1991) and current member of National Bank's Council on Monetary Policy, January 8, 2004, Warsaw.

Juszkiewicz, Ryszard. Former senator (1989–1993) and former director of Chief Commission for the Investigation of Atrocities against the Polish People, January 5, 2004, Mława.

Kalisz, Ryszard. Former head of presidential office (1998) and member of Parliament (SLD) (2001–2005), December 22, 2003, Warsaw.

Kern, Andrzej. Former Sejm member (1989–1993), January 6, 2004, Łódź.

Kieres, Leon. President of Institute of National Memory (IPN), January 16, 2004, Warsaw.

Kochanowski, Janusz. Warsaw University law professor, November 28, 2003, Warsaw.

Konopka, Andrzej. Former Sejm member (1989–1991) and current Supreme Court judge, December 12, 2003, Warsaw.

Kosticki, Jan. President of Szczecin-based Polish League for the Defense of Human Rights (Polska Liga Obrony Praw Człowieka), December 31, 2003, Warsaw.

Kozłowski, Krzysztof. Former internal affairs minister (1990–1991), January 21, 2004, Kraków.

Kozłowski, Stefan. Former Sejm member (1989–1990) and environmental minister (1991–1992), December 30, 2003, Warsaw.

Krasny, Kazimierz. Former Justice Ministry delegate to Special Commission to Investigate the Ministry of Internal Affairs, February 3, 2004, Warsaw.

Krypel, Władysław. Chairman of regional Toruń NSZZ Solidarność, January 28, 2004, Toruń.

Krzyżanowska, Olga. Former Sejm member (1989–2001) and senator (2001–2005), December 18, 2003, Warsaw.

Kulesza, Ryszard. Deputy prosecutor general and director of Chief Commission for the Investigation of Atrocities against the Polish People, December 18, 2003, Warsaw.

Łączkowski, Paweł. Former Sejm member (1989–1993, 1997–2001), January 7, 2004, Poznań.

Lewandowski, Bogdan. SLD Sejm member (1997–2005), December 17, 2003, Warsaw.

Macierewicz, Antoni. Former internal affairs minister (1991–1992), December 22, 2003, Warsaw.

Mazowiecki, Tadeusz. Former prime minister (1989–1991), May 19, 2004, Warsaw.

Michnik, Adam. Former Sejm member (1989–1991) and current editor of *Gazeta Wyborcza*, January 14, 2004, Warsaw.

Moczulski, Leszek. Former Sejm member (KPN) (1991–1997), January 7, 2004, Warsaw.

Monkiewicz, Witold. Director of programs for developing civil society at Foundation for the Development of Local Democracy (Fundacja Rozwoju Demokracji Lokalnej), December 3, 2003, Warsaw.

Niesiołowski, Stefan. Former Sejm member (1989–1993, 1997–2001), January 6, 2004, Łódź.

Olszewski, Jan. Former prime minister (1991–1992), January 26, 2004, Warsaw.

Pałubicki, Janusz. Former Sejm member (1997–2001), January 7, 2004, Poznań.

Paprzycki, Leszek. Former Sejm member (1989–1991) and current president of Supreme Court, December 12, 2003, Warsaw.

Polak, Wojciech. Toruń area local historian, January 28, 2004, Toruń.

Prymas Committee for the Aid of Prisoners and Their Families (Prymasowski Komitet Pomóc Osobom Więzonym i Ich Rodzinom) representative. Martial-law era. January 4, 2004 (via telephone), Warsaw.

Przewłocki, Janusz. Member of historic commission at Union of Siberian Exiles (Związek Sybiraków), February 5, 2004, Warsaw.

Przywara, Danuta. Vice president and co-founder of Polish Helsinki Committee, December 9, 2003, Warsaw.

Radziwiłł, Anna. Former senator (1989–1991) and vice minister of education, January 14, 2004 (via telephone), Warsaw.

Rautio, Sirpa. Head of human rights section at Organization for Security and Co-operation in Europe's Office for Democratic Institutions and Human Rights, December 2, 2003, Warsaw.

Romaszewska, Zofia. Former activist in Committee for the Defense of Workers (KOR, Komitet Obrony Robotników), January 19, 2004, Warsaw.

Romaszewski, Zbigniew. Senator (1989–2005), January 19, 2004, Warsaw.

Staniszewska, Grażyna. Sejm member (1989–2005), December 17, 2003, Warsaw.

Starczewski, Stefan. Co-founder of Polish Helsinki Committee, December 5, 2003, Warsaw.

Stelmachowski, Andrzej. Former senator (1989–1991), January 20, 2004, Warsaw.

Stola, Dariusz. Professor at Polish Academy of Sciences (PAN), November 24, 2003, Warsaw.

Stomma, Stanisław. Former senator (1989–1991), January 15, 2004, Warsaw.

Taylor, Jacek. Former Sejm member (1991–1997) and president of Combatant Affairs Office (1997–2001), January 9, 2004, and January 16, 2004, Warsaw.

Wielowieyski, Andrzej. Senator (1989–2005), January 16, 2004 (via telephone), Warsaw.

Witkowski, Grzegorz. Press spokesman for Combatant Affairs Office, December 12, 2003, Warsaw.

Wujec, Henryk. Former Sejm member (1989–2001) and secretary of Solidarity's 1989 electoral commission (Komitet Obywatelski Solidarności), February 3, 2004, Warsaw.

Zalewski, Jan. Vice president of Union of Soldiers from the National Armed Forces (Związek Żołnierzy Narodowych Sił Zbrojnych), December 3, 2003, Warsaw.

Zoll, Andrzej. Current ombudsman, December 17, 2003, Warsaw.

Serbia and Montenegro

Advisor (former), to Prime Ministers Đinđić and Živković, February 11, 2005, Belgrade.

Aide, to Miroljub Labus, president of G17 Plus, January 17, 2005, Belgrade.

Bandović, Igor. Researcher at Belgrade Center for Human Rights, November 15, 2004, Belgrade.

Biserko, Sonja. Representative of Helsinki Committee for Human Rights in Serbia, December 9, 2004, Belgrade.

Božović, Rebeka. Vice president of Liberal Party, January 28, 2005, Belgrade.

Dimić, Ljubodrag. Former member of truth commission and professor of history at University of Belgrade, December 6, 2004, Belgrade.

Dimitrijević, Vojin. Director of Belgrade Center for Human Rights and former member of Parliament (GSS) and Yugoslav Truth and Reconciliation Commission, December 28, 2004, Belgrade.

Đorđević, Ivan. Former chief of staff (and current advisor) to former Serbian minister of internal affairs Dušan Mihajlović, January 25, 2005, Belgrade.

Đorić, Marijana. Lawyer at International Aid Network, December 23, 2004, Belgrade.

Dukić, Veroljub. Lawyer at Humanitarian Law Center, November 22, 2004, Belgrade.

European Union (EU) diplomat, December 6, 2004, Belgrade.

European Union (EU) official, December 2004, Belgrade.

European Union (EU) representative, November 16, 2004, Belgrade.

Filipović, Miroslav. Vice president of Civic Alliance of Serbia (GSS), February 2, 2005, Belgrade.

Gavrilović, Slobodan. Vice president of Democratic Party (DS), November 30, 2004, Belgrade.

German Government official, December 2004, Belgrade.

Grubač, Momčilo. Former federal minister of justice and current vice president of Democratic Center political party, January 27, 2005, Novi Sad.

Hiber, Dragor. Member of Parliament (Civic Alliance of Serbia, GSS), December 16, 2004, Belgrade.

Humanitarian Law Center members (five), November 9, 2004, Belgrade.

International observer, February 11, 2005, Belgrade.

International Republican Institute (IRI) representative, February 11, 2005, Belgrade.

Janjić, Dušan. Founding member and coordinator of Forum for Ethnic Relations, November 17, 2004, Belgrade.

Janković, Ivan. Former president of Center for Anti-War Action (1996–2003), December 13, 2004, Belgrade.

Jovanović, Čedomir. Former deputy prime minister of Serbia for European Union integration and coordination of reforms, February 3, 2005, Belgrade.

Jovanović, Ivan. National Legal Advisor on War Crimes, Rule of Law-Human Rights Department, OSCE Mission to Serbia and Montenegro, February 8, 2005, Belgrade.

Judges Association of Serbia member, December 13, 2004, Belgrade.

Kandić, Nataša. Director of Humanitarian Law Center, December 29, 2004, Belgrade.

Korać, Žarko. Former deputy prime minister under Đinđić and member of Parliament from Social-Democratic Union, February 4, 2005, Belgrade.

Kovačević, Marko. Youth Organization president and board member at Atlantic Council, Serbia and Montenegro, December 8, 2004, Belgrade.

Kovačević-Vučo, Biljana. President of Lawyers' Committee for Human Rights (Yucom), November 17, 2004, Belgrade.

Licht, Sonja. Former president of Open Society Foundation in Belgrade, December 22, 2004, Belgrade.

Lochary, Robert. Country director of ABA/CEELI in Serbia and Montenegro, December 6, 2004, Belgrade.

Lojpur, Aleksandar. Former coordinator for Yugoslav Truth and Reconciliation Commission, January 10, 2005, Belgrade.

Lučić, Zoran. President of Center for Free Elections and Democracy, November 7, 2004, Belgrade.

Matić, Veran. Editor-in-chief of independent TV/Radio/Internet B92, December 1, 2004, Belgrade.

Matković, Gordana. Former minister of social affairs (2000–2004) and member of Democratic Party (DS), December 9, 2004, Belgrade.

Milenov, Aleksandra. Outreach coordinator for International Criminal Tribunal for Former Yugoslavia, January 19, 2005, Belgrade.

Miljanić, Ana. Co-founder of Center for Cultural De-Contamination, December 9, 2004, Belgrade.

Nakarada, Radmila. Former member of and spokeswoman for Yugoslav Truth and Reconciliation Commission, December 1, 2004, Belgrade.

Nalić, Gradomir. Former human rights advisor to President Vojislav Koštunica and member of DSS, January 25, 2005, Belgrade.

Nosov, Andrej. Executive director of Youth Initiative for Human Rights, December 16, 2004, Belgrade.

Obradović, Vuk. Former deputy prime minister and president of Social Democratic Party, December 20, 2004, Belgrade.

Otpor member (former) and head of a municipal branch, December 3, 2004, Belgrade.

Pesek, Sanja. Serbia deputy director, Freedom House, December 22, 2004, Belgrade.

Petrović, Dušan. Vice president of Democratic Party (DS), December 9, 2004, Belgrade.

Popov, Aleksandar. Director of Center for Regionalism, January 27, 2005, Novi Sad.

Resanović, Aleksandar. Director of Center for Antiwar Action, November 10, 2004, Belgrade.

Samardžic, Slobodan. Political advisor to President (and current Prime Minister) Vojislav Koštunica, December 30, 2004, Belgrade.

Staresinic, Mike. Serbia director, Freedom House, December 22, 2004, Belgrade.

Stojanović, Svetozar. Former member of Yugoslav Truth and Reconciliation Commission and president of Serbian-American Center, December 22, 2004, Belgrade.

St. Protić, Milan. Former Yugoslav ambassador to Washington and vice president of DHSS, December 20, 2004, Belgrade.

U.S. Government official, December 15, 2004, Belgrade.

Vasilevska, Živka. Legal advisor for Non-Governmental Organizations at Center for the Development of Non-Profit Sector, November 17, 2004, Belgrade.

Veljković, Bogdan. President of Association of the Citizens for the Restitution of Confiscated Properties "Beograd," November 29, 2004, Belgrade.

Vukičević, Vladimir. Head of Democratic Party of Serbia's (DSS) International Affairs Department, January 24, 2005, Belgrade.

War crimes prosecutor's office representative, December 17, 2004, Belgrade.

Croatia

Advisor, to President Stepan Mesić, April 1, 2005, Zagreb.

Banac, Ivo. Member of Parliament (former Liberal, now independent), March 17, 2005, Zagreb.

Bing, Albert. Researcher on 1991–1995 Homeland War project (Stvaranje Republike Hrvatske i Domovinski rat), Croatian Historical Institute, April 28, 2005, Zagreb.

Čičak, Ivan. Founder and former president of Croatian Helsinki Committee for Human Rights, March 31, 2005, Zagreb.

Croatian Anti-Fascist Veteran Union representatives (three), March 17, 2005, Zagreb.

European Union (EU) official 1, March 17, 2005, Zagreb.

European Union (EU) official 2, April 28, 2005, Zagreb.

Feldman, Andrea. Head of Open Society Institute (OSI) in Croatia and former vice president of Liberal Party, February 18, 2005, Zagreb.

Gazivoda, Tin. Human Rights Center coordinator, February 17, 2005, and April 1, 2005, Zagreb.

Graovac, Igor. Researcher on 1991–1995 Homeland War project (Stvaranje Republike Hrvatske i Domovinski rat), Croatian Historical Institute, March 18, 2005, Zagreb.

Josipović, Ivo. Member of Parliament (independent) and drafter of 1996 Hague cooperation law, March 18, 2005, Zagreb.

Kašelj, Branka. Executive director of Center for Peace, Non-Violence, and Human Rights in Osijek, April 28, 2005, Zagreb.

Mikić, Ljubomir. President of Center for Peace, Legal Advice, and Psychosocial Assistance, Vukovar, April 29, 2005, Vukovar.

Milošević, Saša. Program director at Serbian Democratic Forum, April 28, 2005, Zagreb.

Pamuković, Nela. Director of Center for Women War Victims (Centar za žene žrtve rata), February 17, 2005, Zagreb.

Paraga, Dobroslav. President of Croatian Party of Rights–1861 (HSP–1861), March 3, 2005, Zagreb.

Piplović, Franjo. Member of Parliament (Democratic Center, DC), March 31, 2005, Zagreb.

Puhovski, Žarko. President of Croatian Helsinki Committee for Human Rights, February 16, 2005, Belgrade, Serbia and Montenegro; follow-up meeting, March 17, 2005, Zagreb.

Pusić, Vesna. Deputy Speaker of Parliament and vice chair of Croatian National Party (HNS), March 31, 2005, Zagreb.

Pusić, Zoran. President of Civil Committee for Human Rights (GOLJP), March 17, 2005, Zagreb.

Račan, Ivica. Former prime minister (2000–2004) and head of Social Democratic Party (SDP), March 4, 2005, Zagreb.

Radelić, Zdenko. Project supervisor of 1991–1995 Homeland War project (Stvaranje Republike Hrvatske i Domovinski rat), Croatian Historical Institute, March 3, 2005, Zagreb.

Rehak, Danijel. Head of Association of Former Croatian Detainees in Serbian Camps, April 29, 2005, Vukovar.

Representative of Croatian human rights organization, February 17, 2005, Zagreb.

Šeparović, Zvonimir. Former justice minister (1999), foreign minister (1991–1992), and law professor, February 18, 2005, Zagreb.

Šimonović, Ivan. Former Croatian representative to United Nations (1998–2002) and current Croatian agent to International Court of Justice, March 18, 2005, Zagreb.

Spajić-Vrkaš, Vedrana. Head of Research and Training Center for Human Rights and Democratic Citizenship, March 18, 2005, Zagreb.

Tauber, Charles. Head of Mission for Southeast Europe, Coalition for Work with Psychotrauma and Peace, April 29, 2005, Vukovar.

Teršelić, Vesna. Executive director of Center for Peace Studies, February 19, 2005, Zagreb.

U.S. Government official, April 2005, Zagreb.

Western diplomat, March 4, 2005, Zagreb.

Uzbekistan

Apellyatziya Regional Human Rights Society official, September 3, 2004, Andijon.

British Government official, February 2004, Tashkent.

Center for Democratic Initiatives (CDI) official, September 7, 2004, Tashkent.

Colby, Marina. Human Rights Program liaison, ABA-CEELI, March 3, 2004, Tashkent.

Committee for the Defense of Human Rights (CDHR) official and Agrarian Party official, March 4, 2004, Tashkent.

Committee for Social Monitoring in the Courts official and former member of Human Rights Society of Uzbekistan (HRSU), September 13, 2004, Tashkent.

Erk Party official 1, September 25, 2004, Vopkent, Bukhara.

Erk Party official 2 and Mazlum official, February 24, 2004, Tashkent.

European Union (EU) official, September 2004, Tashkent.

Ezgulik official and Birlik Party leader, March 11, 2004, Tashkent.

Ezgulik official 1 (Andijon region), September 2, 2004, Andijon.

Ezgulik official 2 (Samarqand region), September 10, 2004, Samarqand.

German Government official, March 2004, Tashkent.

Glaub, Richard. National Democratic Institute country director for Uzbekistan, February 25, 2004, Tashkent.

Gleb (non-elite interviewee), September 2004, Tashkent.

Grzenda, Daniel. Third political secretary, British embassy, Tashkent, February 27, 2004, Tashkent.

Human Rights Program staff attorney, ABA-CEELI, March 3, 2004, Tashkent.

Human Rights Society of Uzbekistan (HRSU) member 1, March 2, 2004, Tashkent.

Human Rights Society of Uzbekistan (HRSU) member 2, March 11, 2004, Tashkent.

Human Rights Society of Uzbekistan (HRSU) official 1 (Andijon region), September 3, 2004, Shaxrixan.

Human Rights Society of Uzbekistan (HRSU) official 2 (Ferghana city), September 4, 2004, Ferghana.

Human Rights Society of Uzbekistan (HRSU) official 3 (Jizak city), September 17, 2004, Tashkent.

Human Rights Society of Uzbekistan (HRSU) official 4 (Jizak region), September 16, 2004, Tashkent.

Human Rights Society of Uzbekistan (HRSU) official 5 (Jizak region) and Birlik Party official, September 16, 2004, Tashkent.

Human Rights Society of Uzbekistan (HRSU) official 6 (national office), March 2, 2004, Tashkent.

Human Rights Society of Uzbekistan (HRSU) official 7 (national office), September 14, 2004, Tashkent.

Human Rights Society of Uzbekistan (HRSU) official 8 (Samarqand region), September 10, 2004, Samarqand.

Human Rights Society of Uzbekistan (HRSU) official 9 (Qoraqolpokiston region), September 16, 2004, Tashkent.

Human Rights Watch researchers, February 26, 2004, Tashkent.

Humanitarian Legal Center official, September 25, 2004, Bukhara, Tashkent.

Independent Human Rights Initiative (IHRI) official 1 (national office), March 3, 2004, Tashkent.

Independent Human Rights Initiative (IHRI) official 2 (Samarqand region), September 9, 2004, Samarqand.

Independent Human Rights Initiative (IHRI) official 3 (Samarqand region), September 9, 2004, Samarqand.

Independent Human Rights Society of Uzbekistan (IHRSU) official 1 (Andijon region), September 3, 2004.

Independent Human Rights Society of Uzbekistan (IHRSU) official 2 (Bukhara region) and Erk Party official, September 25, 2004, Vopkent.

Independent Human Rights Society of Uzbekistan (IHRSU) official 3 (Ferghana region) and Erk Party official, September 4, 2004, Ferghana.

Independent Human Rights Society of Uzbekistan (IHRSU) official 4 (Namangan region) and Erk Party official, September 2, 2004, Namangan.

Independent Human Rights Society of Uzbekistan (IHRSU) official 5 (national office), March 9, 2004, Tashkent.

Independent Human Rights Society of Uzbekistan (IHRSU) official 6 (break-away national office), March 12, 2004, Tashkent.

International Committee of the Red Cross (ICRC) representative, February 24, 2004, Tashkent.

Ismalebbe, Zanofer. Human Rights Development officer for UN Resident Coordinator System, February 26, 2004, Tashkent.

Karimov, Naim. Chairman of Republic of Uzbekistan Charity Fund "In Memory of Victims," September 23, 2004, Tashkent.

Krumm, Reinhard. Head of regional office for Central Asia at Friedrich Ebert Stiftung, March 15, 2004, Tashkent.

Mazlum official 1 (Andijon region), September 2, 2004, Andijon.

Mazlum official 2 (Namangan region), September 2, 2004, Namangan.

Mazlum official 3 (Tashkent region) and Erk Party official, March 12, 2004, Tashkent.

Mezzon member, September 3, 2004, Andijon.

Mezzon official, September 3, 2004, Andijon.

Mothers against the Death Penalty and Torture member, March 16, 2004, Tashkent.

Mothers against the Death Penalty and Torture official, September 15, 2004, Tashkent.

Norbaev, Jasur. Rule-of-Law Program coordinator at Open Society Institute Assistance Foundation in Uzbekistan, February 27, 2004, Tashkent.

Normark, Per. Human Dimension officer, Organization for Security and Co-Operation in Europe Center, March 10, 2004, Tashkent.

Ohunov, Pulat. Deputy head of Birlik Party (in exile in Sweden), September 4, 2004, Shaxrixon.

Oscar, Phyllis. Human Rights Law Clinic liaison, ABA-CEELI, March 3, 2004, Tashkent.

Ozod Dekhkonlar (Free Peasants) Party official, March 16, 2004, Tashkent.

Pawelski, Ele. Freedom House senior program officer, Rights Program, Uzbekistan, March 10, 2004, Tashkent.

Radio Liberty employees (three), March 2, 2004, Tashkent.

Reddish, Peter. Coordinator for European Commission's Europa House, Tashkent, September 23, 2004, Tashkent.

Tuychiev, Hayot. Human rights officer at Freedom House, March 16, 2004, Tashkent.

U.S. Government official 1, February 2004, Tashkent.

U.S. Government official 2, February 2004, Tashkent.

Uzbek Government official, September 2004, Tashkent.
Western diplomat, September 2004, Tashkent.
Western observer 1, March 4, 2004, Tashkent.
Western observer 2, March 16, 2004, Tashkent.

Washington, D.C.

Andersen, Elizabeth. Executive director of Human Rights Watch's Europe and Central Asia division, April 30, 2003.

Benjamin, Robert. Regional director for Central and Eastern Europe at National Democratic Institute, May 14, 2003.

Glahe, Rachel. Senior program associate for Central Asia at ABA-CEELI, May 15, 2003.

Greenwood, Maureen. Advocacy director for Amnesty International, May 15, 2003.

Haltzel, Mike. Senior professional staff member, Senate Foreign Relations Committee (SFRC), May 15, 2003 (via telephone).

Hartmann, Michael. U.S. Institute of Peace senior fellow and first UN-appointed international public prosecutor for Kosovo (February 2000–January 2003), May 7, 2003.

Hefferman, John W. Senior communications associate of Physicians for Human Rights and founder of Coalition for International Justice, May 6, 2003.

Ledsky, Nelson. Senior associate/regional director for Eurasia, National Democratic Institute, May 8, 2003.

Southwick, Michael. Ambassador; principal deputy assistant secretary, U.S. Department of State, Office for Democracy, Human Rights, and Labor, May 9, 2003.

United States Agency for International Development official 1, April 2003.

United States Agency for International Development official 2, May 2003.

U.S. Congress staffer, May 2003.

U.S. Congress staffer at Helsinki Commission, May 2003.

U.S. Department of State official 1, May 2003.

U.S. Department of State official 2, May 2003.

U.S. Government (USG) official 1, April 2003.

U.S. Government (USG) official 2, April 2003.

U.S. Government (USG) official 3, April 2003.

U.S. Government (USG) official 4, April 2003.

U.S. Government (USG) official 5, April 2003.

U.S. Government (USG) official 6, April 2003.
U.S. Government (USG) official 7, April 2003.
U.S. Government (USG) official 8, May 2003.
U.S. Government (USG) official 9, May 2003.
U.S. Government (USG) official 10, May 2003.
U.S. Government (USG) official 11, May 2003.
U.S. Government (USG) official 12, May 2003.
Witte, Eric. Analyst at Coalition for International Justice, May 7, 2003.

Select Bibliography

Adams, Laura. "Tashkent Museum Allows for Public Discussion of Recent Past." *Eurasianet,* November 1, 2002.

———. "Winds of Change in Central Asian Politics." Paper presented at the Center for Russian and East European Studies, University of Michigan, Ann Arbor, October 5, 1995.

Aguilar, Paloma. "Justice, Politics, and Memory in the Spanish Transition." In *The Politics of Memory: Transitional Justice in Democratizing Societies,* edited by Alexandra Barahona De Brito, Carmen Gonzales-Enriquez, and Paloma Aguilar, 92–118. Oxford: Oxford University Press, 2001.

Aguilar, Paloma, and Carsten Humblebaek. "Collective Memory and National Identity in the Spanish Democracy: The Legacies of Francoism and the Civil War." *History and Memory* 14, no. 1–2 (2002): 121–64.

Allison, Graham. "Conceptual Models and the Cuban Missile Crisis." *American Political Science Review* 63, no. 3 (1969): 689–718.

Allison, Graham, and Morton Halperin. "Bureaucratic Politics: A Paradigm and Some Policy Implications." *World Politics* 24 (1972).

Anderson, Christopher. "Economic Voting and Political Context: A Comparative Perspective." *Electoral Studies* 19, no. 2 (2000): 151–70.

Baehr, Peter R. "Controversies in the Current International Human Rights Debate." *Human Rights Review* 2, no. 1 (2000): 7–32.

Bahry, Donna, and Brian Silver. "Intimidation and the Symbolic Uses of Terror in the USSR." *American Political Science Review* 81, no. 4 (1987): 1065–98.

Barahona De Brito, Alexandra. "Truth, Justice, Memory, and Democratization in the Southern Cone." In *The Politics of Memory: Transitional Justice in Democratizing Societies,* edited by Alexandra Barahona De Brito, Carmen Gonzales-

Enriquez, and Paloma Aguilar, 119–60. Oxford: Oxford University Press, 2001.

Barahona De Brito, Alexandra, Carmen Gonzales-Enriquez, and Paloma Aguilar. "Introduction." In *The Politics of Memory: Transitional Justice in Democratizing Societies,* edited by Alexandra Barahona De Brito, Carmen Gonzales-Enriquez, and Paloma Aguilar, 1–39. Oxford: Oxford University Press, 2001.

Bartosek, Karel. "Central and Southeastern Europe." In *The Black Book of Communism,* edited by Stephane Courtois, Nicolas Werth, Jean-Louis Panne, Andrzej Paczkowski, Karel Bartosek and Jean-Louis Margolin, 394–456. Cambridge, Mass.: Harvard University Press, 1999.

BCHR. "Public Opinion in Serbia: Attitudes towards the International Criminal Tribunal for the Former Yugoslavia." Belgrade: Belgrade Center for Human Rights, 2003.

Beissinger, Mark R. "Promoting Democracy: Is Exporting Revolution a Constructive Strategy?" *Dissent* (2006): 18–24.

Benomar, Jamal. "Justice after Transitions." In *Transitional Justice: How Emerging Democracies Reckon with Former Regimes,* edited by Neil J. Kritz, 32–41. Washington, D.C.: United States Institute of Peace Press, 1995.

Bertschi, C. Charles. "Lustration and the Transition to Democracy: The Cases of Poland and Bulgaria." *East European Quarterly* 28, no. 4 (1994): 435.

Best, Geoffrey. "Justice, International Relations, and Human Rights." *International Affairs* (Royal Institute of International Affairs) 71, no. 4 (1995): 775–99.

Bhargava, Rajeev. "Restoring Decency to Barbaric Societies." In *Truth v. Justice: The Morality of Truth Commissions,* edited by Robert I. Rotberg and Dennis Thompson, 45–67. Princeton: Princeton University Press, 2000.

Bielasiak, Jack, and David Blunck. "Past and Present in Transitional Voting: Electoral Choices in Post-Communist Poland." *Party Politics* 8, no. 5 (2002): 563–85.

Blankenburg, Erhard. "The Purge of Lawyers after the Breakdown of the East German Communist Regime." *Law and Social Inquiry* 20 (1995): 223–43.

Bloomfield, David, Teresa Barnes, and Luc Huyse. *Reconciliation after Violent Conflict: A Handbook.* Stockholm: International Institute for Democracy and Electoral Assistance (IDEA), 2003.

Booth, W. James. "The Unforgotten: Memories of Justice." *American Political Science Review* 95, no. 4 (2001): 777–91.

Borisov, Nikolai. "Transformation in the Political Regime in Uzbekistan: Stages and Outcome." *Central Asia and the Caucasus* 6 (2005): 22–32.

Borneman, John. "Apologies as Performative Redress." *SAIS Review* 25, no. 2 (2005): 53–66.

Bueno de Mesquita, Bruce, James D. Morrow, Randolph M. Siverson, and Alastair Smith. "An Institutional Explanation of the Democratic Peace." *American Political Science Review* 93, no. 4 (1999): 791–807.

———. "Policy Failure and Political Survival: The Contribution of Political Institutions." *Journal of Conflict Resolution* 43, no. 2 (1999): 147–61.

Burke-White, William W. "Reframing Impunity: Applying Liberal International Law Theory to an Analysis of Amnesty Legislation." *Harvard International Law Journal* 42 (2001): 467–534.

Burley, Anne-Marie, and Walter Mattli. "Europe before the Court: A Political Theory of Legal Integration." *International Organization* 47, no. 1 (1993): 41–76.

Burstein, Paul. "The Impact of Public Opinion on Public Policy: A Review and an Agenda." *Political Research Quarterly* 56, no. 1 (2003): 29–40.

Cain, Kenneth L. "The Rape of Dinah: Human Rights, Civil War in Liberia, and Evil Triumphant." *Human Rights Quarterly* 21, no. 2 (1999): 265–307.

Calhoun, Noel. "The Ideological Dilemma of Lustration in Poland." *East European Politics and Societies* 16, no. 2 (2002): 494–520.

Carothers, Thomas. "The Backlash against Democracy Promotion: The Autocrats Push Back." *Foreign Affairs* 85, no. 2 (2006).

Carver, Richard. "Called to Account: How African Governments Investigate Human Rights Violations." *African Affairs* 89, no. 356 (1990): 391–415.

CE. "Resolution #1096 on Measures to Dismantle the Heritage of Former Communist Totalitarian Systems," Council of Europe, 1996.

Cepl, Vojtech, and Mark Gillis. "Making Amends after Communism." *Journal of Democracy* 7, no. 4 (1996): 118–24.

Chapman, Audrey R., and Patrick Ball. "The Truth of Truth Commissions: Comparative Lessons from Haiti, South Africa, and Guatemala." *Human Rights Quarterly* 23 (2001): 1–43.

Chayes, Abram, and Antonia Handler Chayes. "On Compliance." *International Organization* 47, no. 2 (1993): 175–205.

Cohen, Dov. "The American National Conversation about (Everything but) Shame." *Social Research* 70, no. 4 (2003): 1075–1108.

Cohen, Stanley. "State Crimes of Previous Regimes: Knowledge, Accountability, and the Policing of the Past." *Law and Social Inquiry* 20 (1995).

Collier, Paul. "Ethnic Diversity: An Economic Analysis." *Economic Policy* 32 (2001): 127–66.

Cooper, Richard. "Economic Interdependence and Foreign Policy in the Seventies." *World Politics* 24 (1972): 159–81.

Corey, Allison, and Sandra F. Joireman. "Retributive Justice: The Gacaca Courts in Rwanda." *African Affairs* 103, no. 410 (2004): 73–89.

Cornell, Stephen B., and Joseph B. Kalt. "Successful Economic Development and the Heterogeneity of Governmental Form on American Indian Reservations." In *Getting Good Government: Capacity-Building in the Public Sectors of Developing Countries,* edited by Merilee Grindle, 257–96. Cambridge, Mass.: HIID/Harvard University Press, 1997.

Cox, Gary W., and Mathew D. McCubbins. "Political Structure and Economic Policy: The Institutional Determinants of Policy Outcomes." In *Presidents, Parliaments, and Policy,* edited by Stephan Haggard and Mathew D. McCubbins, 21–63. Cambridge: Cambridge University Press, 2001.

Crocker, David A. "Reckoning with the Past: A Normative Framework." *Ethics and International Affairs* 13 (1999): 43–64.

———. "Truth Commissions, Transitional Justice, and Civil Society." In *Truth v. Justice: The Morality of Truth Commissions,* edited by Robert I. Rotberg and Dennis Thompson, 99–121. Princeton: Princeton University Press, 2000.

Cvijanovic, Zeljko. "Serbia: Red Beret Revolt." *Balkan Crisis Report #296,* November 13, 2001.

Davenport, Christian. "Multi-Dimensional Threat Perception and State Repression: An Inquiry into Why States Apply Negative Sanctions." *American Journal of Political Science* 39, no. 3 (1995): 683–713.

Davenport, T. R. H. *The Birth of a New South Africa*. Buffalo, N.Y.: University of Toronto Press, 1998.

David, Roman. "Lustration Laws in Action: The Motives and Evaluation of Lustration Policy in the Czech Republic and Poland (1989–2001)." *Law and Social Inquiry* 28, no. 2 (2003): 387–439.

———. "Transitional Injustice? Criteria for Conformity of Lustration to the Right to Political Expression." *Europe-Asia Studies* 56, no. 6 (2004): 789–812.

de Klerk, F. W. *The Last Trek—a New Beginning: The Autobiography*. New York: St. Martin's Press, 1999.

Diamond, Larry Jay. "Thinking about Hybrid Regimes." *Journal of Democracy* 13, no. 2 (2002): 21–35.

Dicklitch, Susan, and Doreen Lwanga. "The Politics of Being Non-Political: Human Rights Organizations and the Creation of a Positive Human Rights Culture in Uganda." *Human Rights Quarterly* 25, no. 2 (2003): 482–509.

di Palma, Giuseppe. "Legitimation from the Top to Civil Society: Politico-Cultural Change in Eastern Europe." *World Politics* 44, no. 1 (1991): 49–80.

Donnelly, Jack. "Human Rights at the United Nations, 1955–1985: The Question of Bias." *International Studies Quarterly* 32, no. 3 (1988): 275–303.

———. "International Human Rights: A Regime Analysis." *International Organization* 40, no. 3 (1986): 599–642.

Doyle, Michael. "Liberalism in World Politics." *American Political Science Review* 80 (1986): 1151–69.

Eades, Lindsay Michie. *The End of Apartheid in South Africa.* Westport, Conn.: Greenwood Press, 1999.

Ekiert, Grzegorz. "Democratization Processes in East Central Europe: A Theoretical Reconsideration." *British Journal of Political Science* 21, no. 3 (1991): 285–313.

———. *The State against Society: Political Crises and Their Aftermath in East Central Europe.* Princeton: Princeton University Press, 1996.

Ellis, Mark. "Purging the Past: The Current State of Lustration Laws in the Former Communist Bloc." *Law and Contemporary Problems* 59, no. 4 (1996).

Elster, Jon. *Closing the Books: Transitional Justice in Historical Perspective.* New York: Cambridge University Press, 2004.

———. "Introduction." In *Retribution and Reparation in the Transition to Democracy,* edited by Jon Elster, 1–14. New York: Cambridge University Press, 2006.

Ergashev, Bakhtier. "The Formation of a Multi-Party System in Uzbekistan: Problems and Prospects." *Central Asia and the Caucasus* 6 (2000): 51–59.

Esquith, Stephen L. "Toward a Democratic Rule of Law: East and West." *Political Theory* 27, no. 3 (1999): 334–56.

Evans, Tony. *U.S. Hegemony and the Project of Universal Human Rights.* New York: St. Martin's Press, 1996.

Fakhritdinov, Bakhodir. "Civilian Movements and Parties in Uzbekistan: Development Trends and Problems." *Central Asia and the Caucasus* 5 (2002): 44–53.

Fearon, James D. "Bargaining, Enforcement, and International Cooperation." *International Organization* 52, no. 2 (1998): 269–305.

Fehrer, Michael. "Terms of Reconciliation." In *Human Rights in Political Transitions: Gettysburg to Bosnia,* edited by Carla Hesse and Robert Post, 325–88. New York: Zone Books, 1999.

Fletcher, Laurel E., and Harvey M. Weinstein. "Violence and Social Repair: Rethinking the Contribution of Justice to Reconciliation." *Human Rights Quarterly* 24, no. 3 (2002): 573–639.

Forsythe, David P. *Human Rights in International Relations.* New York: Cambridge University Press, 2000.

Garret, Stephen A. "Problems of Transitional Justice: The Politics and Principles of Memory." Paper presented at the Annual Meeting of the International Studies Association, Washington, D.C., February 16–20, 1999.

Geddes, Barbara. "What Do We Know about Democratization after 20 Years?" *Annual Review of Political Science* 2 (1999): 115–44.

Gelpi, Christopher. "Crime and Punishment: The Role of Norms in International Crisis Bargaining." *American Political Science Review* 91, no. 2 (1997): 339–60.

Gerring, John. "What Is a Case Study and What Is It Good For?" *American Political Science Review* 98, no. 2 (2004): 341–54.

Gibney, Mark, and Erik Roxstrom. "The Status of State Apologies." *Human Rights Quarterly* 23, no. 4 (2001): 911–39.

Gibson, James L. *Overcoming Apartheid: Can Truth Reconcile a Divided Nation?* New York: Russell Sage Foundation, 2004.

———. "Truth, Justice, and Reconciliation: Judging the Fairness of Amnesty in South Africa." *American Journal of Political Science* 46, no. 3 (2002): 540–56.

Gilligan, James. "Shame, Guilt, and Violence." *Social Research* 70, no. 4 (2003): 1149–80.

Gilligan, Michael J. "Is Enforcement Necessary for Effectiveness? A Model of the International Criminal Regime." *International Organization* 60 (2006): 935–67.

Graybill, Lyn. "To Punish or Pardon: A Comparison of the International Criminal Tribunal for Rwanda and the South African Truth and Reconciliation Commission." *Human Rights Review* 2, no. 4 (1999): 3–18.

Grodsky, Brian. "Direct Pressures for Human Rights in Uzbekistan: Understanding the U.S. Bargaining Position." *Central Asian Survey* 23 (2004): 327–44.

———. "Justice without Transition: Truth Commissions in the Context of Repressive Rule." *Human Rights Review* 9, no. 3 (2008): 281–97.

———. "Looking for Solidarność in Central Asia: The Role of Human Rights Organizations in Political Change." *Slavic Review* 66, no. 3 (2007): 442–62.

———. "The New Game in Central Asia: Comparative Uzbek and Kazakh Foreign Policy." *Journal of Central Asian Studies* 5, no. 2 (2003): 16–31.

———. "On the Other Side of the Curtain: A Reassessment of Non-Elite Human Rights Experiences and Values in Poland." *Human Rights Review* 9, no. 4 (2008): 219–38.

———. "Resource Dependency and Political Opportunity: Explaining the Transformation from Excluded Political Opposition Parties to Human Rights Organizations in Post-Communist Uzbekistan." *Government and Opposition* 42, no. 1 (2007): 96–120.

Gurr, Ted Robert, and Woodrow Wilson School of Public and International Affairs. Center of International Studies. *Why Men Rebel.* Princeton: Princeton University Press, 1970.

Havel, Vaclav, and John Keane. *The Power of the Powerless: Citizens against the State in Central-Eastern Europe.* Armonk, N.Y.: M. E. Sharpe, 1985.

Hayden, Robert M. "'Ethnic Cleansing' and 'Genocide.'" *European Journal of Public Health* 17, no. 6 (2007): 546–47.

Hayner, Priscilla B. "Commissioning the Truth: Further Research Questions." *Third World Quarterly* 17, no. 1 (1996): 19–30.

———. "Fifteen Truth Commissions, 1974 to 1994: A Comparative Study." *Human Rights Quarterly* 16, no. 4 (1994): 597–655.

———. "International Guidelines for the Creation and Operation of Truth Commissions: A Preliminary Proposal." *Law and Contemporary Problems* 59, no. 4 (1996): 173–80.

———. *Unspeakable Truths: Confronting State Terror and Atrocity.* New York: Routledge, 2001.

Held, David. *Global Transformations.* Stanford: Stanford University Press, 1999.

Henderson, Conway. "Conditions Affecting the Use of Political Repression." *Journal of Conflict Resolution* 35, no. 1 (1991): 120–42.

Higley, John, Judith Kullberg, and Jan Pakulski. "The Persistence of Post-Communist Elites." *Journal of Democracy* 7, no. 2 (1996): 133–47.

Hirschman, Albert O. "Exit, Voice, and the State." *World Politics* 31, no. 1 (1978): 90–107.

Holmes, Stephen. "The End of Decommunization." *East European Constitutional Review* 3, no. 3–4 (1994): 33–36.

HRI. "Human Rights Internet: For the Record 2002—the United Nations Human Rights System." Human Rights Internet, www.hri.ca/fortherecord2002/engtext/vol5eng/polandrr.htm.

Hug, Simon, and Thomas Konig. "In View of Ratification: Governmental Preferences and Domestic Constraints at the Amsterdam Intergovernmental Conference." *International Organization* 56, no. 2 (2002): 447–76.

Huntington, Samuel. *The Third Wave: Democratization in the Late Twentieth Century.* Norman: University of Oklahoma Press, 1991.

Huyse, Luc. "Justice after Transition: On the Choices Successor Elites Make in Dealing with the Past." *Law and Social Inquiry* 20, no. 1 (1995): 51–78.

Jackson, John. "The 1994 Election: An Analysis." In *The New South Africa: Prospects for Domestic and International Security,* edited by F. H. Toase and E. J. Yorke, 3–16. New York: St. Martin's Press, 1998.

Jacobs, Lawrence R., Eric D. Lawrence, Robert Y. Shapiro, and Steven S. Smith. "Congressional Leadership of Public Opinion." *Political Science Quarterly* 113, no. 1 (1998): 21–41.

Jacobs, Lawrence R., and Robert Y. Shapiro. "Presidential Manipulation of Polls and Public Opinion: The Nixon Administration and the Pollsters." *Political Science Quarterly* 110, no. 4 (1995–96): 519–38.

Jalcin, Resul. "The Formation of a Multi-Party System in Uzbekistan." *Central Asia and the Caucasus* 5 (2001): 25–35.

Jasiewicz, Krzysztof. "The Political-Party Landscape." *Journal of Democracy* 18, no. 4 (2007): 26–33.

Jaspers, Karl. "The Question of German Guilt." In *Transitional Justice: How Emerging Democracies Reckon with Former Regimes,* edited by Neil J. Kritz, 157–71. Washington, D.C.: United States Institute of Peace Press, 1995.

Joppke, Christian. "Revisionism, Dissidence, Nationalism: Opposition in Leninist Regimes." *British Journal of Sociology* 45, no. 4 (1994): 543–61.

Judt, Tony. "The Past Is Another Country: Myth and Memory in Postwar Europe." In *The Politics of Retribution in Europe: World War II and Its Aftermath,* edited by István Deák, Jan Tomasz Gross, and Tony Judt, 293–323. Princeton: Princeton University Press, 2000.

Kaldor, Mary, and Ivan Vejvoda. "Democratization in Central and East European Countries." *International Affairs* (Royal Institute of International Affairs) 73, no. 1 (1997): 59–82.

Kamali, Maryam. "Accountability for Human Rights Violations: A Comparison of Transitional Justice in East Germany and South Africa." *Columbia Journal of Transnational Law* 40, no. 1 (2001): 89–142.

Kaminski, Marek M., and Monika Nalepa. "Judging Transitional Justice: A New Criterion for Evaluating Truth Revelation Procedures." *Journal of Conflict Resolution* 50, no. 3 (2006): 383–408.

Kamminga, Menno T. "Lessons Learned from the Exercise of Universal Jurisdiction in Respect of Gross Human Rights Offenses." *Human Rights Quarterly* 23 (2001): 940–74.

Kaplan, Robert M. "Boundaries: Dr. Radovan Karadzic: Psychiatrist, Poet, Soccer Coach, and Genocidal Leader." *Australasian Psychiatry* 11, no. 1 (2003).

Kara, Halim. "Reclaiming National Literary Heritage: The Rehabilitation of Abdurauf Fitrat and Abdulhamid Sulaymon Cholpan in Uzbekistan." *Europe-Asia Studies* 54, no. 1 (2002): 123–42.

Karimov, I. A. *Uzbekistan on the Threshold of the Twenty-first Century.* Surrey, Eng.: Curzon, 1997.

Katz, Mark N. "Revolutionary Change in Central Asia." *World Affairs* 168, no. 4 (2007): 157–71.

Keck, Margaret E., and Kathryn Sikkink. *Activists beyond Borders: Advocacy Networks in International Politics.* Ithaca, N.Y.: Cornell University Press, 1998.

Keith, Linda Camp. "The United Nations International Covenant on Civil and Political Rights: Does It Make a Difference in Human Rights Behavior?" *Journal of Peace Research* 6, no. 1 (1999): 95–118.

Keohane, Robert O., and Joseph S. Nye. "Transgovernmental Relations and International Organization." *World Politics* 27 (1974): 39–62.

Kitschelt, Herbert. *Post-Communist Party Systems: Competition, Representation, and Inter-Party Cooperation,* Cambridge Studies in Comparative Politics. Cambridge and New York: Cambridge University Press, 1999.

Klosko, George, Edward N. Muller, and Karl Dieter Opp. "Rebellious Collective Action Revisited." *American Political Science Review* 81, no. 2 (1987): 557–64.

Koch, Jeffrey W. "Political Rhetoric and Political Persuasion: The Changing Structure of Citizens' Preferences on Health Insurance during Policy Debate." *Public Opinion Quarterly* 62, no. 2 (1998): 209–29.

Kraus, Michael. "The Czech Republic's First Decade." *Journal of Democracy* 14, no. 2 (2003): 50–64.

Kritz, Neil J. "Coming to Terms with Atrocities: A Review of Accountability Mechanisms for Mass Violations of Human Rights." *Law and Contemporary Problems* 59, no. 4 (1996): 127–52.

———. "The Dilemmas of Transitional Justice." In *Transitional Justice: How Emerging Democracies Reckon with Former Regimes,* edited by Neil J. Kritz, xix–xxx. Washington, D.C.: United States Institute of Peace Press, 1995.

Kuran, Timur. "Now out of Never: The Element of Surprise in the East European Revolution of 1989." *World Politics* 44, no. 1 (1991): 7–48.

Landsman, Stephan. "Alternative Responses to Serious Human Rights Abuses: Of Prosecution and Truth Commission." *Law and Contemporary Problems* 59, no. 4 (1996): 81–92.

Lave, Charles A., and James G. March. *An Introduction to Models in the Social Sciences.* New York: Harper & Row, 1975.

Lazare, Aaron. *On Apology.* Oxford; New York: Oxford University Press, 2004.

Letki, Natalia. "Lustration and Democratization in East-Central Europe." *Europe-Asia Studies* 54, no. 4 (2002): 529–52.

Lijphart, Arend. "Comparative Politics and the Comparative Method." *American Political Science Review* 65, no. 3 (1971): 682–93.

Lindner, Evelin Gerda. "Humiliation and Human Rights: Mapping a Minefield." *Human Rights Review* 2, no. 3 (2001): 46–63.

Linz, Juan J., and Alfred Stepan. *Problems of Democratic Transition and Consolidation: Southern Europe, South America, and Post-Communist Europe.* Baltimore: Johns Hopkins University Press, 1996.

Los, Maria. "Lustration and Truth Claims: Unfinished Revolutions in Central Europe." *Law and Social Inquiry* 20 (1995): 117–61.

Los, Maria, and Andrzej Zybertowicz. "Is Revolution a Solution?" In *The Rule of Law after Communism*, edited by Martin Krygier and Adam Czarnota, 261–77. Brookfield, Vt.: Dartmouth, 1999.

MacDonald, Oliver. "The Polish Vortex: Solidarity and Socialism." *New Left Review* 139 (1983): 5–48.

Magalhaes, Pedro C. "The Politics of Judicial Reform in Eastern Europe." *Comparative Politics* 32, no. 1 (1999): 43–62.

March, Andrew F. "The Use and Abuse of History: 'National Ideology' as Transcendental Object in Islam Karimov's 'Ideology of National Independence.'" *Central Asian Survey* 21, no. 4 (2002): 371–84.

Mason, T. David, and Dale A. Krane. "The Political Economy of Death Squads: Toward a Theory of the Impact of State-Sanctioned Terror." *International Studies Quarterly* 33 (1989): 175–98.

McCann, James A. "Electoral Choices and Core Value Change: The 1992 Presidential Campaign." *American Journal of Political Science* 41, no. 2 (1997): 564–83.

McFaul, Michael. "The Fourth Wave of Democracy and Dictatorship: Noncooperative Transitions in the Postcommunist World." *World Politics* 54, no. 2 (2002): 212–44.

———. "Transitions from Postcommunism." *Journal of Democracy* 16, no. 3 (2005): 5–19.

McGregor, Lorna. "Individual Accountability in South Africa: Cultural Optimum or Political Façade?" *American Journal of International Law* 95, no. 1 (2001): 32–45.

McKeown, Timothy J. "The Cuban Missile Crisis and Politics as Usual." *Journal of Politics* 62, no. 1 (2000): 70–87.

———. "Reflections on the Collapse of Communism." *Journal of Democracy* 11, no. 1 (2000): 119–26.

Michnik, Adam, and Vaclav Havel. "Confronting the Past: Justice or Revenge?" *Journal of Democracy* 4, no. 1 (1993): 20–27.

Miller, John. "Settling Accounts with a Secret Police: The German Law on the Stasi Records." *Europe-Asia Studies* 50, no. 2 (1998): 305–30.

Milner, Helen. "The Interaction of Domestic and International Politics." In *Double-Edged Diplomacy*, edited by Peter Evans, Harold Jacobson, and Robert Putnam, 207–32. Berkeley: University of California Press, 1993.

Minow, Martha. *Between Vengeance and Forgiveness*. Boston: Beacon Press, 1998.

Moore, Will H. "The Repression of Dissent: A Substitution Model of Government Coercion." *Journal of Conflict Resolution* 44, no. 1 (2000): 107–27.

Moran, John P. "The Communist Torturers of Eastern Europe—Prosecute and Punish or Forgive and Forget." *Communist and Post-Communist Studies* 27, no. 1 (1994): 95–109.

Moravcsik, Andrew. "The Origins of Human Rights Regimes: Democratic Delegation in Postwar Europe." *International Organization* 54, no. 2 (2000): 217–52.

Murphy, Jeffrie G. "Forgiveness and Resentment." In *Forgiveness and Mercy,* edited by Jeffrie G. Murphy and Jean Hampton, 14–34. Cambridge: Cambridge University Press, 1988.

Nalepa, Monika. *Skeletons in the Closet: Transitional Justice in Post-Communist Europe.* Cambridge: Cambridge University Press, 2009.

Nanda, Ved P. "Civil and Political Sanctions as an Accountability Mechanism for Massive Violations of Human Rights." *Denver Journal of International Law and Politics* 26, no. 3 (1998): 389–97.

Nasi W Sejmie I W Senacie: Posłowie I Senatorowie Wybrani Z Listy Solidarności. Warsaw: Oficyna Wydawnicza Volumen, 1990.

Nedelsky, Nadya. "Divergent Responses to a Common Past: Transitional Justice in the Czech Republic and Slovakia." *Theory and Society* 33, no. 1 (2004): 65–115.

Newham, Gareth. "Truth and Reconciliation: Realising the Ideals." *Indicator SA* 12, no. 4 (1995): 7–12.

Nino, Carlos Santiago. *Radical Evil on Trial.* New Haven: Yale University Press, 1996.

Ocampo, Luis Moreno. "Beyond Punishment: Justice in the Wake of Massive Crimes in Argentina." *Journal of International Affairs* 52, no. 2 (1999): 669–89.

O'Donnell, Guillermo, and Philippe C. Schmitter. "Tentative Conclusions about Uncertain Democracies." In *Transitions from Authoritarian Rule: Prospects for Democracy,* edited by Guillermo O'Donnell, Philippe C. Schmitter, and Laurence Whitehead, 3–78. Baltimore: Johns Hopkins University Press, 1986.

Offe, Claus. *Varieties of Transition: The East European and East German Experience.* 1st MIT Press ed., Studies in Contemporary German Social Thought. Cambridge, Mass.: MIT Press, 1997.

Olson, Mancur. "Dictatorship, Democracy, and Development." *American Political Science Review* 87, no. 3 (1993): 567–76.

OSCE. Paper presented at the Perspectives on Responsibility for Grave Violations of Human Rights in the Past, Media Center, Belgrade, December 10, 2004.

Osiel, Mark J. "Why Prosecute? Critics of Punishment for Mass Atrocity." *Human Rights Quarterly* 22, no. 1 (2000): 118–47.

Ost, David. "The Politics of Interest in Post-Communist East Europe." *Theory and Society* 22, no. 4 (1993): 453–85.

———. "The Weakness of Symbolic Strength: Labor and Union Identity in Poland, 1989–2000." In *Workers after Workers' States: Labor and Politics in Postcommunist Eastern Europe,* edited by Stephen Crowley and David Ost, 79–96. Lanham, Md.: Rowman & Littlefield, 2001.

Paczkowski, Andrzej. "Poland, the 'Enemy Nation.'" In *The Black Book of Communism,* edited by Stephane Courtois, Nicolas Werth, Jean-Louis Panne, Andrzej Paczkowski, Karel Bartosek, and Jean-Louis Margolin, 363–93. Cambridge, Mass.: Harvard University Press, 1999.

Payne, Leigh A. "Collaborators and the Politics of Memory in Chile." *Human Rights Review* 2, no. 3 (2001): 8–26.

Pharr, Susan J. *Losing Face: Status Politics in Japan.* Berkeley: University of California Press, 1990.

Pion-Berlin, David. "To Prosecute or to Pardon? Human Rights Decisions in the Latin American Southern Cone." *Human Rights Quarterly* 16, no. 1 (1994): 105–30.

Polish Parliament (*see also* Sejm; Senat). *Dziennik Ustaw.* Nr. 34, poz. 179, 1989.

———. *Dziennik Ustaw.* Nr. 64, poz. 390, 1989.

———. *Dziennik Ustaw.* Nr. 45, poz. 195, 1991.

———. *Dziennik Ustaw.* Nr. 89, poz. 400, 1996.

———. *Dziennik Ustaw.* Nr. 68, poz. 436, 1997.

———. *Dziennik Ustaw.* Nr. 1, poz. 1, 1999.

Posner, Eric A., and Adrian Vermeule. "Transitional Justice as Ordinary Justice." In the Public Law and Legal Theory Working Paper Series. Chicago: University of Chicago Law School, 2003.

———. "Transitional Justice as Ordinary Justice." *Harvard Law Review* 117, no. 3 (2004): 761–825.

Powlick, Philip J. "The Attitudinal Bases for Responsiveness to Public Opinion among American Foreign Policy Officials." *Journal of Conflict Resolution* 35, no. 4 (1991): 611–41.

Powlick, Philip J., and Andrew Z. Katz. "Defining the American Public Opinion/Foreign Policy Nexus." *Mershon International Studies Review* 42, no. 1 (1998): 29–61.

Putnam, Robert. "Diplomacy and Domestic Politics: The Logic of Two-Level Games." *International Organization* 42, no. 3 (1988): 427–60.

Ratner, Steven R., and Jason S. Abrams. *Accountability for Human Rights Atrocities in International Law: Beyond the Nuremberg Legacy.* Oxford: Oxford University Press, 2001.

Reilly, Ben. "Democratic Levers for Conflict Management." In *Democracy and Deep-Rooted Conflict: Options for Negotiators,* edited by Peter Harris, Ben Reilly, and Mark Anstey, 133–342. Stockholm: International Institute for Democracy and Electoral Assistance, 2002.

Riezler, Kurt. "Comment on the Social Psychology of Shame." *American Journal of Sociology* 48, no. 4 (1943): 457–65.

Rigby, Andrew. *Justice and Reconciliation: After the Violence.* Boulder, Colo.: Lynne Rienner Publishers, 2001.

Roehrig, Terence. *The Prosecution of Former Military Leaders in Newly Democratic Nations.* Jefferson, N.C.: McFarland & Company, 2002.

Roht-Arriaza, Naomi. "Combatting Impunity: Some Thoughts on the Way Forward." *Law and Contemporary Problems* 59, no. 4 (1996): 93–102.

———. "The Role of International Actors in National Accountability Processes." In *The Politics of Memory: Transitional Justice in Democratizing Societies,* edited by Alexandra Barahona De Brito, Carmen Gonzales-Enriquez, and Paloma Aguilar, 40–64. Oxford: Oxford University Press, 2001.

Romijn, Peter. "'Restoration of Confidence': The Purge of Local Government in the Netherlands as a Problem of Post-War Reconstruction." In *The Politics of Retribution in Europe: World War II and Its Aftermath,* edited by István Deák, Jan Tomasz Gross, and Tony Judt, 173–93. Princeton: Princeton University Press, 2000.

Rose, Richard, and Doh Chull Shin. "Democratization Backwards: The Problem of Third Wave Democracies." *British Journal of Political Science* 31, no. 2 (2001): 331–54.

Rosenberg, Tina. *The Haunted Land: Facing Europe's Ghosts after Communism.* New York: Random House, 1995.

———. "Overcoming the Legacies of Dictatorship." *Foreign Affairs* 74, no. 3 (1995): 134–53.

Roundtable. "Media Roundtable with Robert Seiple, U.S. Ambassador-at-Large for Religious Freedom," http://www.osce.usia.co.at/ambseiple24may00 .html.

Rudolph, Christopher. "Constructing an Atrocities Regime: The Politics of War Crimes Tribunals." *International Organization* 55, no. 3 (2001): 655–91.

Rudolph, Thomas J. "Institutional Context and the Assignment of Political Responsibility." *Journal of Politics* 65, no. 1 (2003): 190–215.

Rupnik, Jacques. "The Post-Totalitarian Blues." *Journal of Democracy* 6, no. 2 (1995): 61–73.

———. "Totalitarianism Revisited." In *Civil Society and the State: New European Perspectives,* edited by John Keane, 263–90. New York: Verso, 1988.

Sadurski, Wojciech. *Rights before Courts: A Study of Constitutional Courts in Postcommunist States of Central and Eastern Europe.* Norwell, Mass.: Springer, 2005.

Schmitter, Philippe C. "The Consolidation of Democracy and Representation of Social Groups." *American Behavioral Scientist* 35, no. 4/5 (1992): 422–49.

Schwartz, Shalom H., and Anat Bardi. "Influences of Adaptation to Communist Rule on Value Priorities in Eastern Europe." *Political Psychology* 18, no. 2 (1997): 385–410.

Scott, James C. *Weapons of the Weak: Everyday Forms of Peasant Resistance.* New Haven: Yale University Press, 1985.

Searing, Donald D. "Roles, Rules, and Rationality in the New Institutionalism." *American Political Science Review* 85, no. 4 (1991): 1239–60.

Sejm (Poland). *Monitor Polski.* Nr. 21, poz. 327, June 21, 2007.

———. *Sprawozdanie Stenograficzne.* Kadencja X, 4 posiedzenie, 1989, 291–310.

———. *Sprawozdanie Stenograficzne.* Kadencja II, 51 posiedzenie, 1991, 205–6.

———. *Sprawozdanie Stenograficzne.* Kadencja X, 49 posiedzenie, 1991, 156–91.

———. *Sprawozdanie Stenograficzne.* Kadencja X, 52 posiedzenie, 1991, 337–72.

———. *Sprawozdanie Stenograficzne.* Kadencja X, 76 posiedzenie, 1991, 256–70.

———. *Sprawozdanie Stenograficzne.* Kadencja I, 7 posiedzenie, 1992, 158–213.

———. *Sprawozdanie Stenograficzne.* Kadencja III, 39 posiedzenie, 1998, 176–202, 245–46.

Sen, Amartya. "Civilizational Imprisonments: How to Misunderstand Everybody in the World." *The New Republic,* June 10, 2002, 28–33.

Senat (Poland). *Dziennik Ustaw.* Kadencja I, 45 posiedzenie, March 15, 1991, 33–51, 83.

———. *Dziennik Ustaw.* Kadencja I, 45 posiedzenie, April 19, 1991, 166–90.

———. *Monitor Polski.* Nr. 45, poz. 195, April 4, 1991.

———. *Monitor Polski.* Nr. 20, poz. 287, June 18, 1998.

———. *Monitor Polski.* Nr. 59, poz. 799, December 6, 2002.

———. *Sprawozdanie Stenograficzne.* Kadencja I, 4 posiedzenie, August 11, 1989, 64.

———. *Sprawozdanie Stenograficzne.* Kadencja I, 6 posiedzenie, August 30, 1989, 64.

Shapiro, David. "The Tortured, Not the Torturers, Are Ashamed." *Social Research* 70, no. 4 (2003): 1131–48.

Sharman, J. C. *Repression and Resistance in Communist Europe.* BASEES/Routledge-Curzon Series on Russian and East European Studies. London; New York: Routledge Curzon, 2003.

Shweder, Richard A. "Toward a Deep Cultural Psychology of Shame." *Social Research* 70, no. 4 (2003): 1109–30.

Sieder, Rachel. "War, Peace, and Memory Politics in Central America." In *The Politics of Memory: Transitional Justice in Democratizing Societies,* edited by

Alexandra Barahona De Brito, Carmen Gonzales-Enriquez, and Paloma Aguilar, 161–90. Oxford: Oxford University Press, 2001.

Sieff, Michelle, and Leslie Vinjamuri Wright. "Reconciling Order and Justice? New Institutional Solutions in Post-Conflict States." *Journal of International Affairs* 52, no. 2 (1999): 757–79.

Siegelman, Peter. "The Problems of Lustration: Prosecution of Wrongdoers by Democratic Successor Regimes." *Law and Social Inquiry* 20, no. 1 (1995): 1–6.

Simpson, Graeme, and Paul van Zyl. "South Africa's Truth and Reconciliation Commission." *Temps Modernes* 585 (1995): 394–407.

Skapska, Grazyna. "Moral Definitions in Constitutionalism in East Central Europe: Facing Past Human Rights Violations." *International Sociology* 18, no. 1 (2003): 199–218.

Smith, Nick. *I Was Wrong: The Meanings of Apologies.* Cambridge: Cambridge University Press, 2008.

Snyder, Jack, and Leslie Vinjamuri. "Trials and Errors: Principle and Pragmatism in Strategies of International Justice." *International Security* 28, no. 3 (2003/2004): 5–44.

Sriram, Chandra Lekha, and Amy Ross. "Geographies of Crime and Justice: Contemporary Transitional Justice and the Creation of 'Zones of Impunity.'" *International Journal of Transitional Justice* 1, no. 1 (2007): 45–65.

State Department (U.S.). "U.S. Assistance to Uzbekistan—Fiscal Year 2002." United States Department of State, http://www.state.gov/p/eur/rls/fs/15683.htm.

———. "U.S. Assistance to Uzbekistan—Fiscal Year 2003." United States Department of State, http://www.state.gov/p/eur/rls/fs/29494.htm.

Stinchcombe, Arthur L. "Lustration as a Problem of the Social Basis of Constitutionalism." *Law and Social Inquiry* 20 (1995).

Stoner-Weiss, Kathryn. *Local Heroes: The Political Economy of Russian Regional Governance.* Princeton: Princeton University Press, 1997.

Sutter, Daniel. "Settling Old Scores: Potholes along the Transition from Authoritarian Rule." *Journal of Conflict Resolution* 39, no. 1 (1995): 110–28.

Szczerbiak, Aleks. "Dealing with the Communist Past or the Politics of the Present? Lustration in Post-Communist Poland." *Europe-Asia Studies* 54, no. 4 (2002): 553–72.

Tarrow, Sidney. "'Aiming at a Moving Target': Social Science and the Recent Rebellions in Eastern Europe." *PS: Political Science and Politics* 24, no. 1 (1991): 12–20.

———. *Power in Movement: Social Movements, Collective Action, and Politics.* New York: Cambridge University Press, 1994.

Tavuchis, Nicholas. *Mea Culpa: A Sociology of Apology and Reconciliation*. Stanford: Stanford University Press, 1991.

Teitel, Ruti G. "Transitional Justice Genealogy." *Harvard Human Rights Journal* 16 (2003): 69–94.

TRC. "Archbishop Desmond Tutu's Address to the First Gathering of the Truth and Reconciliation Commission." *Truth and Reconciliation Commission (TRC) Press Release,* December 16, 1995.

Tymowski, Andrzej. "The Unwanted Social Revolution: Poland in 1989." *East European Politics and Societies* 7, no. 2 (1993): 169–202.

UN. "Basic Principles and Guidelines on the Right to Reparation for Victims of Gross Violations of Human Rights and Humanitarian Law." United Nations Commission on Human Rights, 1996.

———. "The Right to Restitution, Compensation, and Rehabilitation for Victims of Gross Violations of Human Rights and Fundamental Freedoms." United Nations Commission on Human Rights, 1993.

UNHCHR. "Status of Ratifications for the Principal International Human Rights Treaties." Office of the United Nations High Commissioner for Human Rights, 2004.

UNSC. "The Rule of Law and Transitional Justice in Conflict and Post-Conflict Societies," 1–24. United Nations Security Council, 2004.

USAID. "U.S. Overseas Loans and Grants [Greenbook] 2007." United States Agency for International Development, http://qesdb.cdie.org/gbk/index.html.

USIP. "Serbia Still at the Crossroads." In *Special Report*. United States Institute of Peace, 2002.

Uslaner, Eric M. "Trade Winds, NAFTA, and the Rational Public." *Political Behavior* 20, no. 4 (1998): 341–60.

Uslaner, Eric M., and Ronald E. Weber. "U.S. State Legislators' Opinions and Perceptions of Constituency Attitudes." *Legislative Studies Quarterly* 4, no. 4 (1979): 563–85.

Vaisman, Demian. "Regionalism and Clan Loyalty in the Political Life of Uzbekistan." In *Muslim Eurasia: Conflicting Legacies,* edited by Yaacov Ro'i, 105–22. London; Portland, Ore.: F. Cass, 1995.

Vajda, M. "East-Central European Perspectives." In *Civil Society and the State: New European Perspectives,* edited by John Keane, 333–60. New York: Verso, 1988.

Vinjamuri, Leslie, and Jack Snyder. "Advocacy and Scholarship in the Study of International War Crime Tribunals and Transitional Justice." *Annual Review of Political Science* 7 (2004): 345–62.

Vogelgesang, Sandy. "What Price Principle? U.S. Policy on Human Rights." *Foreign Affairs* 56, no. 4 (1978).

von Kellenbach, Katharina. "Vanishing Acts: Perpetrators in Postwar Germany." *Holocaust and Genocide Studies* 17, no. 2 (2003): 305–29.

Waldmeir, Patti. *Anatomy of a Miracle: The End of Apartheid and the Birth of the New South Africa*. New York: W. W. Norton & Company, 1997.

Walicki, Andrzej S. "Transitional Justice and the Political Struggles in Post-Communist Poland." In *Transitional Justice and the Rule of Law in New Democracies,* edited by A. James McAdams, 185–238. Notre Dame, Ind.: University of Notre Dame Press, 1997.

Wardlaw, Grant. *Political Terrorism: Theory, Tactics, and Counter-Measures.* New York: Cambridge University Press, 1989.

Welsh, Helga A. "Dealing with the Communist Past: Central and East European Experiences after 1990." *Europe-Asia Studies* 48, no. 3 (1996): 413–28.

Werth, Nicolas. "A State against Its People: Violence, Repression, and Terror in the Soviet Union." In *The Black Book of Communism,* edited by Stephane Courtois, Nicolas Werth, Jean-Louis Panne, Andrzej Paczkowski, Karel Bartosek, and Jean-Louis Margolin, 394–456. Cambridge, Mass.: Harvard University Press, 1999.

Williams, Kieran, Brigid Fowler, and Aleks Szczerbiak. "Explaining Lustration in Central Europe: A 'Post-Communist Politics' Approach." *Democratization* 12, no. 1 (2005): 22–43.

Wilson, Richard A. *The Politics of Truth and Reconciliation in South Africa: Legitimizing the Post-Apartheid State.* New York: Cambridge University Press, 2001.

Wilson, Richard J. "Prosecuting Pinochet: International Crimes in Spanish Domestic Law." *Human Rights Quarterly* 21, no. 4 (1999): 927–79.

Wintrobe, Ronald. "The Tinpot and the Totalitarian: An Economic Theory of Dictatorship." *American Political Science Review* 84, no. 3 (1990): 849–72.

Yin, Robert K. *Case Study Research: Design and Methods.* Thousand Oaks, Calif.: Sage Publications, 1994.

Zalaquett, José. "Balancing Ethical Imperatives and Political Constraints: The Dilemma of New Democracies Confronting Past Human Rights Violations." *Hastings Law Journal* 43, no. 1425 (1992): 1424–38.

———. "Confronting Human Rights Violations Committed by Former Governments: Principles Applicable and Political Constraints." In *Transitional Justice: How Emerging Democracies Reckon with Former Regimes,* edited by Neil J. Kritz, 3–31. Washington, D.C.: United States Institute of Peace Press, 1995.

Index

Poland (*cont.*)
    criminal prosecutions, 53, 112–18,
        197, 198, 265n112, 265n115,
        266n116, 266n117
    —elderly defendants, 266n118
    —of judiciary, 267n122
    differences between Sejm and
        Senat, 103–5
    early demands for change, 61
    elite interviews, 83, 85–86
    European Union and, 203
    forced resignations in the political
        world, 260n65
    justice, fall 1989–fall 1991, 121*f*
    justice, summer 1989, 120*f*
    lack of support from public,
        211
    long-term presence of transitional
        justice, 215, 222
    lustration, 70, 73, 199–203
    —behind-the-scenes force, 202
    —Macierewicz list, 200
    —opposition to, 201–2
    —politicization, 65
    media analysis, 81–82
    post-Solidarity elites and justice
        demand, 270n144
    public support-based arguments
        applied to, 90*t,* 101
    purging of human rights abusers
        from public positions, 108–12,
        196, 210
    —within Internal Affairs Ministry,
        261n87
    —judiciary, 108, 110–12,
        267n121
    —reasons for practical immunity
        for abusers, 115
    —Security Services, 108–10

rebuke of the old system, 98–102,
    192–93
rehabilitation and compensation for
    victims, 102–5
—budgetary concerns, 193
relative power arguments applied
    to, 89, 90*t,* 97, 100–101, 105,
    107, 117, 118, 119
representative of Central European
    states, 79
role of secondary actors, 205, 223
role of society in, 208
societal-based relative power
    arguments applied to, 119
statute of limitations, 71, 72, 113
strategic arguments applied to, 90*t,*
    115
truth commission, 97, 105–8, 194,
    195, 196, 209
police. *See also* secret police/services
    fight against corruption vs. fighting
        for human rights, 138
    purges in Serbia, 136–38, 276n95
policy-oriented truth commissions, 47
political environment, contemporary
    justice policies and, 25–26, 220–21
    lustration and, 69–70
Politika (newspaper, Serbia), 81
Popiełuszko, Jerzy, 264n112,
    266n116
postcommunist world uniqueness,
    217
post–World War II era, 19
    purges in, 50
Poveda Burbano, Alfredo, 54
Powell, Colin, 294n25
Poznań, 1956 events
    1996 Sejm resolution in
        remembrance of, 99

opposition attitudes, 184–86
political parties development,
226–27
rebuke of old system, 193
rehabilitation and compensation for
victims, 194
relative power arguments applied
to, 89, 179
representative of Central Asian
states, 79
role of secondary actors, 206
role of society in, 208
Soviet period recalled favorably, 184
truth commission, 179–84, 194,
195–96, 208, 209
United States and, 174–76,
290n11, 291n17, 291n19,
292n20, 293n21, 293n22,
293n24, 295n33
—assistance to opposition and
human rights organizations, 177
—policy shift after September 11,
2001, 175, 292n20
*Uzbekistan on the Threshold of the
Twenty-first Century* (Karimov),
180

variable, dependent
interaction among components of,
221
specification of, 38
underspecification of, 37
victim oriented truth commissions, 47
victim's fund (Uzbekistan), 183
Videla, Jorge, 44
violator regimes and codification of
human rights violations, 42

Wałęsa, Lech, 65, 110
lustration and, 199, 200
"weight of the past" and lustration, 69
Welsh, Helga, 69
Williams, Kieran, 69–70
witch-hunts, fear of, 53
World War II violations
Croatia and, 150, 151
Poland and, 95, 96
Wright, Leslie, 36–37
Wujek miners rights violations
(Poland, 1981), 98
investigation, 264n112
laying of wreath by Jaruzelski,
98–99
retirement of generals and, 260n68

Xalq So'zi (newspaper, Uzbekistan),
298n49
xenophobic right, rise of, 18

Yugoslavia, former, 18. *See also*
Croatia; International Criminal
Tribunal for the former
Yugoslavia; Serbia and
Montenegro
break with Soviet Union in 1948,
123
early communist period, 123
lack of interest in rehabilitation and
compensation, 208
overlap between victims and
abusers over time, 194

Zalaquett, José, 22, 23, 24
Zamora, Rubén, 51
Živković, Zoran, 128

Brian K. Grodsky

is assistant professor of political science at
the University of Maryland, Baltimore County.

.

www.ingramcontent.com/pod-product-compliance
Lightning Source LLC
Chambersburg PA
CBHW071831270326
41929CB00013B/1962